THE OLD TESTAMENT STORY

THE OLD TESTAMENT STORY

Fifth Edition

John H. Tullock

Professor Emeritus
Belmont University

PRENTICE HALL, Upper Saddle River, New Jersey 07458

Library of Congress Cataloging-in-Publication Data

Tullock, John H.
   The Old Testament Story / John H. Tullock. — 5th ed.
     p.   cm.
   Includes bibliographical references and index.
   ISBN 0-13-011293-3
    1. Bible. O.T.—History of Biblical events. 2. Bible. O.T.—
History of contemporary events. 3. Bible. O.T.—Introductions.
I. Title.
BS1197.T78   1999
221.9′5—dc20

          99-19378
          CIP

Editorial Director: Charlyce Jones Owen
Acquisitions Editor: Karita France
Assistant Editor: Emsal Hasan
Production Editor: Louise Rothman
Marketing Manager: Ilse Wolfe
Manufacturing Manager: Nick Sklitsis
Manufacturing Buyer: Ben Smith
Cover Design: Bruce Kenselaar
Cover Art: *Tower of Babel*, Jan Brueghel, Pinacoteca Nazionale, Siena, Italy.
   Copyright Scala/Art Resource, NY

This book was set in 10/12 Palatino by Oakland Publishing Services, Inc.
and was printed and bound by R R Donnelley and Sons, Inc.
The cover was printed by Phoenix Color Corporation

For permission to use copyrighted material, grateful acknowledgment is made to the following
copyright holders: Excerpts from "Akkadian Myths and Epics," trans. by E. A. Speiser; "The Code of
Hammurabi," trans. by Theophile J. Meek; and "Palestinian Inscriptions," trans. by W. F. Albright in *The
Ancient Near East: An Anthology of Texts and Pictures*, by James B. Pritchard (ed.), ©1958 by Princeton
University Press, pp. 70, 165, and 213. Reprinted by permission of Princeton University Press.

© 2000, 1997, 1992, 1987, 1981 by John H. Tullock
Published by Prentice Hall, Inc.
Upper Saddle River, New Jersey 07458

Printed in the United States of America

10 9 8 7 6 5 4 3 2 1

ISBN: 0-13-011293-3

Prentice-Hall International (UK) Limited, *London*
Prentice-Hall of Australia Pty. Limited, *Sydney*
Prentice-Hall Canada Inc., *Toronto*
Prentice-Hall Hispanoamericana, S.A., *Mexico*
Prentice-Hall of India Private Limited, *New Delhi*
Prentice-Hall of Japan, Inc., *Tokyo*
Pearson Education Asia Pte. Ltd., *Singapore*
Editora Prentice-Hall do Brasil, Ltda., *Rio de Janeiro*

To Helen,
the love of my life—
faithful fan for over fifty years—
whose loving support has made
telling the story a joy.

CONTENTS

ENDNOTE AND BIBLIOGRAPHICAL ABBREVIATIONS

AB	*Anchor Bible*
ABD	*Anchor Bible Dictionary*
ABRL	*Anchor Bible Reference Library*
ANE	*The Ancient Near East*
ANET	*The Ancient Near East—An Anthology of Texts and Pictures*
ARCH	*Archaeology*
BA	*Biblical Archaeologist*
BAR	*Biblical Archaeology Review*
BBC	*Broadman Bible Commentary*
BR	*Bible Review*
FOTL	*Forms of Old Testament Literature*
HER	*Hermeneia*
IB	*Interpreter's Bible*
IDB	*Interpreter's Dictionary of the Bible*
INT	*Interpretation*
ITC	*International Theological Commentary*
JBL	*Journal of Biblical Literature*
JBQ	*Jewish Bible Quarterly*
JBR	*Journal of Bible and Religion*
LAI	*Library of Ancient Israel*
LBC	*Layman's Bible Commentary*
LXX	*The Septuagint* (the Greek version of the Hebrew Bible)
KJV	*King James Version of the Bible*

MBA	*MacMillan Bible Atlas*
MCB	*Mercer Commentary on the Bible*
MDB	*Mercer Dictionary of the Bible*
NCBC	*New Century Bible Commentary*
NEA	*Near Eastern Archaeology*
NIB	*New Interpreter's Bible*
NICOT	*New International Commentary on the Old Testament*
NJBC	*New Jerome Bible Commentary*
NOAB	*New Oxford Annotated Bible*
NRSV	*New Revised Standard Version*
OBA	*Oxford Bible Atlas*
OTL	*The Old Testament Library*
TEV	*Today's English Version, or Good News for Modern Man*
WBC	*Word Biblical Commentary*

LIST OF MAPS

PREFACE

Twenty years have passed since that September afternoon in 1977 when I sat down and wrote the first words of what would later become *The Old Testament Story*. My colleagues at Belmont had challenged me to do so, because we were having difficulty finding a text that was suited for the freshman college level.

Now, I prepare this fifth edition to be published at the beginning of a new millennium. I am grateful to God for continuing good health, for my peers in both denominational and state schools who continue to find *The Old Testament Story* useful in their teaching, and to my Belmont colleagues who started me on this journey. I owe a special note of thanks to my former English teacher and now my wife for more than fifty years for her continuing help and encouragement. For the first time, without the aid of a competent secretary, I typed the whole manuscript. I surprised myself at what I was able to accomplish.

Space limitations, and opposing points of view of reviewers have made it impossible to incorporate all suggestions for revisions. After all, the book is now used in the diverse classroom situations found in religious schools and in state college classes. I have tried to balance the differing viewpoints as I have made this revision.

ACKNOWLEDGMENTS

I wish to express my gratitude to Karita France, Emsal Hasan, and Louise Rothman at Prentice Hall and others who have been most helpful in the preparation of this fifth edition. I would also like to thank the reviewers of this edition, Sondra Frisch, San Diego Mesa College, and Robert Ellis, Hardin Simmons University, for their comments. I am particularly grateful to my nephew, Dr. David Tullock, for reading the manuscript and making helpful suggestions. I am also grateful to Mercer University Press for permission to revise two of the maps that are used.

Except for a few phrases from *The Bible in Today's English Version (TEV)* ©1966, 1971, 1976, and the *King James Version,* all scripture quotations are from the *New Revised Standard Version,* ©1989, by the Division of Christian Education of the National Council of Churches of Christ in the U.S.A., and are used by permission. All rights are reserved.

John H. Tullock

Unique FREE online study resource . . .
the *Companion Website*™

www.prenhall.com/Tullock

Prentice Hall's exclusive *Companion Website*™ that accompanies *The Old Testament Story*, 5/e offers unique tools and support that make it easy for students and instructors to integrate this online study guide with the text. The site is a comprehensive resource that is organized according to the chapters within the text and features a variety of learning and teaching modules:

For students:

- **Study Guide Modules** contain a variety of exercises and features designed to help with self-study.

- **Reference Modules** contain *Web Destinations* and *Net Search* options that provide the opportunity to quickly reach information on the web that relates to the content in the text.

- **Communication Modules** include tools such as *Live Chat* and *Message Boards* to facilitate online collaboration and communication.

- **Personalization Modules** include our enhanced **Help** feature that contains a test page for browsers and plug-ins.

For instructors:

- **Syllabus Manager**™ tool provides an easy-to-follow process for creating, posting, and revising a syllabus online that is accessible from any point within the companion website. This resource allows instructors and students to communicate both inside and outside of the classroom at the click of a button.

- **Faculty Module** includes resources for teaching. This may include Lecture Hints, Class Activities, and graphics from text, all coordinated to each chapter. This module is accessed via a password provided by your local Prentice Hall representative.

The *Companion Website*™ makes integrating the Internet into your course exciting and easy. Join us online at the address above and enter a new world of teaching and learning possibilities and opportunities.

Chapter 1 🌿

THE BOOK AND THOSE WHO STUDY IT

"Tell me a story, Daddy," is the frequent plea of the child. It is through stories that we transmit to our children our values, our family traditions, and much of our view of life. So it has always been with humankind, and so it was with ancient Israel. Its stories took many forms: the accounts of the creation of the universe and of people, its legal system, the oracles of its prophets, the songs of its singers, and the wisdom of its sages. All these are part of the Old Testament story.

THE OLD TESTAMENT: WHAT IS IT?

Definition

The Old Testament is first and foremost the Hebrew Bible, the sacred scripture of the people who at differing times in their history have been called Hebrews, Israelites, and Jews. The Old Testament is actually a library of thirty-nine books, produced over a period of more than a thousand years (1200–200 B.C.E.).[1] This was the Bible that was known to Jesus, the apostles, and members of the early Christian church, especially in the period before the fall of Jerusalem to the Romans in 70 C.E., when the church was still viewed as another of the Jewish sects. After 70 C.E., when the collection of Christian writings, which began with some of Paul's letters and the earliest of the Gospels, began to be viewed as inspired and thus having the

1

status of scripture, Christians began to refer to the Hebrew Bible as the Old Covenant or Old Testament and their sacred writings as the New Covenant or New Testament. They took the term "covenant" from the prophet Jeremiah (Jer. 31:31–34).

THE VEHICLES THAT CARRY THE STORY[2]

Narrative.   In our culture, we normally expect narrative to be the means of telling a story. Thus we are not surprised that much of the Old Testament is made up of narrative material. True, that narrative often makes use of or is supplemented by other literary forms: laws, songs, genealogies, and lists. Yet, these forms are woven into the narrative in such a way as to become a vital part of it. Narrative is the principal literary vehicle from Genesis through 2 Kings; in major portions of the prophetic books including Isaiah, Jeremiah, Ezekiel, Jonah, Haggai, Zechariah, and Malachi; in the work of the Chronicler—1,2 Chronicles, Ezra through Nehemiah; and in addition, Esther, Daniel, and Ruth.

What is unusual about all this is that narrative was not a common literary device in other surviving literature from the ancient Near East. Outside of legal codes, most of what is known about its gods, goddesses, legendary heroes, and kings is told in poetry. Poetry's primary function is to impart a sense of emotion and praise for its subject, while narrative serves to give the stories a sense of time and place, to flesh out their characters, and to impart a sense of the flow of life to what is being told.

Note the difference between the use of prose and poetry in the story of Deborah (the prose version in Judges 4 and the poetic version of the same story in Judges 5). While the powerful poetry of Judges 5 conveys the sense of celebration for the LORD's delivery of Israel by the hand of a woman from a powerful enemy, Judges 4 fills in the background of time, place, and circumstance, making it possible to better understand Judges 5.

Legal Materials.   As noted earlier, most Old Testament laws are incorporated in its narratives. This material is found principally in Exodus, Leviticus, Numbers, and Deuteronomy, which contain three major legal codes—the Covenant Code, the Deuteronomic Code, and the Levitical Code. These codes will be more fully identified later.

Poetry.   One would naturally expect Psalms and Song of Songs to be poetry. What might come as a surprise to those who have not used modern translations of the Bible is that large portions of the books of the prophets are also in poetic form.

Wisdom Literature.   While wisdom literature—Proverbs, Job, Ecclesiastes—is almost entirely in poetic form, it is a special category by dint of its subject matter—namely, how to get along in the world and how to deal with some of life's seemingly unanswered questions. In structure, it ranges from extended wisdom poems to short one-line (in Hebrew) proverbs. Except for chapters 1 through 3 and 42:7–16, Job is an extended poetic drama in the form of a dialogue between Job and his friends, followed by two speeches by God. The book of Ecclesiastes is a mixture of prose and poetry.

The Crucial Event

As it now stands, the Old Testament now starts at the beginning of all things—the Creation—but this order is probably not how the story of Israel was first told. All through the Old Testament, the one theme which continually appears is the Exodus. This was the supreme event in Israelite history. Israel became a people through this event and those which followed. Thus it is commemorated in song and story (Exodus to Deuteronomy) and in numerous references in Psalms (such as 66:6; 68:7–18; 78:11–55; 114; 135:8–12; 136:10–22) as well as in other places in the Bible. A classic summary of the story is found in Deuteronomy 26:5–9:

> You shall make this response before the Lord your God: "A wandering Aramean was my ancestor; he went down into Egypt and lived there as an alien, few in number, and there he became a great nation, mighty and populous. When the Egyptians treated us harshly and afflicted us, by imposing hard labor on us, we cried to the LORD, the God of our ancestors; the LORD heard our voice and saw our affliction, our toil, and our oppression. The LORD brought us out of Egypt with a mighty hand and an outstretched arm, with a terrifying display of power, and with signs and wonders; and he brought us into this place and gave us this land, a land flowing with milk and honey."

The Exodus event made Israel aware of itself as a group of people with common experiences that united them. Just as a baby first notices fingers and toes, leading to the awareness of itself as a person, so Israel became aware of itself as a people. When the "Who am I?" question is answered, there inevitably follows the question, "Where did I come from?"

When people begin to ask these kinds of questions, they begin to look at their history—so Israel, in times of literary activity, had historians who gathered together the memories and traditions of the people and began to weave them into a story. In this story, they not only explained their own origins in the Exodus, but also carried that explanation back through the patriarchs to the origin of the human race, and even to the universe itself. As the nation grew, the history was expanded and revised, either in written or oral form. Then, when the tragedy of the Babylonian Exile struck and it looked as though not only historical materials but the words of the prophets, the wisdom materials, and the songs of the people might be lost, a concerted effort was made to gather together and preserve the literary heritage.

HOW IT BEGAN

How did the Old Testament come to be written? Did someone just suddenly decide, "I'm going to write the Old Testament"? Or was it a more complicated process?

To answer this question with certainty is impossible. A New Testament writer for whom the Old Testament was the Bible spoke of how "Holy men of old wrote as they were moved by the Spirit of God" (2 Pet. 1:21). Yet even that statement, setting forth the conviction that God was the initiator of the process that led to the writing, also suggests that the development of the Old Testament was an historical process. The following is a suggested scheme of how the Old Testament may have been developed.

First the Event

Nothing happens without a cause; something must trigger it. The Old Testament grew out of the events and circumstances of the life of the people of Israel. While the Exodus and related events served as the catalyst for the development of the sacred literature of the Israelites, many events before and after that crucial event contributed to the material resources from which the Old Testament was constructed.

Then the Story—the First Interpretation

First, things happened. The people to whom things happened told others about their experiences. Just as every family has a fund of stories about various relatives, much of the Old Testament is made up of stories that came from the oral tradition of the people who were to be known as Israel. Not all the stories, however, were based on actual events. Some stories, known as *etiologies*, for example, were created to answer "why" questions. Other stories, like Jotham's fable about the trees (Judg. 9:7–15), or Samson's riddle (Judg. 14:14), were told to make a point. Telling the stories over the centuries also had its effects on their nature and their subsequent interpretation.

Then the Reinterpretation

When things happen to us, we interpret them in the light of existing circumstances. Later, however, as we look back we may view a particular event in an entirely different way than we did when it happened. Time and circumstances may have given us a different insight into its significance for us. For instance, something once seen as a disaster may later be may looked upon as something very positive and meaningful for us.

Then the History—the Continuing Interpretation

The Old Testament grew from such hindsight. At some point in the life of Israel as a people, someone, or a number of someones, looked back at the past and concluded that God had been at work in the lives of the people—calling their ancestors out of paganism, making himself known to them, leading them from the Tigris and Euphrates River valleys to Palestine and eventually into Egypt and bondage. But even that bondage, a disaster by most normal standards, was God's way of preserving the Israelites as a people. God raised up a leader, Moses, and prepared him, as the adopted son of an Egyptian princess and as a Midianite shepherd, for the difficult job of leading a band of slaves and a mixed multitude of others into the Sinai desert, there to weld this motley group into a people, united in covenant to God.

Furthermore, God led them to a land—a land that had been promised to their ancestors, Abraham, Isaac, and Jacob. After a long and difficult period, the land became theirs. But their troubles were not over. After many years of struggles to achieve some kind of national unity, they finally settled on a monarchy as the kind of government they would have. After a sputtering start under Saul, the storytellers describe a remarkable growth during David's time when the nation reached its greatest territorial limits, which enabled it to withstand any challenge to its territory. Solomon enjoyed the fruits of his father's success, enjoying a time of peace and great economic prosperity. Yet, he sowed seeds of discontent that would come to full flower under his son Rehoboam, whose unwise policies resulted in the kingdom splitting into two separate states.

For two centuries, the two parts of the once-proud kingdom of David limped along—sometimes as enemies, sometimes as allies. At times in their periods of friendship, they combined forces to bring a measure of prosperity to their people, but for most of the time they were like pawns, toyed with by the great powers of the time—Egypt and Assyria. Finally, in 721 B.C.E., Israel, the Northern Kingdom, was blotted out of existence by the Assyrian giant, who destroyed its cities and deported all that was left of its upper classes, replacing them with foreigners who were to intermarry with the poor people left in the land, which produced the Samaritans.

Judah, the Southern Kingdom, struggled on for just over a century, but it too fell, this time to Babylonia, the nation that had succeeded Assyria as the terror of the Near East.

As had been the case with Israel, most of the members of Judah's surviving leadership was deported, but different factors were at work that allowed the people to keep their identity. The prophets had warned that such an occurrence was likely if Judah persisted in its wrongdoing. Seemingly, the stability of the government in the south gave the people a greater sense of unity which helped them to hold together in the time of national disaster. Then, too, the Babylonians seem to have contributed to the situation by settling the people in communities where they could follow the advice of the prophet Jeremiah and live as normal a life as possible (Jer. 29).

In response to the trauma of the Exile and the threat of annihilation, Jewish scholars began in earnest to collect and shape the literature of the people. While history writing may have begun earlier, the Exile gave the work a new sense of urgency. Along with the writing of history, poetry was collected, the law was codified, and the words of the great prophets were arranged and preserved. Much of the Old Testament as we now know it took shape during the Exile and immediately afterward.

With the people now convinced of the importance of the preservation of their traditions, the period following the Exile, while not a time of glory, was a time of collection, preservation, and interpretation which reached its climax in the final canonization of the Old Testament early in the Christian era.

HOW IT DEVELOPED

The Process

Did the process of forming the literature of the Old Testament begin during the Exile? The answer most certainly is "No."

The development of the Old Testament may be compared to a river and its tributaries. A river does not begin full-sized. Rather it is a combination of dozens of smaller streams which have joined together to form the river. So it was with the Old Testament. Some will be quick to point out that it began with God. Even so, God worked through human agents, and it is the work of these human agents that is being discussed.

The first tiny streams were the oral traditions: the poems of victory, the stories of the ancestors; the memories of great events that were treasured, gathered, and passed on for many generations. These oral treasures were the means by which families preserved their values and their sense of who they were. Not only did they remember heroes, they remembered villains as well. Both played roles in events the community deemed important. Thus the people preserved the stories—from exalted stories such as that of the call of the patriarch Abraham from the paganism of Ur of the Chaldees, to less-than-exalted stories such as the account of how Jacob outwitted his brother Esau and his father Isaac to secure the birthright and the blessing. The most-told story of all, however, was of God's marvelous delivery of their ancestors during the flight from Egypt. The storyteller was the teacher and the story was the medium through which he taught.

At shrines where clans (extended families) gathered for worship, the stories were combined into larger units to form cycles of tradition, each with its own distinctive point of view. Finally, someone conceived the idea, by what religious people call inspiration, that the stories of God's dealings with the people needed to be written down or put into a complete story so they could be preserved.

The Written Story

When the smaller streams of tradition were combined to form a connected story is a matter of dispute. More conservative scholars argue for a date as early as the time of Moses. Other scholars see the smaller streams of tradition continuing either in an oral or written form until the time of David and Solomon, before attempts were made to write a history of Israel. They see the process as taking place in stages, designated by letters of the alphabet. This theory was given classic expression by Julius Wellhausen in the nineteenth century. It embraces not only the Pentateuch (Genesis through Deuteronomy), or Torah, but also all the major historical books: Joshua through 2 Kings, as well as 1, 2 Chronicles; Ezra and Nehemiah.

According to this view, that stream of tradition which began with the Exodus stories was chosen as the mainstream. To it were added the stories of the *patriarchs* ("first fathers") and the stories of the creation. This edition of the history of Israel (characterized by referring to God by the personal name Yahweh and designated by scholars by the letter J) was made up largely of materials from the southern part of Israel. It flowed on for a hundred years of so until it was joined by another stream of materials from the northern part of the country, identified by the use of a more general or "family" name for God—Elohim, designated by the letter E. These materials started with stories about Abraham, but they became so mingled with the mainstream that it is difficult to determine just how much each contributed to the total volume.

The next tributary was of such volume and force that it became dominant in the historical materials. During the reign of Josiah, king of Judah (640–609 B.C.E.), "the book of the law" was found in the temple when repairs were being made (2 Kings 22:8). Scholars conclude, on the basis of the religious reforms which followed and which seemed to be based on the contents of the book of the law, that this book was essentially the Book of Deuteronomy. Some argue that Deuteronomy was written not more than one hundred years before its discovery. Yet it is usually agreed that a major part of the materials it contains are from an earlier time.

Like a river whose whole character is changed by the joining of a major tributary, so the character of the presentation of the history of Israel is changed by the reform growing out of the discovery of the Deuteronomic materials designated by the letter D. Beginning particularly with the book of Judges, Israel's history is interpreted in a distinct fashion. It is viewed as following a cycle: Israel *sins*, *judgment* comes through the oppression of an enemy, Israel *repents*, God raises up a leader to *deliver* the people from their enemies. To see a clear example of this, read Judges 3:7–11. Less obvious examples are found in the history of the monarchy (1,2 Sam.: 1,2 Kings).

The exile in Babylon (586–538 B.C.E.) and the years following saw a floodtide of materials enter the stream. Because the danger of the extinction of the people brought a new reverence for the sacred traditions and a zeal for preserving the sacred literature, the people established a unifying symbol. *Torah*, now expanded to mean not only the Pentateuch but also the history and sayings of the great prophets, the wisdom of the sages, and the sacred songs of the people, gave them a sense of unity and purpose that was to enable them to survive many centuries of adversity.

Just as today, when the dangers of losing natural beauty have led to government action to preserve some streams as scenic rivers, so the Jews moved to preserve their most meaningful literature by designating it as sacred. The final contributors to this literary river were the priests of the exilic and postexilic periods. They gave the material its final form designated by the letter P through an editorial process and through collecting those books known as the Writings, including the last edition of the history of Israel as found in 1, 2 Chronicles, Ezra, and Nehemiah. All that remained was the climax of the process of canonization by sometime prior to 100 C.E. So, as the river finally reaches the ocean, the Hebrew Bible became the possession of the world through the Jewish community and its major offspring, Christianity.

The Final Product: The Canon.[3]   The word *canon* originally referred to a reed used for measuring, such as a yardstick. When applied to literature, it has come to mean a body of writings that, for religious folk, are held to be sacred because *they contain God's message to the faithful.* The process by which these books achieved that status is thus called *canonization.* For Jews and Christians alike, then, the Old Testament or Hebrew Bible is sacred literature.

The Hebrew Canon.   Though the process of canonization took place over a long period of time, the Hebrew canon is usually spoken of as developing as follows:

1. 400 B.C.E.   The *Torah* (Genesis through Deuteronomy), or Law, achieved sacred status.
2. 200 B.C.E.   The *Nebi'im*, or Prophets, were canonical. There was a two-fold division of the Prophets:
   a. The Former Prophets: the books of Joshua; Judges; 1,2 Samuel; 1,2 Kings.
   b. The Latter Prophets: Isaiah, Jeremiah, Ezekiel, and the Twelve, generally known to Christians as the Minor Prophets.
3. 100 C.E.   Not later than this date, the *Kethubim*, or Writings, had achieved canonical status. These include: Psalms; Job; Proverbs; Ecclesiastes; Song of Songs; Lamentations; 1,2 Chronicles; Ezra; Nehemiah; Ruth; Esther; Daniel.

The question might legitimately be asked, "Why were these books included and not others?" That there were others is abundantly clear. The Dead Sea Scrolls alone had manuscripts and fragments of nearly a thousand religious writings, and other Jewish sects developed their own sacred books. Basically two tests determined what books would be in the Old Testament canon. These primarily were the tests of time and usage. The literature, oral and written, that continued to speak to the believing community over the years was judged to have the breath of the Divine about it. Admittedly, the survival of the community that used the literature also had to be a factor in the development of the canon.

Until recently, it was widely held that the rabbis of Jamnia, an academy established by Johanan ben Zakkai after the fall of Jerusalem in 70 C.E., had in effect declared the canon closed around 100 C.E.. This is increasingly challenged today by those who would argue that there are indications that the canon closed much earlier, perhaps as early as the Maccabean period (150 B.C.E.). They cite evidence from the Dead Sea Scrolls to bolster this conclusion. It is also now believed that Jamnia was not nearly so authoritative as the later church councils were. At most, the rabbis simply were recognizing the canon as accepted by the Pharisees, that branch of Judaism most closely associated with the Jerusalem Temple.

The Septuagint.   The Greek translation of the Hebrew Bible, used by the Jewish community of Alexandria in Egypt, differed from the Hebrew canon as to what books should be included in the *Kethubim*. It contained some fifteen extra books: 1,2 Esdras; Tobit; Judith; the Additions to the Book of Esther; the Wisdom of Solomon; Ecclesiasticus, or the Wisdom of Jesus, Son of Sirach; Baruch; the Letter of Jeremiah; the Prayer of Azariah and the Song of the Three Jews; Susanna; Bel and the Dragon; the Prayer of Manasseh; and 1,2 Maccabees. Roman Catholics refer to these as Deuterocanonicals. Eastern Orthodox Catholics accept these, plus 3,4 Maccabees and Psalm 151 as part of their canon.

The Septuagint influenced the great fourth-century scholar Jerome in his Vulgate translation, which became the standard Latin version of the Bible for many centuries. Thus, both Roman Catholic and Eastern Orthodox Bibles include the Apocrypha in their canon. While other Christians do not consider the books of the Apocrypha canonical, most modern translations include them since they are studied for their contribution to understanding the history of the period in which they developed.

WORK OF SCHOLARS

How do we know that the Old Testament developed in this or any other way? That it exists is ample evidence that it developed somewhere, somehow, and at some time. Since there are no time machines to transport us back through the ages to watch the Bible being written, we must depend upon those who can discover and interpret clues about its beginnings and growth.

But the questions arise, "Why go to all that trouble?" "Why not just accept it as it is?" Those who ask such questions probably would agree that one needs to understand the Old Testament—or the Bible as a whole, for that matter—as well as possible. Just as we can understand others better if we understand their background, so we can understand the Bible better if we understand its background. If we study the results of their efforts, all varieties of biblical scholars can contribute to our understanding of the Bible. These include textual specialists or theologians; form critics or archaeologists; literary historians or redaction critics; those who look at particular parts or those who try to look at the message of the Bible as a whole. We need then to describe briefly some (but not all) of the kinds of scholarship that are used to aid us in understanding and interpreting the Bible.

Textual Criticism

First are those scholars whose concern is the biblical text itself. Sometimes called lower criticism, the concerns of textual criticism is of basic importance to all who study the Bible seriously for any reason, since no one possesses a single original copy of any book of the Bible, either in the Old or New Testament. The oldest complete copy of any Old Testament book is a manuscript of the Book of Isaiah, found among the Dead Sea Scrolls, which dates to about the time of Christ. This means that the original copy of the Book of Isaiah was written several hundred years before the Dead Sea Scroll Isaiah was copied.

On the other hand, there are more copies of biblical manuscripts than of any other kinds of ancient manuscripts. There is far more manuscript evidence for the prophets of Israel than there is for Plato and Aristotle. That such a profusion of manuscripts exists creates something of a problem, however, in that they differ in places. This is where the talents of the textual scholar are put to work. Through a vast knowledge of the ancient languages, the textual specialist is able to compare the various manuscripts and thus bring us closer to what the original copies said. It should be pointed out the most of the variants in the text involve only about 5 percent of the total material.

Literary and Historical Studies

In the second place, there are scholars who study the text from the literary and historical standpoint. While there is a great degree of unanimity about the aims of textual criticism, there is far less agreement about the results, or in some cases, even the need for literary or higher criticism. Literary and historical studies are directed toward three basic concerns: source (was there an author or authors?); form (in what form or style was the composition written or spoken?); and history (how did the present book develop?).

The first concern can be illustrated by the question: Who wrote the Pentateuch? Perhaps no other question in biblical studies has evoked a wider variety of responses than this one.

Mosaic Authorship of the Pentateuch.   Scholars who are more conservative say Moses wrote the Pentateuch, and it was he who joined the tiny streams of tradition into a major tributary. Even here there is variation, some say that Moses used available traditions while others advocate the view that Moses received the totality of the material through divine revelation. As evidence of Mosaic authorship, the long Jewish tradition that Moses was the author of these books is noted. To further support this view, numerous Old Testament passages are cited, among them being Deuteronomy 31:9,24; 1 Kings 2:3; 2 Kings 14:6; 2 Kings 23:25; Malachi 4:4; Joshua 8:31; Nehemiah 8:1; and 2 Chronicles 25:4; 35:12. In addition, Jesus' statements in Luke 24:27,44 are also cited as evidence of Mosaic authorship. Differences in writing styles in the text are explained by saying that Moses used different scribes, giving to them the sense of what was to be said, with the scribes putting it in their own idiom.[4]

The Documentary Hypothesis

The Mosaic authorship of the Pentateuch began to be questioned as early as the twelfth century by certain Jewish rabbis. Then, in the 1700s two individuals, H. B. Witter, a German pastor (d. 1711), and Jean Astruc, a French physician (d. 1753), noticed the alternation of the divine names *Elohim* in Genesis 1 and *Yahweh Elohim* in Genesis 2. Others then noticed, among other things, third person references to Moses; repetitions (Gen. 12, 20, 26; Exod. 20, 24; Deut. 5); and differing names for the same place or person (Mt. Sinai and Mt. Horeb; Jethro and Reuel).

All this led to the classical expression of the Documentary or JEDP hypothesis in the late nineteenth century by Julius Wellhausen, a German biblical scholar. It proposed that Israel's history was written in four stages:

J. A history using *Yahweh* as the principal name for God, written in time of Solomon or shortly thereafter.

E. A history using *Elohim* as the principal name for God, written around 750 B.C.E.

D. A history influenced by the finding of the Book of Deuteronomy during the reign of Josiah (621 B.C.E.). This history is generally dated around 550 B.C.E.

P. A history written by the priests around 450 B.C.E. adding legal materials related to worship and genealogical lists.

This hypothesis was based on the assumption that Israelite society evolved out of a primitive view of the universe and became more complex as it developed. It needs to be noted that this view arose in the same period as the one when Darwin's *Origin of Species* was written.

Modifications of Wellhausen's Views

Form Criticism.[5]   Another German scholar introduced the first important modification of Wellhausen's views. Instead of emphasizing completed documents, Hermann Gunkel shifted the emphasis to the building blocks of those documents—the oral stories, poems, legal materials, wisdom sayings—that the author(s) used to put the final product together. This is called *form criticism*—the study of the smallest units that make up the larger text. Form critics look for the distinctive types of speech patterns that characterize a certain kind of life situation. For example, a person who has had a lifetime involvement in sports, either as a fan or as a participant, is likely to use figures of speech from sports to describe other aspects of life. So one might say after failing to achieve a goal, "I struck out!" Israel's prophets, familiar with the legal activity they saw taking place in the city gate, were fond of using legal language to describe God's judgment on the people. As an illustration of this, read Micah 6:1–8 where one finds an indictment (6:1–2), the case presented against the defendant (6:3–5), the defense (6:6–7), and the verdict (6:8).

Oral Tradition.   A further challenge to Wellhausen came from a group of Scandinavian scholars led by Ivan Engnell. Coming from a culture where oral literature was a part of their heritage, they challenged Wellhausen at two points: (1) the age of the materials and (2) the nature of the "documents." Where Wellhausen proposed that each of the "histories" (J, E, D, or P) reflected the time in which it was written, Engnell and his colleagues argued that the basic materials from which J, E, D, and P were developed were much older than the documents themselves, having been a part of the oral tradition of the Israelite people (see the Song of Deborah, Judges 5, as an example). Even the so-called documents could have been passed down in oral form before being recorded in written form. This, in turn, has led to an area of study that attempts to trace the history of these traditions.

Redaction Criticism

Redaction criticism studies how various sources were combined into larger units. Three kinds of sources were used: written, oral, and what might be called editorial additions. The redactor was a theologian with a message that was shaped by the units of material that were selected and by the narrative transitions that were added. An example of this would be the story of David's life (1 Samuel 16 to 1 Kings 2:12, and 1 Chronicles 10:1–29:30). While the Chronicler's history repeats much of the materials found in 1 Samuel and 1 Kings, there are important omissions—i.e., David's affair with Bathsheba. By the Chronicler's time (the postexilic period), David was seen as the ideal king, so much so that the Jews envisioned a new day when a new David, the Messiah, would come to deliver Israel from its enemies. So the redactor, or editor, saw no good purpose in bringing up David's indiscretion with Bathsheba.

Present Trends in Old Testament Studies

A marked shift in emphasis has occurred in Old Testament studies in recent years. There has been a movement away from examining the pieces that make up the literature to an examination of the finished product. This has taken two forms in particular: (1) those studies that examine the text for its literary merit, and (2) those studies that center around the question of what the finished text had to say to the particular audiences to which it was addressed.

The Bible as Literature.   Differing from earlier work, the Bible as a whole is examined as a work of literary force and authority. It is seen as a work that demonstrates "the remarkable ingenuity of biblical authors" in creating literature which is so entirely credible that it should have shaped the minds and lives of intelligent men and women for two millenia and more. The text is not only read for its beauty but also for its meaning as a whole.[6]

Canonical Criticism.   These critics have the same aim as those who study the Bible as literature, insofar as the criticism emphasizes the canonized text. Where it differs is in the assumption that a given segment, when it took its final form, was designed to speak to problems of that time. As one well-known critical scholar recently has asked, "Should we not ask what the final author (or authors) of the *book* wanted to tell the reader?"[7] The redactor or editor was much like a student writing a dissertation. A subject is selected, and sources are examined and selected to support the thesis that is being proposed. Thus the editors or redactors were theologians who had something to say, who selected the materials from available sources, and, when needed, created materials that supported the point or points that were to be made in the finished product.

The Sociohistorical Approach.   There is a growing interest in how common folk lived. Sources for this type of approach include physical remains such as garbage pits and village ruins; written sources, including the biblical texts and texts from similar ancient sources; and comparisons with similar present-day societies. A major problem with which this approach has to deal is this: in comparing Israelite society to other societies, just how similar is the society in question to ancient Israelite society? Furthermore, most archaeological evidence is mute and thus is subject to often conflicting interpretations. Despite these problems, this approach makes valuable contributions to our understanding of Israelite society.[8]

Developers of the Finished Product.   Present-day scholars emphasize the role of three major groups in the development of the narrative materials in the Old Testament (Genesis–Numbers; Deuteronomy–2 Kings; 1,2 Chronicles–Ezra–Nehemiah). First, the priestly redactors are credited with giving Genesis through Numbers its final form since much of the material, apart from Genesis, is concerned with legal and cultic matters, the areas of special interest to the priest. Secondly, the Deuteronomistic editors are seen as being responsible for Joshua through 2 Kings, with Deuteronomy as the bridge between the Genesis to Numbers narrative and what is commonly called the Deuteronomic History. The latter influence may spill over into the narrative portions of Jeremiah. Finally, the Chronicler(s) were responsible for 1,2 Chronicles, Ezra, and Nehemiah.

ARCHAEOLOGY AS A TOOL
FOR UNDERSTANDING

Archaeology is increasingly in the news. Whether it is the report of the inscriptional reference to the "house of David",[9] the uncovering of a complete city gate in the ancient Canaanite city of Laish,[10] or the making of popular movies that portray a breed of archaeologist that is as outdated as the horse-drawn carriage, archaeology is a subject that draws attention.

Since archaeology is a term that is often misunderstood, certain questions should be examined: "What is archaeology?" "How does the archaeologist know where to dig?" "What methods are used in digging?" "What is the value of archaeology?"

Basic Matters

The Purpose of Archaeology. Contrary to the popular image of an archaeologist as a fortune hunter, archaeology is a serious scientific discipline, dedicated to the search for truth about ancient cultures by studying the material remains of those cultures. Those remains may be such simple things as broken pottery, animal bones, seeds, remains of buildings, and, if the archaeologist is fortunate, written materials. Biblical archaeologists particularly are interested in the peoples mentioned in the biblical story, and especially the Israelites. Even here, the archaeologist does not set out to prove the Bible. Instead, the purpose is to shed light on the Bible by trying to understand its people and their culture more thoroughly.

The Practice of Archaeology. Sites in biblical lands are called *tells*. These are flat-topped hills, built up over centuries of construction and destruction on basically the same site. Such sites were limited in number because of the lack of available water sources. The discovery of how to make lime plaster made possible the development of cisterns, cavities dug into the soft rock and then plastered to make them waterproof so rainwater could be stored in them. This made it possible to build in an area that previously had been inaccessible. The important city of Samaria was one such site.

The tell is divided into squares, 5 meters by 5 meters. Only selected squares are excavated, for two reasons: (1) the limits of financial resources and manpower, and (2) the need to leave areas for later scholars to examine when increased knowledge may lead to a more accurate evaluation of what was found. As the selected squares are excavated, only a few inches of soil are removed at a time. The sides of the square are kept as straight as possible, and adjoining squares are separated by a dirt wall or *balk*. This is essential in determining the various levels of occupation. Any important finds are photographed, and charts are kept as to their exact location in the square.

Formerly, the emphasis was on digging such areas as the city gate because this was the center of governmental functions; the areas where worship was carried on; the homes of the city's rulers—palaces and monumental buildings. Present-day archaeologists, while not ignoring these important features of tells, are turning more and more attention to the dwellings of the common people to determine how they lived and the types of societies they had.

The Skills and Tools of Archaeology.   The basic tools of the trade are hand tools because excavation must be done carefully and systematically. Such small tools as trowels, hand picks, and a variety of brushes are used to carefully expose the finds. Earth that is removed is sifted for smaller items that might escape visual detection. Interpretation of what is found involves many scientific disciplines— physical and cultural anthropologists to study physical changes and social organizations; paleobotanists and paleozoologists to study the remains of ancient plant and animal life, to name a few.

Electronic gear of various sorts is increasingly important. The computer is used for recording and analyzing data, while ground-penetrating radar, echo sound,

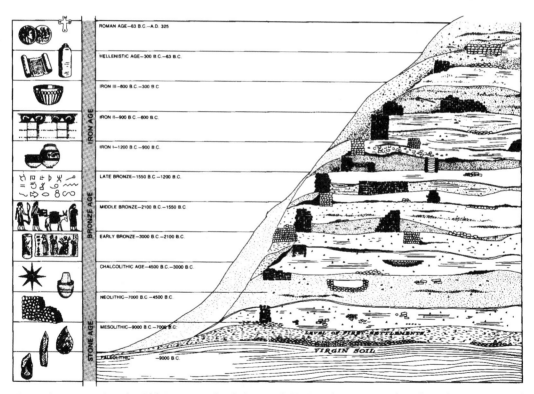

From *Compass Points for Old Testament Study* by Mark H. Lovelace. © 1972 by Abingdon Press. Used by permission.

Figure 1–1.   Cultural and archaeological ages of the past in Palestine. This illustration shows how a *tell* was built up by layers, over the centuries, as cities were built and destroyed.

and other such techniques are used for at least two purposes: to determine those areas where digging would be most fruitful; and to detect underground structures where it is not possible to dig, or where there is neither time nor resources available to dig.[11]

Such electronic tools are especially useful in area surveys, a major emphasis in present-day archaeological work. In years past, such surveys consisted of examining surface features of tells. Judgments were made on the basis of such features as the occupants of the tell and when they occupied it. With modern electronic tools, a much wider range of data can be collected, leading to much sounder judgments about the nature of a given site.

Dating What Is Found.   One of the early techniques for dating was developed by two pioneer archaelogists, Sir Flinders Petrie and William F. Albright. They noticed that pottery found at the same level of tells over an area had the same basic features. From this, they developed a method of dating, based on the changes in pottery. Epigraphical dating is based on written materials, and involves the changing styles of letter formation. Broken pottery was the most convenient material upon which to write, particularly in Israel. Formerly it was scrubbed to discover writing, but now it has been discovered that simply dipping it in water is the better method.[12] The carbon-14 test can be used on any plant-based samples of surviving materials. For example, both epigraphy and carbon-14 tests were used to date the Dead Sea Scrolls.

Important Discoveries

Following are a few examples of discoveries that have had an impact on biblical studies.[13]

The Rosetta Stone.   This trilingual inscription, discovered in 1801 by an engineer in Napoleon's army, made possible the translation of thousands of previously unreadable Egyptian inscriptions. While its impact on the interpretation of the Bible is indirect, nevertheless, it gave insight into the history of a people who were intimately involved with the Israelites.

The Gilgamesh Epic.   In the mid-nineteenth century, Austen Henry Layard, a British explorer discovered an ancient Assyrian library at Nineveh. Later, while translating the clay tablets, George Adam Smith, a young assistant at the British Museum, came across a flood story that had remarkable parallels to the biblical flood story. Unfortunately, the tablet was broken. Subsequently, Smith returned to the site of the discovery, and within five days of digging found a tablet containing the rest of the story. This story, whose hero is Gilgamesh, predates the biblical story, which suggests that the biblical storyteller was familiar with it and used materials from it for his own purposes.

The Beni Hasan Mural. This wall painting, found in a large rock-hewn tomb near the village of Beni Hasan, 150 miles north of Cairo, dates to the early nineteenth century B.C.E.. The picture portrays a group of Asiatics who have come to Egypt either to trade or to seek mining rights. From where in Asia they originate is unclear, but the picture suggests the type of trading relationships described in the stories of the patriarchs in Genesis.

The Gezer High Place. Discovered by R. A. S. Macalister in 1902, this site has been interpreted as being from times ranging from 2500 B.C.E. to 1600 B.C.E. It consists of a series of ten upright stone pillars and a large rectangular block of stone with a depression cut into its top. While the purpose of the basin is something of a mystery, the most likely explanation for the upright stones is that they served as witnesses of some sort of covenant ceremony, as described in the story of the confrontation of Jacob and Laban (Genesis 31:43–54; see also Joshua 24:25–27).

An Ivory Knife Handle from Megiddo. This ivory knife handle from the twelfth century B.C.E. has two scenes incribed on it. One depicts an Egyptian pharaoh, possible Ramesses III (1182–1151 B.C.E.) returning victorious from battle, driving captives, interpreted by some as being ancestors of the Israelites. A second

Photo by Hershel Shanks courtesy of *Biblical Archaeology Review*.

Figure 1–2. The Gezer High Place.

scene shows the Pharaoh seated on his throne, surrounded by his courtiers. It is a picture of luxury not unlike the court of Solomon. It also has similarities to the throne in Solomon's Temple (1 Kings 6:23–28; Exodus 25:17–22).

The Dead Sea Scrolls. Undoubtedly the most famous archaeological discovery of this century, it began in 1947 when a Bedouin boy found the first manuscripts in a cave near the Dead Sea. When experts recognized their value, a systematic examination was made of other caves in the area, leading to the discovery of a veritable treasure of both biblical and nonbiblical manuscripts. This discovery made available manuscripts or portions of manuscripts of every Old Testament book except two, some of which are 1000 years older than previously known manuscripts. In addition, there are manuscripts from nearly one thousand nonbiblical books.

The Purpose and Value of Archaeology

A major aim of archaeology is to discover as much as possible about ancient peoples. Ideally, the archaeologist does not set out to prove anything but tries to let the evidence speak for itself. Sometimes it speaks for what is described in the Bible, at others it is neutral, while at other times it is contrary to what the Bible describes. If one turns up written materials, the task of interpretation is clarified somewhat. Most of the evidence that is found, however, is mute. That is the reason why often in archaeology two interpreters will take the same evidence and reach seemingly opposite conclusions.

Despite these limitations, because of the work of archaeologists, we know more about the lives of the peoples of biblical times than we discern from reading the Bible alone. We know the kinds of houses they lived in, their customs, what languages they spoke, the foods they ate, and even how they made out property deeds. More importantly, we are far richer in the manuscript evidence for biblical books, and our ability to understand these texts is far greater, thanks to archaeological discoveries. All in all, it has proven to be a useful tool in biblical interpretation.

Why Study the Old Testament?

People study the Old Testament for a variety of reasons. Many people study it as an aid to understanding our language and culture, since much of our great literature has been influenced by Old Testament themes and figures of speech. Even nonreligious people read such Old Testament books as Job, Proverbs, or Psalms with appreciation for their literary merit.

But for devout Jews and Christians alike, there is a sense of the sacred about the Old Testament or Hebrew Bible. They view it as inspired literature—inspired on a higher and different level from other great literary works. But even so, there are different interpretations as to how the Bible was inspired. Some would hold

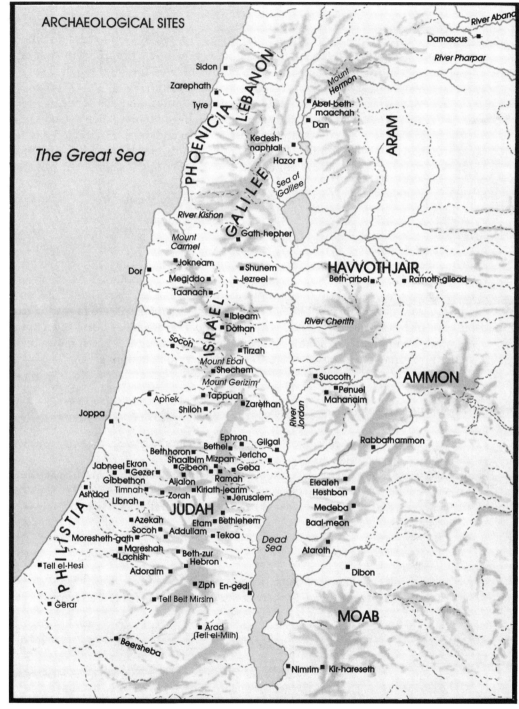

ARCHAEOLOGICAL SITES

Artwork by Margaret Jordan Brown © Mercer University Press.

Figure 1–3. Archaeological sites

that every word in the original manuscripts was dictated by God to persons whose only function was to write it down in the idiom of their own time. Others view biblical inspiration as a process in which persons encountered the Divine in their everyday living and wrote down their reaction to that encounter.

Such a view would say that God's power is unlimited, and this surely includes the power of self-revelation, and thus inspiration is the human reaction to God's self-revelation. The biblical writers' abilities, however, to understand what God was revealing definitely were limited, and that limitation is reflected in what is written about what God has done or is doing in the world. The Old Testament mirrors the strengths and weaknesses of those people whose experiences are portrayed, including their understanding and misunderstanding of the nature of God and of God's will for their lives. For instance, the Christian apostle Paul accepted slavery as a part of his world and gave instructions about how slaves were to behave. Today, we do not accept nor do we believe that God approves of slavery. What has changed—God's will about slavery or our understanding? The obvious answer is that God has not changed—rather our understanding of God's will has changed. But even in this realization that a biblical character could misunderstand God's will, we learn one of the great lessons of our faith—that we, too, are prone to error but can still be effective servants of God. This is part of what has been called "progressive revelation." As William Neil has observed, "The Bible is essentially a book about our human situation in a bewildering and perplexing universe."[14]

STUDY QUESTIONS

1. What do we mean when we speak of the Old Testament and how did the term originate?
2. What do the abbreviations B.C.E. and C.E. mean?
3. What is unusual about the fact that the Old Testament has much narrative material?
4. Why did the Israelites begin their story with the Exodus?
5. How were the early traditions about Israel developed and passed on from generation to generation?
6. What are etiologies?
7. What were the high points of Israel's story beginning with the Exodus and ending with the Babylonian Exile?
8. What are the three divisions of the Hebrew canon?
9. How did the Septuagint affect how various Christian groups view the biblical canon today?
10. What is the basic concern of textual criticism?
11. With what three things are literary and historical studies of the biblical text concerned?
12. What evidences are cited to argue for the Mosaic authorship of the Pentateuch (Genesis through Deuteronomy)?
13. Identify: (a) H. B. Witter and Jean Astruc; (b) Julius Wellhausen; (c) Hermann Gunkel; (d) form criticism; (e) Ivan Engnell; (f) oral tradition; (g) redaction criticism.
14. What major shift in emphasis has taken place in Old Testament studies in recent years?
15. What three groups of redactors or editors are believed to have been responsible for the final form of the Old Testament as we now know it?
16. What is the basic purpose of archaeology?

17. How are archaeological dig sites selected?
18. What are some ways that modern technology is making a contribution to archaeology?
19. What are the strengths and weaknesses in using archaeology in biblical interpretation?
20. Learn at least one important fact about each of the archaeological examples given in this chapter.
21. Something to think about: How do the inspiration of other great literature and the inspiration of the Hebrew Bible differ? Or do they?

ENDNOTES

1. In keeping with more recent practices, B.C.E., "before the Common Era" and C.E., "the Common Era" are used in this text instead of B.C. and A.D.
2. For this insight, I am indebted to Tamara Cohn Eskenazi, "Torah as Narrative and Narrative as Torah," in *Old Testament Interpretation: Past, Present, and Future—Essays in Honor of Gene M. Tucker*, edited by James Luther Mays, David L. Petersen, and Kent Harold Richards (Nashville: Abingdon Press, 1995), 14.
3. On the problem of the formation of the canon, see Daniel J. Harrington, "Introduction to the Canon," *NIB* I, esp. 7–13. See also John J. Collins, "Before the Canon: Scriptures in Second Temple Judaism," in James L. Mays, et al., op. cit., 225–241. For a look at how the differing order of the Hebrew Bible by Jews and Christians affects the interpretation of various books, see James A. Sanders, "'Spinning' the Bible: How Judaism and Christianity Shape the Canon Differently," *BR* XIV, 3 (June, 1998), 22–29.
4. For a concise discussion of the traditional view, see G. Herbert Livingston, *The Pentateuch in Its Cultural Environment* (Grand Rapids: Baker Book House, 1974), 218–220.
5. *Critic* and *criticism* are used here to mean "one who analyzes" and "the analysis of" the materials for the purpose of coming to a better understanding of them. It does not imply a destructive purpose.
6. James L. Crenshaw, "The Bible as Literature," *MDB*, 515–519, is a good survey of this field of study. Two books that use this approach are: Robert Alter and Frank Kermode, *Introduction to the Literary Guide to the Bible* (Cambridge, MA: Belknap Press, 1987); and Brian Peckham, *History and Prophecy: The Development of the Late Judean Literary Traditions* (New York: Doubleday, 1993).
7. A major work based on this interest is Ranier Albertz, *A History of Israelite Religion in the Old Testament Period*. Trans. by John Bowden (Louisville: Westminster John Knox Press, 1994), 2 vols.
8. Victor H. Matthews, *Manners and Customs in the Bible: An Illustrated Guide to Daily Life in Bible Times* (Peabody, Mass.: Hendrickson Publishers, 1988) is a comprehensive work on this aspect of biblical life.
9. "David Found at Dan," *BAR* 20,2 (March/April, 1994), 26–39.
10. Avraham Biran, "The Discovery of the Middle Bronze Gate at Dan," *BA* 44, 1 (November, 1981), 139–144.
11. A fascinating example of this is described by Dan Bahat, "Jerusalem Down Under: Tunneling Along Herod's Temple Wall," *BAR* 21, 6 (Nov./Dec., 1995), 30–47. See also Thomas E. Levy, "From Camels to Computers: A Short History of Archaeological Method," *BAR* 21, 4 (July/August, 1995), 44–51, 64.
12. James L. Crenshaw, *Education in Ancient Israel: Across the Deadening Silence* (New York: Doubleday, 1998), 39f.
13. For a number of these examples, I am indebted to Michael D. Coogan, "10 Great Finds," *BAR* 21, 3 (May/June, 1995), 36–47.
14. William Neil, *The Rediscovery of the Bible* (London: Hodder and Stoughton, Ltd., 1954), 9.

Chapter 2 🌿

THE GEOGRAPHICAL
AND HISTORICAL SETTING
FOR THE OLD TESTAMENT
PRIOR TO 1200 B.C.E.

In a remarkable photograph taken from the *Gemini XI* spacecraft in 1966, the biblical world from Egypt to Mesopotamia is captured in one magnificent view. One is struck by the dry, barren look that characterizes much of this area, called the Near East. And dry it is. Deserts abound—the Arabian Desert is on the East, the desert of the Sinai Peninsula is to the south, and the great Sahara Desert in North Africa pushes its way right up to the banks of the Nile River in Egypt. Only where there were rivers was there settled life in early times. These rivers furnished water for drinking and for the irrigation that made possible the development of agriculture. Other regions might have in the occasional oasis enough water for nomadic herdsmen, but these oases were so far apart that desert travel was limited until the domestication of the camel. Nomads until late in the second millenium B.C.E. traveled by ass or donkey and thus were limited in their range.

THE FERTILE CRESCENT

The watered areas of the Near East form a rough crescent-shaped pattern known as the Fertile Crescent. This fertile strip of land begins in the east at the Persian Gulf and runs northwestward, taking in the valleys of the Tigris and Euphrates. North of this region high mountains form a barrier between the rivers and what we know today as southern Russia. Mesopotamia, the name given to this region, means literally, "in the midst of, or between, rivers." The mountains continue in the northwest, separating Mesopotamia from Asia Minor and the Mediterranean Sea.

The center of the Fertile Crescent was Syria-Palestine, a narrow bank of fertile land caught in a vise between the Arabian Desert and the Mediterranean Sea. All the major roads from Africa to Asia passed through this narrow strip of land, thus making it a prize to be seized by the great powers of the time.

The southern end of the crescent was Egypt, the land of the Nile. Isolated from other major civilizations by deserts and distance, it developed one of the earliest and most powerful civilizations.

MESOPOTAMIA

3000 to 2000 B.C.E.

The Sumerians.   These people, named for their major area, Sumer, occupied a number of city-states that dominated the lower Mesopotamian region from 3150 to 2350 B.C.E. and again from 2060 to 1950 B.C.E. In this later period, Ur, one of the truly great cities of the ancient world, was dominant. The Sumerians invented the earliest known form of writing (cuneiform) and introduced counting by sixties (the method we use to count seconds and minutes). They were conquered by the Elamites.[1]

The Akkadians.   The first empire builder was Sargon of Akkad, who interrupted the Sumerian dominance of Mesopotamia in 2350 B.C.E., establishing an empire that would last until 2180 B.C.E. His people, the Akkadians, were Semites, a people from whom the later Israelites came. The Akkadians moved northwest into Mesopotamia from the Arabian Peninsula. Their language and literature continued to dominate Mesopotamia through their heirs, the Babylonians and the Assyrians. Through archaeology it has come to us, and it furnishes a wealth of knowledge about the religious and cultural life of the region.

2000 to 1500 B.C.E.

The Amorites (Arameans).   These people, known as "Westerners," were originally seminomadic tribesmen from Arabia. In the 200 years after 2000 B.C.E., they appeared all over the Fertile Crescent, causing great disruptions. After some time they settled down, building new towns in northern and western Palestine and establishing two strong states in Mesopotamia around 1800 B.C.E.—Mari, located in the northwest and Babylonia, in south-central Mesopotamia. Babylonia's most famous king was Hammurabi, best known for his famous law codes. From Mari we have the Mari Tablets, which shed light on many patriarchal customs.

Like the Akkadians, the Amorites were Semitic people. Their invasion of the Fertile Crescent was during the same general time of the Hebrew patriarchs, Abraham, Isaac, and Jacob. What has been learned about them through archaeology fits in well with the descriptions of the lifestyle of the patriarchs.

Figure 2–1. The Fertile Crescent from *Gemini XI.*

Courtesy of the National Aeronautics and Space Administration.

The Hurrians.   The Amorite states also passed away, being succeeded by the Hurrians, or Horites as the Old Testament calls them. They absorbed the Amorite population into a state called Mitanni, and they also absorbed much of the Amorite culture. Fortunately, many of their writings were preserved on clay tablets at Nuzi, one of their major cities. The discovery of these tablets has helped clear up many obscure passages in the Old Testament.

1500 to 1000 B.C.E.

Arameans and Habiru.   Again, as it had happened five hundred years before, the Fertile Crescent was overrun by seminomads from Arabia. Among them were people referred to as *Apiru* or *Habiru*. Who they were has been the subject of much discussion. They appeared in many roles—as outlaws, as hired soldiers or mercenaries, as slaves, as seminomadic wanderers. The similarity of their name to the word *Hebrew* makes it tempting to say they were the Hebrews. However, references to them come from places all over the Fertile Crescent, so they cannot be one and the same. *Habiru* refers to a much broader range of people. On the other hand,

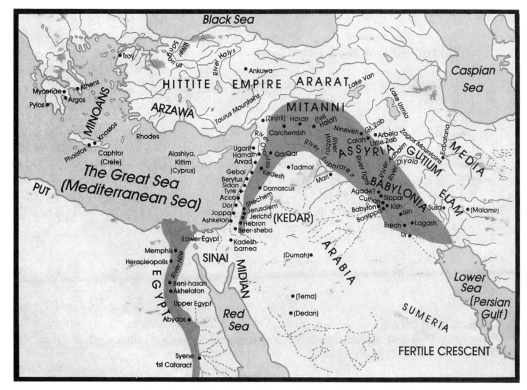

Artwork by Margaret Jordan Brown. © Mercer University Press.

Figure 2–2.   The Fertile Crescent.

the Hebrews seem to have belonged to the same class of people. In other words, not all *Habiru* were Hebrews, but the Hebrews seem to have been *Habiru*. They were a social class from which the Hebrews came.

ASIA MINOR

The Hittites.   While it actually lay outside the bounds of the Fertile Crescent, Asia Minor was to play a very influential role in biblical history, especially in the Christian era. For many years, however, it was thought that it had little or no role in Old Testament history. Now we know that central Asia Minor was the center of the Hittite Empire. The Hittites are known in the Old Testament as the "sons of Heth." Their capital was Hattusa. They pushed down from Asia into what is known now as Lebanon and Syria around 1400 B.C.E., having won the area from the Mitanni. Their greatest threat was to the power of Egypt, which controlled Palestine during that time.[2]

EGYPT

3000 to 2000 B.C.E.

The part of Egypt comprising the fertile area—a narrow strip of land along the Nile River—looks like a crooked tree with a fan-shaped top representing the Nile Delta. There the river breaks up into many branches before entering the Mediterranean Sea. This delta region was a tempting target for hungry nomads throughout biblical history, for its well-watered lands produced food and pasturage in abundance when other areas were devastated by drought.

At the same time, Egypt's separation from the rest of the Fertile Crescent by the land bridge of Palestine and the Sinai Desert enabled its civilization to develop with a minimum of interruption from outside forces. This early period, before 2000 B.C.E. was the time of the building of the great pyramids.

2000 to 1000 B.C.E.

Genesis 12:10–20 tells the story of Abram (Abraham) taking his family to Egypt. This kind of emigration was common at that time. It also came at the time when the Fertile Crescent was experiencing the invasions by the Amorites, the Semitic tribesmen from Arabia.

From 1720 to 1570 B.C.E. Egypt was ruled by the Hyksos, or "foreigners." The Hyksos were a people who were among the first to use chariots and cavalry units for warfare. They also built cities with a distinctive kind of protective wall. These walls had a steep slope, or *glacis*, extending from the base of the wall, which made it difficult for aggressors to attack the wall. Their kingdom included both Egypt and Palestine.

The Hyksos were overthrown by the eighteenth Egyptian dynasty, founded by Ahmose I. In the centuries that followed, the Egyptians dominated Palestine. Their rule there was opposed by the Hurrian (Horite) kingdom of Mitanni, or *Naharin*. Later, the Hittites took control of the Hurrian Empire, but Egypt was still able to control Palestine proper until late in the 1200s B.C.E. Egypt's last great rulers were Seti I (1308–1290 B.C.E.) and Ramses II (1290–1224 B.C.E.). These pharaohs often are associated with the Hebrew exodus from Egypt.

SYRIA-PHOENICIA

3000 to 2000 B.C.E.

Syria, bounded on the west by the Mediterranean Sea and on the east by the Arabian Desert, is the northern portion of the land bridge connecting Mesopotamia, Asia Minor, and Egypt. Its southern boundaries during the period of the Israelite kingdoms varied from period to period but generally were marked by Mt. Hermon, whose melting snows furnish water for the major sources of the Jordan River.

Courtesy of H. Armstrong Roberts.

Figure 2–3. The Sphinx and the Great Pyramid—symbols of the grandeur of ancient Egypt.

As part of the corridor connecting the continents, Syria's populations varied with each new outbreak of migration and conquest. Until recently, no major civilization was known to have existed in Syria before 2000 B.C.E. Now, however, the discoveries at Ebla in northern Syria have radically changed that assessment. Ebla seems to have flourished in two periods, the first of which was from 2400 to 2250 B.C.E. During this time, it was strong enough to challenge the empire of Sargon of Akkad, who had the first great Near Eastern empire. The first period of Ebla's prosperity ended when the city was conquered and burned by the Akkadian ruler Namar-Sin. Ebla flourished again between 2000 and 1600 B.C.E., as is evidenced by the discovery of an elaborate palace complex. It is certain that the eventual decipherment and translation of thousands of tablets found in the Ebla excavations will add much to our knowledge of ancient Syria in the second and third millenia. The initial suggestion, however, that they would have great significance for Old Testament studies, now seems to be far less certain.[3]

2000 to 1000 B.C.E.

The southwestern coast of Syria, known in biblical times as Phoenicia and Lebanon, was one of the major strongholds of the Canaanite populations so frequently mentioned in the Old Testament. Possessing the finest natural harbors in the eastern end of the Mediterranean Sea, coupled with an abundance of fine timber and a lack of agricultural land, its economy was based on the sea. The Phoenicians developed a merchant fleet that became, in effect, the navy and merchant fleet of the Israelite kings, David, Solomon, Omri, and Ahab, who had trade agreements with the local kings, especially the kings of Tyre. In addition, Israelite building programs used Phoenician architects, craftsmen, and vast quantities of the famous "cedars of Lebanon."

Farther north lay the city of Ugarit, center for Canaanite culture and learning around 1400 B.C.E. Here were discovered the Ras Shamra texts, which, like the Dead Sea Scrolls, opened up new areas of understanding in Old Testament studies.

The most famous of all Syrian cities was and is Damascus, which was already an old city in the time of the patriarchs. Through it passed the traders, wanderers, and armies of the ancient world.

PALESTINE

Its Importance

Possibly no geographical area in the Western world holds a greater fascination for more people than does Palestine. For three great religions it is the "Holy Land." Its strategic location made it the object of a continual tug-of-war among the ancient empires. Each one coveted its territory, not because it possessed vast land or rich resources, but simply because anyone going anywhere north or south in the ancient Near East had to cross Palestine to get there. On the West the barrier was the Mediterranean Sea. Although some small ships sailed its waters, it was not a major means of travel for many centuries. To the east lay the vast reaches of the Arabian Desert, virtually impassable to the donkey-riding traders of early times. The famous ship of the desert, the camel, did not come into common use until after 1000 B.C.E. Thus all land traffic between Africa, Asia Minor, and Mesopotamia was funneled through Palestine.

Geographical Features

As one moves eastward from the Mediterranean coastal area, four major divisions of the land are evident. First is the coastal plain itself. The plain, broader in the southern region, becomes more narrow, generally speaking, as one goes northward. In the south it is known as the Plain of Philistia after its most famous inhabitants, the Philistines. They were a seafaring people who settled there, either after having been repulsed in an attack on Egypt, or as mercenaries placed there by the Egyptians after being conquered by them.[4] They had five major cities—Gaza, Ashdod, Ashkelon, Ekron, and Gath. Not until David's time was the area under Israelite control.

The northern border of the Philistine territory was the Yarkon River, one of the few free-flowing streams in Palestine. From the Yarkon north to Mt. Carmel was the Plain of Sharon, covered in biblical times by forests. It, too, came under Israelite control rather late.

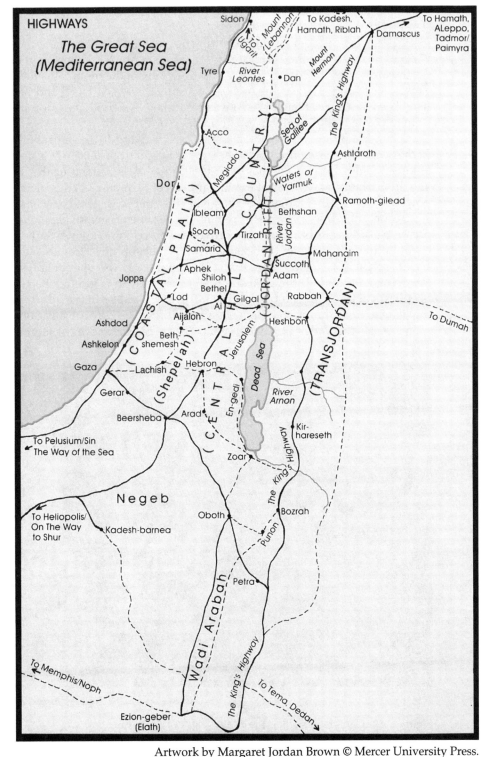

Artwork by Margaret Jordan Brown © Mercer University Press.

Figure 2–4. The Highways of Palestine and Major Divisions.

Mt. Carmel, a major landmark jutting out into the Mediterranean, divided the Plain of Sharon from the Plain of Acco, or Acre, a much smaller plain extending northward to the "Ladder of Tyre," where once again the mountains meet the sea. This latter feature marked the boundary at times between Israel and its northern neighbors. While the Plain of Acco was controlled by David, Solomon had to give it up to pay his building debts to Hiram, king of Tyre.

The second major division as one moves eastward is the central hill country. In the north, the hills of upper Galilee vary in height from 2000 to 3000 feet, whereas lower Galilee farther south has hills of 2000 feet or less. Separating the Galilee hills and the Carmel range is the flat triangular Plain of Megiddo. On this plain stood the powerful city of Megiddo, one of the great cities of the ancient Near East.

As one moves southward, the mountains become progressively higher, pierced occasionally by valleys, running west to east. This region is known as the hill country of Ephraim in much of biblical history. Further south it becomes the hill country of Judah. This region actually has two parts: (1) the Shephelah, an area of low-lying hills, and (2) the plateau on which Jerusalem is located. Separating the Shephelah and the Judean plateau is a north-south valley that made approaching the plateau from the coastal plain especially difficult. There are basically four approaches: (1) the Valley of Aijalon, which is the easiest and most famous; (2) the

Louis Goldman/Rapho/Photo Researchers.

Figure 2–5.   Coral reefs such as these, and a lack of deep water, effectively prevented the Israelites from developing seaports.

Valley of Sorek; (3) the Valley of Azekah; and (4) the Valley of Elah. The latter three were more narrow and deep, making major movements, such as by armies, more difficult. In biblical times, if whoever controlled the plateau also controlled the Valley of Aijalon, many of the major defensive problems were solved.[5]

South of Judah, the hill country begins to decrease in altitude. In the south is the Negev, an area of rather flat land, primarily suited for raising sheep and limited agriculture. Beyond the Negev lies the Sinai Desert.

The third division, the Jordan Rift, is a deep scar in the earth that stretches from the base of Mt. Hermon in the north all the way through Palestine and eventually into East Africa. In Palestine it is the channel for the Jordan River; the Sea of Galilee, its only large body of fresh water; and the Dead Sea, one of the world's most unusual lakes.

The Jordan, appropriately named the "down-rusher," is formed from a number of smaller sources—the primary ones being the Snir, the Dan, and the Banias Rivers—that rise near Mt. Hermon. In earlier times the Jordan flowed into Lake Huleh—a swampy area now drained for agriculture—before dropping rather rapidly into the Sea of Galilee. By the time the Jordan reaches the Sea of Galilee, it is already more than six hundred feet below the level of the Mediterranean. From the Sea of Galilee to the Dead Sea is 65 miles, but, by the time the waters of the Jordan

Courtesy of C. May / H. Armstrong Roberts.

Figure 2–6. A view of the rough terrain of the central hill country of Palestine.

Figure 2–7. The Negev, lying between the sown land and the desert, was the home of pastoral groups such as the Amalekites.

Eric Hartmann/Magnum Photos.

reach the Dead Sea they have traveled 135 miles because of the meandering nature of the stream. Unlike the Nile and the Tigris-Euphrates Rivers, whose waters give life to the land through which they pass, until modern times the Jordan's waters have contributed little to sustain life along its path. There were two reasons for this: (1) Unlike the other rivers, its valley was formed by earthquake, not carved out by the river itself. Because of this, instead of deep rich loam that is characteristic of valleys carved by rivers, the Jordan Valley soil is of such a nature that it is not suitable for agriculture. (2) In addition, the Jordan floods at the wrong time of the year so that it would wash away any crops planted along its banks (see Josh. 3:15). These and other reasons also prevent the Jordan or its valley from being used for travel.

At the deepest point of the great rift valley through which the river flows lies the Dead Sea, whose surface is more than 1300 feet below the level of the Mediterranean. The Dead Sea is a taker, giving up nothing without a struggle. As a result, it has such a high concentration of natural pollution that very little life can exist in its waters.[6]

South of the Dead Sea the rift valley is known as the Arabah. Rising gradually from the Dead Sea, it eventually begins to slope downward again until it reaches the Gulf of Aqabah, an arm of the Red Sea.

The fourth division of the land is the Transjordan Plateau. To the north opposite the Huleh Valley and the Sea of Galilee was the region known in biblical times as Bashan. The ownership of Bashan, known for its fine cattle, was under constant dispute between the Israelite kingdoms and Syria. It has been in the newspaper headlines in recent years under its modern name, the Golan Heights.

Across the Jordan from the hill country of Ephraim lay the territory of Gilead. Through it ran another major tributary of the Jordan, the Jabbok River. It was at one of the fords of the Jabbok that Jacob had his famous wrestling match (Gen 32:22–32).

The hill country of Gilead descends to form a broad plateau area. Traditionally called Moab, it bordered the Dead Sea and was ideal sheep country. Its broad, flat plains are broken only by an occasional stream, the chief one being the Arnon River.

The Brook Zered, which enters the Arabah at the southern end of the Dead Sea, was the traditional border between Moab and Edom. The Edomite territory was more rugged and less suited to pastoral or agricultural development than the other parts of Transjordan. This area often went for long periods with no major settlements. Those who did settle there were famous as traders and merchants.

J. Allan Cash/Rapho/Photo Researchers Inc.

Figure 2–8.   An aerial view of the Jordan River as it follows a serpentine path to the Dead Sea.

Major Roads

The chief value of Palestine to the ancient world powers lay in two major roads which crossed its territory. The most important was called "the Way of the Philistines," or "the Way of the Sea." In Roman times, it was called the *Via Maris.*[7] As its name suggests, it followed the seacoast as it ran northeastward from Egypt, passing through the important Philistine cities of Gaza and Ashdod. As it neared the northern boundaries of the Philistine territory, it had to swing eastward toward the foothills to avoid the swamps caused by the blockage of the Yarkon River by shifting sands. Proceeding northward, it passed through the Carmel range near Megiddo and across the plain, skirting the Sea of Galilee and crossing the Jordan near Hazor, the largest city in ancient Palestine. From there it continued northeastward through Damascus and on to Mesopotamia.

Photograph by Richard T. Nowitz.

Figure 2–9.   "We will not pass through field or vineyard . . . we will go along the King's Highway" (Num. 20:17). The King's Highway approaches Madaba (biblical Medeba) on the ancient border between Moab and Ammon. Today a modern road follows the ancient caravan route.

The desire to control this road was motivated by two things—power and money. It was the major invasion route followed by armies from Mesopotamia, Egypt, and Asia Minor. A nation controlling the road beyond its borders could expect greater safety for the empire. Furthermore, the caravans which traveled over it were made to pay for that privilege, thus providing a rich source of revenue for the country that controlled it.

To a lesser degree the same was true of the major north-south route east of the Jordan River—the King's Highway. Beginning with a major trans-Sinai route from Egypt to Edom, the King's Highway proceeded northward until it, too, came to Damascus. It was this route that Israel followed in part as it came out of the desert to invade Palestine.

While not of international importance like the *Via Maris* and the King's Highway, a number of secondary roads were of importance for travel within the land. Perhaps the most significant of these was the route which ran through the hill country, connecting such strategic points as Shechem, Bethel, Jerusalem, Hebron, and Beersheba. A major cross-country route ran from the Plain of Acre through Megiddo and on to the Jordan River, via the Valley of Jezreel. In the South, routes into the central hill country followed the Valleys of Aijalon and Elah.

STUDY QUESTIONS

1. What is the Fertile Crescent and what areas does it cover?
2. Identify: Sumerians, Akkadians, Amorites, Hurrians, Arameans, *Habiru*, Hittites.
3. What was the importance of the Nile River for ancient Egypt?
4. Who were the Hyksos? What role are they believed to have played in the early history of Israel?
5. Why has Ebla been in the news in recent years?
6. Why are Ugarit and the Ras Shamra texts important for Old Testament studies?
7. What are the four major divisions of Palestine, West to East?
8. How did the Shephelah function in biblical times to protect the area of Judah?
9. Why was the Jordan River of little positive importance in Old Testament times?
10. What were the two major North-South roads in ancient Palestine and why were they so important?

ENDNOTES

1. William W. Hallo, "Sumerian Literature: Background to the Bible," *BR* IV, 3 (June, 1988), 29.
2. A complete issue of *BA* 53, 2 and 3, (June/September, 1989) is devoted to articles on the Hittites.
3. For a comprehensive summary on the Ebla discoveries, see Robert D. Biggs, "Ebla Tablets," *ABD* II, 263–270. See also

Stephen M. Hooks, "Ebla," *MDB* 225–227.
4. For opposing points of view on this issue, see Bryant G. Wood, "The Philistines Enter Canaan—Were They Egyptian Lackeys or Invading Conquerors?" *BAR* XVII (November/December, (1991), 44–52, who argues that they were conquerors; and Itamar Singer, "How

Did the Philistines Enter Canaan," *BAR* XVIII November/December, 1992), 44–46, who argues that they were Egyptian mercenaries.

5. Harold Brodsky, "The Shephelah—Guardian of Judea," *BR* III (Winter, 1987), 48–50.

6. _____, "The Jordan—Symbol of Spiritual Transition," *BR* VIII (June, 1992), 34–43, 52.

7. Barry J. Beitzel, "The *Via Maris* in Literary and Cartographic Sources," *BA* 54, 2 (June, 1991), 64–75, argues that *Via Maris* referred to an East-West road rather than the major North-South coastal road.

Chapter 3 🔥

ISRAEL LOOKS
AT THE BEGINNINGS

THE BEGINNINGS

Genesis is a Greek translation of the Hebrew title for this book—*bᵉreshith*. This Hebrew phrase means "in beginning." Genesis not only introduces the Pentateuch or Torah but the whole of the Hebrew Bible or *Tanak*. *Tanak* is a word formed by using the first letters of the name for the three divisions of the canon: *Torah, Nebi'im* and *Kethubim*.

Genesis naturally falls into two parts: 1–11, the Creation, the Fall, and the consequences of the Fall; and 12–50, the patriarchs or ancestors of Israel—Abraham, Isaac, Jacob, and Joseph. Whoever was responsible for the final form of this book obviously had access to a variety of materials—creation stories, genealogical lists, flood stories, sagas, and other popular stories. Priestly concerns are evident in emphases on religious ceremonies, such as covenant making and circumcision (Gen. 17). The primary purpose of the book is theological—to say that Israel was brought into being by the LORD God, the Creator of the Universe.

The Primeval History

The primeval history, as Genesis 1–11 is often called, is a different kind of history. It is different, first of all, because it is based on oral traditions passed along over a long period of time. It is different also because of the way it speaks of God's direct relationship to people, unlike the style of a modern historian. After all, there was no television camera to record the events of creation for the 6 o'clock news.

The nature of this material, then, is theological—that is, it speaks of God's activity in creation. It is the product of Israel's thoughts about how the world came into being, expressed in the oral traditions that were a part of Israel's heritage.

Israel's neighbors also had creation stories. One of the most famous stories goes back to the Akkadians, who dominated Mesopotamia from 2350 B.C.E. to 2060 B.C.E. Because it comes to us from the Babylonians, it is called the Babylonian creation epic, or *enuma elish*, after the opening words of the text.

Enuma Elish

This myth describes how the gods were the offspring of Tiamat and Apsu in chaos. Later, there is warfare among the gods and goddesses, caused by the fact that Apsu (the lover of Tiamat) had been killed by Ea. Tiamat vowed to get revenge on Ea. Ea trembled in fear at the possibility of having to face Tiamat, so he turned to Anshar, his father, for advice. It was decided that Marduk, the strong man of the gods, would face Tiamat. As his price for taking on that responsibility, Marduk demanded first place among the gods. Anshar, mortally afraid of Tiamat, agreed.

Taking along the four winds to help him, Marduk went out to meet Tiamat. She came out at him with her mouth open, intending to devour him. That was her fatal mistake. Marduk unleashed the four winds, who entered her mouth, blowing her up like a balloon. Then, Marduk took his sword and sliced her into halves like a grapefruit. The upper half of her body he used for the dome of the heavens, and the lower half he used to create the earth. They then killed her latest lover, Kingu, and made man out of his blood.[1]

The Israelite Understanding of Creation

The Old Testament is filled with references to creation. Such is the case of Psalm 104:1b–8, where God is described as follows:

> You are clothed with honor and majesty,
>   wrapped in light as with a garment.
> You stretch out the heavens like a tent,
>   you set the beams of your chambers on the waters,
> You make the clouds your chariot,
>   you ride on the wings of the wind,
> You make the winds your messengers,
>   fire and flame your ministers.
>
> You set the earth on its foundations,
>   so it shall never be shaken.

You cover it with the deep as a garment;
    the waters stood above the mountains.
At your rebuke they flee;
    at the sound of your thunder they take to flight.
They rose up to the mountains, ran down to the valleys
    to the place that you appointed for them.
You set a boundary that they may not pass,
    so that they might not again cover the earth.

The concepts used by the Psalmist reflect images present in the world of that time.

The influence of Israel's world can best be seen, however, in the Genesis creation story. Both Genesis 1:1–2:4a and the *enuma elish* speak of the watery chaos, covered by darkness, which precedes the work of creation; they follow something of the same order of creation—firmament, land, sun and moon, humanity—and in each, the creator rests after the work is finished. But as is often true, the agreements in detail are not nearly so significant as the differences. After all, all humans are similar—their differences make them unique.

Genesis I:I-2:4a

This account of creation, the product of centuries of theological reflection, was put into its final form by the priestly theologians of Israel. Well aware of other creation stories, they expressd the conviction that the God of Israel was the only God and the creator of the visible universe.[2] In the myths, the gods arose out of the creative process. This was not so for Israel. God did not arise from creation—God was the Creator! There is no speculation about God's beginning; Israel assumed that God was and had always been. Thus the emphasis in Israel's creation story is more on God than on what was created.

"In the beginning, God created the heavens and the earth" (1:1) is a summary statement of all that is to follow. God (called *Elohim*) is *transcendent* (separated from the material universe) and powerful (God speaks and things come into being). There is no struggle to bring order to chaos, but the majestic God calls things into existence. Like the notes of a symphony, certain phrases appear and reappear; "and God said," "God called (named)," "God saw that it was good," "God made," "And there was evening, and there was morning."

There seems to be a conscious effort to counter the Near Eastern creation myths. In contrast to the struggle waged between Marduk and Tiamat, God is in complete control of creation. The heavenly bodies—the sun, the moon, and the stars (1:14–19), worshiped as gods by Israel's neighbors—are created (1:14). They get their light from God, not from their own powers. The earth, furthermore, looked upon as the mother goddess by many ancient people, has no power to give life except as God commands (1:21). Finally, humanity, the crown of creation, is made in God's image and is commissioned by God to be caretaker of creation (1:26-27).

For two reasons, the statement, "Let *us* make humankind in *our* image and after *our* likeness (1:26) is one which has drawn much attention: (1) because of the personal pronouns "us" and "our," and (2) because of the meaning of the expression "image of God."

Three possible explanations of the use of the plural pronouns are advanced. (1) Since the word for God (*Elohim*) is a plural form, the use of the plural pronoun is expected. The problem with this expanation is that *Elohim* is used in other places with the singular pronoun. (2) It is simply the equivalent of "Let's do it" as if to say, "I will do it" (Isa. 6:8). (3) God is pictured as a king, addressing a heavenly court or council, expressing to those who serve him what he wants done.[3]

The meaning of the expression "image of God" has caused much ink to be used. That the ancient Hebrews thought of God as having certain physical traits cannot be denied since numerous references are made to such in the Old Testament. The temptation is to see "image" and "likeness" in these terms, but it surely goes deeper than a physical image. One aspect of the image seems to lie in the statement that humankind, like God, who is the ruler over all creation, is given power to rule over the earth. The privilege of naming the animals signifies power over them. Another aspect of the image of God must lie in the statement that humankind is endowed by God with intelligence and the power of creativity.

Genesis 2:4b–2:25

In reading this version of Israel's creation story, the first thing to notice is that God is referred to as the "LORD God" (2:4) (Hebrew: *Yahweh Elohim*). Some would call this the Yahwistic version of creation since it uses Israel's personal name for God, *Yahweh*. Its simplicity and directness seem to indicate that it is much older than the more highly developed account in 1:1–2:4a. The main interest is the creation of humanity, which is placed first. The creation of the world is already assumed to have taken place.

The patterned kind of story found in 1:1–2:4a is missing in this account. God's creative acts, furthermore, are described in human terms. To say that "the LORD God *formed* man from the dust," "*breathed* into his nostrils the breath of life," "*planted* a garden," and "*took* the man and put him in the garden" is to speak in what is called *anthropomorphic language*, that is, "to describe God in human terms." God is pictured as acting in human ways as he made human beings, talked with them, and, like a concerned father, disciplined them when they did wrong (Gen. 3).

Just as an exalted view of God in Genesis 1:1–2:4a (which theologians call *transcendence*) is needed so that God will be reverenced and respected by the worshiper, so a more personal view of God (a view which theologians speak of as *immanence*), emphasizes God's nearness and concern for the worshiper. These two views of God must be kept in proper relationship to each other. If transcendence is overemphasized, God becomes so far removed as to have little or no interest in humankind. An overly trancendent view makes any personal relationship with the Deity a farce.

On the other hand, an overly "humanized" Deity can lead to overfamiliarity, with the result that God becomes a "big Daddy" or "the man upstairs." Extreme "humanization" of God also makes the Deity irrelevant. A balance between the two extremes more nearly represents the biblical view.

The man created by God from the dust of the earth and given life by the breath of God is not created for idleness. Instead, he is placed in the garden that the LORD God has "planted" and given the responsibility for its cultivation (2:15). As tenant, he has privileges, but he also has responsibilities. The man, from the first, has his "do's" and "do not's," and the major "do not" is "Do not eat of the tree of the knowledge of good and evil" (2:17). He is given power over the animals, symbolized by the privilege of naming them (2:19–20); but power does not satisfy the basic human need for companionship. So woman is created, and man is complete (2:23). Made for each other, they have nothing to hide (2:25).

The Fall (Gen. 3:1–24)

Man's glory is also his undoing. Created in God's image, his *hubris* ("pride or arrogance") moves him to substitute his judgment for that of God. This sense of pride underlies the appeal of the serpent to the woman when he tells her that if she eats the forbidden fruit, she will "be like God, knowing good and evil" (3:5). The ancient storyteller had a marvelous understanding of human nature. His description of the forbidden fruit's appeal to Eve's appetite ("good for food"), to her sense of beauty ("a delight to the eyes"), and to her sense of pride ("the desire to make one wise," 3:6), shows how well he understood the nature of temptation. If he lived today, he probably could make a fortune in advertising.

The woman falls for the serpent's line so quickly that she is hooked before she realizes what is happening. The man, no less gullible than the woman, falls for the same line. Suddenly, they are ashamed of what they see in each other and so they try to cover their nakedness with clothing made of leaves (3:7).

Discovery of man's disobedience brings God's displeasure. Since man wants to be like God, he has to take the responsibility for his action. Now, he hides from God, who created him and gave him paradise (3:10). As a further result of their disobedience, man and woman are banished from the garden and separated from God. They are in this together. Work becomes a burden, and life loses much of its joy (3:17–20).

The biblical writer here has given his view of man's basic problem in relation to God. Adam (mankind) wants to be God, but the Creator cannot and will not yield his unlimited authority to his creation. Man has been given as much power as he can handle wisely. To give him more would be disastrous for him, so limits have to be established (3:24).

Cain and Abel (Gen. 4:1–26)

As a large stone dropped in a calm body of water begins a series of ever-widening circles that do not stop until they reach the shore, so the first sin is described as creating even more disastrous consequences as its influence passes from generation to generation. Guilt and suspicion between husband and wife pay off in brother killing brother in the next generation. The murder was instigated by jealousy on Cain's part over Abel's more acceptable sacrifice. Sin so alienated Cain from Abel that personal feelings had greater value than a human life, but murder will not stay hidden. The ancients believed that when a body was not properly buried, as would be usual in the case of murder, the blood of the victim that contained the life would cry to God until justice was done (4:10). Try as he might, Cain could not escape the consequence of his sin (4:13). Even so, God showed mercy by giving Cain a protective mark (4:15).

But Cain's murder of Abel was only a beginning. By the time of Lamech, human life was so worthless that Lamech could brag: "I killed a man for wounding me, a young man for striking me." (4:23).

Adam's Descendants

The narrator ties the stories of creation to the story of the flood by "the list of the descendants of Adam" (Gen. 5).

Flood Stories and the Flood (Gen. 5:32–9:19)

Flood stories are a part of the traditions of many peoples. The biblical flood story (which properly begins with the introduction of Noah and his sons in 5:32) shares common features with two accounts of a great flood in Mesopotamia—the Gilgamesh Epic and the Atrahasis Epic.

The Gilgamesh Epic. Gilgamesh, the hero, seeks the secret of eternal life. He goes to Utnapishtim, who tells him how the gods tried to destroy humanity with the great flood. Ea, one of the gods, had warned Utnapishtim, who escaped by building an ark. The flood was so great that even the gods themselves thought they were going to be destroyed.

When the waters receded a bit, the ark landed on Mount Nisir. Utnapishtim sent out a dove and a raven to see if the waters had receded sufficiently for him to leave the ark. When the flood was over, he made a sacrifice:

> The gods smelled the sweet savor,
> The gods crowded like flies about the sacrifice.[4]

The Atrahasis Epic. This epic, first published in 1922, also comes from the Babylonians. Like the biblical account, it starts first with the creation story. The people are so numerous and noisy that the gods decide to destroy them. A number of solutions are tried—plague, drought, famine—but none is satisfactory. Finally, a flood is called for, after which a new kind of world will appear, in which various means will be used to control the population.[5]

The Flood (Gen. 5:32–8:22).   The story of the marriage of the "sons of God" and the "daughters of men" (6:1–4) serves as the background for the biblical account of the flood because it illustrates the conclusion reached in 6:5:

> The LORD saw that the wickedness of humankind was great on the earth, and that every inclination of the thoughts of their hearts was only evil continually.

The reference to the "sons of God" reflects an ancient belief that marriage between divine men and human women produced a race of giants (6:4). Here the older story is given new meaning by serving as an illustration of the depths of human sinfulness that results in the flood.[6]

That Israel also had at least two different flood traditions can be seen when one separates the passages using LORD from those using *God*.[7] Each series of passages tells a story of the flood. The two have been blended without regard to duplications.[8]

Numerous attempts have been made to confirm the flood story by archaeology. None of these attempts has been conclusive, including well-publicized attempts to find the ark.[9] The importance of the flood story does not depend on the archaeologist, or on anyone else for that matter. The ancient storyteller did not let variations in the traditions he received deter him from his purpose of weaving these materials together to say what he wanted to say about God. For him, the story of Noah is a vehicle to tell about (1) God's judgment on sin which had so affected creation; (2) God's concern to preserve what was begun in creation; and (3) God's reaching out to humankind in covenant.

Unlike the Atrahasis Epic, in which people had become so numerous and noisy that the gods decided to destroy them, Israel's theologians see destruction resulting from corruption that arises from people's abuse of the created order. The covenant brings law and structure to society where such has not existed before. The shedding of blood especially is singled out as taboo.

It seems that for the priestly theologians this polluting of the land by the shedding of human blood may well have been the "wickedness" that led to the desire by God to start anew.[10]

The Covenant (Gen. 9:1–17).   Noah represented a new beginning. Like Adam, he was told to "be fruitful and multiply and fill the earth" (9:1, 7), but earth was no longer a paradise where people and beasts lived in harmony—the beasts feared humans, who were made master over them. Humanity, which had shed blood so freely, was now made accountable in a more stringent way for the shedding of blood (9:6).

God made a covenant, or contract, with Noah and his descendants which said that humanity would never again be destroyed by a flood. This covenant, or agreement between parties, was initiated by God, not Noah, and was evidence of divine mercy extended to the survivors of the flood. The rainbow was given as an everlasting symbol of the contract between the Creator and his creatures (9:8–17).

The Noah narratives end with the story involving a drunken Noah pronouncing a curse upon one of his sons who saw him naked. Somehow, the curse fell upon his grandson Canaan (9:18–27). Curses such as this were believed to have the power within them to carry out what was threatened. Likewise, blessings given in special times of life were believed to have this power.

Again, the narrator inserted a genealogy (Gen. 10) to introduce a new segment of the story. One purpose is to say something about the geography of the ancient Near East sometime in the period of the second millenium (2000–1000 B.C.E.). A second purpose is to express the author's conviction that the human race was a unity growing out of its descent from Noah. This serves, then, as a background for what follows in Genesis 11.

The Tower of Babel (Gen. 11:1–9)

Humanity was united not only in language (11:1) but also in determination to rebel against God. This rebellion took the form of building a tower to reach the heavens, where the challenge to God could be made (11:4). The rebellion was nipped in the bud, however. People lost their ability to communicate with one another when their language, which had bound them together, became a barrier—a babble which began with Babel. The ancient Israelites probably saw the great *ziggurats*, or pyramidlike towers, in Babylon, built originally as worship centers for Babylonian deities. From them they concluded that this had caused God to confuse people by giving them many languages instead of one.

Summary (Gen. 1–11)

Throughout these chapters, the narrator has been dealing with humanity on a universal scale. This has been the story of every person and a continuing fascination with sin. It is the story also of God's continuing efforts to deal with sin—both by means of judgment upon it and by his merciful guidance to those sinners who struggle to overcome it.

Again, a genealogy marks a new phase of the story. The floodlights are darkened, and a lone spotlight focuses on a figure who now comes on the stage to introduce the drama of a people chosen from all of humanity to be the bearers of the message of God to the mass of humanity. But before there was a people, there was a man—Abraham.

THE PATRIARCHS[11]

Introduction

With the story of Abraham, the Israelite storytellers move from the broad sweeping view of history to concentrate on people of a more vital interest to their own story. Left behind for a time are the genealogies designed to cover long spans of time. Genesis 12–50 is dominated by four men—Abraham, Isaac, Jacob, and Joseph. This period is known as the period of the patriarchs—literally the time of the "first fathers."

The Time.   There is no universal agreement as to the dating of the patriarchs. Yet the names, customs, and mode of life seem to fit into what is known of the first half of the second millenium B.C.E. They would seem to be connected to the rise of Amorite influence in this region. While there is no absolute proof for these conclusions, evidence seems to point to the probability that these stories are, in the main, authentic memories about real people. Abraham's journey from Ur of the Chaldees (Gen. 12) usually is associated with the movement of the Amorites from Mesopotamia into Palestine in the nineteenth and eighteenth centuries B.C.E.[12]

Joseph, the last of the four major figures in Genesis 12–50, is often associated with the Hyksos rule in Egypt. The Hyksos were foreign rulers of Egypt who conquered the country in the eighteenth century B.C.E. and established a dynasty that ruled for more than 150 years. Like the Hebrews (as the Israelites were first known), the Hyksos had among them many people of Semitic origin. They made extensive use of chariot warfare. They built cities whose fortifications included walls with a steep ramp, or glacis, designed to prevent easy approaches to the walls. If Joseph did come in this period, the patriarchs would be dated from about 2000 to 1550 B.C.E.

Their Lifestyle.   The picture given of Abraham, Isaac, and Jacob is that of people who habitually moved about. Yet it was not an aimless wandering; instead, they seem to have followed a yearly cycle, based on the availability of pasturage for their flocks. During the dry season they would move into the empty spaces in the central hill country, where, among other things, they could graze in the cut-over grain fields. There they remained until the rains came. They might even plant a grain crop on unclaimed land to be harvested when they returned after the grasses in the Negev had died out. For this reason, they were not nomads in the modern sense of the term. Their chief beast of burden was the ass or donkey. Camels were not yet in general use.[13]

In contrast to our limited families of today (consisting of parents, or a parent, and on rare occasions a grandparent or grandparents) the patriarchs were heads of extended families consisting of wives, children, relatives of varying degrees, and servants—most of whom undoubtedly were slaves. A man's wealth was measured in terms of the number of wives, sons, and cattle he possessed (see Job 1). For all these persons, the patriarch was the chief decision maker. He determined whom his sons married and which of his sons would succeed him as patriarch. While it was customary for the eldest son to become the patriarch, it was not always so.

Abraham, the First of the "First" Fathers

To discover what Abraham was like some 4000 years ago is no easy task. Although numerous stories have him as the major character, they lack many of the ingredients necessary for the writing of history. These narratives, called "sagas", have a real person at the core, but what we can actually learn about the details of his life are quite limited. No dates are given and no events that can be confirmed in an independent study are mentioned. No archaeologist has dug up a tablet saying, "Abraham slept here." Nevertheless, we do have the biblical stories—stories that at least suggest that behind those stories was a great personality claimed by three great world religions—Judaism, Christianity, and Islam. Our purpose is to learn from the stories as they are.

From Ur to Egypt (Gen. 12).   The stories of the patriarchs are religious history. Persons, places, and events are secondary to what the LORD is doing through those persons, places, and events. Abraham (called Abram until Gen. 17:5), a native of Ur of the Chaldees in southeastern Mesopotamia (on what is today the Persian Gulf), moved to Haran in Northwestern Mesopotamia while he was still in the clan of Terah, his father. There, Terah died and Abraham became the patriarch (11:31–32).

In Haran, life took a new direction. Abraham was called by the LORD to leave the familiar faces of his kinsmen and the well-watered areas of northwestern Mesopotamia to go to a new land that the LORD would show him. It was a promise that carried with it universal meaning. Abraham would receive the blessing of a land, numerous descendants, and divine protection; and through him all the nations were to be blessed (12:1–3). This promise was repeated with differing emphases several times in the Abraham stories (Gen. 12:7; 13:14–17; 15:17–21; 17:1–21).

While the biblical narratives present Abraham as a man of God, they certainly do not present him as a plaster saint. Driven to Egypt by famine conditions in Palestine, he persuaded his wife to lie about her relationship to him, resulting in her being chosen for the Pharaoh's harem. When the truth is discovered, Abraham and his people are expelled from the land (12:10–20) to face the rigors of the famine.

Conflict and Covenant (Gen. 13–16).   Abraham settled in the Negev, the southern region of Judah, between the sown land and the desert region of Sinai. Here, possibly as a caravaneer—i. e., a trader—he gained great wealth in the form of herds of animals. Conflict between his herdsmen and those of his nephew Lot arose, causing a parting of the ways. Lot chose the well-watered valley of the Jordan, while Abraham chose the hill country. Conflict and crisis brought a reaffirmation of the promise from the LORD of numerous descendants and possession of the land (13:14–17).

Another kind of conflict is described in Genesis 14. Abraham appears as no ordinary desert chieftain but as one who was powerful enough to challenge the rulers of the area. Lot, captured in warfare between a group of kings, was carried off to northern Syria. Abraham, with his personal army of 318 men ("born in his house") rescued Lot. On his return Abraham paid tithes to Melchizedek, the king of Salem (later known as Jerusalem). The name used for God was *El Elyon*, "God Most High." His later descendants could point to Abraham's association with Jerusalem when it became David's capital city to validate their claim to it.[14]

Social and physical conflict is followed by mental conflict (15:1–21). No child had blessed the marriage of Abraham and Sarah. Their only heir was a foreign slave, Eliezer of Damascus, whom Abraham adopted as his heir. Such a custom is known from the Nuzi tablets (about 1500 B.C.E.). Abraham agonized about his lack of a son by Sarah, and the LORD reassurred him. Then followed a strange ceremony.

A sacrifice was made, but not on the usual altar. Instead, the larger animals were cut in half, the halves being laid on the ground opposite each other. As the sun sank in the west, Abraham went to sleep. The vision came as a dream. The LORD spoke of the Egyptian sojourn. A smoking pot and a flaming torch passed between the split animals, and the covenant was made. The boundaries of the land, essentially as they stood in the time of David, were described to Abraham.

Domestic conflict arose when, in keeping with custom, Sarah gave Abraham her maid Hagar as a secondary wife, or concubine, so that Hagar could have a child for her by proxy (16:1–15). Hagar's instant fertility gave her a feeling of superiority over her barren mistress (16:1–4). Hagar then had to flee from the wrath of Sarah. Hagar's son, Ishmael, was said to have been the father of the Ishmaelites, who roamed the southern desert areas of Palestine (16: 5–15).

The Covenant and Circumcision.   Here one finds another view of the covenant. First, another name for God is used. He is *El Shaddai* "God Almighty" (17:1).[15] Then Abraham, called Abram to this point, is now called Abraham, "the father of a multitude" (17:5). In addition, circumcision (the cutting off of the male foreskin), is described as the symbol of the covenant with God. Sarah, (formerly Sarai) also underwent a name change, and assurance was once more given that she would be the mother of Abraham's heir and successor as patriarch. All these elements suggest the emphases one might expect of the priests, causing this to be considered by many as the priestly version of the covenant story.

The Promise of New Life and Forebodings of Doom (Gen. 18–19).   The promise of a son and heir finally moved toward its fulfillment. The patriarch looked out from his tent one day to see three strangers approaching. True to his cultural sense of courtesy, he invited them in and gave them water to wash their dusty, tired feet. He spread for them "a morsel of bread," which in reality was bread, cheese, milk, and meat (18:1–8). In the story of the three strangers, the narrator described a theophany—the appearance of the divine to a human being.

The divine visitors had some good news and some bad news. First, they told Abraham that in the spring Sarah would bear a child. This struck Sarah, who was well past the age of childbearing, as somewhat ridiculous. Her giggles, as she hid behind the tent door, reached the ears of the divine messenger, who heard her and gave her a gentle rebuke (18:9–15).

Then came the bad news. Abraham was told of the doom of Sodom and Gomorrah, the licentious cities in the Dead Sea area, where Lot lived. Despite Abraham's plea (18:16–33), judgment fell and only Lot and his children escaped (19:1–23).

The description of the destruction of these cities suggests that an earthquake occurred, which resulted in the sinking of the land. The fire and brimstone were burning gases and sulfur, both common in this region (19:24–29). Geologists recently proposed that a massive earthquake "liquified the rocks and the soil the cities were built upon, toppling all the buildings." The site was then covered by the waters of the Dead Sea.[16]

The last picture of Lot is a sad one. Old and drunk, he is debauched by his own daughters (19:30–38).

Isaac and Ishmael (Gen. 21). After another incident involving Sarah, which sounds much like Abraham's experience with the Pharaoh of Egypt (see Gen. 12:10–20; 20:1–18), the long-expected child, Isaac, was born. Conflict again arose between Sarah (old enough to be her son's great-grandmother) and Hagar (the slave wife and mother of Ishmael). Jealousy forced Hagar to flee so that Isaac would have preeminence. Here again, the word used to refer to the divine being changes to *Elohim*, "God." In yet another narrative concerning conflict with a local chieftain, Abimelech, the term *El Olam* (the everlasting God) is introduced. The shifting of terms may indicate that these are parallel traditions, that is, the same story coming from different tribes or clans. This could especially be true of the Sarah-Hagar conflict stories.

The Test (Gen. 22). The high point of the Abraham drama was played out on a mountain, "in the land of Moriah." Later, according to tradition, Solomon's temple would be built on this site. The passage emphasizes that "God tested Abraham" by commanding that Isaac be offered as a sacrifice to God. Abraham obeys, but at the climactic moment, just as he is about to take his son's life, his attention is drawn to a ram caught in a nearby thicket. The ram serves as the sacrifice instead.

Three possible interpretations have been offered for this incident. Some see it as a parable, the point of which is that God does not require human sacrifice. That this interpretation has some validity is seen by the fact that human sacrifice never played the important role in Israelite religion that it did in other religions. A second line of interpretation sees Isaac as representing Israel and its relationship to God. The dominant interpretation, however, sees it as enshrining Abraham in the history of religion as the man of faith, revered by three great world religions—Judaism, Christianity, and Islam.[17]

Sarah's Death and Burial (Gen. 23). When Sarah died, a burial place had to be bought. Abraham went to the village elders and there engaged in a typical bargaining session, complete with flowery phrases and exaggerated gestures. Finally, a purchase price was named—after the owner had offered to "give" the land and the cave of Macpelah to Abraham, and, in the process, obligating Abraham to buy more property than he wanted. Today, the traditional site of the burial at Hebron is a sacred site to both Muslim and Jew.

A Wife for Isaac (Gen. 24:1–25:18).   Before Abraham died, he had to see that Isaac had a wife. The practice of the parents choosing a bride for their son is still followed in some cultures. Abraham sent his trusted servant Eliezer back to Haran to find a wife for Isaac. Here we are introduced to the wily Laban, the brother of Rebekah, Isaac's future wife. While the storyteller credits the Lord with pointing out the right girl, Laban was quite willing to give up his sister when he saw the rich gifts Abraham had sent for the bride price (24:53–61).

As in Genesis 1–11, a genealogy is used to summarize and conclude the Abraham story (25:1–18).

Isaac, the Link between Abraham and Jacob

Of the patriarchs, Isaac receives the least attention. He is pictured as an introvert—a shy, quiet, meditative person dominated by the stronger personalities around him. Such a person was Rebekah, his wife. The choosing of Rebekah as Isaac's wife and her subsequent domination of her husband receives more attention in the tradition than does Isaac himself (24:15–61; 25:20–24; 26:6–11; 27:5–17).

One of the stories about Isaac is suspiciously like those about Abraham. He was said to have caused Rebekah to lie about their relationship to prevent trouble with a local chieftain, Abimelech (26:6–11; 12:10–20; 20:1–18). As in the past, the covenant was reaffirmed also with Isaac (26:1–5, 23–25). He did not have to wait as long for an heir as had Abraham, however.

Jacob, the Supplanter

Most of the stories about Jacob are the kinds of stories one prefers to tell about a relative who is long-since dead. If he were alive, one would only whisper about his escapades at family gatherings and hope that the neighbors had not found out about the wayward son's latest caper.

Jacob and Esau.   Jacob was a twin of Esau. Esau was born first, but Jacob's later reputation as a schemer was such that the tradition arose that he had hold of Esau's heel when Esau was born, trying to pull him back so Jacob could come out of the womb first (25:19–26).

Esau was an outdoorsman and a man who lived by impulse. Jacob, on the other hand, was more like his father but with the cunning of his strong-willed mother. Esau, as the elder of the two sons, was first in line to be the patriarch. In addition to the birthright, one had to secure the blessing of the partiarch as he approached death in order to have the right to succeed him (25:27–28).

The blessing was important because the spoken word, in primitive societies, was viewed as having much more power than it has today. The ancients believed that a blessing or curse carried with it a sort of self-fulfilling power. Neither was given lightly, nor were they taken lightly. The blessing was greatly desired, and the curse was greatly feared.

It was for this reason, then, that Jacob—in trying to get the right to be patriarch himself over the firstborn Esau—had to secure both the birthright and the blessing. He had failed to get out ahead of Esau, but that was not his last attempt to get ahead of him!

Buying the Birthright (Gen. 25:29–34).   The birthright was his first goal. Esau, slave of his appetites, fell into Jacob's trap like a hungry bird. Coming from an exhausting and probably futile hunt, Esau smelled the red bean soup Jacob was cooking. When he asked Jacob for food, Jacob set a high price—Esau's birthright. Esau, listening more to his hunger pangs than to his head, agreed. And so on a solemn oath, Esau sold Jacob his future for a bowl of bean soup (25:33).

Stealing the Blessing (Gen. 27:1–45).   But the birthright was not enough. Jacob still had to have Isaac's blessing. On his side, he had a very powerful ally—his mother, Rebekah. Isaac favored Esau, perhaps because he saw in him those characteristics of strength and self-confidence he lacked and secretly longed to have. Isaac, as the saying goes, enjoyed poor health. Troubled by eye disease (a common malady in the Near East) and other ailments (either real or imagined), he feared that death might overtake him at any time. He decided, therefore, that the time had come to pass on to his older son the responsibility of being patriarch. Calling Esau in, he gave him instructions to prepare for him a dish of wild game and bring it to him. Then he would bless Esau (27:1–4).

As Esau left to hunt game, Rebekah (who overheard the conversation) immediately gave Jacob instructions to kill a young goat and bring it to her. Taking the goat, she made stew, dressed Jacob in Esau's clothes, and put fresh goat skins on Jacob's arms and neck so he would be hairy like Esau (27:5–17).

When Jacob went to Isaac, claiming to be Esau, Isaac was suspicious because the voice did not sound right. If it were Esau, he had returned rather quickly. Calling Jacob to him, Isaac felt his now-hairy arms and neck, and ate the savory stew. As he kissed Jacob prior to the blessing, he smelled his clothes. The voice was Jacob's, but the body odor was Esau's! And so the blind Isaac—deceived by his sense of taste, feel, and smell—blessed the deceiver. Jacob left with a blessing Isaac could not take back, even though Esau soon came in and Isaac learned the truth of what had been done (27:18–45).

Jacob on the Run (Gen. 27:46–28:22).   Rebekah, having overheard Esau's threats to kill Jacob, immediately persuaded Isaac to send Jacob to her brother Laban's house in Haran to escape the wrath of Esau. Taking the road northward through the central hill country, Jacob came to a place in the barren rocky hills north of present-day Jerusalem. Using one of the numerous limestone rocks for a pillow, he tried to get some sleep. In a dream, the LORD appeared to him, saying:

> I am the LORD, the God of Abraham your father and the God of Isaac; the land on which you lie I will give to you and to your offspring; and your offspring will be like the dust of the earth . . . and all the families of the earth shall be blessed in you and in your offspring (28:13–14).

Jacob was awed by the experience. But even though he set up a memorial stone, he only committed himself to serve the LORD as his God if he returned to his father's house safely (28:18–22).

Jacob and Laban: An Amateur versus a Professional (Gen. 29:1–30).[18]   On coming to the territory of Laban, Jacob met his cousin Rachel at the well where sheep were watered. One look was all it took! He fell hopelessly in love with Rachel. Laban, shrewd man of the world, sized up the situation. Before Jacob knew it, he was committed to work seven years for the privilege of marrying Rachel since he had no money for the bride price. What seems to have been involved here was a kind of herding contract where Jacob agreed to work as a herdsman for Laban for seven years in return for the privilege of marrying Rachel.

When the seven years had passed and Jacob went forward to claim his wage, he received a shocking surprise. Custom decreed that the veiled bride be brought to the groom's tent under the cover of darkness. So it was that Jacob only saw his new bride after the honeymoon night was over. His bride was not Rachel! It was her unattractive older sister Leah.

Jacob, with murder in his eyes, was pacified by his new father-in-law with the promise that when the seven-day celebration of his marriage to Leah was over, he could marry Rachel. Of course, after the second wedding was over, he had to work an additional seven years to pay for her (29:27–30).

Jacob and Laban: The Tables Turned (Gen: 30:1–31:55).   The years passed, and Jacob, the father of many children, had learned well his lessons from Laban. Getting Laban to agree to let him have any animal that was not white, Jacob used a mixture of folk medicine (30:37–39) and shrewd observation to cause more of the animals to be born spotted, speckled, or black. While Laban was away, Jacob gathered his family and flocks and left the territory. Laban followed in angry pursuit when he found out what had happened. Before he caught up with Jacob, God appeared to Laban in a dream and told him not to harm Jacob (30:40–31:24).

As a result, when Laban caught up with Jacob he could only bluster and accuse Jacob of stealing his household idols (31:30). Possession of the symbols gave the possessor claim to the family property.

Rachel, however, not Jacob, had taken the idols. While her reason is not given, she may have taken them to get back at her father, who had not given her a proper dowry at marriage. A woman's dowry was her social security in her old age. When Laban came searching for them in her tent, she was seated on a camel's saddle where the idols were hidden. She kept him from finding them by saying she could not rise because "the way of women is upon me." (31:35). In this narrative, there are two new ways of referring to God. In 31:42, God is called the *"God of my father,* the God of Abraham, and the *Fear of Isaac."*

In parting, a memorial stone was set up and a solemn oath was taken, calling on the "God of Abraham and the God of Nahor, the God of their father, [to] judge between us" (31:52–54). This ceremony, a kind of covenant, was sealed by the oath-taking and the sharing of a meal. It basically was a plea to the gods, as guarantors of the covenant, to keep an eye on Jacob and Laban so they would not cheat each other again (31:25–55).

Jacob and Esau: A Man Faces His Past (Gen. 32:1–33:20). The biblical narrative did not gloss over the weaknesses of the ancestors, neither with Abraham nor with Jacob, whose sons gave their names to the twelve tribes of Israel. The narrator believes in divine retribution, that is, that evil will be punished. Abraham's lies to the Egyptians concerning Sarah resulted in expulsion from Egypt to face the risk of starvation in the famine conditions of Palestine. Likewise, Jacob's past came back to haunt him.

Traveling down the King's Highway, the major north-south route east of the Jordan, Jacob realized he would soon enter the territory of Esau. First, he sent messengers to Esau to tell him he was coming (32:2–5). When he received word that Esau, with an army of 400, was coming to meet him, he divided his forces and flocks, hoping an attack on the forward group would give the second group a chance to escape (32:6–8). The prayer of a man facing death and destruction was quite different from the prayer of the brash young man who had stolen his brother's blessing (28:20–22).

Another part of Jacob's strategy was to send an impressive gift to Esau. But even this was not enough to still his fears. We are told of a strange experience in the night where Jacob wrestled with a man (32:13–24). This, in part, suggests a theophany (an appearance of the divine); but it also suggests that Jacob's inner struggle was reaching a climax.[19] From the experience, Jacob derives a new name (Israel) symbolic of a changed man. So that he would remember the experience, he received an injury that caused him to limp (32:25–32).

Jacob was the picture of abject humility when he met Esau. Surprisingly, Esau (now a prosperous desert chieftain) was generous to his brother who had cheated him. They parted, Esau going south to Seir, and Jacob going westward into the hill country near the ancient city of Shechem (33:1–20).

Trouble at Shechem (Gen. 34). In a rare story about a woman, the narrator tells of the rape of Dinah (Jacob and Leah's daughter) and the subsequent vengeance taken by Simeon and Levi, two of Jacob's sons. The story is of interest for two reasons: (1) Levi is mentioned as of a secular tribe, indicating that this story is quite old, since in later history, Levi is of the priestly tribe. (2) It is believed that this story is included here to indicate why Shechem did not have to be conquered by the Israelites when they came out of Egypt. This would be because some of the tribes of Jacob remained near Shechem and did not go to Egypt.[20]

Back to Bethel and Two Genealogies (Gen. 35–36). The major stories in which Jacob plays a leading role end with the story of his return to Bethel, where he had experienced God's presence some twenty years or more before. His wives were instructed to put away foreign gods in preparation for worship (35:2), just as Joshua was to do to the tribes of Israel many years later (Josh. 24). Next, another story of Jacob's name change is associated with worship at Bethel (35:9–15). Finally, there is the account of Rachel's death. The cycle of stories, as is true throughout Genesis, is brought to a close by extended genealogies of Jacob (35:16–19, with the note that Isaac finally died!) and Esau (Gen. 36). Jacob's story is interrupted by the story of Joseph and the beginning of Egyptian bondage.

Photo by Ken Touchton.

Figure 3–1.   "The same night he arose . . . and crossed the ford of the Jabbok" (Gen. 32:22). This site on the Jabbok River is the traditional site of Jacob's nighttime struggles prior to meeting his brother Esau.

Joseph: From Patriarch's Son to Prime Minister

The story of Joseph takes the form of a novella, or miniature novel. It is as if the storyteller has taken the Joseph traditions and sketched a novel he is going to write. He introduces his hero, Joseph; the villains, his brothers. Then Joseph goes through a series of reverses and advances, climaxing with a suspense-filled scene where Joseph, the prime minister of Egypt, reveals his identity to his brothers who thought he was long-since dead.

The stories concerning Joseph differ in many ways from the stories of the patriarchs. First of all, they have about them certain of the characteristics of wisdom stories in the Near East: (1) the theme of the stories is that goodness is always rewarded and evil is always punished, which is a major theme of the Book of Proverbs; (2) The theme of the oppressed, righteous man who overcomes all obstacles and comes out on top, particularly because he possesses the wisdom to interpret dreams, is like that found in the stories concerning Daniel.

A second difference in these stories is in how God communicates with Joseph. Here there are no divine messengers—no theophanies. Instead, God guides Joseph through the events and circumstances of life.

A third major difference is in the background reflected by the Joseph stories. It is an Egyptian background. The names of the characters, the bestowing of the signet ring and the gold chain as symbols of Joseph's office, and the emphasis on dreams—these and other matters are known from Egyptian records to be characteristic of Egyptian civilization.

Finally, these stories differ in that they are more than a collection of stories. Here, there is a more unified single story, without the repeating of similar tales, as was true in the Abraham-Isaac-Jacob cycle of stories. The only interruption is for the Judah-Tamar story (Gen. 38).

A Fancy Coat and Angry Brothers (Gen. 37:1–36).   Joseph, the eleventh of Jacob's twelve sons, was his father's favorite. He relished the position, lording it over his older brothers by showing off his fancy clothes and telling them of dreams in which he came out superior to them.

Rough shepherds that they were, they decided to take drastic action to squelch their obnoxious younger brother. Some wanted to kill him, but Reuben prevailed to put him into a pit in the dry country, hoping later to rescue him. Instead, he was sold to a caravan, either to the Ishmaelites (35:25, 27) or Midianites (35:28, 36). (Here is one of the few places that the text shows a blending of traditions.) Eventually he was sold in Egypt to Potiphar, an officer of the pharaoh.

Judah and Tamar (Gen. 38).   A rather uncomplimentary story about Joseph's brother Judah interrupts the Joseph narrative. Judah failed to observe the law of custom regarding the obligation to give his widowed daughter-in-law another of his sons as her husband. The purpose of the "law of the levirate" was that the name of a dead husband who died without a male heir should have his name preserved in the naming of the first son of the second marriage. The second husband was to be his brother or his nearest surviving relative. This arose from the fact that there was no belief in life after death in that time and one could only continue to exist through his sons. Judah, having failed to give his daughter-in-law a proper husband, was subsequently tricked by Tamar into having a child by her, by playing the role of a prostitute. When Judah found out she was pregnant, he accused her of prostitution, only to find out that he was the one who was guilty of having sexual relations with her. Why this story is here is not clear, but it does fill in a time gap in the story of Joseph.

Joseph Loses Another Cloak and Lands in Jail (Gen. 39:1–20).   Years passed, and Joseph was put in charge of Potiphar's business. Mrs. Potiphar tried to seduce the handsome young servant. He refused her advances, and as he ran away, she seized his cloak and yelled, "Rape!" As a result, Joseph landed in jail.

Joseph the Prisoner and Interpreter of Dreams (Gen. 39:21–41:36).   Joseph, ever the man of responsibility, soon became a trusted prison aide (39:22). When the king's butler and baker, imprisoned because they were in disfavor, had strange dreams, Joseph interpreted them correctly. As he predicted, the butler was restored and the baker was hanged. The butler forgot Joseph after promising to reward him (40:1–23).

Then the Pharaoh began to have strange dreams. When all his wise men failed to interpret them, the butler finally remembered Joseph. Joseph was called before the pharaoh, where he interpreted the dreams as predicting Egypt would have seven years of plenty to be followed by seven years of famine. The pharaoh was so impressed by Joseph's wisdom that the former chief prison trusty was made prime minister of Egypt. He was put in charge of preparations for the great famine (41:1–36).[21]

Joseph and His Brothers Again (42–45).   The famine came. Joseph's brothers came to Egypt to buy grain, not realizing that their obnoxious younger brother was now Egypt's chief grain salesman. They did not recognize him (42:8), but Joseph knew them and began a series of tests to find out what sort of characters they now were. First, he accused them of being spies (42:9). Vowing their innocence, they agreed to leave one of their number (Simeon) as a surety until they could return home and bring Benjamin, their younger brother, with them, as Joseph demanded. On the way home, they found all their money in their grain sacks (42:1–38).

When the continuing famine made a return trip to Egypt mandatory, Joseph's demand that Benjamin be brought aroused strong objections from the aged Jacob. To win his father's reluctant approval for the trip, Judah solemnly vowed to Jacob that Benjamin would be kept safe at the cost of his (Judah's) own life (43:9). When they arrived in Egypt with Benjamin, Simeon was released. Following his release, the brothers were invited to eat in Joseph's house, with Benjamin receiving special treatment (43:34).

Joseph's testing of the brothers was not at an end, however. He gave orders that when they made their grain purchases, his personal cup was to be hidden in

Benjamin's sack. Joseph's soldiers then pursued them, brought them back, and the missing cup was found in Benjamin's sack. Judah, who had played such a prominent role in disposing of Joseph many years before made a stirring plea for his younger brother, citing the drastic effect the failure of Benjamin's return would have on their father (44:18-34). Joseph, now convinced that his brothers had suffered enough, revealed his true identity to them (45:1–4). Rather than blaming them for their mistreatment of him, he interpreted it as the providential work of God, who sent him to Egypt to preserve them (45:7).

The Family in Egypt (Gen. 46–50). The brothers returned to Palestine and brought their father to Egypt. His meeting with the pharaoh involved some verbal sparring to determine who was the elder of the two. Since Jacob was, he had to pronounce a blessing on the pharaoh (47:7–12). Some see this as evidence that the Egyptian ruler was a Semite, as was Jacob, since a native Egyptian would not seek blessing from a Semite, whom he would hold in contempt. This would have taken place, then, during the Hyksos rule (1720–1570 B.C.E.) since they were Semites.[22]

Genesis ends with the blessing of Jacob's sons (Gen. 49), the story of Jacob's death and burial, and finally Joseph's death, preceded by his request not to be buried in Egypt (Gen. 50).

Summary on the Patriarchs

The patriarchal history was composed by later historians from traditions from different times and different places. The many names for God that have been noted, the different versions of the same story, the different emphases in the accounts of the covenant, and the shifting back and forth of certain personal names (Jacob, Israel)—all these indicate something of the variety of sources that were used. But to concentrate on the differences would be to miss the main purpose the writers had in mind. As in Genesis 1–11, Genesis 12–50 has much to say about God and the divine relationship to the world, but more particularly to a people—Israel.

The later Israelites were convinced that they were a people divinely chosen to fulfill God's purpose in the world. That choice was embodied in a particular man, Abraham, and was symbolized by the covenant, a binding contract between God and Abraham that involved Abraham's loyalty to God and God's blessing of Abraham, and through him to his descendants. The covenant was reaffirmed to each succeeding patriarch, but it also demanded their commitment to it . Thus, Jacob had to be purified through long years of subjection to the wiles of Laban and the frightening confrontation with Esau before he could be called Israel, "prince of God." The writers knew that God had to work through imperfect people because those were the only kinds of people available. Through the long years, God was preparing (1) a person, (2) a family, and finally (3) a people to serve the divine purpose in the world.

STUDY QUESTIONS

1. When one says, "The primary purpose of Genesis is theological," what does that mean? Does that necessarily exclude other purposes?

2. How does the biblical story of creation differ from other such stories?

3. Compare the images of God in 1:1–2a to 2:4b–3:25. What do they say about Israel's understanding of God?

4. What role did *hubris* play in the story of the Fall (Genesis 3)?

5. Identify: (a) *enuma elish;* (b) Atrahasis Epic; (c) Gilgamesh Epic; (d) covenant; (e) ziggurat.

6. What is the theological importance to the biblical flood story?

7. If one assumes that the Tower of Babel is an etiology, what "why?" questions would it answer?

8. What factors contribute to a dating of the patriarchs in the period from 2000 B.C.E. to 1500 B.C.E.?

9. The patriarchs were head of extended families or clans. What does this mean?

10. How are the covenant accounts in Genesis 13:14–17; 15:17–21; and 17:1–21 alike and how do they differ?

11. Genesis 14 is often said to be different from the other Abram narratives. Read it carefully and see if you can understand why such a statement should be made.

12. Trace the theme of conflict between Sarah and Hagar in the Abraham stories.

13. If Abraham were living today and attempted to sacrifice his son, how would you view it? Why should your view be different in the light of his times?

14. Define *theophany.*

15. In what ways did Abraham try to gain an heir other than through Sarah giving birth?

16. How do you account for the similarities between the stories about Sarah and the Pharaoh (Gen. 12:14–20), Sarah and Abimelech (20:10–20), and Rebekah and Abimelech (26:6–11)?

17. In a good Bible dictionary, read about "blessing" and "curse." See how they relate to the Jacob-Esau stories.

18. Why do you suppose the biblical storyteller glorifies Jacob's deceptive ways?

19. How can one understand Jacob's willingness to work for Laban for such a long while?

20. What result, other than a change of name, came from Jacob's experience at the Jabbok River?

21. How do the stories about Joseph differ from other patriarchal stories?

22. Why is Joseph usually associated with the Hyksos rulers of Egypt?

23. How is one to understand Joseph's treatment of his brothers, once he got the upper hand?

24. What reason does Genesis 45 give for Joseph's experiences?

ENDNOTES

1. For all the gory details see James B. Pritchard, ed., *ANET* (Princeton: Princeton University Press, 1958), 30–39.

2. Compare the view of God here to that found in Isaiah 40:12–31.

3. See 1 Kings 22:19–23; Zechariah 3:1–2; Job 1–2. For a good discussion of this problem, see Bruce Vawter, *On Genesis: New Reading* (Garden City, N.Y.: Double-day, 1977), 53ff. See also Edward M. Curtis, "Image of God," *ABD* III, 389–391.

4. Pritchard, *ANE* 70.

5. Wilford G. Lambert and A. R. Millard, *Atrahasis: The Babylonian Story of the Flood* (New York: Oxford University Press, 1969) is the most recent translation.

6. For an extended discussion of the matter, see Ronald S. Hendel, "When the Sons

of God Cavorted with the Daughters of Men," *BR* III, 2 (Summer, 1987), 8–13.

7. God (Priestly version): 6:1–4, 9–22; 7:11–8:5, 13–19. LORD (Yahwist version): 6:5–8; 7:1–10; 8:6–12, 20–22.

8. See Vawter, *On Genesis*, 115, for a list of duplications.

9. For a serious discussion of wood samples for Mount Ararat, see Lloyd R. Bailey, "Wood from Mount 'Ararat': Noah's Ark?" *BA* 40, 4 (December, 1977), 137–146). On the significance of the flood story, see by the same author, *Noah: The Person in History and Tradition* (Columbia, S. C: University of South Carolina Press, 1989).

10. See Tikva Frymer-Kensky, "The Atrahasis Epic and Its Significance for Our Understanding of Genesis 1–9, *BA* 40, 4 (December, 1977), 147–155.

11. For two somewhat contradictory yet related articles on the background of the patriarchal age, see Kenneth Kitchen, "The Patriarchal Age: Myth or History?" *BAR* 21, 2 (March/April, 1995), 48–56 and Ronald Hendel, "Finding Historical Memories in the Patriarchal Narrative," *BAR* 21, 4 (July-August 1995), 53–59, 70–71. For a radically contrary view, see J. Van Seters, *Abraham in History and Tradition* (New Haven: Yale University Press, 1975).

12. For a contrary view suggesting that Abraham came from Asia Minor, see Cyrus H. Gordon, "Where Is Abraham's Ur?" *BAR* III, 2 (June, 1977), 21–22, 52.

13. For this and other characteristics of patriarchal life, see Victor H. Matthews, *Manners and Customs in the Bible* (Peabody, Mass.: Henrickson, 1988), 1–32.

14. For a discussion of the relationship of Genesis to the rest of the Abram cycle, see E. A. Speiser, "Genesis," in *AB* 1, 105–109.

15. On the meaning of this and other names for God in Genesis, see Ranier Albertz, *A History of Israelite Religion in the Old Testament Period*, I, John Bowden, trans. (Louisville: Westminster/John Knox Press, 1994), 29–32.

16. This report on an article by Graham Harris and Anthony Beardow was written by Associated Press reporter Edith M. Lederer, "Geologists Say Quake Destroyed Sodom, Gomorrah," *The Chattanooga News-Free-Press*, December 19, 1995.

17. For the many ways this passage has been interpreted, see Robin M. Jensen, "This Binding or Sacrifice of Isaac—How Jews and Christians See Differently," *BR* IX, 5(October, 1993), 42–51; and an alternative by Lippman Bodoff, "God Tests Abraham," *op. cit.*, 53–56, 62.

18. Martha A. Morrison, "The Jacob and Laban Narratives in Light of Near Eastern Sources," *BA* 45, 3(Summer, 1983), 155–164, is an excellent article on the Jacob-Laban stories, while Samuel Dresner, "Rachel and Leah: Sibling Rivalry or the Triumph of Piety and Compassion?" *BR* VI, 2 (April, 1990), 26, points out that the names of Leah's sons reflect the desire to be loved by her husband, while the names of Rachel's sons reflect her desire to be a mother.

19. Jack Miles, "Jacob's Wrestling Match: Was It An Angel or Esau?" *BR* (October, 1998), 22–23, makes an interesting argument that it was Esau with whom Jacob wrestled.

20. Gordon Tucker, "Jacob's Terrible Burden," *BR* X, 3 (June, 1994), 20–28, argues that Jacob felt that his oath to Laban was the cause of Rachel's premature death, as well as his problems with Joseph and Benjamin.

21. Richard Elliott Friedman, *Who Wrote the Bible*, 62 f., suggests the story of Dinah was told by the Judahites to embarass the tribe of Ephraim, and that the story of Judah's incestuous relationship with his daughter-in-law Tamar (Genesis 37) was designed to embarass the tribe of Judah.

22. Nahum M. Sarna, "Exploring Exodus: The Oppression," *BA* 49, 2 (June, 1986), 70, points out that the Joseph stories fit well in what is known as the Hyksos period (1720–1570 B.C.E.). "The Second Intermediate Period in Egyptian history is marked by a strong Semitic presence."

Chapter 4 🌿

ISRAEL BECOMES A PEOPLE

Exodus and Wilderness

THE BOOK OF ISRAEL'S BEGINNINGS

In the Hebrew Bible, Exodus is called *w^eeleh sh^emot*, "these are the names," refer-ring to the twelve sons of Jacob. It also has been called "the book of the departure from Egypt," by the LXX, or Septuagint, from which our title "Exodus" is derived.

Exodus begins Israel's story with Moses, his preparation, his elevation to the leadership of his people by the LORD's hand, and the Exodus (1:1–13:16). It contin-ues with the wilderness experiences (13:17–18:27), and it ends with the giving of the law at Sinai, including the Covenant Code and the story of the completion of the tabernacle (19:1–40:38).[1]

THE IMPORTANCE OF THE EXODUS STORY

What the Fourth of July is to the citizens of the United States, Bastille Day is to the French, and the Magna Carta is to the English, the Exodus was to the Israelites. The Israelite writers have mentioned the Exodus more than any other event in their his-tory. In the Book of Psalms, for instance, the Exodus theme is sounded again and again. A good example is Psalm 105. After recounting the plagues, the psalmist says:

> Then he brought Israel out with silver and gold,
>   and there was no one among their tribes who stumbled.
> Egypt was glad when they departed,
>   for the dread of them had fallen upon it.

> He spread a cloud for a covering,
> and fire to give light by night.
> They asked, and he brought quails,
> and gave them food from heaven in abundance.
> He opened the rock, and the water gushed out;
> it flowed through the desert like a river.
> For he remembered his holy promise,
> and Abraham, his servant. (Ps. 105:37–42)

THE NATURE OF THE EXODUS AND THE EXODUS MATERIALS

The picture that emerges from a superficial reading of the narrative portions of the Books of Exodus and Numbers gives the familiar outline of the Exodus as most people know it—the sojourn in Egypt; the birth and preparation of Moses; the Exodus with its dramatic delivery of the Israelites at the sea; the wilderness wanderings and the rebellious murmurings of the people; the giving of the Law at Sinai; and the subsequent experiences of the people in the years before the invasion of Palestine.

The picture given is, however, the simplified version of a much more complicated process. None of my own ancestors came to America prior to the American Revolution. Yet I, like most Americans, speak of our "founding fathers" as if I actually had an ancestor among the early settlers at Jamestown or Plymouth. Likewise, later Israelites, and even present-day Jews, speak as though they are all direct descendants of the people Moses led out of Egypt. Yet, as Joshua 24:14ff. indicates, what became Israel actually was a diverse group, composed of people of a Semitic background as well as non-Semites, including people of the land who never had been in Egypt. This is supported by a careful reading of the Book of Exodus which shows how various sources have been brought together to tell what the LORD had done for Israel. While Moses is the major human character in the Exodus narratives, they are designed not to glorify Moses but to glorify the LORD, the God of Israel. It was the LORD of history and the master of the created order who brought Israel out of Egypt. The narration of the Exodus events was a central theme in the worship of Israel, and no word of praise was too elaborate to describe what the LORD did in bringing Israel from Egyptian slavery.[2]

MOSES: BIRTH AND WILDERNESS YEARS

Changed Times and Changed Circumstances (Exod. 1)

Joseph could not live forever, nor could one expect the Hyksos rulers to dominate Egypt forever. Joseph died and the Hyksos were overthrown. As native Egyptians regained the government, the circumstances of the Hebrews changed. The Hebrews had been settled in northeastern Egypt east of the delta, where the Nile broke up into a number of branches like the fingers on a hand. The area known as Goshen was suitable for the grazing of sheep and cattle of the tent-dwelling Hebrews.

Since such a thing as birth control was unknown to the Israelites, and since the mention of such an idea would have been an insult, the original seventy people who came with Jacob enthusiastically followed the command to " multiply and replenish the earth." This alarmed the rulers of Egypt, who, in typical political exaggeration, said that the people of Israel were "too many and too mighty for us" (1:9). This was their justification for enslaving the Hebrews for building projects at the cities of Pithom and Raamses (1:11).

Dating the Exodus

Dating the Exodus is not the simple matter it once seemed to be. In earlier times, the reference in 1 Kings 6:1 in which Solomon is said to have begun the temple 480 years after the people escaped from Egypt was used as a basis for dating the event at *circa* 1450 B.C.E.[3] Other interpreters took the 480 year figure to be symbolic, and using other archaeological, biblical, and historical evidences, arrived at a date of 1290 B.C.E. for the Exodus and 1250 B.C.E. for the conquest of Palestine. These evidences include: (1) the building of the cities of Pithom and Raamses which most likely occurred during the reigns of Seti I (1304–1290 B.C.E.) and Rameses (1290–1224 B.C.E.); (2) archaeological evidence of the violent overthrow of certain Palestinian cities between 1300 and 1200 B.C.E.; and (3) the Stela of Merneptah, a stone monument set up by Pharaoh Merneptah (1224–1211 B.C.E.) on which he boasts of defeating Israel in Palestine. This is the first known nonbiblical reference to Israel as a people. As shall be seen when the conquest is discussed hereafter, there is by no means universal agreement on the dates, nor even of the nature of both the Exodus and the conquest. Both these matters are undergoing strenuous scholarly examination, giving rise to a wide variety of possible explanations. It is safe to say, however, that while the biblical accounts of the Exodus and the conquest may be a simplified version of a much more complex series of events, the stories of Moses and Joshua were adopted by all Israelites as their stories.

One of the highlights of the first chapter of Exodus is the story of the Hebrew midwives who are ordered by the pharaoh to assist his program of genocide by killing all the male Hebrew babies. Instead, at the risk of their own lives, they sidestepped the ruler's orders, permitting the boys to live. This information is of twofold importance: (1) it highlights how two brave women played a pivotal role in shaping the destiny of a people, and (2) it is a factor in determining the number of people involved in the exodus, since two midwives could not serve an overwhelmingly large population.

Moses' Birth and Early Manhood (Exod. 2)[4]

If the Exodus was Israel's Declaration of Independence, then Moses was Israel's George Washington, Thomas Jefferson, and Continental Congress all rolled into one. While there are no records of the man Moses outside the Bible, the marks he left on the nation and the traditions that grew up around his name are proof enough of the reality and the greatness of the man. True to an honest portrayal of its characters, the Bible lays out Moses' strengths and weaknesses with equal frankness. The story of Moses is the story of a people; without him, the people would not have been.

In the story of Moses' birth and childhood, brave women also play vital roles. His mother saves him by putting him in a small boat made of reeds. After the daughter of the pharaoh discovers the baby, his sister maneuvers her back to his mother to serve as his nursemaid.[5]

Famous men with humble beginnings is a familiar theme in ancient literature. There is a story about Sargon, the king of Akkad, that is similar to the story of Moses. Sargon's mother also hid him in the river in a basket. A major difference is that Sargon was a royal son whose mother had fallen into disfavor in the royal court. He was found and reared as a gardener, while Moses, a slave, was found and reared in the royal court.[6]

For Israel, this was a lesson on the providence of God. Growing up in the pharaoh's household, yet with his own mother as his nursemaid, Moses had feelings for the problems of his people. Those feelings came out in a violent manner one day when he saw an Egyptian beating a Hebrew. Thinking no one was looking, he killed the Egyptian and buried his body in the sand (2:11–12). But his secret got out. Trying to break up a fight between two Hebrews, he was taunted by one of the men about killing the Egyptian (2:13–15).

Realizing he was in difficulty, Moses fled across the Sinai Peninsula to Midian. While Midian is thought to have been located to the east of the Sinai Peninsula, in the time of Moses, the name may also have been applied to parts of the Sinai region. There, in manner strangely like Jacob's encounter with Rachel, Moses met Zipporah, the daughter of a Midianite priest (called Reuel in one story (2:18) but Jethro in another (3:1)). Moses married into the Midianite clan and began the life of a family man (2:15b–22). Meanwhile, back in Egypt, things were going from bad to worse (2:23–25).

The Call of Moses (Exod. 3:1–4:17)

Moses was not destined to be a shepherd all his life. His solitary job through the years had given him a knowledge of the desert that was to be invaluable in the work of leading the people from Egypt. It was not conscious preparation on Moses' part. Rather, for the storyteller, it was the providence of God working to prepare the man for the work he was to do.

Those years of preparation came to an end on a mountain called Horeb in one tradition (3:1) and Sinai in another (19:11). While pasturing his flocks, Moses suddenly became aware of a bush that was aflame, seemingly without burning up. As he went near for a closer look, he became aware of a "presence." Out of this experience came Moses' call to lead the people out of Egypt. This call experience is significant because it was said to be the time when God revealed his personal name to Moses. Of the two major terms used by Israel to speak of God, *Elohim* was what one might call the general, or, to use a common analogy, the "family" name for God. It was not only used to refer to the one God but also might be used to refer to any god, or gods (3:1–5).

The name *YHWH* (translated "I AM WHO I AM" by the New Revised Standard Version in Exodus 3:14 but elsewhere as the "LORD"), which was revealed first to Moses on the mountain, was the personal name of God. For example, there might be a large family of Fafoofniks, but only one Fafoofnik with the personal name Abercrombie. Thus there were many *elohims* but only one *YHWH*.

The proper pronunciation and meaning of the name *YHWH* is subject to much debate since it ceased to be pronounced sometime after the Babylonian Exile. It is believed, however, that it was pronounced *Yahweh*. In Jewish religious services today, the tetragrammaton, *YHWH*, is not pronounced since to pronounce it wrongly would defile the holiness of God. A substitute word *Adonai* (translated LORD), is used. This practice of using LORD for *YHWH* is followed in this textbook. Its meaning is variously interpreted: I AM WHO I AM, I WILL BE WHO I WILL BE, I CAUSE TO BE WHAT IS. Each translation has strong arguments in its favor.

Moses' Excuses

When God called Moses, Moses was told that this was the God of the patriarchs (3:6). While Moses was awestruck, he was not so awed that he could not argue, especially when the LORD said, "I will send you to Pharaoh that you may bring my people, the Israelites, out of Egypt." Moses immediately began to make excuses: (1) The excuse: "Who am I that I should go?" (3:11); the answer: "You will have the LORD's presence with you, and he will bring the people to this mountain" (3:12). (2) The excuse: "Who are you that you are sending me?" (3:13); the answer: "You shall say, 'YHWH [the LORD], the God of Abraham, of Isaac, and of Jacob has sent me" (3:14–22). The excuse: "But they will not believe me (4:1); the answer: "I will give you signs—a rod changed to a snake, a leprous hand healed" (4:2–9). (4) The final excuse: "LORD, I cannot talk!" (4:10); the answer: "I will give you your eloquent brother Aaron to be your spokesman" (4:14–17).

On the Road to Egypt (Exod. 4:18–31)

His excuses in tatters by the divine answers, Moses set out for Egypt, with the blessing of Jethro. The story of the return to Egypt contains a strange incident (4:24–26). At a lodging place in the wilderness, it is said that the LORD attempted to kill Moses. He was saved when Zipporah, his wife, circumcised their son and touched Moses with the bloody foreskin, saying, "Truly, you are a bridegroom of blood to me!" While the meaning of this ancient story is unclear, it probably indicated that he was not properly circumcised. Furthermore, in much of the Old Testament the LORD is looked upon as the cause of everything. This is reflected in the saying of the prophet Amos: "Can disaster befall the city, unless the LORD has done it?" (Amos 3:6). The idea of an evil force in the world outside of God's control that caused bad things to happen did not come into prominence until the postexilic period of Israel's history. The Hebrews did believe in demons, but the demons were under divine control. For this reason, this may reflect the idea of a demonic attack on Moses. Why it is included here is uncertain.[7]

Aaron, hearing that Moses was returning to Egypt, met him on the way. Moses briefed him on what they were to do. As soon as the brothers got to Egypt, Aaron, in turn, told the Hebrews what was to happen.

MOSES: THE STRUGGLE WITH PHARAOH

The Struggle Begins: Moses and Aaron before the Pharaoh (Exod. 5:1–6:1)

The task before Moses and Aaron was not an easy one. As an excuse to get the people out of Egypt, they asked the pharaoh to let the people take a three days journey into the wilderness to worship. The pharaoh's reaction was outright rejection of the request and an increase in the workload on the Hebrews (5:1–9). They, in turn, vented their anger on Moses and Aaron, calling down the LORD's judgment upon them (5:20–21). Moses complained to the LORD, who assured him there would soon be action.[8]

Moses' Call, the Covenant and a Genealogy (Exod. 6:2–7:7)

Ancient covenants were of at least two types: (1) the *suzerainty treaty* was an agreement or contract between a superior party and an inferior party. The superior party (in this case, God) set forth the terms of the agreement since he had the power to do so. The superior party could obligate himself only if he chose to do so; the inferior party had no choice. Divine mercy and honor obligated God to meet the terms set forth. (2) The *parity treaty* was an agreement between equals where both parties contributed to the agreement and both bore equal obligations to see that it was preserved.[9]

Another version of the call of Moses is given here with a strong emphasis on the suzerainty covenant made with the patriarchs. Abraham, Isaac, and Jacob knew God as *El Shaddai* (God Almighty) and not as *YHWH* (the LORD) (6:2–3). The people were to be reminded of the earlier covenant to assure that God would (1) deliver them from Egypt, (2) make them God's people, (3) be their God, and (4) give them their own land. As usual, when Moses told the people, they ignored him. When he complained to God, he was told to keep telling them (6:4–15).

This priestly version of the call of Moses and Aaron includes a genealogy to establish their credentials. Perhaps of greater significance here is the statement in 7:1 concerning Aaron's role in relation to Moses. In the account of Moses' call in 3:1–4:17, Moses had complained of his speech problems. Here, Moses voices the same complaint (6:30), and is told, "See, I have made you like God to Pharaoh, and your brother Aaron shall be your prophet"(7:1). This word *prophet* was the same term used to describe the great prophets of Israel. Just as Aaron spoke for Moses, so the prophets spoke for God.

The Going Gets Rough: The Plagues (Exod. 7:8–11:10)

The stage was set for the struggle to free the Hebrews. It was not just a struggle between human powers; rather it was a struggle between the LORD and the gods of Egypt, in the person of their earthly representative, the divine pharaoh. Since the gods of Egypt were associated with the Nile, Moses chose to challenge them on their home court, so to speak.

After an opening round in which the Egyptian magicians duplicated the actions of Moses and Aaron (the use of serpent magic, the reddening of the Nile, and the plague of the frogs), the Egyptian magicians surrendered, saying, "This is the finger of God" (8:19). From that point on, the plagues increased in intensity until the climax was reached with the death of the first-born and the escape from Egypt.

The number of plagues varies according to the source. Psalms 78:43–51 lists eight plagues. It is believed to be based on an old epic source (or J according to the Documentary Hypothesis) and emphasizes the role of Moses in Exodus. Psalm 105:27–36 seemingly is based on the priestly tradition that magnifies Aaron's role. Exodus shows evidence of both traditions.[10]

The plagues were evidence for later Israel that the LORD had been at work on their behalf, using divine power over nature to convince the pharaoh that he must free them from bondage. Israel's later retelling of the events did not have as its primary purpose recording history for twentieth-century readers, but "as a celebration of God's great victory whereby he is glorified and acknowledged as sole sovereign and power."[11] This is not to deny that the accounts of the plagues grew out of actual events but rather that Israel was more concerned about praising God than it was about writing history.

The Plagues as Miracle.   *Miracle* is a term often used in religious circles. A rather common element in many definitions of miracle is that it is something that happens which cannot be explained by ordinary means. A believer in God would say it is evidence of God's power. But any definition of the miraculous that requires that the happening must not be explainable in human terms means that once it can be explained, it will no longer be a miracle. Our great-great-grandfathers would say that television is a miracle, but to us it is a common, everyday fact of life. We do not look at it as a miracle. One's inability to explain an event, therefore, is not a reliable standard for judging whether or not it is miraculous.

All definitions of miracle start with the basic idea that it is a religious interpretation of an event. If this is true, then whether an event is miraculous or not depends, to a certain extent, on the person who views that event. It has been illustrated in this fashion: A bear was chasing a man through Yellowstone Park. The man ran across the site of the Old Faithful Geyser, which erupts every sixty minutes or so. The bear, close behind, crossed the geyser the split second it erupted, throwing him high into the air and killing him. To the onlookers, it was a spectacular event; to the man, it was a miracle; but to the bear, it was a catastrophe.[12]

To develop a workable definition of miracle, it is necessary to examine the Israelite view of God's relationship to the world. According to the creation story in Genesis 1–2, the world was created through God's power. It is God's world, and he is active in it, bringing both judgment (as in the case of Sodom and Gomorrah) and blessing (the promise to Abraham). Nothing happens in the world except as God wills it to happen. To the Israelite, there was no such thing as a natural event. God was in everything—whether it was a storm, a drought, or a baby's birth. In short, the biblical writers—especially the Old Testament writers—did not make the distinction between natural and supernatural that we make.

The biblical writers used miracles to "call attention to something else that's going on that is even more important than the miracle." For example, the importance of the burning bush (Exodus 3:2–5) was to direct Moses' attention to God rather than to the bush itself.[13]

In this light, the plagues were viewed by the Israelites as the activity of God because God is active in everything. Two things characterized them as miraculous for Israel: (1) Moses predicted them, and (2) their timing was right for Israel's needs. Had these same events happened at a different time or under different circumstances, Israel might well have interpreted them in an entirely different light. A miracle, then, could be defined as follows: any event, which, when seen through the eyes of faith, strengthens the faith of the believer.

The Plagues: God at Work Through Nature.[14]   Granted that the plague narratives were developed primarily to be used in worship, the fact that they reflect the kinds of natual phenomena one would find in Egypt rather than in Palestine testifies to their authenticity. In fact, at least the first six plagues can be associated with the annual flooding of the Nile River during the period from August to March. The first plague, the reddening of the Nile, has been interpreted two ways: (1) a literal view that the waters actually changed to blood, or (2), a view that the condition may have arisen from one of two natural causes—from red soil washed down from the Ethiopian highlands, or from a blood-red algae, similar to the one which causes the so-called red tide in the coastal waters of Florida. Regardless of the cause, for Israel it was the LORD who changed the life-giving waters of the Nile into the stinking river of death (7:14–24).

Frogs, the second plague (7:25–8:15), were common when the Nile flooded, leaving stagnant pools where their long strings of eggs could hatch into tadpoles and then change into young frogs. The unusual flooding conditions brought enormous numbers of frogs, far more than the ibises, birds that lived on frogs, could eat. The frogs, forced from the polluted water, carried with them germs that killed them. Although the stench of their rotting carcasses polluted the air, "Pharaoh . . . hardened his heart" and would not let the people go (8:15).

The third plague, called gnats by the New Revised Standard Version (NRSV) (8:16–19), more likely were mosquitos,[15] bred in the stagnant pools of water. This was too much for the Egyptian magicians, who acknowledged that Israel's God was more powerful than theirs (8:19). The fourth plague, flies (8:20–24), bred in the filth of the primitive living conditions of ancient villages, were naturally attracted to the piles of dead and decaying frogs.

When this plague hit Egypt, the pharaoh relented a bit. Calling Moses in, he told Moses he would release the people from working long enough to have their worship services, but only on the condition that they remain in Egypt. Moses refused to compromise. Pharaoh then agreed that the people could leave the country to sacrifice if Moses would pray for an end to the plagues. Moses agreed to pray; but when the flies disappeared, the pharaoh changed his mind.

The time was now late December or early January, when flies disappear from Egypt because of changes in weather conditions. Goshen, where the Hebrews lived, was much cooler because of the sea breezes. For this reason, the Hebrews would not have had the flies, which are common in the rest of the country.

The fifth plague, a disease of livestock (9:1–12), came in January when livestock was turned out to graze in the fields after the waters receded. The disease that killed the frogs probably was anthrax, which is also fatal to livestock. Grazing where the dead frogs had been, they became diseased and died. The Hebrew's livestock was spared because the land of Goshen was the last to dry out after the flood, so their animals were still in their stalls.

The flies of the fourth plague probably contributed to the sixth plague, which consisted of painful boils on both men and animals. The flies were not the common housefly so familiar to Americans but a tropical fly that bit the legs of men and of animals. It would have served as a carrier for the virus that caused the boils. The fact that the magicians "could not stand before Moses" (9:11) could quite literally mean that their feet and legs were most affected by the boils.[16]

After a speech in which Moses told the pharaoh of the LORD's patience with him (9:13–21), Moses warned the pharaoh that since he had not released the Hebrews, a devastating hailstorm would come. This seventh plague came in a violent thunderstorm accompanied by both hail and lightning (9:13–26). A heavy hailstorm can be devastating to plant life and even to animals, especially younger animals. Moses had warned the pharaoh to keep his people and their remaining animals inside because of the danger (9:19). Since hailstorms usually are limited in scope, Goshen was once again spared.

The ruined crops brought the prospect of famine and softened the pharaoh's resolution not to let the Hebrews leave. It hardened again rather quickly when the storm ended (9:27–35).

Pharaoh's Compromise Offer and the Eighth and Ninth Plagues (Exod. 10:1–11:10). Pharaoh's advisers urged him to give in to the demands of Moses and Aaron, but the proud ruler did not want to admit complete defeat. Calling the Hebrew leaders in, he offered a series of compromises. He asked Moses who was to go. Moses replied that all their families and flocks had to go. The pharaoh offered his first compromise: "Go, but take only the men."

The LORD's reply through Moses was a plague of locusts. These insects, a variety of grasshopper, have been a plague of Africa and the Eastern countries throughout recorded history. Their devastation is chillingly described by the prophet Joel:

> What the cutting locust left,
>   the swarming locust has eaten.
> What the swarming locust left,
>   the hopping locust has eaten.
> What the hopping locust left,
>   the destroying locust has eaten.
>
> It (the locust) has laid waste my vines,
>   and splintered my fig trees;
> it has stripped off their bark
>   and thrown it down;
>   their branches have turned white.
>
> The fields are devastated,
>   the ground mourns;
> for the grain is destroyed,
>   the wine dries up,
>   the oil fails.
>
>   Joel 1:4, 7, 10.

The locusts were blown into the land by a strong east wind, the dread *sirocco*, which blew in from the Sinai Desert. Another wind, called a "strong sea breeze" by the Hebrew text and thus a north wind in Egypt, caused the plague to be lifted when Moses prayed (10:18–20). But when the pressure let up, the pharaoh was back to his old ways.

The ninth plague (10:21–29) " a darkness that can be felt" (10:21), was in some ways the most disturbing of all. The probable cause was the blinding sandstorms that come with the March winds from the Sahara Desert. The darkness blotted out the sun, or Amun Re, the chief deity among the Egyptian gods. Amun Re's daily march across the heavens was the greatest constant in Egyptian life and, as such, was a symbol of life itself. For the LORD to prevent Amun Re from rising for three days was a clear demonstration that the LORD was more powerful than Amun Re.

Since the pharaohs also were thought to be divine, the expression, "the LORD hardened Pharaoh's heart" also had a religious connotation. One of the three words translated "hardened" (*kaved*, 10:1) literally means "to make heavy." The Egyptian notion of the final judgment was that one's heart was weighed on a balance with a feather as a counterweight. If one's heart was pure, there was a balance and the person entered eternal life. If, however, one's heart outweighed the feather, the person was devoured by the goddess Amenit. To say that the pharaoh had a hard (heavy) heart meant that he was no deity. Instead, he was no more than an ordinary mortal whose '"heavy" heart would lead to his destruction at the hands of the LORD of all creation.[17]

Pharaoh summoned Moses and Aaron to deal with them again. This time he offered to let them take their families, but they had to leave their herds. Moses quickly rejected any compromise: "Not a hoof shall be left behind," he declared (10:24–26). After all, one could not have a sacrifice without a victim. With that rejection, Moses was ordered from the presence of the pharaoh.

The Final Plague: The Death of the Firstborn (Exod. 11:1–10, 12:29–32). While timing was the significant factor in the first nine plagues, causing them to be "wonders" in the eyes of the Hebrews, both the timing and the selective nature of the tenth plague made it the climactic event for Israel. The firstborn son was the most important child, especially from a practical standpoint. This was illustrated by Jacob's devious actions designed to secure the rights of the firstborn for himself. To lose the firstborn was (and still is) a devasating psychological blow to a family, and

Figure 4–1. "Then Pharaoh said to (Moses), 'Get away from me. . . . do not see my face again.' " (Exod. 10:28). This statue is a representation of Rameses II, believed to be the pharaoh of the Exodus.

Ernest Manewal/Black Star.

more especially in ancient days if the firstborn was a son. For the firstborn son of the pharaoh, who considered himself to be divine, this would be the crowning blow in the struggle between the LORD and the gods of Egypt.

Some might question whether every firstborn child and animal actually died (11:5). It must be remembered that these traditions passed through many generations before they were written down. Their use of "all" and "every" was much like our own; that is, to indicate that a large number of people, especially children, died. The death rates among children in parts of Africa today still runs 60 to 70 percent for those under ten years of age. Still, there are unexplainable elements of this plague which made it a "wonder" to the Israelites (11:10).

The Meaning of the Plagues. How are the plagues to be interpreted? A basic assumption is that whatever one's understanding of what actually happened and how it happened, for Israel the plagues were a manifestation of the power of God, the mighty act that the LORD had done in Egypt (Exod. 14:31). Beyond that basic assumption, two lines of interpretation that have been proposed are: (1) they were attacks against the deities of Egypt (Num. 33:4); and (2) they were meant to teach Israel that the God of creation was the God who had delivered them from Egypt. The latter interpretation is suggested by the Sabbath commandment as found in Deuteronomy 5:15.

The interpretation that they were attacks on the Egyptian deities can be summarized as follows:

Plague	*Deity or Deities against Whom the Plague Was Directed*
1. Nile turned to blood	Khnum—creator of water and life; or Hapi—the Nile God; or Osiris—the Nile was his bloodstream
2. Frogs	Heket—goddess of childbirth whose symbol was the frog
3. Lice	No known deity
4. Flies	No known deity
5. Pestilence in cattle	Hathor—mother and sky goddess whose symbol was the cow; or Apis—the bull god
6. Boils	No known deity
7. Hail	Seth—god of wind and storms
8. Locusts	Isis—goddess of life; or Min—goddess of fertility and vegetation and protector of crops
9. Darkness	The sun deities, Amon-Re, Atum, or Horus
10. Death of the firstborn	Osiris—judge of the dead and patron deity of the pharaoh

A second way to interpret the plagues is to view them as a reversal of creation intended to make Israel aware of God's power. He who had brought order out of chaos in creation had now turned the orderly life of Egypt back to chaos. The climactic act was the drowning of the Egyptian army in the waters of chaos at the sea.[18]

THE EXODUS

Preparation for the Passover (Exod. 12:1–28)

The Passover, which was later combined with the Feast of Unleavened Bread, became the festival for celebrating the Exodus. In reality, the festival itself probably was older than the Exodus, having been a spring festival of shepherds among Israel's ancestors. After the Exodus, the festival was taken over to celebrate the momentous event and was given a new interpretation. The Feast of Unleavened Bread, a celebration of the barley harvest, was joined with Passover to make an eight-day festival.

Such festivals were a vital part of Israelite religious tradition, which continues to this day in Judaism. In the celebration of Passover-Unleavened Bread, the worshiper relived the events of the Exodus. The aim was to make the Exodus the experience of each new generation, and the ritual even today is designed to help the worshiper to identify with the Exodus generation.

Passover was (and is) a family festival, a meal that consisted of roast lamb that had been killed with the proper ritual. It was eaten at night with unleavened bread and bitter herbs (12:3–12). The blood of the lamb was to be sprinkled on the doorposts and lintel to signify that an Israelite lived there (12:13). The instructions for the Feast of Unleavened Bread reflect a later time since it involved eating unleavened bread over a seven-day period to remind the people that since they left Egypt in a hurry, they had no time to let the dough rise (12:14–20).

Forward! March! (Exod. 12:29–42)

The last blow was struck! Pharaoh had had enough! Summoning Moses and Aaron, he told them to take their families and animals and leave. Their Egyptian neighbors also were anxious for the Israelites to leave, even giving them jewelry and clothing. From Raamses they set out to Succoth, a company of Israelites accompanied by a "mixed crowd" (12:38), who presumably were non-Israelite.

How Many Went?

How big was the group that left Egypt? English translations say, "Six hundred thousand men . . . besides women and children" (12:37). If the average family was only five persons, this would mean more than three million persons. This figure is too high for a number of reasons: (1) Not discounting God's power to sustain them in the desert, nevertheless, under ordinary circumstances, the Sinai would never sustain life for that many people. (2) This is more people than have lived in Palestine (except for modern times) at almost any time in its history. (3) The word translated *thousands* can be translated several ways. Its most likely meaning is a village or district which provides soldiers. Thus a more likely figure is 6,000 men and a total not exceeding 25,000 to 30,000 people. Some would see this figure as a census figure during Davidic times.[19]

The smaller number is more in keeping with the fact that only two midwives were needed by the Hebrews (1:15–22). They really would have difficulty delivering babies in a population of three million. Even 6,000 families would keep them busy in a time of unrestrained pregnancy.[20]

Which Way Did They Go?

The route of the Exodus would be simple to trace if all the places mentioned could be identified. They did not travel the easiest route, designated in Exodus 13:17 by a later name, "the way of the Land of the Philistines." This was the international road from Egypt up the Palestinian coast to all points north and east. This route, lined with Egyptian fortresses, was too risky. Instead, they went the "roundabout way of the wilderness toward the Red Sea"(13:18 NRSV). This translation, "Red Sea," is based on the Greek version of the Old Testament. The Hebrew text says,

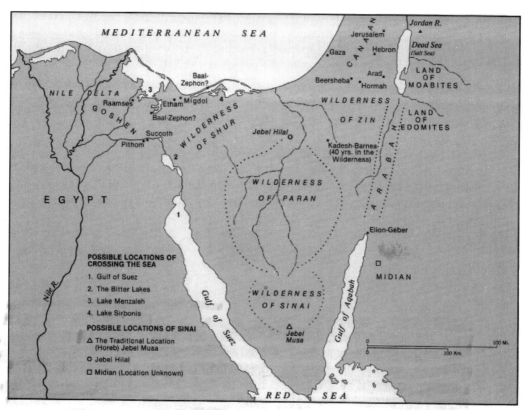

Figure 4–2. The Exodus and Sinai.

"Yam Suph, 'Sea of Reeds.'" The possibilities for the body of water actually crossed are: (1) what we know as the Gulf of Suez, which is an extension of the Red Sea; (2) the Bitter Lakes, a shallow, marshy area north of the Gulf of Suez along what is now the route of the Suez Canal; (3) Lake Menzelah, an arm of the Mediterranean into which today the Suez Canal empties; and (4) Lake Sirbonis, cut off from the Mediterranean Sea by a narrow sandy strip of land and located on the northern Sinai Coast. Each identification has its difficulties. The first is too far south of the identifiable sites located in northern Egypt. The second has somewhat the same problem. The third possibility is shown as the crossing place on many modern maps because of the tentative identification of two or three key sites. If present-day archaeological site identifications are correct, the fourth possibility has strong arguments in its favor. Pithom, Raamses, Succoth, Etham, Migdon, and Baal-Zephon all have been identified and lead directly to the strip of land surrounding Lake Sirbonis.[21]

If the fourth hypothesis is true, when the forces of the pharaoh overtook the Israelites, they had their backs to the Mediterranean Sea. He pursued them out onto the narrow strip of land along the lagoon. Finally, they came to the inlet separating them from land again. Night came and with it a strong east wind. Exodus 14:21 says, "The LORD drove the sea back by a strong east wind all night . . . and the waters were divided."

When the morning came, the east wind, which perhaps contributed to an unusually low tide, had left the land so dry that the frightened Israelites could pass over to the mainland again. By the time they had crossed, the returning waters swallowed up the heavy Egyptian chariots in the sea (14:1–31).

Regardless of where the crossing took place, the important point for Israel is found in the words of the biblical writer, who says:

> Thus the LORD saved Israel that day from the Egyptians. . . . Israel saw the great work that the LORD did against the Egyptians. So the people feared the LORD and believed in the LORD and his servant Moses (14:30–31).

Sing Praises to the LORD (Exod. 15:1–21)

The importance of the Exodus to the Israelites is shown by the many songs that commemorate the event. One such song is found in Exodus 15:1–18. This was a later song, probably used in festivals celebrating the Exodus. It was based, however, on the song of Miriam, Moses' sister (Exod. 15:21):

> I will sing to the LORD, for he has triumphed gloriously;
> horse and rider, he has thrown into the sea.

This short poem, celebrating the LORD's victory through the forces of nature over the Pharaoh, comes from a time very near the actual event.

TROUBLES IN THE WILDERNESS

Which Way to Sinai?

The destination of the Israelites was Mt. Sinai (Horeb), where the LORD had appeared to Moses. Unfortunately, there had never been any long-term settlements in the Sinai region except for a few military outposts guarding mining operations of the Egyptians and at one or two major oases. For this reason, there can be little or no archaeological verification of sites mentioned in the biblical record. The traditional location of Mt. Sinai is Jebel Musa (Mt. Moses) in the southern end of the Sinai Peninsula. On this mountain is St. Catherines's Monastary, founded in 527 C.E. to mark the traditional site. A second possibility is Jebel Hilal, thirty miles west of Kadesh Barnea, the large oasis in the northeastern Sinai region, which served as the base for the wilderness wanderings. A third possibility is the region of Midian, east of the Sinai Peninsula near the Gulf of Aqabah. This was a volcanic region, and the "pillar of fire and cloud" (14:24) may refer to an active volcano.[22]

The traditional location would require a route on the west side of the Sinai Desert along the Gulf of Suez. It would also seem to presuppose the location of the Red Sea (Sea of Reeds) as either the Bitter Lakes or the Gulf of Suez. The third and fourth theories, however, lend support to a northern route. The evidence for neither location is decisive.

Trouble on the Way (Exod. 15:22–17:7)

The Sinai Desert very quickly put to the test the leadership skills of Moses. Egypt, even with its slavery, did provide at least a minimum of food and plenty of water to drink. In contrast, the Sinai made Egypt look like the Garden of Eden. First, the stagnant pools of water they found at Marah caused complaint. Moses threw the bark or leaves of a desert shrub into the water to make it drinkable (15:22–26). Soon they found an oasis at Elim which had plenty of fresh water (15:27).

The next complaint was food. The supplies they brought from Egypt began to run low, and the complaints increased (16:1–13). Again the LORD through nature met the needs of the people through (1) manna and (2) quail. Manna was the secretion of a tiny scale insect, still eaten today by the Bedouin. Quail, similar to the American bird, often fall exhausted in the Northern Sinai after migratory flights over the Mediterranean. They can be captured easily by hand during this time (16:4–36).

Water again became a problem. Moses' experience as a desert sheepherder once more stood him in good stead, for he found a water-bearing rock that satisfied the thirst of the people (17:1–7).

The Amalekite Raid (Exod. 17:8–16)

An even greater danger was ahead. At Rephedim, the people were attacked by the Amalekites, a fierce tribe of desert dwellers. The task of leading the people to battle was given to Joshua, the son of Nun, who one day would become the leader. While Moses held up his rod, the battle favored the Israelites; but when his arms fell down, the tide of the battle changed. The effect of the rod was psychological since it reminded the people how the LORD had defeated the pharaoh, who was much more powerful than the Amalekites (17:8–16). The Israelites won the battle, and Moses found a general.

A Father-in-law's Advice (Exod. 18:1–27)

The people came at last to Sinai. Soon afterward, Moses' family—accompanied by his father-in-law Jethro—joined him there. It did not take the older man long to see that Moses was overworking himself, trying to do everything for the people. Calling Moses aside, he advised him to set up a system whereby the people would be divided into groups of ten, fifty, one hundred, and one thousand. A leader would be responsible for the handling of all problems that arose in his group. If he could not handle them, he would consult the leader of the larger unit of which his smaller group was a part. That way, only the most pressing problems reached Moses. This allowed him to devote his time to the more important work of interceding with God for the people and teaching them God's laws (18:17–27).

This tradition of the influence of Jethro on Moses may be evidence of other influences. Some have suggested that even the personal name for God (*YHWH*) may have originated with Jethro's clan. At present, however, there is no conclusive proof of it.

SINAI AND THE GIVING OF THE LAW

Israel's Constitutional Convention (Exod. 19–24)

Moses finally reached one of his major goals: he brought the people to Sinai. It was there that the constitution of the Israelite people was made and ratified. Through Moses the people were told, "If you will obey my voice and keep my covenant, you shall be a treasured possession out of all peoples." If they met the conditions, they were to be a "priestly kingdom and a holy nation" (19:5–6). To be a holy people meant to be a people set apart for special service for the LORD, since holiness carries with it the idea of separation.

When he came down from the mountain, Moses called the leaders of the people and told them the conditions of the covenant. They agreed to do as the LORD commanded (19:7–8). Then, instructions were given for the all-important covenant-making ceremony. Elaborate preparations relating to cleanliness and sexual abstinence had to be made (19:10–11, 14–15). Boundaries were established around the holy mountain so the people would not come too close. The ancient belief in the power and awesomeness of the Holy was evidenced by the threats of death by stoning to anyone who violated the boundaries around the sacred mountain (19:12–13).

On the great day came thunder and lightning from the cloud-shrouded mountain, accompanied by the loud blast of the *shophar*, a trumpet made of ram's horn. Descriptions of the appearance of God (theophany) in the setting of the thunderstorm are common in the Old Testament (Judg. 5:4–5; Ps. 18:8–15; 29:3–9). The summons came for Moses to go up the mountain. At the LORD's command he then descended and brought Aaron back up the mountain with him (19:16–25).

The Ten Words (Exod. 20:10–17; see also Deut. 5:16–21)

As they now stand, the Ten Commandments (known as the Ten Words in Judaism) are expanded from the earliest form, which is believed to have consisted of ten concise statements:

Photograph © Broadman Films. Used by permission.

Figure 4–3. "On the third new moon after the Israelites had gone out of...Egypt...they came into the wilderness of Sinai" (Exod. 19:1). Jebel Musa, the traditional site of Mt. Sinai, is located in this range of mountains.

1. You shall have no other gods (*elohim*) before me.
2. You shall not make for yourself a graven image.
3. You shall not take the name of the LORD your God in vain.
4. Remember the Sabbath day and keep it holy.
5. Honor your father and your mother.
6. You shall not murder.
7. You shall not commit adultery.
8. You shall not steal.
9. You shall not bear false witness against your neighbor.
10. You shall not covet.

As evidence that the Commandments in their longer form represent an expansion, one needs to compare the version found in Deuteronomy 5:6–21 and, more particularly, the Fourth, Fifth, and Tenth Commandments, with the version in Exodus. The Fifth Commandment says:

Exodus 20:12
Honor your father and your mother, so that your days may be long in the land that the LORD your God is giving you.

Deuteronomy 5:16
Honor your father and your mother, *as the* LORD *your God commanded you,* so that your days may be long *and that it may go well with you* in the land that the LORD your God is giving you.

A more important difference is to be found in the Tenth Commandment:

Exodus 20:17
You shall not covet your neighbor's house; you shall not covet your neighbor's wife, or male or female slave, or ox, or donkey or anything that belongs to your neighbor.

Deuteronomy 5:21
Neither shall you covet your neighbor's *wife.* Neither shall you desire your neighbor's *house, or field,* or male or female slave, or ox, or donkey, or anything that belongs to your neighbor.

These differences are such that they suggest a changing view of the Commandments in their applications to specific situations. The Tenth Commandment, in particular, reflects either a change in the status of women, or possibly, a difference in their status (in a later time) from one section of the country to another.

For Israel, the Ten Commandments were the constitution, the laying down of the basic principles from which a legal system would develop. A common way of looking at the Commandments sees them as reflecting the two poles of Israel's existence as a people. (1) Commandments 1 to 4 are concerned with Israel's relationship to God: absolute loyalty, imageless worship, reverence for the Name (*YHWH*), and regular worship. (2) Commandments 5 to 10 deal with the Israelites' relationship to the social order: family solidarity, reverence for life, respect for property, truthfulness in speech, and a proper attitude toward others and their property. No other set of moral principles has been so influential in Western legal systems.

Absolute Law and Case Law

The Ten Commandments were also unique in their form. They are stated as absolutes; that is, they allow for no contradictions. This kind of law is known as *apodictic* law and was rarely found in the ancient Near East outside the Israelite law codes. A second type of law is *casuistic* or case law. It, too, was found in Israel but also was common in other law codes. Case law stated a condition and told what the penalty was if the condition existed.

The Ten Commandments and Covenant Ceremonies

When the covenant ceremony in which Israel accepted the obligations of the Ten Commandments as the basic law of its existence is compared with covenant ceremonies of other peoples, some interesting parallels appear. Among the Hittites, a fourteenth century B.C.E. people from Asia Minor, there were suzerainty treaties (covenants involving a stronger and weaker party) that had six major elements: (1) a prologue identifying the maker of the covenant; (2) a historical record stating why the suzerain or lord had a right to make the covenant; (3) the conditions of the covenant; (4) the requirement for preservation and the periodic public reading of the text; (5) a list of the gods who were witnesses to the covenant; and (6) curses and blessings directed toward those who kept and who neglected the covenant.[23]

Exodus 20:2

Prologue:	"I am the LORD your God."
Historical record:	"who brought you up out of the land of Egypt, out of the house of slavery."

Exodus 20: 3–17

Stipulations:	The Ten Commandments

Exodus 24:4,7

Preservation and public readings:	"And Moses wrote down all the words of the LORD. . . . Then he took the book of the covenant, and read it in the hearing of the people; and they said, 'All that the LORD has spoken we will do, and we will be obedient.' "
List of gods as witnesses:	These obviously would not appear in light of the First Commandment.
Blessings and curses:	These do not appear in connection with the Ten Commandments, but Deuteronomy 27:11–26 preserves a cursing ceremony which may have originated in a covenant-renewal festival where each generation accepted the obligations of the Ten Commandments and the laws that grew out of them.

The Covenant and Israelite Life.   Two covenants competed for Israel's attention during her history—the Sinai covenant and the Davidic covenant. The latter covenant would not come into existence for another three centuries. While there might not be universal agreement as to what happened at Sinai, that something of supreme importance for Israel as a people did happen is attested to by the persistence of the covenant idea in Israelite life. Israel became the people of the LORD through divine grace, and the LORD became their God—Ruler, Patriarch, Savior, and Judge.

The covenant was kept alive by a reenactment of the covenant ceremony, at times in a systematic fashion, at other times sporadically. Joshua 24 is an example of the type of thing that must have happened in such ceremonies. Nehemiah 8 describes the revival of such a ceremony after what appears to have been a long period when no such reenactment had taken place. Perhaps a major stumbling block for the Sinai covenant, however, was the fact that it was supplanted by the Davidic covenant during the period of the monarchy. While the two covenants were of different natures—David's covenant having to do with the continuation of his line on the throne of the kingdom, while Sinai was of a moral and ethical nature—David's kind of covenant offered a type of security that did not make moral demands on the people and thus was more readily accepted. Another problem was the assimilation of a large non-Israelite population into the kingdom as the result of David's conquests. Consequently, a large part of the population neither knew or cared about Sinai. The Ten Commandments' demand for absolute loyalty to the LORD and the expectation that every Israelite would treat every other follower of the LORD as a family member were lost in the vast changes that took place during that time. An additional factor was the change in the economic circumstances. Society became more stratified with the passing years, with more and more power being concentrated in the hands of fewer people. As a result, the old family ideal fell by the wayside.

Yet in spite of the difficulties it faced over the years, the Sinai covenant would not die, but continued to come alive at opportune times in Israel's history. Some even see it as the glue that held Israel together.[24]

THE PRINCIPLES MADE PRACTICAL: THE LAW CODES

Just as the Constitution was the beginning of the United States legal system, so the Ten Commandments were the beginning of law for Israel, not the finished product. The working out of the principles took the form of laws. These laws are found in three major codes, or groups, in the Old Testament. The Covenant Code (Exod. 20:22–23:33); the Deuteronomic Code (Deut. 5:1–28:68); and the Priestly Code (principally in the book of Leviticus, but with some laws in Exodus and Numbers). The narratives present the laws as if all of them were directly given to Moses, but closer examination reveals that they developed over a long period of time. Moses was the lawgiver in the sense that the basic principles from which all the laws of Israel were to come were given through him.

The Covenant Code (Exod. 20:22–23:33)

This probably was the oldest Israelite code but not the oldest Near Eastern code. There were a number of older Near Eastern codes, the best known being the Code of Hammurabi, which dates from the nineteenth century B.C.E. There are laws from Hammurabi's Code that are very similar to laws in Israelite codes. Compare, for example, the laws concerning dangerous oxen:

Hammurabi's Code

If a seignor's ox was a gorer and . . . {it was} . . . made . . . known to him that it was a gorer, but he did not pad its horns (or) tie up his ox, and it gored to death a member of the aristocracy, he shall give one-half mina of silver.[25]

Covenant Code

If the ox has been accustomed to gore in the past, and the owner has been warned but has not restrained it, and it kills a man or a woman, the ox shall be stoned, and its owner shall be put to death. If a ransom is imposed on the owner then the owner shall pay whatever is imposed for the redemption of the victim's life (Exod. 21:29–30).

The Covenant Code contains laws designed for a society in which agriculture was the major means of earning a living—a condition that did not exist for Israel until it entered the land of Canaan. It contained laws that are classed as civil or criminal laws, but religion was such a basic part of its lifestyle that religious offenses were subject to criminal penalties. A brief summary of the contents is as follows:

20:22–23	A repetition of the commandment concerning idols
20:24–26	A demand for only earthen altars or altars of uncut stones in opposition to the elaborate altars of the Canaanites
21:1–11	Regulations concerning slaves, male and female
21:12–32	Crimes against fellow Israelites and their penalties
21:33–22:17	Laws governing property
22:18–23:9	Miscellaneous laws, many of which relate to the treatment of the weak and defenseless, that is, (1) the treatment of strangers, widows, and orphans (22:21–24); (2) the lending of money to the poor (22:25–27); (3) another warning against oppressing the weak (23:9).
23:10–19	The sabbatical year, the sabbath, and the three major feasts
23:20–33	A promise of success in the conquest if the law is faithfully kept

priest regulations
(2a)

The Priestly Code

Unlike the Covenant Code and the Deuteronomic Code, the Priestly Code is much more complex and scattered. For this reason, only some outstanding sections of this code will be mentioned. While it follows the Covenant Code in the biblical order, it actually came later than either of the other codes, probably reaching its final form sometime during, or immediately after, the Babylonian Exile. Like the other two codes, it is comprised of a mixture of earlier and later laws. A major difference was that the Priestly Code was primarily concerned with proper worship. For example, in Exodus 25–31 a detailed description of (1) the ark and (2) the tabernacle is given. The ark (described in Exodus 25) was a rather elaborate wooden box, carried on two long staves or poles that passed through rings on the corners of the box. It was approximately 45 inches long, 27 inches wide, and 27 inches high, overlaid with gold with a mercy seat on top, with winged figures on each end. This seat represented the throne of God, and as such, symbolized the presence of God among the people. It was thought to be especially effective when carried with the people as they fought their enemies.

The tabernacle (Exod. 26–27) was a tent of skins in which the ark was kept. The tent was surrounded by a fence of skins that formed a sort of courtyard. Inside the tent were two rooms, made by a curtain across one end. The larger room was the Holy Place. Its furnishings were (1) a table for the "bread of the Presence" (25:23–30), which was one of the sacrificial offerings; (2) a seven-branched lamp called the *menorah* (25:31–40); and (3) the altar for burning incense (3) 26:1–10). The priests entered the Holy Place daily in carrying out their duties.

The smaller room, separated from the Holy Place by a curtain, was the Most Holy Place or Holy of Holies. Here the Ark of the Covenant was kept. Only the High Priest could enter the Holy of Holies, and then on only one day in the year— *Yom Kippur,* the Day of Atonement. His activity on that day was for the purpose of securing forgiveness of the people's sins.

Much attention is devoted in the Priestly Code to the priests and their activities. An example of this is Exodus 28:1–29:46, which is devoted to a description of the priestly garments and to the ordination of Aaron and his sons. Leviticus 6:1–9:24 discusses the function of the priest in sacrifices and then turns again to the dedication of Aaron and his sons to the priesthood.

These examples should serve to emphasize the important role the priest played in ancient Israel. In the patriarchal days, the patriarch himself functioned as the priest. When Israel became a distinct people, the priesthood became a separate group of men whose sole job was to function as priests. While the descriptions found in the law codes may well reflect a later, more developed priestly establishment, there can be little doubt that the priesthood played a role in Israelite life in the wilderness.

The power of the priest lay in the belief that he controlled access to God. He was the expert in communicating with the awesome Deity, who brought Israel out of Egypt. The power controlled by the priest carried with it the temptation to corruption; but the continued existence and positive influence of Israelite religion over many centuries must be credited, in part, to the integrity of many of the priests.

(handwritten margin note: Why Sacrifices)

Sacrifice and Sacrifices.   One of the main functions of the priests was to carry out the sacrifices described in the laws. Since most of the people were illiterate, sacrifice was a visual aid to worship. Its effectiveness as an aid to worship depended, in large measure, upon how it was viewed. Three basic views of sacrifice prevailed in ancient societies: (1) that sacrifice was made to appease an angry deity—in short, to bribe him/her; (2) that sacrifice was an act of communion whereby the worshiper had fellowship with the deity; (3) that sacrifice was a gift to the deity, as an act of praise. The sacrifice of an animal was regarded as substituting for the life of a human being, but it had a deeper meaning than mere substitution.

(handwritten margin note: Sacrafices to the Isrealites)

What then, did it mean when an Israelite had sinned and brought a sacrifice to be offered at the altar? Basic to any understanding of this question is the conception of one's relatedness to all that he had including family and possessions. One's land and possessions were bound up with his life because they were the means of sustaining life. Naboth's reluctance to surrender his land to Ahab, even for a fair price, is a vivid illustration of this feeling of oneness which the Israelite had for land and possessions (1 Kings 21:3). It is also illustrated by the destruction of Achan, his family, and all his possessions, because he had sinned (Joshua 7:25). All he had was contaminated by his sin because it was thought of as being a part of him. When one brought an animal to sacrifice it, it was his possession and therefore was a part of himself. He laid his hands on its head to symbolize his identity (oneness) with it (Leviticus 1:4). When its blood was shed in the ritual, the life that was given was his life given symbolically. It was not a substitute; it was the offerer giving of himself.[26]

(handwritten margin note: Kinds of Sacrafices)

The major kinds of sacrifice are described in Leviticus 1:1–6:7.[27] (1) The whole burnt offering was the major daily sacrifice and had as its purpose making the people right with God, that is, atoning for sin (1:1–17). (2) Cereal offerings were peace offerings, expressing thanks for the produce of the land (2:1–16). (3) In contrast to the whole burnt offering was the peace offering. The animal was slain, its blood was thrown against the altar, the fat and internal organs were burned, and the meat was eaten by the priests and the worshipers in an act of communion (3:1–17). (4) The sin offering for "any one {who} sins unwittingly" was a whole burnt offering (4:1–5:13). (5) The guilt offering involved not only a sacrifice but an act of restoring any loss that had resulted from sin (5:14–6:7).

Holidays and Holy Days. (Lev. 23:1–44).   (1) Passover-Unleavened Bread, which came in March or April, was to celebrate the Exodus events. (2) The Feast of Weeks, which celebrated the grain harvest, came fifty days after Passover, which is why it is called Pentecost (Greek for "fiftieth") in the New Testament (Acts 2:1). (3) The Feast of Booths (Tabernacles) came in the early Fall and celebrated the fruit harvest. (4) The most solemn day of the year was the Day of Atonement, when the High Priest entered the Holy of Holies in the Tabernacle to make atonement for the sins of the people (Lev. 16:1–34).

The Holiness Code (Lev. 17–26). Mention needs to be made of one other major section of the Priestly Code. Leviticus, Chapters 17 through 26, constitute a major section containing many ancient traditions grouped around the theme of Israel's need to be a holy people, set apart and dedicated to the service of God. Chapter 19, in particular, highlights the idea of holiness as embodied in the famous line, "You shall love your neighbor as yourself" (19:18).

The Deuteronomic Code

The Deuteronomic Code, found in the Book of Deuteronomy, was first discovered during the reign of Josiah in Judah in 621 B.C.E., many centuries after the Exodus. But, like the Covenant Code and the Priestly Code which came after it, it contained many ancient laws as well as laws that were brought into being much nearer the time of its discovery. It, too, had a version of the Ten Commandments (5:6–27). As its title Deuteronomy ("second law") suggests, it was a restatement of the law; in short, a sort of updating or modernizing of the law to fit a changed situation. For this reason, old laws still usable were kept while new laws, suitable for new conditions that had arisen, were added. It may be summarized as follows:

5:1–11:32	The Ten Commandments and exhortations to keep them
12:1–31	The command to have all worship in one central sanctuary
12:32–13:18	The awfulness of idolatry
14:1–15:23	Regulations for a holy people: Warnings against pagan customs, regulations about clean and unclean animals, the law of the tithe, the sabbatical year as related to debts and slavery of Hebrews, offering of first-born animals
16:1–17	The major festivals: Passover-Unleavened Bread; Festival of Weeks (Pentecost in the New Testament) or grain harvest festival; and Festival of Booths or Tabernacles, which celebrated the fruit harvest
16:18–17:20	Rules for the administration of justice
18:1–22	How to worship God in a proper manner
19:1–21	Legal problems: manslaughter, property fraud, proper evidence for determining guilt in a crime
20:1–20	How to conduct a holy war
21:1–23:14	Various laws concerning unsolved murder, treatment of captive women, disrespect for parental authority, rules for hanging a man, responsibilities for a man's lost property, a woman's use of a man's clothes, protection of bird life, building codes, the mixing of unlike things, relations between the sexes, relations to outcasts and other people, proper sanitary procedures
23:15–25:19	Humanitarian and religious laws: runaway slaves, cult prostitutes, taking of interest on loans, making vows to God, respect for property, divorce procedures, the newly married, taking security for debts, stealing, rules for the leper, extending credit, relation to the poor and needy, individual responsibility, the sojourner and the widow, law of punishment, just payment for services, law of the levirate marriage, dirty fighting, false weights and measures, relations with the Amalekites
26:1–19; 28:1–68	Rules for worship: the service of first fruits, the tithing ceremony; a plea to observe the law and the consequences for failing to do so

Summary of Deu.

THE TEN COMMANDMENTS AND THE CODES

By taking one of the Commandments and showing how it was used in the codes, one perhaps can see the differences which the passage of time brought in the interpretation of the Commandments. The Sixth Commandment is "You shall not murder." See how the three codes treat this commandment in the following comparison:

Covenant Code
(Exod. 21:12–14)

Whoever strikes a person mortally shall be put to death. If it was not premeditated, but came about by an act of God, then I will appoint for you a place to which the killer may flee. But if someone willfully attacks and kills another by treachery, you shall take the killer from my altar for execution.

Deuteronomic Code
(Deut. 19:4–6; 11–13)

Now this is the case of a homicide who might flee there and live, that is, someone who has killed another person unintentionally when the two had not been at enmity before: Suppose someone goes into the forest with another to cut wood, and when one swings the ax to cut down a tree, the head slips from the handle and strikes the other person who then dies; the killer may flee to one of these cities and live. But if the distance is too great, the avenger of blood . . . might pursue and overtake and put the killer to death, although the death sentence was not deserved, since the two had not been at enmity before. . . .

But if someone at enmity with another lies in wait and attacks and takes the life of that person, and flees into one of these cities, then the elders of the killer's city shall send to have the culprit taken from there and handed over to the avenger of blood to be put to death. Show no pity; you shall purge the guilt of innocent blood from Israel, so that it may go well with you.

Priestly Code
(Num. 35:11–12; 16–25a)

Then you shall select cities of refuge for you, so that a slayer who kills a person without intent may flee there. The cities shall be for you a refuge from the avenger, so that the slayer may not die until there is a trial before the congregation.

But anyone who strikes another with an iron object, and death ensues, is a murderer; the murderer shall be put to death. Or anyone who strikes another with a stone in hand that could cause death, and death ensues, is a murderer; the murderer shall be put to death. Or anyone who strikes another with a weapon of wood in hand that could cause death, and death ensues, is a murderer; the murderer shall be put to death. The avenger of blood is the one who shall put the murderer to death; when they meet, the avenger of blood shall execute the sentence. Likewise, if someone pushes another from hatred, or hurls something at another, lying in wait, and death ensues, or in enmity strikes another with the hand, and death ensues, then the one who struck the blow shall be put to death; that person is a murderer; the avenger of blood shall put the murderer to death, when they meet.

But if someone pushes another suddenly without enmity, or hurls any object without lying in wait, or, while handling any stone that could cause death, unintentionally drops it on another and death ensues, though they were not enemies, and no harm was intended, then the congregation shall judge between the slayer and the avenger of blood, in accordance with these ordinances; and the congregation shall rescue the slayer from the avenger of blood.

AFTER THE CONVENTION WAS OVER

The Covenant Broken (Exod. 32)

The people's commitment to the covenant did not erase their proneness to rebellion. When Moses delayed coming down from the mountain, they assumed the worst had happened and demanded he make images for them to serve as gods. Aaron did as they requested, trying still to point them to the LORD (32:1–6). This incident reflects a theme common throughout Israel's history, that is, the temptation to dilute the religion of the God of Sinai with the popular religions of the time. Moses' magnificent prayer of intercession following the LORD's threat to destroy the rebels revealed the depth of the man's commitment to his people (32:7–14). That love for the people did not keep him from a wrathful explosion when he came down from the mountain and found the people dancing around a golden calf. In a fit of temper, he threw down the tablets on which the Commandments were written, literally breaking the Ten Commandments! The calf, probably a gold-covered wooden frame, was destroyed (32:15–20).

Moses then turned to Aaron, whose excuse sounded as pathetic as that of a small boy caught with his hand in the cookie jar! There followed a violent purge of the rebels, led by the Levites. Moses again made intercession for the people and received the command to be on the road toward the Promised Land again (32:21–35); the covenant was renewed, and the promise was repeated (34:1–16).

On the Road to Kadesh-Barnea (Num. 10:11–12:26)

Following the report of a census (Num 1:1–4:9)—giving the book its name, based on the Latin *numeri* (Hebrew *b*e*midbar*, "in the wilderness")—another section of the Priestly Code (5:1–6:27) and narratives concerning the tabernacle, the account of the journey resumes.[28] A song that was sung on the march is preserved in 10:35–36:

> Arise, O LORD, and let your enemies be scattered,
>   and your foes flee before you. . . .
> Return, O LORD of the ten thousand thousands of Israel.

But the songs did not muffle the complaints, whether it was food (11:4–35), or Aaron and Miriam's complaint about Moses' Cushite wife. It seems even Moses had to deal with racial prejudice.

Spying Out the Land (Num. 13:1–33)

A second major time of decision had arrived. The march had brought the people to the southern reaches of the Negev, Palestines's southernmost habitable region. This was the most logical place from which to launch an invasion of the land.

Choosing twelve men (a representative from each tribe), Moses sent them northward into the hill country to estimate the chances of a successful invasion (13:1–24). The returning spies gave a glowing report of the richness of the land, especially when compared with the barren territory through which they had come. But for ten of the men, the minuses in the form of walled cities far outweighed the pluses. In view of the disadvantages, they gave a majority report which counseled against an invasion (13:28–29, 32–33). Caleb and Joshua gave a strong minority report, recommending an invasion (13:30–31).

The Invasion Nobody Believed Would Succeed—And It Didn't (Num 14:1–45)

Rebellion flared once again, coming almost to the point of Moses and Aaron being stoned by the people (14:1–10a). Moses, in turn, had to plead with the LORD to keep the people from being destroyed, appealing to the LORD's sense of honor (14:10b–19). The rebellion condemned that generation to the wilderness, except Caleb and Joshua (14:20–38).

A plague convinced the people that an invasion was imperative, although Moses warned that it was doomed to failure. He was right, for the Israelites suffered defeat at the hands of the Amalekites and Canaanites (14:39–45). Some Israelites probably stayed in the northern Negev, however, joining forces with the Joshua-led group some forty years later when it invaded from east of the Jordan. After this failure, Kadesh-Barnea became the base of operations for the main body of Israelites for the next generation.

The Kadesh Years and More Priestly Laws (Num. 15:1–19:22)

The Israelite storyteller gave little attention to what happened in the years at Kadesh-Barnea. Chapter 15 contains laws concerning offerings and an incident about a man who violated the Sabbath law on work (15:1–41). The major headline was the rebellion led by a quartet named Korah, Dathan, Abiram, and On (16:1–19). Their subsequent punishment , as well as that of their whole families, illustrates the concept of corporate responsibility, a commonly held view in biblical times. It held that a man's actions affected his whole family either for good or ill. They shared his guilt or glory (16:20–50).

There follows another section of the Priestly Code, dealing with priestly stories and duties, as well as the ritual for purifying a person made unclean by contact with a corpse (17:1–13).

ON THE MARCH AGAIN

Bound for the Promised Land (Num. 20:1–21:9)

The passage of time brought the passing of the older generation, including Miriam and Aaron. Miriam died before Israel left Kadesh-Barnea (20:1). Time did not lessen the rebelliousness of the people, however. As they moved away from the oasis at Kadesh to continue their movement toward the land promised to them, lack of water—an ever-present problem when they were on the move—brought still another crisis. Moses, commanded by the LORD to speak to a rock to find water, seems to have struck it in anger, bringing the LORD's judgment that Moses, too, would die on the trail and would never enter Canaan (20:2–13).

Trouble not only came from within but also from external forces. Failing in attempts to invade Canaan from the south, Moses then proposed to cross the Arabah, the continuation of the great Rift valley south of the Dead Sea, and to follow the King's Highway northward through the territories of Edom and Moab. Contacting the king of Edom, Moses promised to pass through the land peaceably, paying for any water used. The Edomites refused passage, however, and threatened to attack Israel (20:14–21).

Aaron died and was buried on Mt. Hor. This only left Moses of the first-generation leaders (20:22–29). Eventually, the people set out in the direction of the Gulf of Aqabah (called the Red Sea) in an attempt to go around Edom. They encountered numerous poisonous snakes on the way. Moses was instructed to make a bronze serpent and to make the people look at it to be healed when they were bitten (21:4–9). In this same general area in a Midianite archaeological site, such a bronze snake was found. This suggests that such a technique was used among the Midianites in the case of snakebite. It is evidence, furthermore, of a possible ancient relationship between Israel and Midian.[29]

The Moabites and Balaam (Num. 21:10–24:25)

Unable to go around Edom, the Israelites turned northward along the Arabah, coming at last to the southern end of the Dead Sea. Passing along through the valley of the Brook Zered, which served as the border between Edom and Moab, they finally

Courtesy of the Israel Government Tourist Office.

Figure 4–4. "Then they came to Elim, where there were twelve springs of water and seventy palm trees" (Exod. 15:27). Oases, like Elim and the one pictured here, were essential for Israel's survival in the Sinai Peninsula.

were able to get to the major caravan road, the King's Highway (21:10–20). Not wanting trouble with the Moabites, Moses asked permission to pass though the territory peaceably. When the king refused, Israel attacked, took control of much of the Moabite kingdom, and even took some Ammonite territory north of Moab (21:21–35).

At this point entered the prophet Balaam, one of those characters about whom the Israelites were to talk for many generations. As a matter of fact, not only did the Israelites talk about this famous prophet, but others did also. We now know of Balaam apart from the biblical text through inscriptions that have been found in Transjordan. That this is the same prophet spoken of in Numbers 22 through 24 is shown by the fact that he is identified in these inscriptions as "Balaam, the son of Beor" (*cf.* Num. 22:5). The inscriptions also speak of him receiving his oracles at night as in Numbers 22:8, 19. Unlike in the Bible, however, he is further described as "seer of the gods," who speak to him at night. This would indicate that he was by no means an Israelite prophet nor a follower of *YHWH* (the Lord). There is mention also of goddesses, another idea foreign to Israelite religion. As in the biblical account, he is pictured as one who pronounces curses.[30] It is in light of these texts, then, that the Balaam stories in Numbers will be examined.

Desperate for a way to stop the marauding Israelites, Moab's king Balak sent for the famous Balaam, a Mesopotamian holy man. Balak wanted Balaam to curse the Israelites so that they could not defeat his armies (22:1–6). Taking money with them, Balak's messengers came to Balaam, who told them he would give them an answer in the morning. The next morning, he told them that the LORD would not let him go (22:7–14). After reporting to Balak, the messengers came back with a much larger sum of money. This time Balaam agreed to go under the instructions to do as God told him (22:15–21).

At this point the text seems to contradict itself. After saying that Balaam went on God's command (22:20), it says that God was angry with him for going (22:22). It must be remembered that God was believed to cause everything. Thus, for him to cause a person to commit an action and then be angry at him for doing it was not viewed as an inconsistency on God's part. If we were telling the story, we probably would say that the large sum of money offered to Balaam was what changed his mind. This resulted in God being angry with him for going with the Moabites.

Then follows the most famous part of the story. Saddling his donkey, Balaam set out to go to Moab. On the way, strange things began to happen. The donkey, seeing things that Balaam did not see, ran off the road and crushed Balaam's foot against a stone wall. Finally, the donkey lay down in the road. Balaam, who had been beating the donkey for its seeming stubbornness, suddenly heard the donkey speak up in its own defense (22:22–30). To top it off, the LORD spoke out in defense of the donkey, telling Balaam that he had been trying to get his attention through the donkey. Balaam was told he was to go with the Moabites (22:31–35). Did anyone else hear what the donkey and God said to Balaam? The text is silent at this point.

When Balaam came to the Moabites, he made preparations to carry out the request of Balak. But, try as he might, each time he started to pronounce a curse, a blessing was pronounced on Israel. Needless to say, Balak was most unhappy. He soon sent Balaam back the way he came (22:36–24:25).

Trouble at Peor (Num. 25:1–17)

While the Israelites were in Moabite territory, they encountered the worship of fertility gods. These were nature deities believed to have the power to make the crops grow. This type of worship, which was to be a major problem for Israel through much of the prexilic period, involved so-called holy women, who played the role of goddesses in sacred prostitution. The Israelite men were attracted to the worship, so much so that one man brought a Moabite prostitute into camp. An epidemic, probably a venereal disease, broke out in the camp. Again, radical action was taken, in which Moses ordered the execution of anyone who had patronized the fertility cult. In this way, the disease was checked.

Miscellaneous Materials (Num. 26–36)

The latter part of the Book of Numbers contains a variety of materials: a census (26:1–65); an incident concerning the inheritance of property by women (27:1–11); Joshua appointed Moses' successor (27:12–23); rules concerning offerings for the major holidays—the Sabbath, the New Moon, Passover-Unleavened Bread, Feast of Weeks or Grain Harvest, the New Year's Festival, the Day of Atonement, and the Feast of Booths or Fruit Harvest (28:1–29:40); the law of vows ((30:1–6); holy war against Midian (31:1–54); the story of assigning territory east of the Jordan to the tribes of Reuben, Gad, and Manasseh (32:1–42); a summary of the journey from Egypt to Moab (33:1–56); a discussion of the territorial boundaries of the people in Canaan (34:1–29); a discussion of the Levitical cities and the cities of refuge (35:1–34); and finally a discussion of a married woman's inheritance (36:1–13).

Two things are of importance here: holy war (Num. 31), which will be dealt with later, and route of the march described in Numbers 33. Some archaeologists argue that the cities mentioned— Iyyim, Dibon, Almon-Diblathaim and Abel-Shittim—did not exist when the Exodus is thought to have taken place. Yet, Egyptian temple lists from this period list most of them as existing cities in the same order that Numbers lists them.[31]

Deuteronomy's Contribution to the Wilderness Story

The name *Deuteronomy* comes from the Greek name of the book and means "the second law." The Hebrew title means "These are the words," based on the first verse of the book. The word *Deuteronomy* is very descriptive of the contents of this book because 1:1–4:49 is a summary statement of the wilderness wanderings of Israel, presented in the form of an address to the people on the plains of Moab.[32]

The second major section (5:1–26:19; 28:1–68) has already been discussed under the section on the law codes. Two major themes in this section deserve more lengthy comment: (1) the command for a single place for worship and (2) the concept of holy war.

The command to have a single place of worship is found in 12:5, 11, 18, 21. In its original time and context, it probably referred to either Shiloh or Shechem. Both seem to have served as the major worship center at one time or another. When the essentials of what is known today as Deuteronomy were discovered, or rediscovered, in the time of King Josiah (621 B.C.E.), the references to a single place of worship were taken to mean Jerusalem. By this time, Jerusalem was the capital of all that remained of the Israelite kingdoms. Even more important was the fact that the Temple was located there and was controlled by a powerful and influential priesthood.

The second important theme was the holy war. The Hebrew word is *cherem*, sometimes translated as "the ban." The key passage is Deuteronomy 20:16–18:

> But as for the towns of these peoples that the LORD your God is giving you as an inheritance, you must not let anything that breathes remain alive. You shall annihilate them—the Hittites and the Amorites, the Canaanites and the Perizzites, the Hivites and the Jebusites—just as the LORD your God has commanded, so that they may not teach you to do all the abhorrent things that they do for their gods, and you thus sin against the LORD your God.

The justification for such an action is found in 20:18, which says, in effect, that the people of the land were like an infection in the body. It must be gotten rid of, even though the solution is a radical one. Similarly, today the amputation of a limb is viewed as a radical solution to a physical ailment. Yet, at times, it is the only solution to the problem.

But the question arises, "How does one justify such actions?" The simple answer is that there is no way it can be justified. The best one can do is to understand that the Israelites practiced holy war in a time when many nations practiced holy war. They justified their actions in the same manner as those who slaughter their neighbors in religious and ethnic wars do to this day. We can only try to understand why it was the way it was without giving our approval.

Deuteronomy's Place in the Canon

It has long been recognized that Deuteronomy stands at a crucial juncture in the canon. While tradition has numbered it with Genesis through Numbers as part of the Torah or Pentateuch, it also has marked affinities with the books that follow it—Joshua, Judges, 1 and 2 Samuel, 1 and 2 Kings. Because themes from Deuteronomy play a prominent role in these latter books, scholars call them the "Deuteronomic History." At the same time, Deuteronomy recapitulates Exodus through Numbers and answers questions about the fate of Moses. Thus it serves as a bridge between the Pentateuch and the books that follow it.

The Old Passes—the New Comes (Deut. 29:1—34:12)

As in other Pentateuchal materials, Deuteronomy has a strong emphasis on the covenant. The description of a covenant ceremony in Moab is found in 29:1–29. This was a part of the third major section of Deuteronomy and is followed by an exhortation which could be titled "The Two Ways" (30:1–20). In it the people were given the choice of blessing or curse, depending on whether they chose the good way of obedience to the LORD or the way of disobedience.

After Deuteronomy's version of the choosing of Moses' successor (31:1–8), there is a command to have a ceremony of covenant renewal every seven years at the time of the Feast of Booths (31:9–29). Much debate has taken place among Old Testament scholars about whether in early Israel this ceremony was like a New Year's festival celebrated by the Babylonians. There is little direct evidence for such a festival in Israel; therefore, drawing a definite conclusion from parallels is not possible. The important point is that such a ceremony of covenant renewal was designed to make the covenant meaningful for each generation.

Deuteronomy concludes with two songs: (1) a song not unlike those found in the Book of Psalms, seemingly used in celebrations of the Exodus events (32:1–43); and (2) a deathbed blessing similar to the blessing of Jacob in Genesis 49 (33:1–29).

Moses, the servant of the LORD, saw the land of promise; but he died on Mt. Pisgah. The final words of the Book of Deuteronomy serve as his epitaph:

> Never since has there arisen a prophet in Israel like Moses, whom the LORD knew face to face. He was unequaled for all the signs and wonders that the LORD sent him to perform in the land of Egypt, against Pharaoh and all his servants and his entire land, and for all the mighty deeds and all the terrifying displays of power that Moses performed in the sight of all Israel. (Dt. 34:10–12)

THEMES IN THE PENTATEUCH

Even if one grants that the Pentateuch is developed from many sources over several hundred years, two questions remain: "What is the ruling purpose behind its final form?" and "What major themes are used to enunciate this purpose?"

As for the first question, the obvious answer is that the Pentateuch gave Israel an explanation for its existence as a people. The themes used to enunciate this purpose include the following:

1. The LORD is creator of the heavens and the the earth, including humankind, to whom he has given lordship over the earth both to use and to preserve.
2. Humankind violated the LORD's trust by rebellion and thus sinned, provoking the LORD's judgment.
3. Israel's connection to the LORD, creation, humankind, and sin was through the patriarchs.
4. The LORD made a covenant with Abraham, the first patriarch, that demanded loyalty to the LORD on Abraham's part. The LORD, in turn, promised that Abraham's descendants would become a people who would receive a land, if they kept the covenant.
5. Exodus through Deuteronomy describes the fulfillment of the first part of the promise—the creation of a people.
6. The Pentateuch ends with the anticipation of the fulfillment of the second part of the covenant—the giving of the land.

STUDY QUESTIONS

1. What major events in Israel's story are described in the book of Exodus?
2. What evidences are cited for dating the Exodus in the 1300–1200 B.C.E. time period?
3. For Israel, what role did the LORD play in the events of the Exodus?
4. How did Moses' life experiences, up to and including his call on Mt. Horeb, prepare him for his leadership role?
5. What meanings can the name *YHWH* have?
6. Compare Aaron's role as described in Exodus 4:10–31 to that of 6:2–7:7. What differences, if any, do you detect? How can they be explained?
7. What is the distinction between a suzerainty treaty or covenant and a parity treaty or covenant?
8. Define *miracle* and describe the function of the miraculous.
9. What sort of Egyptian natural phenomena testify as to the reality of the plagues?

10. In what two ways did the ninth plague strike at the pharaoh's power?
11. What are two ways to interpret the plagues?
12. Although they are now associated with the Exodus, what were the probable origins of the festivals of Passover and Unleavened Bread?
13. Why is it not likely that 3,000,000 people were involved in the Exodus?
14. Where are the four possible places for the crossing of the sea?
15. Where was Sinai?
16. What is the relationship between the Song of Moses (Exodus 15:1–18) and the Song of Miriam (15:21)?
17. How did Jethro help Moses with the problem of overwork?
18. Identify: (a) Amalekites (b) apodictic (c) casuistic
19. Look up "covenant" in a Bible dictionary and determine its role in Israelite religion.
20. What are the three major law codes in the Pentateuch and how are they related to the Ten Commandments?
21. Why is Moses called the lawgiver?
22. What characterizes the three law codes?
23. What seems to have been the intent of sacrifice in early Israel, and how was that intent changed over the years?
24. Why did Israel fail in its attempt to invade Canaan from the South?
25. What extrabiblical evidence is there for the prophet Balaam?
26. How do the Balaam stories illustrate the ancient belief in the power of the spoken word?
27. How is one to understand Deuteronomy's humanitarian strain in light of the instructions for holy war?
28. Why is Deuteronomy's place in the canon unique?
29. What are the major themes of the Pentateuch?
30. Why do you suppose the Pentateuch was written?
31. Other important words and phrases to know: Elohim, El Shaddai, prophet, Yam Suph, Yom Kippur.

ENDNOTES

1. For a succinct introduction to Exodus, see John I. Durham, "Exodus," in *MCB*, 127–129.
2. While some who would minimize the historical value of the biblical narratives concerning the Exodus and conquest of the land are able to marshal some convincing arguments for a different scenario of the formation of Israel as a people, their greatest weakness in every case is how to account for the development of the worship of Yahweh as the God of Israel, whatever Israel's roots. Someone or something had to be responsible, and the personality of a Moses and the events described in Exodus are much better than whatever alternatives have been proposed to this point.
3. For arguments for dating the Exodus in the 14th century during the reign of Horemheb, with Amenhotep III as the pharoah of the oppression, see Joseph Adler, "Dating the Exodus: A New Perspective," in *JBQ* XXXIII, 1 (January-March, 1995), 44–51.
4. For an excellent work on the life of Moses , see Dewey Beegle, *Moses, the Servant of Yahweh* (Grand Rapids: Wm. B. Eerdmans, 1972).
5. Tikva Frymer-Kensky, "Forgotten Heroines of the Exodus: The Exclusion of Women from Moses' Vision," *BR* XIII, 6 (December, 1997), 38–44, points out how the patriarchal system obscured the important roles women played in significant events of biblical history.

6. J. B. Pritchard, ed., *ANET* 85.
7. See Durham, ""Exodus," *MDB* 135 for a "reasonable guess" as to the meaning of this incident.
8. On conditions during the oppression, see Nahum Sarna, "Exploring Exodus: The Oppression," *BA* 49, 2 (June, 1986), 69–79. See also Hershel Shanks, "An Ancient Israelite House in Egypt?" *BAR* 19, 4 (July-August 1993), 44–45.
9. On covenants, see John H. Hayes, "Covenant," *MCB* 178–181; George E. Mendenhall and Gary A. Herion, "Covenant," *ABD* I, 1179–1202.
10. See Bernhard W. Anderson, *Understanding the Old Testament*, 4th ed. (Englewood Cliffs, NJ: Prentice Hall, 1986), 70, for a chart comparing the different traditions.
11. L. Mihelic and G. Ernest Wright, "Plagues in Exodus," in *IDB* III, 822. Also Karen R. Joines, "Plagues," *MDB* 692.
12. From Chester Warren Quimby, "Straight from the Classroom," *JBR* XXI, 1 (1953), 62.
13. I am indebted to David Noel Freedman, "Did God Play a Dirty Trick on Jonah at the End?" *BR* VI, 4 (August, 1990), 27, for this insight.
14. For this interpretation of the plagues, see Greta Hort, "The Plagues in Egypt," *Zeitschrift für die Altestamentliche Wissenschaft* 69 (1956), 84–103. She proposes that they represent a chain of events occurring from August to March. This is also the position of Beegle, *Moses,* 97–118.
15. Beegle, *Moses,* 106.
16. Ibid., 111.
17. On the Egyptian background of this material, see John E. Currid, "Why Did God Harden Pharaoh's Heart?" *BR* XI, 6 (December, 1993), 46–51, esp. 49–50.
18. This is based on Ziony Zevit, "Three Ways to Look at the Plagues," *BR,* VI, 3 (June, 1990), 16–23, 42.
19. G. Ernest Wright, *Biblical Archaeology,* rev. ed. (Philadelphia: Westminster, 1962), 66–67 discusses this problem.
20. For other views about the midwives and conditions of the oppression, see Sarna, "Exploring Exodus: The Oppression," 68–70.
21. From Martin Noth, *The History of Israel,* 2nd ed. (New York: Harper and Row, 1960), 115ff. See also Gaalyah Cornfeld and David Noel Freedman, *Archaeology of the Bible: Book by Book* (New York: Harper and Row, 1976), 38–41.
22. This theory on Sinai's location was brought to my attention by the late J. Philip Hyatt at Vanderbilt University. For other alternatives, see Cornfeld and Freedman, *Archaeology of the Bible,* 40.
23. Mendenhall and Herion, "Covenant," *ABD* 1, 1179–1194.
24. Walter Eichrodt, *Theology of the Old Testament,* 2 vols, trans. J. A. Baker (Louisville: Westminster/John Knox, 1961, 1967) sees the covenant as the dominant idea in Israel's history.
25. Pritchard, *ANE* 165.
26. John H. Tullock, *Blood-Vengeance Among the Israelites in the Light of Its Near Eastern Background* (Ann Arbor: University Microfilms, 1966), 165.
27. On the nature of Leviticus, " the priestly book," (LXX), or *wayyiqra'* "and he called," (Hebrew Bible), see W. H. Bellinger, Jr., "Leviticus, Book of," *MDB* 511f.
28. See Claude Mariottini, "Numbers, Book of," *MDB* 621.
29. Suzanne Singer, "From These Hills," *BAR* IV (June 1978), 16–27.
30. Andrew Lemaire, "Fragments of the Book of Balaam Found at Deir Alla," *BAR* XI, 5 (September-October 1985), 26–39. See also Jacob Hoftijzer, "The Prophet Balaam in a 6th Century Aramaic Inscription," *BA* 39, 1 (March 1976), 11–17. Lemaire would date the texts to the eighth century B.C.E.
31. For a fuller discussion, see Charles R. Krahmalkov, "Exodus Itinerary Confirmed by Egyptian Evidence," *BAR* XX, 5 (September-October 1994), 54–62.
32. John H. Tullock, "Deuteronomy," *MCB* 201.

Chapter 5 🖋

ISRAEL GAINS A HOME

Joshua and Judges

TWO VIEWS OF THE CONQUEST—JOSHUA AND JUDGES

Currently, a number of theories are advanced to explain how Israel conquered Palestine. Joshua 1–12 gives a picture of a lightning campaign, yet Joshua 23:4–5 says after the land is supposedly won:

> I have allotted to you as an inheritance...those nations that remain. . . . The LORD your God will push them back before you . . . and you shall possess their land.

The Book of Judges then opens with the question, "Who shall go up first for us against the Canaanites, to fight against them?" (Judg. 1:1). Judges then goes on to describe a continuing struggle to wrest the land from the enemy, stretching over more than a century since much of the land was unconquered. The Israelites first controlled parts of the hill country, while the Philistines occupied the coastal plain and valleys, frequently putting the Israelites in jeopardy. They were preserved only by the leadership of charismatic chieftains—called "judges"—who arose to inspire the people to victory when the hour seemed darkest.

A total of thirteen judges are mentioned, some meriting only a verse or two, while the exploits of others, such as Deborah, Gideon, and Samson cover several chapters. The book ends with the story of a tragic civil war.

In keeping with the purpose of this text, the accounts of Joshua and Judges will be examined as they now stand. When this has been done, present views of the conquest will be discussed.

THE INTERNATIONAL SCENE

Conditions in Palestine in the period 1300 to 1100 B.C.E. had changed considerably from those of previous centuries. Canaan, later known as Palestine, had been dominated by the Egyptians for a long time. By the time of Joshua's entry into the land, however, Egypt and the Hittites of Asia Minor, the two contenders for control of the vital land bridge between Asia and Africa had fought an exhausting war. Egypt probably was the winner, but she was left weakened. This was during the reign of Ramses II around 1285 B.C.E. The Exodus may have taken place about that time.

Another problem facing Egypt was an invasion by the "Sea Peoples," invaders who seem to have come from the area of modern Greece. Merneptah (1224–1211 B.C.E.), the son of Ramses II, succeeded in driving the invaders off, but after his death the Egyptian Empire went into a rapid decline. As noted earlier, Merneptah mentions the Israelites in a monument for a battle fought in 1220 B.C.E.

The "Sea Peoples," driven out of Egypt, settled on the southern coast of Canaan and became known as the Philistines. It was from them that Canaan got the name Palestine. Israel's major problem was to fight the people of the land since the Egyptians, the Hittites of Asia Minor, and the Assyrians of the Mesopotamian region were too weak to interfere in Canaan in the twelfth century.

THE INVASION OF CANAAN

Preparations for the Invasion (Josh. 1:1–2:24)

Israel's new leader was no newcomer to responsibility. As a soldier, Joshua had proven his ability as a leader in the battle against the Amalekites (Exod. 17:8–16). As one of the twelve spies, he had already gotten a first-hand look at the territory to be invaded. He had come away firmly convinced that it could be conquered despite the fact that only one other of the twelve (Caleb) agreed with him (Num. 13:1–33). Assured of the LORD's presence and leadership (1:1–18), he began the preparations for the invasion.

First, he ordered the people who were to cross the Jordan to prepare themselves. Then, he placed them under strict orders of obedience to his authority (1:10–18). Next, he sent two spies to Jericho to bring back information about the enemy. As a natural cover-up, they went to the house of a prostitute named Rahab. The ruse did not work because the king of Jericho sent men to Rahab's house to try to find them. She had hidden them, however, and was able to convince the king's men that they were not in the house. Since her house was located on the city wall, she was able to let them down by a rope on the outside of the wall. Returning to Joshua, they gave their report (2:1–24).

The Waters Part Again (Josh. 3:1–5:1)

There followed another of the remarkable series of timely events that Israel saw as the "wonder" of God. Several miles above Jericho stood the city of Adam or Adamah. At this site the Jordan follows its twisting path between high clay banks. At times, the river undercuts the banks so that they fall into the river, forming a natural dam that holds it in check for several hours. When Israel needed it to happen, it did. As the biblical writer describes it:

> When the people set out from their tents to cross over the Jordan, the priests bearing the ark of the covenant were in front of the people. Now the Jordan overflows all its banks throughout the time of harvest. So when those who bore the ark had come to the Jordan, and the feet of the priests bearing the ark were dipped in the edge of the water, the waters flowing down from above stood still, rising up in a single heap far off at Adam, the city that is beside Zarethan, while those flowing toward the sea of the Arabah, the Dead Sea, were wholly cut off. Then the people crossed over opposite Jericho (3:14–16).

The ark of the covenant, symbol of the LORD's presence with the Israelites, was carried to the midst of the riverbed to remind them that it was the LORD's doings that were enabling them to cross the flooded river (3:17).

The passage through the Jordan was commemorated by a pile of stones set up as a memorial to the event. They were to serve as a teaching aid so that when children of future generations asked, "What do these stones mean?" the elders would tell them of the LORD God's deliverance of the people (4:1–5:1).

And the Walls Came Tumbling Down (Josh. 5:2–6:27)

After crossing the Jordan, all the men and boys underwent circumcision as an act of consecration to the LORD (5:2–12). When they had recovered, preparations got underway for the attack on Jericho. In a vision, Joshua saw "the commander of the army of the LORD." There are elements here that parallel Moses' vision on the mountain (Exod. 3). Joshua was assured of divine leadership in the days ahead (5:13–15).

Jericho, the first major target of the Israelites after they crossed the Jordan, is one of the world's oldest continuously existing cities. Located just north of the Dead Sea, this well-watered oasis was settled at least as early as 7000 B.C.E. Much archaeological effort has been spent in excavating Jericho, and interpretations about the results have run the gamut. An early excavator, John Garstang, interpreted the evidence as supporting the biblical account. Then Dame Kathleen Kenyon concluded that there was little evidence that Jericho was even a city when Joshua was supposed to have conquered it. Now, a new assessment of Kenyon's excavations by Bryant Wood, an American archaeologist, has led him to conclude that Jericho was indeed conquered in the manner described in the Book of Joshua, aided by an earthquake.

The major problem arises in relating this to Joshua's conquest. Wood dates this fall at 1400 B.C.E., too early for Joshua by most estimates. The whole question as to the nature of the Exodus and conquest is in such a state of flux, however, that it is difficult to reach any firm conclusions at this time.[1]

In the description of the fall of the city there are some significant features. For one thing, the religious nature of Israelite warfare can be seen in the act of carrying the ark of the covenant around the walls of the besieged city, accompanied by the raucous blaring of the ram's horn trumpets (Hebrew *shopharim*) (6:1–11). In the second place, the prominent role the number 7 plays in the story shows the importance of numerology in Hebrew thought. In addition to 7, the numbers 1, 3, 4, 10, and 12 and their multiples had significance other than their numerical value. Seven symbolized completeness, 10 perfection, and 12 completeness (6:12–16).

Of great significance is the fact that this was a holy war. Everything was to be destroyed as an act of dedication to God. Only the prostitute, Rahab, who had helped the spies, was to be spared (6:17–25). Finally, when the city was conquered, a curse was pronounced on it to prevent its rebuilding (6:26–27).

Trouble in the Camp (Josh. 7:1–26)

As harsh as the requirements of the holy war were, an incident involving an Israelite would make it seem even more harsh. Strict rules governed the disposal of goods that were captured in the holy war. A violation of the ban on the taking of spoils for personal use was punishable by death to the offender. In the battle for Ai, a stronghold in the hill country west of Jericho, the Israelites were driven back. Unknown to Joshua, Achan, one of the warriors, had taken certain banned objects at Jericho (7:1): a beautiful robe, a large number of silver coins, and a bar of gold. Unfortunately for Achan, the word of his crime—in modern parlance—was "leaked" to Joshua, though, at first, the name of the culprit was not revealed. Knowledge that someone had gotten by with violating the ban seems to have had a divisive effect on the army, resulting in a stinging defeat at Ai (7:2–5).

Joshua was perplexed, feeling the LORD had let him down (7:6–9). Then Joshua became aware that this was not the case, but rather, someone had violated the ban (7:10–15). An investigation revealed Achan as the culprit, and, in due course, he confessed his sin (7:16–26).

By our standards of justice, what followed would seem to be unjust, for the text says:

And Joshua and all Israel took Achan . . . and the silver, the mantle, and the bar of gold, with his sons and daughters, with his oxen, donkeys, and sheep, and his tent and all that he had. . . . And all Israel stoned him to death; they burned them with fire, cast stones on them (7:24–25).

Why did his family have to suffer the consequences of his sin? Because of a view that is best described by the term *corporate personality*. In this view, a person was not seen as an individual but as part of a larger unit—the family, the tribe, or clan. Our society emphasizes the importance of the individual. Early Israelite society emphasized the importance of the group. Because of this, whatever action a person took was thought to affect not only himself but the group as a whole, either positively or negatively. For this reason, Achan's guilt had to be shared by the group of which he was a part. It affected not only those related to him, but also whatever he possessed. The destruction of Achan, his family, and his possessions was looked upon as the only way to clear the larger group, the people as a whole, of Achan's sin. When the punishment was carried out, the battle was renewed and was won (8:1–29).[2] There follows an account of building an altar on Mt. Ebal in the Shechem area. It may possibly belong with Joshua 23–24, where an account of a covenant ceremony is given. It will be discussed there (8:30–35).

Those Tricky Gibeonites (Josh. 9:1–27)

Gibeon, some six to seven miles northeast of the present city of Jerusalem, was typical of the small Canaanite villages of the time. Having heard of the brutal Israelite conquest of the nearby towns, the Gibeonites decided that they would rather not have to face such a fate. They put on their most ragged clothes and worn-out sandals, took stale bread and wineskins that were brittle with age, and set out for the Israelite camp. When they arrived, they told the Israelites a fanciful tale, designed to appeal to the Israelite ego, about how they had heard of the greatness of the Israelites, but more especially the greatness of their God (9:3–10). As a result, they said they had set out to find these people who worshiped the LORD in order to make a covenant with them.

The Israelites were completely taken in by their story. Without any investigation, the made a covenant with the Gibeonites. They confirmed the covenant with a covenant meal and by taking a solemn oath. Under the terms of the covenant, the Gibeonites were to be spared and thus would become part of Israel (9:11–15).

After the covenant was made, the truth came out. Their word having been given, the Israelites could not change the terms except to make the Gibeonites "hewers of wood and drawers of water for the congregation and for the altar of the LORD" (9:27). This is one of the few breaks in the idealized picture of the conquest, and it reveals an important fact—namely, that many of the people who later counted in Israel never came from Egypt and were joined to Israel by covenant in the worship of the LORD.

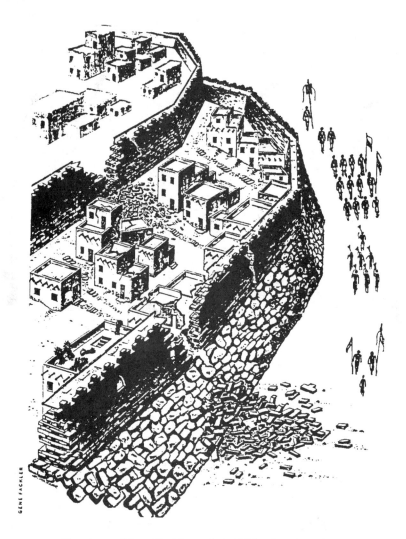

Courtesy of Gene Fackler and the Biblical Archaeology Review.

Figure 5–1.   "So the priests blew the trumpets. As soon as the men
heard it, they gave a loud shout, and the walls col-
lapsed" (Josh. 7:20 *TEV*). An artist's sketch, based on
biblical descriptions and archaeological interpretations,
of the collapse of the mud brick walls of Jericho, creating ramps for the Israelites to enter the city.

The Five Kings of the South (Josh. 10:1–27)

The local kings, more like self-appointed rulers of small towns of a few hundred people, became alarmed over Israelite successes. Five of them joined forces,
including the kings of Jerusalem, Hebron, Eglon, Lachish, and Jarmuth (10:3). The

battle took place in the Valley of Aijalon. This valley was one of the few routes from the coastal plain up into the southern section of the central hill country. The attack, which probably came at dawn, was aided by a violent hailstorm that lasted into the day. The great hailstones killed many of the enemy and caused the Israelite minstrels to sing a song about the sun standing still at Gibeon (10:1–14).

The kings were captured, and a symbolic ceremony was conducted in which the Israelite leaders placed their feet on the kings' necks. As they did, Joshua charged the leaders to be strong. He promised that the LORD would lead them to be just as successful against all of Israel's enemies if they remained faithful to the LORD (10:15–27).

Joshua's Conquests (Josh. 10:28–12:24)

The view of the conquest presented by the Book of Joshua is an idealized version. As will be seen later in the Book of Judges, Joshua's campaigns were not quite the smashing successes they appear to be in Joshua's accounts. In the main, success was confined to the hill country, with most of the plains, valleys, and coastal cities remaining under the control of the Canaanites and Philistines. Summary statements of Joshua's accomplishments are found in 10:28–43 and 11:16–12:24. It was a war of extermination with the LORD's assistance, as explained by 11:20:

> For it was the LORD's doing to harden their hearts so that they would come against Israel in battle, in order that they might be utterly destroyed, and might receive no mercy but be exterminated, just as the LORD had commanded Moses.

The battle against one city in particular has been singled out—the battle against Hazor, the metropolis of early Palestine, located some ten miles north of the Sea of Galilee. The great mound of Hazor is the largest archaeological site in Palestine, covering more than two hundred acres. By comparison, the average size of a city mound, or *tell*, is five to ten acres; a tell of thirty acres is considered to be large (11:10–11). Archaeological work at Hazor has tended to confirm the destructive attack of the Israelites in keeping with the biblical account.[3]

DIVIDING THE LAND AND RENEWING THE COVENANT

The Dividing of the Land (Josh. 13:1–21:45)

While Joshua speaks as though the land is already conquered, the boundaries described in 13–21, in reality, represented the territory each tribe was responsible to conquer, not what it had already captured.

Of special interest are the cities assigned to the Levites (21:1–42). They had no territorial boundaries, but they were to receive cities within each of the territories, centrally located to provide (1) accessible worship centers, and (2) centers for the

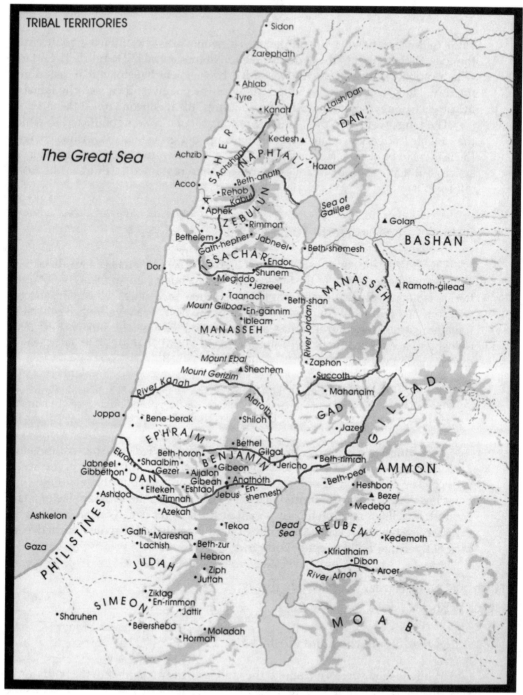

Artwork by Margaret Jordan Brown ©) Mercer University Press.

Figure 5–2. The division of the land (Josh. 13:1–19:51).

administration of justice, including refuge centers where an accused killer could come until some disposition could be made of the case. Otherwise, the killer would be at the mercy of the "avenger of blood," a member of the family against whom the crime had been committed. Under the family law of custom, the avenger was judge, jury, and executioner when there was no ruling state to carry out punishment for crimes against a family member.

The Altar That Was Not an Altar

An insight into how the early Israelites dealt with problems that arose between tribes can be seen in the story of an altar built by the tribes east of the Jordan. When word came back to the tribes in the west, an alarm was raised. Such an altar would seem to violate a ban on worshiping anywhere except at one central shrine, which in those days probably was Shechem or Shiloh (22:12). In a tribal assembly it was decided to send Phineas, a priest, accompanied by ten tribal representatives, to investigate the situation. When they inquired of the Reubenites, Gadites, and the half tribe of Manasseh, they were told that the altar was a memorial, "a witness between us and you . . . that we do perform the service of the LORD in his presence with our burnt offerings and sacrifices and offerings of well-being" (22:27). Satisfied about the purpose of the altar, the tribal representatives returned and the planned attack was averted (22:30–34).

Joshua's Farewell and a Covenant-Renewal Ceremony (Josh. 23:1–24:28; see also Josh. 8:30–35 and Deut. 27:1–26)

A recognition that Joshua's conquest is not complete appears in Joshua's farewell address to the Israelite leaders. The LORD God had given them the land from the Jordan to the "Great Sea in the west," and he would enable them to conquer the people who still occupied the land provided Israel was faithful to God's law as given to Moses (23:1–13). Unfaithfulness would lead to loss of life and land (23:14–16).

The climax of Joshua's story is the covenant-renewal ceremony described in Joshua 24:1–28. The site of the ceremony was Shechem, an ancient religious center (Gen. 34) located at the head of a pass between Mount Gerizim and Mount Ebal in the central section of the hill country. Shechem is not mentioned among the cities conquered by Joshua, possibly because the natives of the area were somehow related to the Israelites and had joined Israel by covenant in which they agreed to worship the LORD.

Deuteronomy 27:1–8 contains a command for the people to set up a memorial on Mount Ebal when they entered the land. Joshua 8: 30–35 describes the fulfillment of this command and goes on to describe briefly a covenant-renewal ceremony.

An altar was built, sacrifices were offered, a copy of the law was written and read to the people, and a ceremony of blessing and cursing was carried out, with half the Levites standing on Mount Gerizim and the other half standing on Mount Ebal (Josh. 8:33; but see Deut. 27:12–13 where all the tribes are mentioned, with Levi as a secular tribe).

Shechem, then, obviously had strong traditions connecting it to the early days of Israel's history. The covenant-renewal ceremony at Shechem described in Joshua 24 has about it many of the same elements of the suzerainty (superior-inferior) treaty. The important men of Israel gathered at the sanctuary (24:1). Joshua recounted the LORD's call to the patriarchs, how the people were brought out of Egypt under the leadership of Moses and Aaron, and into the land of Canaan (24:2–13). After reminding them of the LORD's blessing, Joshua called on them to accept the obligations of the covenant. Joshua 24:14–15 indicates that not all the people present were descendants of those who came out of Egypt, for he spoke of those who were worshiping "the gods your ancestors served . . . beyond the River or the gods of the Amorites in whose land you dwell." A careful reading of this passage suggests that at least four groups were present: (1) the Joshua-led Israelites; (2) Israelites who had filtered into the land apart from those led by Joshua; (3) Semitic peoples who had never been to Egypt but who shared the patriarchal traditions with Israel; and (4) non-Semitic peoples who joined Israel by covenant. The most numerous among these undoubtedly were the Canaanites.

The Influence of Canaanite Religion. That Canaanite religious practices were much more influential in the development of Israelite religion than was formerly thought is becoming more widely recognized today. This is because (1) the number of people entering Palestine from the outside is now believed to have been much fewer than once was thought, and consequently (2) the Canaanite population was much larger than earlier thought, especially since the views of the nature of the conquest have changed substantially. Among those elements adapted from Canaanite religion by the Israelites would be the divine name *El* as the equivalent to *YHWH*, and three festivals that originally were agricultural in nature—Tabernacles, Weeks, and Unleavened Bread. Outside the religious sphere, Israel's adoption of the kingship undoubtedly was influenced by the Canaanites (1 Sam. 8:20; Psa. 110:4).[4]

Among the negative effects on Israelite religion were those practices adopted from the worship of Baal, the Canaanite god of the storm. Baalism was based on the wet-dry cycle of the year, common in Palestine. According to the Baal myth, Baal and Anat were brother and sister, but also lovers. Baal was killed by his enemy, Mot, the god of death. Mot devoured Baal. Because Baal made the earth productive, his death caused vegetation to die (the dry season). Anat, or Asherah as the Old Testament calls her (1 Kings 16:33), went looking for Baal. When Mot bragged that he had killed Baal, Anat seized Mot, killed him, and made chopped meat of him, scattering the bits of his flesh on the fields as food for the birds. When Mot died, Baal came alive again. Sexual union between the lovers followed, and fertility returned with the rainy season.[5]

Summary on Joshua's Version of the Conquest

In the strict sense, the complete story of the conquest is not told in the Book of Joshua. This is not its purpose. Instead, its purpose is to glorify the LORD by giving examples of the marvelous way he led the people to the land that had been promised to the patriarchs. The book says, further, that any failure was a failure on the part of Israel to walk in faith with God. This is part of the theme spoken of first in Deuteronomy and which finds its clearest expression in the Book of Judges. Because of its origin in Deuteronomy, it is known as the Deuteronomic theme. As we look at Judges, this theme will become more evident.

ANOTHER LOOK AT THE CONQUEST

On with the Conquest (Judg. 1:1–2:5)

Once the territory had been assigned to the tribes, the hard part began. Warfare lasted for many years. In reality, the boundaries described in Joshua were never achieved until the time of David. Judah asked the tribe of Simeon to join with it in the conquest of southern Palestine. The impression is given (1:8) that they conquered Jerusalem, but in a later account David is named as its conqueror. There is also the mention of the capture of three cities of the Philistines: Gaza, Ashkelon, and Ekron. The Septuagint, however, specifically says that these cities were not captured. As a whole, this section is a record of the failure of the majority of the tribes to conquer the territory assigned to them. For the biblical historian, the military failure was brought on by the failure to keep the LORD's covenant. Failure would continue to haunt them as long as they were unfaithful to the covenant.

A Preview of the Book of Judges (Judg. 2:6–3:6)

After a description of the death and burial of Joshua comes a verse that is reminiscent of Exodus 1:1: "Now a new king arose—who did not know Joseph." Judges 2:10 says in part, "Another generation grew up after them, who did not know the LORD or the work he had done for Israel."

The basic pattern of the Book of Judges starts with this theme and is based on a four-part sermon, a concise form of which is found in Judges 3:7–11: (1) "The Israelites did what was evil in the sight of the LORD" (3:7); (2) "the anger of the LORD was kindled against Israel" and an enemy oppressed them (3:8); (3) "when the Israelites cried out to the LORD, (4) the LORD raised up a deliverer for the Israelites" (3:9).

First of all, the theme of sin-punishment-repentance-deliverance is the Deuteronomic theme. It is so named because scholars believe the books beginning with Joshua and extending through 2 Kings (with the exception of Ruth) were put in their present form during the Babylonian exile by Jewish historians who had been influenced by the Book of Deuteronomy. In 621 B.C.E., during the reign of Josiah, a major portion of Deuteronomy, with its strong emphasis upon the necessity of Israel's faithfulness to the covenant, had been found during a major repair of the Jerusalem Temple. Its discovery had led to a strong religious revival for a time; but after Josiah's death the revival quickly died. A few years later, the Babylonians invaded and carried many of the Israelites into captivity. The historians of Israel concluded that their troubles stemmed from the failure to be faithful to the covenant. The whole history of the people, furthermore, from the time of the entry into the land, had been marred by this same unfaithfulness to the covenant. Thus, their version of the history of Israel was interpreted in the light of this conviction.

In the second place, it is in this section of the book that the judges are first mentioned. From the description in 2:16: "Then the LORD raised up judges who delivered them out of the power of those who plundered them," one can discover the major function of the judges of the Book of Judges; namely, they were military leaders. They have been described as "charismatic military leaders," meaning that they were persons who had qualities that inspired others to follow wherever they led.

Since Israel was composed of twelve tribes, however, no one of them was able to get all the people to follow his or her leadership. At this time, the tribe was more important than the people as a whole. There was little, if any, national unity. It was not until the monarchy of David that tribal feeling began to take second place to national feeling. Even then, tribal feelings were not completely dead.

THE PERIOD OF THE JUDGES

Othniel (Judg. 3:7–11)

Othniel was a minor judge who was said to have delivered Israel from "King Cushan-rishathaim of Aram." This king is not known from any historical record, so he must have been a minor king.

Ehud, the Left-Handed Benjaminite (Judg. 3:12–30)

The oppressor was Eglon, king of Moab. Ehud, of the tribe of Benjamin, was chosen to take an annual payment to Eglon, to keep him from attacking the Israelites. In preparation for his visit, Ehud strapped a short sword to the inside of his right thigh. After the money had been paid, he sought a private conference with the king. When they were alone, Ehud drew his sword and stabbed Eglon in the belly:

> the hilt also went in after the blade, and the fat closed over the blade, for he did not draw the sword out of his belly; and the dirt came out (3:22).

Ehud's bold assassination of Eglon rallied the Ephraimites around him so that the Moabite oppression was ended (3:26–30).

Shamgar, the Man with the Goad (Judg. 3:31)

The oppressors were the Philistines. Shamgar is said to have used an ox-goad, a sharpened stick used to prod the oxen as they plowed the fields, to kill 600 Philistines.

Deborah and Barak: Women's Liberation in the Twelfth Century B.C.E. (Judg. 4:1–5:31)

Much has been written about the low status of women in ancient times, but the story of Deborah is an indication that outstanding women had a way of making their mark. Two versions are given of Deborah's story—a later prose version appears in Judges 4:1–24 and the original poetic version is found in 5:1–31.

The two accounts differ somewhat. The prose story speaks of Jabin, the king of Hazor, as Israel's oppressor (4:2). According to Joshua 11, Joshua defeated Jabin and destroyed Hazor some years earlier. The poetic account does not name Jabin, nor does it mention Hazor. Only Sisera, a general, is mentioned.

Deborah, described as a prophetess (4:4), was judging Israel near Bethel in the hill country of Ephraim (4:5). She seems to have functioned as an adviser on personal matters and in settling disputes between contending parties. The oppression was so bad that:

> In the days of Shamgar son of Anath,
>   in the days of Jael, caravans ceased
>   and travelers kept to the byways.
> The peasantry prospered in Israel,
>   they grew fat on plunder,
>   because you arose, Deborah,
>   arose as a mother in Israel.

Deborah's role was to rally the people to fight against the enemy. Barak served as her general, but he refused to go unless she went with him. She agreed, but she told him that a woman would get the glory for winning the battle (4:6–10).

The poetic version calls the roll of the tribes who joined in the battle that took place on Mount Tabor, located at the apex of the triangular plain of Megiddo or Esdralon. After speaking of Ephraim, Benjamin, Machir, Zebulun, and Issachar as tribes who contributed soldiers to the cause, the poet speaks of those who refused to join:

> Among the clans of Reuben
>   there were great searchings of heart.
> Why did you tarry among the sheepfolds,
>   to hear the piping for the flocks?
>   . . . .
> Gilead stayed beyond the Jordan;
>   and Dan, why did he abide with the ships?

> Asher sat still at the coast of the sea,
>   settling down by his landings (5:15d–17).[6]

The Canaanites, equipped with heavy war chariots (4:3), were drawn up on the level plain, while the ill-equipped Israelites were on the slopes of Mount Tabor. A heavy storm broke. The Kishon River, usually no more than a trickle of water, became a raging torrent. It flooded the plain and turned it into a miry swamp. The heavy iron chariots, so fearsome on solid ground, became liabilities instead of assets. The Israelites rushed down the mountain to cut the enemy to pieces (4:13–16; 5:19–21).

When he saw how the battle tide had turned, Sisera decided to take care of the most important person he knew—himself. He fled on foot from the battlefield. After some time, he came to the tent of a Kenite named Heber. Jael, Heber's wife, was at home. When Sisera asked for refuge in her tent, Jael, true to the law of custom, invited him in and gave him refreshments. While he was eating and drinking, she killed him by driving a tent peg through his skull. Like the gunfighter in the western movie:

> He sank, he fell,
>   he lay still at her feet,
> at her feet, he sank, he fell;
>   where he sank, there he fell dead (5:27)

The poetic version ends with a picture of Sisera's mother looking for him, not knowing that he is dead. The closing line is:

> So perish all your enemies, O LORD (5:31).

Gideon: The Master of the Surprise Attack (Judg. 6:1–8-35)

More stories are told about Gideon than about any other judge except Samson. The oppressors were the Midianites, who were aided by the hated Amalekites and "the people from the East" (6:3). In their raids, they (like the locusts) destroyed crops, bringing famine on the land (6:1–6).

The people cried to the LORD, who reminded them through a prophet that they had been unfaithful to him (6:7–10).

Deliverance began when Gideon, a member of the tribe of Manasseh, received a divine visitor, who told him he was chosen to lead the war against the Midianites (6:11–24).

The first thing he did was destroy his own father's altar to Baal, the chief deity of the Canaanite fertility cult. In its place he built an altar to the LORD and made a sacrifice on it (6:25–32).

Photo courtesy of Comstock.

Figure 5–3. "{Deborah} summoned Barak . . . and said to him, 'The
LORD . . . commands you, 'Go take position at Mount
Tabor' " (Judg. 4:6). Barak and his men rushed down
from the slopes of Mount Tabor to destroy the forces of
Sisera, whose iron chariots were bogged down on the
muddy plain.

Next, he prepared to attack the Midianites. He first sent messengers through
the country, calling for volunteers to fight. Then he asked God for a sign to show
that God approved what Gideon was doing. When the sign was positive, he then
prepared his forces for battle (6:33–40).

Because there were too many volunteers, Gideon gave a series of tests to reduce
the number. Only three hundred were left when the testing was over (7:1–8). These

three hundred men gathered in the hills surrounding the main Midianite camp, located in a valley. Gideon divided his small army into three parts, giving each soldier a torch, a pitcher to cover it with, and a ram's horn trumpet (7:9–18).

He stationed his men at strategic places, where they waited until the Midianites were asleep. When the signal was given, they raced down from the hills, waving their torches and yelling, "A sword for the LORD and for Gideon" (7:20). The Midianites, awakened from their sleep, probably thought all the Israelites in the world were attacking them. They fled in terror and confusion. Gideon's men were then joined by the others in pursuit of the disorganized Midianites (7:19–8:3).

As the battle ended, Gideon captured two Midianite chieftains, Zeba and Zalmunna, who had killed two of his brothers. Gideon tried to disgrace them by telling his teenage son to kill them. This deeply offended Zeba and Zalmunna. They said to Gideon, "You come and kill us; for as a man is, so is his strength" (8:21). What this meant was, "Kill us yourself. A man has a right to be killed by one who is his equal." This sense of rank and honor was common in ancient societies and is still strong in many Eastern societies today. The fear of disgrace was greater than the fear of death (8:4–21).

Returning home from the defeat of the Midianites, Gideon was so popular that the people tried to make him king. He refused, but he made a religious image, possibly to commemorate the victory, and urged the people to follow the LORD. Instead, the image he made became an idol the people worshiped. He died, shunned by the people whom he rescued (8:22–35).

Abimelech: A Nobody Who Thought He Was Somebody (Judg. 9:1–25)

Abimelech, Gideon's son by a slave wife, was his father's opposite, a "mock judge." While Gideon did not seek power, Abimelech did; God called Gideon, but Abimelech called himself; Gideon died with honor; Abimelech died in disgrace.[7] After skillfully manipulating the leaders of Shechem into supporting him financially and otherwise, he hired a group of thugs and slaughtered all his brothers except one. Then he had himself proclaimed king (9:1–6).

The brother who had escaped Abimelech's thugs was Jotham, Gideon's youngest son. Climbing to the top of Mount Ebal, he shouted down to the Shechemites and told them "The Fable of the Trees." The moral was this: when good men fail to act, evil men will act with evil results. Their response to Gideon's leadership had been to choose the worst of his sons to rule over them, simply because he was related to them. He further warned that the results of their foolishness would soon be obvious (9:7–21).

Rebellion, led by Gaal, the son of Ebed, was not long in coming. He stirred up the Shechemites against Abimelech, but Abimelech's supporters in the city betrayed Gaal, causing his defeat (9:22–41). Abimelech then burned the city of Shechem, including a large number of people who had taken refuge in the Tower of Shechem

(9:42–49). Abimelech's victory was short-lived, however. In his attempt to capture a tower at Thebez, a woman dropped a millstone on his head. To avoid the disgrace of being killed by a woman, he asked his armor bearer to kill him, which he did (9:50–57).[8]

Jephthah: A Man Who Made a Foolish Vow and Kept It (Judg. 10:6–12:7)

Two minor judges, Tola (10:1–2), and Jair (10:3–5), are mentioned before Jephthah is introduced. Israel had been unfaithful again. Gilead, a Transjordan tribe, had fallen under the heel of the Ammonites, who also crossed the Jordan to raid southern Palestine (10:6–9).

Repenting of their unfaithfulness, the people pleaded for deliverance, promising to support anyone who would lead them (10:10–18). For a leader, they chose an unlikely prospect. Jephthah was the son of a harlot, cast out by his half-brothers because of his illegitimate birth. He became an outlaw, probably raiding caravans on the King's Highway (11:1–3).

The Gileadites, desperate for someone to lead them, went to Jephthah and pleaded with him to become their leader. He agreed on the condition that should he be successful, he would become the permanent head of the tribe. This done, Jephthah rallied the people around him and prepared for war. Before he began the battle, he vowed that if he were successful, he would sacrifice to the LORD the first thing he saw when he returned from the battle.

He was successful. When he returned, the first thing he saw was his daughter. He kept his vow, thus giving the only clear example in the Old Testament of an Israelite practicing human sacrifice to the LORD (11:29–40). Such a practice was strongly denounced by all the great prophets of Israel.

Not all battles were fought against non-Israelites. The Ephraimites again became jealous (as they did in the case of Gideon) because they had not shared in the glory of Jephthah's victory. They decided, therefore, to attack Jephthah and the Gileadites—but they got the worst of the battle. As the fugitives from the battle tried to slip back across the Jordan, the Gileadites, who controlled the crossing places, made each person prove where he was from by giving a password. If he said, "Shibboleth," he was released for he was not an Ephraimite. If, however, he said "Sibboleth," he was seized and killed, for only those who spoke the Ephraimite dialect pronounced the Hebrew *sh* sound as an *s* (12:1–7).

Samson: A Brilliant Failure (Judg. 13:1–16:31)

Three other minor judges—Ibzan (12:8–10), Elon (12:11–12), and Abdon (12:13–15)—are mentioned before Samson is introduced. The most important thing about any of them was the large size of their families.

The Samson stories are introduced with a familiar theme: "The Israelites again did what was evil in the sight of the LORD." Oppression came from the Philistines, who would be Israel's mortal enemies until David conquered them.

The Philistines controlled the southern Palestinian coast from five strong cities: Gaza, Ashdod, Ashkelon, Ekron, and Gath. They came to Palestine around 1200 B.C.E. and, religion aside, theirs was a much more highly developed society than that of the Israelites. Their pottery was a buff-colored, white-slipped decorated ware that has been found in a number of Philistine archaeological sites. In contrast, Israelite pottery from the same period (the early Iron Age) was very crude and rough. More important, the Philistines possessed the secret of smelting iron, giving them weapons for war far superior to the stone and bronze weapons of the Israelites. Israel did not possess such weapons at least until the time of David.

The pressure begun in Samson's time would mount until it would do what none of the judges had been able to do—namely, to drive the stubbornly independent Israelite tribes into uniting under a single leader. Samson had a flair for the dramatic. This trait might have made him the leader, but unfortunately, he possessed neither the will nor the character to be such a leader.

The story of Samson has the familiar theme of the barren wife, who, after many years, bears a son. Because of the pledge made by his mother before his birth, Samson was a Nazirite. The Nazirite vow required that a person (1) not cut his hair, (2) not drink wine, and (3) not touch a dead body (13:1–25).

Samson's home was in the foothill country, bordering on the Philistine territory. His mother's pledge that he would be a Nazirite did not keep him from growing up as a domineering and arrogant young man, one who was accustomed to having what he wanted. The first thing he wanted was to marry a Philistine woman, an unthinkable thing for a well-brought-up young Israelite man. But Samson knew what he wanted, so his browbeaten parents gave in. The Israelite storyteller interpreted it as the LORD's way of getting an excuse for Samson to strike a blow at the Philistines (14:1–4).

On the way to see the girl, a young lion attacked Samson. Samson killed the lion and left the carcass by the roadside. Later, as he came back, he found a swarm of bees in the body of the lion. When the wedding festivities were taking place, Samson made a bet with the Philistine men that he could give them a riddle they could not solve. If they solved it within the seven-day period of the feast, he would give them thirty linen garments and thirty festal garments. The riddle was:

> Out of the eater came something to eat,
>   Out of the strong came something sweet (14:14).

Unsuccessful at first, the young men threatened Samson's bride, telling her they would kill her if she did not get the answer from Samson and tell them. She tried a number of ways to get the answer. Finally she used the ultimate weapoon—tears—and he told her.

When the Philistines gave him the correct answer he immediately knew his wife had told them (14:19).

> Then the Spirit of the LORD rushed on him, and he went down to Ashkelon. He killed thirty men of the town, took their spoil, and gave the festal garments to those who explained the riddle.

Note that Samson's great strength is said to be because "the Spirit of the LORD rushed on him," in keeping with the idea that all things were from the LORD (14:5–20).

Thus began a series of conflicts between Samson and the Philistines. His wife was given to another man, causing Samson to get his vengeance by setting the grain fields on fire by tying torches to foxes' tails and loosing them in the fields. (Today, a sign of a fox with a torch tied to its tail is the Israeli roadside warning against carelessness with fire.) In revenge, the Philistines burned his ex-wife and her father to death (15:1–8).

Next, they put pressure on the men of Judah to capture Samson for them; else they would make war against Judah. Samson allowed himself to be captured, but once he was handed over to the Philistines, he broke the ropes that bound him. Seizing the jawbone of an ass, he cut a deadly swath with it, leaving dead Philistines in his path (15:9–20).

His passions kept getting him in trouble. A harlot in Gaza almost caused him to be captured (16:1–3). Then came Delilah, a temptress from the Vale of Sorek, who would finally lay him low. Completely under Philistine control, she set out to lead Samson to his downfall. Some lines from the Book of Proverbs describe his response:

> With much seductive speech she persuades him;
>   with her smooth talk she compels him.
> Right away he follows her,
>   and goes like an ox to the slaughter,
> or bounds like a stag toward a trap
>   until an arrow pierces its entrails.
> He is like a bird rushing into a snare,
>   not knowing it will cost him his life (Prov. 7:21–23).

She began a campaign to find the secret of his strength. He played along with her, giving her misleading answers each time. Each failure on her part frustrated her even more. Finally, her tears flowed and the secret was told—his strength lay in his hair. All that was left was for her to tell the Philistines, then lull Samson to sleep so she could cut his hair (16:4–19).

The magic was gone for Samson. When he awoke, the Spirit of the LORD was gone. He had abused the power, and he had lost it. He was blinded and put to doing menial work in a prison (16:20–22).

Samson died dramatically. When he was brought out to entertain Philistine notables in the shrine of the Philistine god Dagon, his strength returned long enough for him to pull the temple down on himself and the worshipers (16:23–31). His epitaph could well have been: "So those he killed at his death were more than those he had killed during his life (16:30c)."

THERE WAS NO KING IN ISRAEL: THREE STORIES

Micah and the Levite (Judg. 17:1–13)

The final chapters of Judges illustrate the troubled and confused times preceding the establishment of the monarchy. Religious confusion is illustrated by the story of a man named Micah, who confessed to his mother that he had stolen eleven hundred silver coins from her. When he confessed to her, she gave the coins to him. He, in turn, had an idol made to worship (17:1–6). A traveling Levite passed through and Micah hired him to be his priest, on the assumption that a Levite would make his worship legitimate (17:7–13).

The Move of the Tribe of Dan (Judg. 18:1–31)

The pressure exerted by the Philistines is illustrated by Judges 18. The tribe of Dan had been assigned a territory lying between Judah and Ephraim, Israel's two most powerful tribes, and the dreaded Philistines. They sent out spies to locate a new place to settle. Eventually, they came to a place in northern Palestine, where the sources of the Jordan River arose at the base of Mt. Hermon. On their return, they discovered Micah, the Levite, and his idol. When the tribe moved northward, they took Micah's idol and his priest and set up a shrine in the new territory that they captured (18:1–31).

The Levite and the Sin of Benjamin (Judg. 19:1–21:25)

A strange but fascinating story closes the Book of Judges. A Levite living in Ephraim had to go to bring back his slave wife after she ran away to her father's home (19:1–9). On the way back, they thought of stopping at Jebus (Jerusalem) for the night, but decided against it since it was not an Israelite city. Instead, they went on to Gibeah, a Benjaminite city near Jerusalem. They were invited into the home of an elderly Ephraimite who lived in Gibeah, after no Benjaminite had extended hospitality to them (19:10–22).

During the night, some local men demanded that their host give up the Levite so they could have sex with him. This was a *nabalah,* the vilest offense imaginable

(19:23). When they threatened violence, the Levite finally gave them his slave wife, whom they raped repeatedly. The next morning her dead body was found at the door (19:22–28).

Taking her body home, he cut it into twelve pieces and sent one piece to each tribe (19:29–30). This seems to have been the signal for an emergency meeting for all the tribes. Saul, in later years, cut up a team of oxen to call the people to war against the Ammonites (1 Sam. 11:7).

The tribal leaders, along with their soldiers, assembled at Mizpah. The Levite told what had happened. A decision was made to attack Gibeah to punish its people for allowing such a crime to happen there (20:1–11). First, however, they gave the tribe of Benjamin (in whose territory Gibeah was located) a chance to surrender the men who had committed the crime. Instead, the Benjaminites took up arms against the other tribes in defense of Gibeah (20:12–17).

At first, the battle favored the Benjaminites (20:18–28). Finally, however, they were soundly defeated and their towns were burned to the ground (20:29–48).

The victory turned to ashes when the other tribes realized that they had practically wiped out one of the twelve tribes. Another assembly was called at Bethel to deal with the situation. What was needed was wives for the surviving Benjaminite men so they could raise families. Yet a vow had been taken that none of the other tribes would permit their women to marry a Benjaminite.

What could be done? A two-part solution was advanced. First, the city of Jabesh-Gilead in Transjordan had not supported the war against Benjamin. Because of this, the city was attacked and four hundred young girls were taken and given to the Benjaminites for wives (21:1–15).

When this did not fill the need, a second solution was put into effect. Each year at Shiloh there was a dance for the grape harvest. The men who needed wives were told to hide in the vineyards, so that when the young girls came dancing through the vineyard, each man could grab a girl and carry her away. This solved the problem, allowing Benjamin to survive as a tribe in Israel (21:16–24).

SUMMARY OF THE BOOK OF JUDGES

The Book of Judges is summarized quite well by its final verse: "In those days there was no king in Israel; all the people did what was right in their own eyes" (21:25).

The final chapters illustrate that theme, but they also say some important things about the times and the ways the tribes functioned in emergencies. It was a time of developing crisis as the Philistines began to exert more pressure on the Israelite territories. The Israelites were poorly organized and were not really prepared to respond to the Philistine threat.

Yet, as the story of the Levite and his concubine shows, there seems to have been a kind of organization among the tribes. The term *amphictyony,* used of a league of tribes in Greece, has been used to describe it. That such a league existed in Israel before the time of the monarchy has been increasingly questioned. If so, its purpose would have been two-fold: (1) to bring the tribes together for major religious ceremonies, such as the covenant-renewal ceremony (Josh. 24); (2) to call the tribes together for war when a situation arose that demanded it. In this latter sense, the chief priest functioned like one of the judges because war was a matter of religion also. The opening chapters of 1 Samuel show two such priest-judges in action—Eli and Samuel.

RECENT VIEWS OF THE CONQUEST

The conquest of Palestine (Canaan) presently is one of the most widely discussed subjects in biblical studies. As has already been seen, Joshua and Judges seem to give two different views of the conquest. Added to this, the archaeological evidence, like most archaeological data, suffers from two major limitations: (1) most excavations cover only a small fraction of the total area of any given site, thus limiting what we can know about the site; and (2), most of what is found is non-verbal (that is, pottery, wall and house foundations, animal bones, the village garbage, etc.) and must be interpreted. As a result, different scholars take much the same evidence and reach widely differing conclusions from that evidence. Nowhere is this more evident than in views of the conquest. They follow at least four major models.

An Invasion.   There are those who see the evidence as supporting basically the biblical picture in Joshua, with a violent attack on the land from the eastern desert region. They point out Lachish, Bethel, and Hazor as cities destroyed in the second half of the thirteenth century B.C.E.[9]

A Peaceful Infiltration.   Others propose that the Israelites were clans or clan-groups of sheep and goat herders who moved into the cultivated areas, especially in the central hill country, when vegetation was too scarce on the desert fringes. Gradually, they began to settle in unoccupied areas and became farmers. It was only later, when they came in conflict with the Canaanites, that they captured the larger cities.[10]

A Peasant's Revolt.   Others theorize that most of the Israelites were Canaanite peasant farmers for whom herding was a secondary occupation. Mixed in with them were a few people of desert origin who had the Exodus-Wilderness stories as part of their tradition. These lower-class people gained power by revolting against their Canaanite overlords. In addition, they used treaties, intermarriage, settlement on unoccupied land, and a commitment to Yahwism to unite them and give them identity. This theory sees the lower-class people moving from the cities on the coast into the scarcely populated hill country.[11]

Canaanites Turned Israelites. While in a sense this is a variation of the peasant's revolt, it rests on seemingly sounder archaeological foundations. Based on surveys in Transjordan and the central hill country which indicate that there was an east to west movement in the development of villages believed to be the first Israelite settlements, it has been proposed that the Israelites really were Canaanite farmers who centuries earlier were forced by changing social and economic conditions to become herdsmen living on the desert fringe. Then, around 1250 B.C.E., the Palestinian coastal cities declined, depriving the herdsmen of their markets. They then gradually moved back into the hill country, established villages, and became farmers, becoming what we know as Israelites. Since this proposal only deals with the economic and social aspects of the settlement, the question of religious development is left open.[12]

Yet, for the Biblical interpreter, the religious question is the crucial question. The questions concerning the nature of the conquest probably never will be resolved to everyone's satisfaction. It certainly was more complicated than a superficial reading of Joshua and Judges suggests. Elements of all the major theories may have actually been present. That question aside, the religion of Israel started somewhere, somehow, and under the leadership of someone. No nonbiblical evidence can cancel the imprint of a Moses on the people who became known as the Israelites.

STUDY QUESTIONS

1. Why does one have to read both Joshua and Judges to get a more balanced view of the conquest?
2. Who were the "Sea Peoples" and how were they to affect the history of Israel?
3. How does the description of the battle for Jericho indicate the religious nature of the story?
4. How does the story of Achan illustrate the principles of Holy War?
5. How does the story of the Gibeonites illustrate the importance of a covenant?
6. What does the story of the covenant-renewal ceremony at Shechem tell us about the makeup of the people of Israel?
7. What was the value of covenant-renewal ceremonies?
8. What elements of Israel's religion may have been borrowed from the Canaanites? Was all such borrowing necessarily bad?
9. What is the Deuteronomic theme and why is it so named?
10. What is meant by saying the judges were "charismatic leaders"?
11. What role did women play in the defeat of Sisera?
12. What was the basis of Gideon's strategy against the Midianites?
13. What is the meaning of Jotham's fable (Judges 9:7–15)?

14. In light of the story in Genesis 22, how do you interpret Jephthah's vow that resulted in the sacrifice of his daughter?
15. Evaluate Samson's role as a judge.
16. What set of circumstances finally served to unite the Israelite tribes?
17. In the current debate over the nature of the Exodus and conquest, be able to identify and summarize the major theories.
18. Terms to know: Holy war, corporate personality, amphictyony, nazirite.

ENDNOTES

1. Bryant G. Wood, "Did the Israelites Conquer Jericho? A New Look at the Evidence," *BAR* XVI, 2 (March/April, 1990), 44–57. For another view of the Joshua conquest stories, see Yigael Yadin, "Is the Biblical Account of the Israelite Conquest Historically Reliable?" *BAR* VIII, 2(March/April, 1982), 22.
2. J. W. Rogerson, "Corporate Personality," *ABD* I, 1156–1157.
3. Yigael Yadin, *Hazor: The Rediscovery of a Great Citadel of the Bible* (London: Weidenfeld and Nicholson, 1975) is a fascinating study of this famous site from an archaeological standpoint. See also Abraham Rabinovich and Neil A. Silberman, "The Burning of Hazor," *ARCH* 51, 3, (May/June, 1998), 50–55, for an updated assessment of Yadin's work.
4. John Day, "Canaan, Religion of," *ABD* I, 831–837.
5. Along with many other stories about Baal, this is part of the Ugaritic materials from the fourteenth century B.C.E. Translations may be found in Pritchard, *ANE* 92–118.
6. Lawrence E. Stager, "The Song of Deborah: Why Some Tribes Answered the Call and Others Did Not," *BAR* XV, 1 (January/February, 1989), 51–64, points out that the tribes that followed Deborah were farmers, while those who didn't were seafarers, whose living depended upon a good relationship with the Canaanites.
7. This insight into the story of Abimelech is from Wesley A. Kort, *Story, Text and Scripture* (University Park: Pennsylvania State University Press, 1988), 32.
8. For a look at archaeological evidences from Shechem during the period of the judges, see Gaalyah Cornfeld and David Noel Freedman, eds., *Archaeology of the Bible: Book by Book* (New York: Harper and Row, 1976), 77–79.
9. Strong advocates of this view were Yadin, "Is the Account of the Israelite Conquest Reliable?" 16–23; and Abraham Malamat, "How Inferior Israelite Forces Conquered Fortified Canaanite Cities," *BAR* VIII, 2 (March/April, 1982), 24f.
10. First proposed by Albrecht Alt, it is summarized by Manfred Weippert, *The Settlement of the Tribes in Palestine: A Summary of Recent Scholarly Debate,* trans. James D. Martin (Napierville, IL: Alec R. Allenson, 1970).
11. Advocated by Norman K. Gottwald, *The Tribes of Yahweh* (Maryknoll, NY: Orbis, 1979).
12. First propounded by Israel Finkelstein, the most recent expression of this theory is by Neil Asher Silberman, "Who Were the Israelites?" *ARCH* 45, 2 (March/April, 1992), 22–30. He also gives a summary of the other positions.

Chapter 6

ISRAEL GAINS A KING

Samuel and Saul

SAMUEL: THE JUDGE WHO APPOINTED KINGS

Things looked dark for Israel. Although no threat was posed from Mesopotamia or Asia Minor, a more immediate threat stood right on her doorstep. The Philistines were increasingly warlike and in a mood to expand their holdings in Palestine. The Israelites controlled the land near them and the Philistines could only increase their territory at the expense of Israel. The Israelites had to fight the Philistines, and to survive the Philistine threat, they had to unite. To unite, there had to be leadership. That leadership came from a man who was to dominate Israelite life for many years—as a priest and as chief judge of Israel, as a prophet and as a wise counselor, as a maker of kings and as a breaker of kings. His name was Samuel.

THE SOURCES FOR THE HISTORY
OF THE ISRAELITE KINGDOMS

Four books—1 and 2 Samuel, 1 and 2 Kings—make up the Deuteronomic history of the Israelite kingdoms. Originally, they were two books but probably were divided so as to keep the scrolls upon which they were written from becoming too large to handle. The Books of 1 and 2 Samuel have only three major characters—Samuel, Saul, and David. The Books of Kings then deal with all the other kings, beginning with the death of David and the rise of Solomon. Since 1, 2 Samuel and 1,2 Kings were the final product of a long process of history writing, the Deuteronomic historians had to have sources. This can be seen by the fact that 2 Kings 25:27–30 tells of the release of King Jehoiachin from a Babylonian prison in 560 B.C.E. Since Samuel lived in the mid-eleventh century (1050 B.C.E.), this means that the history went through a long process of writing before the final version was finished sometime after 560 B.C.E.

Some of the sources used can be determined by reading the materials. One such source is found in 2 Samuel 9–20 and 1 Kings 1–2. It has been called the Court History of David and obviously was written by someone close to David's court. As such, it gives us a picture of David unique among the descriptions of the reigns of ancient kings. It is part of a larger block of material referred to by scholars as the Early Source—a source that believed that kingship was good for Israel. Another, or Late Source, which came from a time after David and Solomon when the kings had become despotic, gives a negative view of the monarchy. Including conflicting viewpoints like this may reflect the true state of affairs concerning the monarchy—that from the very beginning there were those individuals who saw the monarchy as the means of salvation for Israel, while others had the equally strong view that it could only lead to ruin for the people.

There is another version of the history that is different from the version found in 1, 2 Samuel and 1, 2 Kings. This version is found in 1, 2 Chronicles, a history of Israel written sometime after the Babylonian Exile. Many passages in Chronicles are lifted word for word from the Samuel to Kings history; yet are important differences. David's weaknesses are glossed over in Chronicles, as are the weaknesses of other Judean kings such as Manasseh. Much attention is given to genealogies and to the activities of the priests and of other Temple officials. There is also a different theological viewpoint. Whereas 2 Samuel 24:1 says the LORD caused David to number the people, 1 Chronicles 21:1 says "Satan" caused David to number them. Even with these differences, 1, 2 Chronicles preserves valuable supplemental information about Israel's history.

Samuel: His Birth and Dedication (1 Sam. 1:1–2:10)

Hannah, the favorite wife of Elkanah (an Ephriamite), bore one of the heaviest burdens an Israelite woman could bear—she was childless. Peninah, the other wife, was fruitful and lorded her success in childbearing over Hannah. It was a bitter pill for Hannah to swallow (1:1–8).

On an annual trip to Shiloh for one of the major festivals, Hannah was so distraught and earnest in prayer that Eli, the head of the shrine, thought she was drunk. When he started to scold her for her supposed drunkenness, Hannah told him of her distress. Eli, in turn, assured her that her prayer would be answered. (1:9–18).

Eli must have known something, for Hannah was soon pregnant. In due time, the promised son was born. Hannah did not go to the festival until Samuel was able to eat solid foods. Then she took him, offered a sacrifice, and dedicated him to serve the LORD at the Shiloh shrine (1:19–28). As a part of the description of that service, there is a beautiful psalm of thanksgiving called the Song of Hannah. Later, parts of this poem are quoted in the Song of Mary in Luke 1:46–55 (2:1–10) in which Mary expresses her joy at the promise of the birth of Jesus.

Samuel: His Training and Call to Service (I Sam. 2:11–4:1)

Samuel was left with Eli, who was to train him for the priesthood (2:11). Unfortunately, Eli's sons, who served as priests at the shrine, were poor examples. The Hebrew text calls them "the sons of Belial," a term of cursing and condemnation (2:12). They were greedy, irreverent, and immoral (2:13–17, 22). Because of this situation, a prophet (a man of God) came to Eli and told him that his family would lose the privilege of serving at the shrine because his sons had abused their office as priests and leaders (2:22–36). Despite the bad examples before him, Samuel grew "both in stature and in favor with the LORD and with the people" (2:26).

The corruption at the Shiloh shrine was a symptom of the times. "The word of the LORD was rare in those days; visions were not widespread" (3:1). The Deuteronomic historian saw the lack of moral integrity in the family of Eli, Israel's most important leader, as contributing to a state of religious apathy throughout the country. Few people were in a spiritual condition to receive a revelation from God.

Then came Samuel's call from the LORD. He was still a young boy when he heard the LORD speak to him in the night. Thinking Eli was calling him, he awakened the old man to ask what it was he wanted. Eli told him that he had not called. Samuel heard the voice once again and once more went to Eli, with the same result. The third time, Eli told him that the LORD must have been calling. Then Samuel answered and was told that he eventually would replace Eli. Eli's family, furthermore, would meet with disaster. (3:2–14).

When Samuel arose in the morning, he tried to avoid telling Eli what had happened. When Eli insisted on being told, however, Samuel related his vision to Eli. Gradually the word spread that Samuel was a prophet in Israel (3:15–4:1a). As a prophet, he was looked upon as one who had direct access to God and who acted as God's earthly spokesman. For this reason, the prophets introduced their messages, not with "I say," but, "Thus says the LORD." (A fuller discussion of prophets and prophecy will come later.)

THE BEGINNING OF THE PHILISTINE WARS

The Battle of Ebenezer (I Sam. 4:1–22)

Israel's internal confusion, coupled with the increasing Philistine strength, finally led to a full-scale attack by the Philistines. The Philistine army massed at Aphek, where the great international trade road was forced inland by the swamps caused by the slow-flowing Yarkon River. At Aphek, the hill country was only a short distance away. The Israelites were camped at Ebenezer on the edge of the hills.

The Philistine war plan was to cut the country in half by driving through the mountains to the Jordan. Since the Philistines had iron weapons that were far superior to anything the Israelites had, the prospects for Israel looked bleak.

The first day's battle ended with heavy losses for Israel. In desperation, they decided to invoke the memories of the holy war the next day by carrying the ark of the covenant before them into battle. But since the holy object was borne by Eli's two unholy sons, Hophni and Phineas, even the ark could not change the tide of the battle (4:1–5).

The result was a disaster for Israel. The Philistines were inspired to fight harder. Not only did they defeat the Israelites, but they killed Hophni and Phineas and captured the ark (4:6–11). When a messenger took the word to Eli, the shock was so great that it killed him also (4:12–18). Last of all, the wife of Phineas died as she gave birth to a son. Before she died, she gave him the name "Ichabod," symbolic of the disastrous day. The child's name meant, "The glory (the presence of God) has departed" (4:19–22).

Photo courtesy of Comstock.

Figure 6–1.   "[The Israelites] encamped at Ebenezer, and the Philistines encamped at Aphek" (1 Sam. 4:1d). Aphek was a strategic point on the great coastal highway. The remains of a sixteenth century Turkish fort now occupy much of the site.

That Troublesome Ark (I Sam. 5:1–6:21)

The Philistines carried the ark, symbol of the presence of Israel's God, home in triumph. Before long, however, they wished they had never seen it. First, they put it in the temple of their chief deity, Dagon, as a symbol of Dagon's superiority to the LORD. The next morning, Dagon's image was lying face-down on the floor (5:1–5).

Next, a plague struck Ashdod. People began to have skin tumors. The people at Ashdod decided the people of Gath had a right to keep the battle prize for a while, so they sent the ark there. The Gathites, too, broke out in sores. They decided that the people at Ekron would surely want to see the famous ark. The disaster was repeated. Panic mounted in the Philistine towns (5:6–12).

They then decided that the ark was bad luck and that the only thing to do was to send it back where it belonged. Since no one volunteered to carry it back home, they decided upon a plan. They hitched two cows to a cart, placed the ark on the cart, put an offering of gold with the ark to appease the Israelite God, and turned the cows loose, heading them toward Beth-Shemesh in Israelite territory (6:1–13).

When the ark was found by the Israelites, the cart was broken up and the cattle were sacrificed. A number of Israelites died, however, perhaps because the holy ark was not handled properly. Ancient people feared holy things so much that such a fear could actually cause death. A similar thing happens today among people who believe in voodoo, macumba, or similar rites (6:14–20).

While the text is silent about the matter, Shiloh must have fallen while the ark was held by the Philistines. The ark was taken to a private home in Kiriath-Jearim after being returned to the Israelites (6:21–7:2). It was to remain there until David became king and had it moved to Jerusalem (2 Sam. 6:2; 1 Chron. 15:1–29).

THE ROLES SAMUEL PLAYED

It is difficult to realize the importance of Samuel for the history of Israel. Just as the plagues, the crossing of the sea, the stopping of the Jordan, and the great storm that brought victory to the forces of Deborah and Barak were evidence of the LORD's action in natural events that convinced Israel of his providential care for them, so Samuel must rank with Abraham, Moses, and David as a leader who was provided at a time when Israel was in great need. He was a man who played many roles on the stage of Israel's history.

Samuel, the Judge (I Sam. 7:3–17)

Samuel was a judge with a difference. He was, first of all, a spiritual leader who reminded the people of their obligation to live by the covenant (7:3–4). Furthermore, he did not lack leadership ability in military matters since he was able to hold the Philistines in check much of his career (7:5–14). But he was more than a military man. He was a judge in the modern sense of the term—one who administered justice. He single-handedly functioned as Israel's supreme court, going on a circuit in four major cities in the hill country—Bethel, Gilgal, Mizpah, and Ramah (7:15–17).

Samuel, the Prophet (I Sam. 8:1–9:14)

The picture of Samuel given in 8:1–22 is in keeping with the sense of responsibility of Israel's great prophets. Theirs was the job of speaking God's message to the people, warning them of the consequences of their decisions and of the responsibilities that came when decisions were made. Chapter 8 reflects the strong resistance that existed in Israel to the idea of the kingship. Such a feeling continued long after the monarchy was established. In some ways, certain of the prophets reflected the anti-kingship feeling with their condemnation of the reigning monarch.[1] Thus 1 Samuel 8:4–22 has Samuel telling the people of the dangers that they would face if they had a king. The people did not listen, but instead they insisted that a king be chosen for them. Finally, the LORD and Samuel gave in (8:22).

It was in his role as prophet that Samuel first met Saul, the son of Kish. Like the hero in a romantic movie, Saul was tall, dark, and handsome:

> There was not a man among the people of Israel more handsome than he; he stood head and shoulders above everyone else (9:2).

Saul was sent out by his father to find some donkeys that had strayed away. After searching for some time without success, Saul, at his servant's suggestion, went to consult the famous prophet Samuel at his home in Ramah.

Samuel seemingly had what is called "second sight" or the powers of clairvoyance. As such, he was called *the seer* (9:9), a term used to describe many of the early prophets, who functioned more as fortune-tellers than as spokesmen on the moral issues of the time. As a prophet, Samuel seemed to function in both roles: (1) as a moral spokesman, and (2) as a clairvoyant who could help find lost objects. It was, then, as a clairvoyant that Samuel first met Saul (9:3–14).

Samuel, the King-Maker (I Sam. 9:15–10:27)

Saul was so impressive on first sight that Samuel was convinced that he was the LORD's choice to be the king. Saul's journey to find his father's donkeys, then, brought a rather shocking result. Samuel told Saul that the donkeys were already at home. Then, he invited Saul to a banquet at the shrine. When Saul arrived, thirty persons were present. He, an obscure young man from one of Israel's smallest and weakest tribes, was given the seat of honor and was served the choicest portion of the meat (9:15–24).

Undoubtedly, Saul was mystified by all this. But the greatest surprise was yet to come. After spending the night in Ramah as Samuel's guest, Saul prepared to return home. Samuel, going with him to the outskirts of the village, asked Saul to send his servant on ahead so the two of them could be alone. When the servant had gone, Samuel took a vial of olive oil, poured it on Saul's head, and told him he was to be Israel's first king (9:25–10:1).

The Meaning of Anointing

Samuel's act of anointing Saul marked the king as God's man. It was an act separate and apart from the actual installation of the king, especially in the early monarchy. Saul was not crowned for a week after he was anointed (10:8). David, who succeeded Saul, was anointed by Samuel several years before he actually became king. Later on, anointing was probably a part of the coronation of the king; or, at most, it came only a short time before.

When Israel had no king, the terms *to anoint* and *the anointed one* took on a new meaning. Israel looked back at its days of glory. David, her greatest king, became the example of the kind of king Israel wanted in a future time of glory, which she believed the LORD would bring. Because of that hope the term *mashiach*, "the anointed one," was chosen to speak of a hoped-for king. When *mashiach* was put into Greek letters, it became *Messias*, which, in turn, became "Messiah" in English. Furthermore, when *mashiach* was translated into Greek by Christian writers, it became *Christos*, which becomes "Christ" in English. Thus the title, "the Christ," which was applied to Jesus of Nazareth by early Christians, came to mean "God's Chosen One," or "God's Anointed One."[2]

After Samuel had anointed Saul, he told him to return home for seven days. On the way, certain signs would be given to him that he was the LORD's choice as king. One of them would be that he would meet a group of ecstatic prophets. When he did, he would be overwhelmed by the "Spirit of the LORD," which would cause him to prophesy with them. These prophets represented another kind of prophet— those who went around in groups and whose prophesying was accompanied by various expressions of extreme emotionalism, such as trances, mass hysteria, and emotional frenzy (10:2–8).

While things happened as Samuel had said, it led to some people ridiculing Saul. The question, "Is Saul also among the prophets?" (10:11) was asked in a mocking tone rather than a tone of approval (10:9–13). When his uncle asked him where he had been, Saul told of his visit to Samuel, but said nothing about being anointed to be king (10:14–16). This basic shyness would be a major problem for Saul throughout his life.

Even when Samuel called the tribal league together at Mizpah to approve his selection of Saul as king, Saul showed the same kind of shyness. When he finally was confirmed and certified by Samuel as the LORD's choice, the people had to search for him. He was found hiding among the baggage, an act which certainly caused many to be slow in following him as king. Others, however, gave their wholehearted support to him (10:17–27).

SAUL: THE LAST JUDGE AND THE FIRST KING
(1020–1000 B.C.E.)³

Saul Becomes a Hero (I Sam. 11:1–15)

Saul made no move to exert his authority as king even though he had been crowned in a public ceremony. Instead, he went on leading the life of an Israelite farmer until circumstances forced him to take action. Jabesh-Gilead, a town located just east of the Jordan River and about twenty-five miles south of the Lake of Chinnereth (Sea of Galilee), came under attack by the Ammonites, led by King Nahash (the "Snake").⁴ Finding themselves in dire straits, to avoid wholesale slaughter by the superior Ammonite forces, the men of Jabesh-Gilead asked for terms of peace. The Ammonites agreed, but only on the condition that they could gouge out the right eyes of all the men of the town.⁵ After asking for seven days to consider the proposition, the elders managed to get the messengers to Saul at Gibeah to seek his help (11:1–4).

On hearing of their predicament, Saul reacted strongly, for "the Spirit of God came upon Saul in power" (11:6). Taking the team of oxen with which he had been plowing, he killed them, cut them into twelve parts, and sent one piece to the leaders of each of the tribes. This was the signal to mobilize for war. Men responded quickly to his call, especially from the tribe of Judah (11:8; *cf*. Judg.19:29). Dividing his forces into three groups, he attacked the Ammonites early in the morning and routed them. Saul's successful troops, inspired by his leadership, were ready to turn their wrath upon those Israelites who had refused to support Saul, but he would not let them do so. Saul was confirmed as king in a service of celebration (11:5–15).

Samuel Accounts for His Ministry (I Sam. 12:1–25)

This version of Samuel's farewell address contains familiar themes. First, the sense of honor and honesty characteristic of the themes of Israel's great prophets can be seen in Samuel's demand for the people to testify against him if they knew of any act of fraud or dishonesty he had commited (12:1–5).

A second theme that appears thoughout the Old Testament is a recounting of the wonderful works the LORD had done on Israel's behalf in the Exodus and Conquest; in the exploits of the judges (note that Samuel is mentioned in the past tense [12:11], which suggests the influence of a later hand); and Saul's victory over the Ammonites (12:6–12). Woven into this account is the Deuteronomic theme—sin, punishment, repentance, and deliverance (vss. 9–11). The qualms about the kingship are reflected in the warning that no king could lead them to be successful if they were not faithful to the LORD (12:13–17).

A thunderstorm added emphasis to Samuel's warning and gave occasion to repeat the warning that "righteousness brings blessing—sin brings punishment" (12:18–25).

The Nature of Saul's Kingship

Saul was not a king in the usual sense of the word. He might be described as a more powerful judge, who, because of the circumstances, was able to gain the majority support of the people. More important, he seems to have gained at least the qualified support of the "establishment"—tribal chieftains, chief priests, and prophets.[6] Part of that support grew out of the fact that Saul was an impressive man physically, and obviously he had certain personality traits, which on first impression caused people to follow him. He remained a man of the people who never got the "big head." The fact also that he was from a small tribe and not from one of the two dominant tribes, Ephraim or Judah, may have added to his support from all the other tribes.

His residence, the remains of which have been uncovered at Gibeah (Tell en-Nashbeh), was not elaborate. Instead, it was a rough stone fortress designed not for luxury but as a stronghold for defense against an enemy attack.

This fear of an enemy attack, coming from the Philistines, was in itself a major element in Saul's support. Israel faced the real possibility of being destroyed by the Philistines unless they united and, at that moment, Saul offered the best hope for rescue from the Philistine danger.

But an even more important factor than either Saul's abilities or the Philistine threat was the influence of Samuel. He was old, but he was still a man of great influence. He had been influential enough to put an obscure Benjaminite on the throne of Israel. But in the long run, all these factors were not able to make Saul successful because of his own personal flaws that hindered him from the beginning. The withdrawal of Samuel's support, the increasing popularity of his son-in-law David, encouraged by Jonathan, and his deep sense of insecurity growing out of his family background would eventually destroy him. Some see him as a tragic figure; others agree with the assessment that he was "a bungler from the beginning."[7]

The Length of Saul's Reign (1 Sam. 13:1)

The length of Saul's reign is uncertain since a number is missing in the Hebrew text, which simply says, "he reigned . . . and two years over Israel" (13:1). Most scholars would say he ruled about twenty-two years.[8] If one takes the biblical evidence, twelve years might be more logical. The ark was captured by the Philistines some time before Saul began to reign. According to 1 Samuel 7:2, it was kept in Kirath-Jearim "some twenty years." It was taken to Jerusalem in the early part of David's reign (2 Sam. 6:1–15), but David reigned for over seven years at Hebron before Jerusalem was captured (2 Sam. 5:5). If this twenty years is to be taken literally or even as meaning around twenty years, it would seem to limit Saul's reign to no more than twelve years.

Saul's Early Success Against the Philistines
(1 Sam. 13:2–4)

Saul gained more support through some early victories over the Philistines. Much of his success came from the courage and skilled leadership of his son Jonathan, who led the army to victory at Geba (located about five miles northeast of Gibeah). The reference to the battle for Geba shows how the Philistines had penetrated the central hill country as part of their strategy to cut the country in two (13:2–4).

Saul's Mistake at Gilgal (1 Sam. 13:5–15a)

Samuel's support of Saul began to erode rather quickly. Like an elderly person who insists that someone should take his place and then resents it when someone does, Samuel had made his farewell speech, but he was not about to give up all his power. He insisted, as chief religious official of the kingdom, that no battle should take place without the proper religious ceremonies.

Things came to a head when Saul gathered his army at Gilgal for an attack on the Philistines. He was impatient to get started. But, although he waited seven days for Samuel to come, Samuel did not appear. With his troops scattering, Saul decided to take matters into his own hands. He offered the burnt offering himself, only to have Samuel appear just as he finished (13:5–10).

When Samuel asked Saul why he had not waited, Saul said that the people were getting impatient. Samuel rebuked him, told him that he had disobeyed God, and, as a result, his kingdom would not continue (13:11–15a).

Jonathan's Heroics at Michmash
(1 Sam. 13:15b–14:15)

Saul had only six hundred soldiers at Gilgal (near Jericho) to face the large Philistine force encamped at Michmash, about ten to twelve miles west. The problem was compounded by the fact that the Philistines had far superior weapons, and only Saul and Jonathan among the Israelites had iron swords (13:22). The narrative makes the problem more vivid by telling how any Israelite who had an iron tool or weapon had to take it to the Philistines to have it sharpened. Imagine what would happen if an Israelite went to the Philistines and said, "I want to start a war with you tomorrow. Would you sharpen my sword?" (13:15b–23).

Courage and ingenuity saved the day for Israel. Jonathan and his armor-bearer crept up a narrow pass overlooking the Philistine camp, then stood up and called to the Philistines to get their attention. They had already agreed that if the Philistines came up to challenge them it would be a sign that the LORD would give them victory. They fought the Philistines in the narrow pass so that they had only to fight a few at a time. Jonathan would knock them down, and his servant would finish them off. The Philistines became so demoralized by Jonathan's success that they fled in fear. An earth tremor added to the Philistine panic (14:1–15).

Saul Blunders Again (I Sam. 14:16–46)

Word got back to the camp about the uproar Jonathan was causing among the Philistines. Although Saul started to consult the priest, so many of his men were rushing to join the battle that he went on without the required religious ceremony being performed. Before he went, however, he did a rash thing by ordering that no one was to eat anything until the Philistines were defeated. To do so would bring death by execution (14:16–24).

Jonathan, unaware of the order, came upon some honey in the forest. After he had eaten some of it, one of the men following him told him of Saul's oath to kill anyone who ate before the battle was won. Jonathan openly criticized his father for taking a foolish oath since the people were weak with exhaustion. As a result of their hunger, when the battle was over, they seized cattle and killed them, eating blood with the meat (14:25–32). This was in direct violation of an ancient taboo among the Israelites. Leviticus 17:14 says:

> For the life of every creature—its blood is its life; therefore I have said to the people of Israel: You shall not eat the blood of any creature, for the life of every creature is its blood; whoever eats it shall be cut off.

This principle led to the development in Israel, and later Judaism, of rules about the proper way to kill animals for food. Such rules are still observed by many Jews today.

Saul ordered the people to stop what they were doing. He took it upon himself to make an altar to offer a sacrifice for them. He also saw that they were fed properly (14:33–35).

Afterward, Saul wanted to continue the battle on into the night, but the priest suggested that he ask for a sign from God. When no sign was forthcoming, Saul took it to mean that someone had violated the oath. To find the culprit, he consulted the Urim and Thummim. These probably were two marked stones thrown to get yes or no answers to questions. In our day, this would be considered a game of chance; but it was not thought to be such in Saul's time. The LORD controlled how the holy stones fell, and in this manner, God's will was revealed. The first question was,"Did some of the people violate the oath?" The Urim and Thummim said, "No." When the question related to Saul and Jonathan, the answer pointed to Jonathan (14:36–42).

Saul would have killed Jonathan had the people not overruled him. Jonathan was a hero to them, and it was unthinkable that he should be killed for his father's foolish vow. Either an animal was sacrificed in his place, or perhaps someone may even have volunteered to die for him. Either way, Saul lost the people's confidence by his bad judgment (14:43–46).

Saul Disobeys Samuel Again (1 Sam. 15:1–35)

After a summary statement about Saul's military activities (14:47–52), the story of Saul's final break with Samuel is told. Samuel brought an oracle from the LORD telling Samuel to wage a holy war against the Amalekites. He was to "utterly destroy all that they have; do not spare them, but kill both man and woman, child and infant, ox and sheep, camel and donkey" (15:3).

The Amalekites, who lived in the Negev and the upper Sinai, had attacked the Israelites when Israel came out of Egypt. As a result, there seems to have been a long-standing hatred between the two groups. On the other hand, the Kenites, who had been friendly to Israel and lived in this same territory, were given warning of the attack so they could move out of the area of the battle (15:1–6).

When the attack took place, Saul did not keep all the holy war provisions. For one thing, he did not kill Agag, the Amalekite king. Nor did he destroy their herds. Instead, he took them as spoils of war (15:7–9).

When Samuel found out about Saul's disobedience, he rebuked Saul. Saul excused himself by saying that he had only taken the best of the animals for a sacrifice to the LORD. Saul's motive may have been to win the favor of his soldiers whose faith in him was already badly shaken. Sacrifices other than the whole burnt offering allowed the offerers the rare chance to eat all the meat they wanted. Sacrifice days literally were feast days, and they were looked forward to with great anticipation by the average man. Samuel's rebuke, however, was based on the principle that Israel was to live in total commitment to the LORD, including the carrying out of the rules of the holy war (15:10–20).

To Saul' excuse that the people had taken the animals to offer a sacrifice, Samuel replied with perhaps the best-remembered statement in the Saul stories:

> Has the LORD as great delight in burnt offerings and sacrifices,
>   as in obeying the voice of the LORD?
> Surely, to obey is better than sacrifice,
>   and to heed than the fat of rams.

The questioning of the meaning of sacrifice without the proper attitude was to be repeated with even stronger emphasis by Israel's great prophets. Some would even go so far as to question the need for sacrifice.[9] (15:21–23).

With this final act of rebellion, Samuel withdrew his support from Saul. He refused to speak to him again, although it is said that he "grieved for Saul" (15:35). Saul might be likened to a son whose father wanted him to be strong and independent. When the son strove to make his own decisions and to show his independence—in the eyes of the father, at least—he always made a mess of whatever he did. Because the father was always looking over the son's shoulder, both the son and the father ended up wondering what went wrong (15:24–35).

SAUL AND DAVID

The Anointing of David (I Sam. 16:1–13)

Samuel's work was not done. Having told Saul that he would be the last of his family to rule Israel, he set out to find the LORD's next choice to be king.

This time he went to Bethlehem in Judah to find the future king. He was led to the family of Jesse, a sheepherder. Here, Samuel called for Jesse to parade all his sons before him so he could select the one the LORD had chosen. Several young men appeared before him, but he did not feel that any of them was the correct choice. He asked if there were others and was told that only the youngest, who was watching the sheep, was missing. When David was brought, Samuel knew that he was the one and proceeded to anoint him (16:1–13).

Saul and David Meet (I Sam. 16:14–23)

The damage to Saul's ego inflicted by Samuel's rejection was too much for his weak personality. He was thrown into deep depression, caused by an "evil spirit from the LORD." His servants thought that music might help him, so they suggested that someone be found to play the harp for him. David's reputation as a musician had reached Saul's court, with the result that David was brought in to play for Saul (16:14–23).

David and Goliath (I Sam. 17:1–58)

The story of David and Goliath is well known, but it has problems.[10] One of the chief ones is that 2 Samuel 21:19 says:

> Elhanan, the son of Jaareoregim, the Bethlehemite, slew Goliath the Gittite, the shaft of whose spear was like a weaver's beam.

The passage in which this verse appears (2 Sam. 21:18–22), however, may suggest a possible solution since it speaks of four giant Philistine soldiers. Thus the most logical solution is that both Elhanan and David slew giants, but that the name of one of them has been lost from the Samuel tradition. First Chronicles 20:5, furthermore, tries to deal with the inconsistency by saying that Elhanan slew "Lahmi the brother of Goliath the Gittite."

Another problem seen by scholars is that 17:55–58 seems to suggest that Saul did not know David. One explanation given is that the story of David's playing the harp for Saul is based on a different tradition from that of the Goliath story and that there were two different versions of how David met Saul. Another possible explanation is that Saul's unbalanced mental state would account for his failure to recognize David as the one who played for him.

The story itself is a familiar one. Things were going badly for Israel in a battle with the Philistines in the Valley of Elah. This valley was located in southern Judah and was one of four such valleys that provided access into the hill country from the coastal plain. Without the access these valleys provided, going from the coast to the hills would have been virtually impossible. The control of the valleys, then, was essential to the defense of the Israelite positions in the hills.

The two armies had taken up positions opposite each other with the valley in between. The Philistines challenged the Israelites to send someone to fight their champion, the giant Goliath, who was said to be ten feet tall. No one from Israel dared to take up the challenge, even though Saul had offered his daughter in marriage to anyone who would successfully fight Goliath (17:1–10, 25).

David, who had come to the battlefield to bring supplies to his brothers who were serving in the army, was astounded to find that no Israelite was willing to risk his life for the honor of his people (17:11–27). As a result, David, despite the sneering of his brother Eliab (17:28–30), volunteered to fight Goliath.

Saul, relieved to have someone to meet Goliath's challenge, offered David his armor. David refused, however, choosing not to sacrifice his mobility for whatever protection Saul's armor might offer. After all, a 10-ft. giant would be considerably less agile than the much-smaller David (17:31–39). Instead, he chose to use his favorite weapon, the sling, to fell his victim (17:40).

The sling consisted of a leather pouch to which two leather strings were attached. A stone weighing several ounces was placed in the pouch. The strings were held in such a way that when the slinger whirled the sling rapidly, he could turn loose one string and send the rock toward the target. One practiced in the use of the sling could be quite accurate and deadly. Ancient armies regularly used the sling as a weapon.

David's well-aimed rock hit the giant between the eyes, knocking him to the ground unconscious. It was then a simple matter to take Goliath's sword and finish the job by beheading him. David's success led to an Israelite rout of the Philistines (17:41–58).

David in the Family of Saul (I Sam. 18:1–30)

When he entered the king's court, things changed radically for the Bethlehem shepherd boy. First, he gained a friend. Jonathan, Saul's son and general, was instantly attracted to David (18:1–5). David's success as a warrior preceded him, for the women of the village were dancing in the streets and singing his praises. Saul, insecure as he was, became jealous of David. Slipping again into a period of mental disturbance, he attempted to kill David while David was playing music for him (18:6–11).

Saul then attempted to get rid of David by putting him in charge of an army squadron, hoping he would be killed in battle. Instead, this gave David further opportunity to add to his exploits and to gain more admiration from the people (18:12–16).

After reneging on the promise to give David his older daughter's hand in marriage, Saul then proposed that David marry Michal, his younger daughter. To earn this right, however, he had to kill one hundred Philistines and bring their foreskins as proof of what he had done. David believed in doing the job right: he brought back two hundred foreskins (18:20–30)!

David Flees Saul's Murderous Intentions (I Sam. 19:1–21:15)

After a while, David began to feel Saul's rejection of him, especially after Jonathan told him of Saul's orders that he be killed (19:1–7). Continued attempts were made on David's life (19:8–17), causing him finally to flee to Samuel at Ramah. When Saul sent messengers to capture David, the awesome sense of God's presence with Samuel made them unable to carry out Saul's orders. Finally, Saul himself went. But he, too, was overcome just as he had been after his anointing by Samuel (19:18–24).

David saw that the situation was impossible and decided to separate himself from Saul's household. Jonathan agreed to take word to Saul that David had gone to Bethlehem for a feast day (20:1–6). Jonathan, furthermore, was to note Saul's reaction to David's absence and then give David a signal about whether he felt it safe for David to return. Saul became violent, showing Jonathan that it was unsafe for David to return. By their prearranged signal, Jonathan let David know that Saul was determined to kill him (20:7–42).

In his flight from Saul, David came to Nob, just east of Jerusalem. Pretending he was on a mission for the king, he persuaded the priest Ahimelech to give him some of the leftover holy bread, usually only eaten by the priests. He also persuaded Ahimelech to give him the sword of Goliath that was kept at the shrine. Leaving Nob, he went to Philistine territory, but he was recognized there. To avoid being killed, he pretended to be a madman (21:1–15).

DAVID, THE OUTLAW

The years following his escape from Saul saw David in the rather questionable position of being an ally to the Philistines while at the same time proclaiming his loyalty to his own people. His power base was Judah, whose rough terrain furnished an abundance of hiding places for his forces, which were continually being reinforced by people who were becoming disillusioned with Saul.

Preparations for the Struggle with Saul

Word that David had broken with Saul brought many discontented men to his side (22:1–2). As a precaution against an attack on his family, David took his father and mother and asked the king of Moab to protect them (22:3–5).

The Massacre at Nob (I Sam. 22:6–23)

In the meantime, Saul was intensifying his efforts to kill David. Unfortunately, he heard that the priests at Nob had aided David. As a result, he ordered their deaths. But he did not stop with the priests—he also ordered that Nob be treated as an enemy city in the holy war; it was to be completely wiped out. When the Israelite soldiers refused to do it, Saul hired mercenaries led by Doeg, an Edomite, to do the dirty work. The only survivor, Abiathar, a priest, escaped to tell David what had happened (22:6–23).

Running from Saul (I Sam. 23:1–24:22)

David and his men attacked the Philistines who were about to seize Keilah, a Judean village. Instead of being grateful for David's help, however, the villagers were ready to surrender him to Saul's wrath (23:1–14).

David fled, with Saul in pursuit, to the area south of Hebron. There Jonathan found David, but assured him that he would keep David's whereabouts a secret from Saul. They reaffirmed their personal friendship by a covenant (23:15–18). In the meantime, spies brought word of David's hiding place, causing Saul to set out after him. Just as he was closing in on David in the rough, hilly country of the Arabah, word came of a Philistine attack, drawing Saul away (23:19–29).

Next, Saul heard that David was at Engedi, an oasis on the western side of the Dead Sea. While Saul pursued David, he stopped in a cave "to relieve himself" (24:3), not knowing that David was hiding in the cave. While Saul was there, David crept up and cut off a piece of the robe that Saul probably had taken off. He resisted the temptation to kill Saul, however.

When Saul left the cave, David called to him and told him that he had not taken the opportunity to kill him. Saul was so shaken by the event that he admitted he had wronged David. He exacted a promise from David not to kill his family after David became king (24:1–22).

David, the Outlaw

Gaining Two Wives and Losing One (1 Sam. 25:1–44). If one translated a description of David's activity into our modern idiom, it could be said that he was president and chairman of the board of the South Judah Protection Agency. He furnished the Judean villages and the more nomadic Israelites of the area with protection from raids by the Amalekites and other non-Israelite groups who also traveled about in the area. For this service he expected gratitude in the form of food and other provisions for his rather sizeable personal army. Some contributed willingly, if not cheerfully, while others were more difficult to convince of their need for David's services. One such attempt to collect eventually ended rather surprisingly.

That the biblical storytellers had a great sense of humor is often reflected in the names they give certain characters. Like our nicknames, such as "Slim" or "Stone Face," the names they used were part of the meaning they wished to convey in the story. Such a name was given to a sheepman from Carmel in the Judean wilderness near the Dead Sea. The narrator calls him Nabal, meaning " vile thing." While this could have been his name, it is more likely that it is just a descriptive term applied to him to describe his nasty personality.

Nabal had large herds of sheep and goats—three thousand sheep and one thousand goats—that David had protected from raiders. When he sent word to Nabal that he would appreciate a nice gift in gratitude for his services, all he got was an insulting message to the effect that Nabal had nothing to give a renegade who had broken away from his master (25:1–13).

David, proud and hot-tempered also, immediately set out to pay back the insult by a show of force. At this point in the story, Nabal's wife Abigail, a woman of intelligence as well as beauty (25:3), decided something had to be done to head off David. She was wise enough to realize that (1) David's request was reasonable, and (2) he would not stand such an insult without retaliation (25:14–17).

Unknown to her husband, who probably was busy counting his sheep, she prepared a generous gift of food and drink and set out with her servants to head David off before he descended in fury upon their camp.

Abigail had figured correctly. When she met David, she used an unbeatable combination of flattery, food, and an appeal to his religious instincts. She convinced David that what he was about to do was foolish. Since he had received the supplies he had originally sought, he returned to his headquarters (25:18–35).

When Abigail returned, she found Nabal on a drinking binge. The next morning, when his hangover was upon him, she told him what had happened. The shock caused a sudden attack in the form of a paralytic stroke. The text says, "He became like a stone" (25:37). He died ten days later (25:36–38).

When David heard of Nabal's death, he thanked the LORD for keeping him from a foolish attack on a fellow Judean. Such a thing would have given his detractors fuel for the flame and would have alienated others who looked on him as a hero.

Abigail, now a widow with three thousand sheep and a thousand goats, was so attractive that David felt he must marry her to show her his gratitude for her thoughtful action on his behalf. Abigail was willing, so the marriage was carried out. He also married Ahinoam from Jezreel, but lost Saul's daughter Michal, whom Saul had given to another man when David fled. This was an act designed to insult David, since to invade a man's harem could cost one his life.[11] At the time, David could do little about the insult (25:39–44).

Another Version of Saul's Escape from David (I Sam. 26:1–25)

This story has many parallels to 24:1–22, but it differs in important details. David and two of his men slipped into Saul's camp and took Saul's spear and water jug. As in the previous story, David refused to kill Saul. David went to the top of a nearby mountain and shouted down to Abner, Saul's general, accusing him of being careless in protecting Saul. Saul answered and admitted he had wronged David.

David joins the Philistines (1 Sam. 27:1–28:2). This story, telling of David's alliance with the king of Gath, takes care to put David's action in as good a light as possible. It shows how David walked a thin line in claiming to have the interest of his people at heart while acting as the bodyguard for the Philistine king. In addition, it did keep him safe from Saul.

THE END OF SAUL'S REIGN

Saul and the Witch of Endor (I Sam. 28:3–25)

Saul was desperate. The Philistines had moved from Aphek, in the central coastal plain, to Shunem, near Mount Gilboa, where Saul's troops were assembled. There was an air of doom about Saul as the Philistine army gathered for the battle that would come next day. Samuel was dead, David was in the camp of the enemy, and Saul was overwhelmed by his lifelong sense of inadequacy. When he tried to get some sort of leadership from the religious officials, no word was available. He could not dream up a solution, the Urim and Thummim would not fall right, and his prophets claimed that the LORD had nothing to say (28:3–6).

Finally, he sought a medium (or witch) who supposedly could call up the dead. To find one was difficult since most of them had been banished by his own order (28:3). Finally, a medium was found in the nearby village of Endor. He sought her out at night and asked her to call up Samuel for him. She claimed to be in contact with Samuel, but the message she conveyed to Saul was a message of doom. He was reminded of his failures as a king and was told that he and his sons would die the next day (28:7–19).[12]

Saul was terrified and fell to the ground. Finally, the woman persuaded him to eat. After resting for a time, he left (28:20–25).

Where Was David? (I Sam. 29:1–11)

Instead of proceeding immediately to the story of the battle for Mount Gilboa, the narrative switches back to David, probably to make it clear that he had no part in the death of Saul. David had been asked by Achish, the king of Gath, to go with him to fight Saul. He had consented. The other Philistine kings, knowing of David's background and popularity among the Judeans, objected vigorously. As a result, David and his forces were sent back to their base.

A Raid on David's Camp (I Sam. 30:1–31)

While David was away, there was an Amalekite raid on his camp at Ziklag in the Judean foothills (30:1–6). David set out to pursue the raiders. When he returned from a successful attack on them, some of his men did not want to share any of the spoils of battle with those who had stayed behind to guard the camp. David ruled that every man should receive an equal share. Furthermore, he shared the spoils with the elders of Judah (30:7–31).

The Death of Saul (I Sam. 31:1–14)

Saul and his sons died in the battle on Mount Gilboa. Saul, mortally wounded, committed suicide. The Philistines hanged the bodies of Saul and his sons on the wall of Beth-Shan. The people of Jabesh-Gilead stole the bodies during the night and disposed of them properly.

Figure 6–2. "They put {Saul's} armor in the temple of Astarte, and they fastened his body to the wall of Beth-Shan" (1 Sam. 31:10). Tell Beth-Shan, in the valley of Jezreel, was the site of an ancient city that guarded an important crossing of the Jordan.

SAMUEL AND SAUL: A SUMMARY

Samuel and Saul bridge the gap between the judges and the monarchy. Of the two, Samuel was the dominant figure. Saul, while possessing some admirable qualities, lacked the essential quality of self-confidence. This deficiency, coupled with Samuel's domineering ways, made Saul into an emotional cripple and thus a tragic figure.

With Saul's death and that of his more talented son, Jonathan, the Israelites faced a crisis in leadership just as the superior military power of the Philistines threatened their very existence. Israel had a leadership vacuum waiting to be filled. That vacuum would be filled with David's rise to power.

STUDY QUESTIONS

1. What was the attitude toward the monarchy in the Early and Late Sources of the books of Samuel and Kings?
2. What was the Court History of David? How did it differ from usual accounts of the reigns of ancient kings?
3. In what ways are the birth stories of Samuel (1 Sam. 1:1–2:11) and that of Isaac (Gen. 18:9–11; 21:1–8) similar?
4. Why was Samuel turned over to Eli at such an early age?
5. What roles did Samuel play as a leader in Israel?
6. What series of events caused Israel to unite and eventually to choose a king?
7. What was the significance of the ceremony of anointing?
8. Why should Samuel be described as a "king-maker" and as a "king-breaker"?
9. Why was Saul chosen as king over Israel?
10. What were Saul's strengths and weaknesses as a king?
11. How did Saul gain Samuel's disfavor?
12. After he was anointed by Samuel, how soon did David become king?
13. What are the two different versions as to how Saul and David met? What does this seem to say about the sources used in writing the Deuteronomic history?
14. What was David's relationship to Saul?
15. Why did David not kill Saul and take over the kingdom?
16. What does the story of David and Abigail tell about his relations to the people during his outlaw period?
17. Why did David join forces with the Philistines?
18. How would you evaluate the kingship of Saul?
19. Terms to know: seer, *meshiach.*

ENDNOTES

1. See Jeremiah 22:10–30; see also Amos 6:1–14, where criticism is directed toward the ruling class.
2. One of the earliest uses of this title was to refer to King Cyrus of Persia (Isaiah 45:1 LXX). For a description of anointing the king , see Sigmund Mowinckel, *He That Cometh* (Nashville: Abingdon Press, 1954), 63f.
3. This date, as well as the dates for David and Solomon, is approximate and may vary as much as ten years in the differ-

ent chronologies. Dates are more accurate for later kings.

4. Since the term is insulting, this probably was given him by the Israelites. See Larry G. Herr, "Whatever Happened to the Ammonites?" *BAR* XIX, 6 (November/ December, 1993), 28.

5. For an explanation for such mutilation, see Victor H. Matthews, *Manners and Customs in the Bible* (Peabody, Mass: Hendrickson, 1988), 66.

6. Richard Eliott Friedman, *Who Wrote the Bible?* (New York: Harper & Row, 1987), 37, points out that Israel's kingship was dependent upon the consent of these three groups.

7. Kenneth I. Cohen, "King Saul: A Bungler from the Beginning," *BAR* X, 5 (October,

1994), 34–39, 52, argues that not only Saul's personality but also his background condemned him from the start.

8. See the chronological chart on pages 386–388.

9. Isaiah 1:12–17.

10. On these stories, see Emanuel Tov, "The David and Goliath Saga," *BR* II, 4 (Winter, 1986), 34–41.

11. See Solomon's treatment of his brother Adonijah when Adonijah asked permission to marry Abishag, David's wife, who became part of Solomon's harem (1 Kings 2:19–27).

12. For a discussion of Israelite views of the afterlife, see Bernhard Lang, "Afterlife," *BR* V, 1 (February, 1988), 12–23.

Chapter 7 🌿

ISRAEL'S TIME OF GLORY

David and Solomon

Mordecai's question to Esther, "Who knows? Perhaps you have come to the kingdom for such a time as this?" could well have been said of David. Israel was crying out for leadership. Ishbaal, Saul's son and successor was too weak to ever unite the people behind him. David, already popular among the southern tribes, was the only person with the charisma and intelligence needed to build a national following. His genuine piety, combined with a shrewd political sense, would quickly propel him to the top. His son Solomon inherited his father's leadership qualities and was able to build on the foundations that David had laid.[1]

DAVID: KING OVER JUDAH (1000–993 B.C.E.)

David's Reactions to Saul's Death (2 Sam. 1:1–27)

David was at Ziklag when the news of Saul's death on Mt. Gilboa came to him. The messenger told David he had found Saul still alive but that he had killed Saul as Saul had asked him to do. He had brought Saul's crown and armband as proof that Saul was dead.

David's reaction to the story was severe. He ordered the messenger's death because he had claimed to have killed Saul, the "Lord's anointed" (1:14). The messenger was not helped by the fact that he was an Amalekite. In view of the different story told in 1 Samuel 31, it would seem that this story either (1) is from another tradition, or (2) that the Amalekite made up his role in Saul's death to gain David's reward for eliminating the last barrier to David's becoming king (1:1–16).

David's lament over Saul and Jonathan came from the Book of Jashar. This book, which now is lost, seems to have been a collection of traditional songs used by biblical writers. While the lament speaks of both Saul and Jonathan, the feeling expressed for Jonathan was in keeping with the accounts of their strong bonds of friendship (1:17–27).

David as King of Judah (2 Sam. 2:1–11)

By popular consent, David was anointed king of Judah at Hebron (2:1–4a). David commended the people of Jabesh-Gilead for their bravery in stealing the bodies of Saul and Jonathan from Beth-Shean and giving them an honorable burial (2:4b–7).

In the meantime, Abner (Saul's general) had placed Saul's son, Ishbaal (1 Chr. 8:33) on the throne. The Israelite narrators, however, changed Ishbaal's name to Ishbosheth to show their contempt for him since Ishbaal ("Baal's man") was a Baal worshiper. Because of this they called him "man of shame" (Ishbosheth). He ruled from Transjordan over the northern tribes (2:8–11).

Photo courtesy of Comstock.

Figure 7–1. "And Joab . . . and the servants of David . . . met {Abner and the servants of Ishbaal} at the pool of Gibeon" (2 Sam. 2:13). This circular hole, cut into solid limestone, contained a rock-hewn staircase leading down to a water source many feet below the surface.

Civil War (2 Sam. 2:12–32). Before long, a civil war broke out at the "pool of Gibeon." The battle started when the forces of Abner and of Joab, David's general, met there. A wrestling match was proposed for twelve men from each side, but it turned deadly when swords were used instead. Asahel, Joab's brother, ran after Abner as he fled the scene. Abner warned Asahel to stop, but when he failed to do so, Abner killed him. Joab pursued Abner's forces until they took a stand, causing Joab to withdraw (2:12–32).

Abner Asks for Peace (2 Sam. 3:1–21). Abner soon became disillusioned with Ishbosheth. This was evidenced in two ways. First, Abner committed treason by taking a woman from Saul's harem as his slave wife. Ishbosheth, who by custom had inherited his father's harem, was too weak to do anything about it (3:1–11). Second, Abner went to David and offered to surrender the rest of the country to him. He wanted to make a covenant with David, but David first demanded that Michal, his former wife, be given back to him. Abner did this and the covenant was made (3:12–21).

Joab Murders Abner (2 Sam. 3:22–39). As Abner was leaving the meeting with David, Joab met him. Calling him aside as if to have a conversation, Joab stabbed and killed Abner. His justification was that Abner had killed his brother and he was acting as Asahel's avenger. This was a violation of customary law, however, since killing in war was not subject to the rule of blood vengeance. Abner and David had a covenant that made David responsible to avenge Abner's murder. While he lamented Abner, David's excuse was that Joab and his brother were too strong for him to do anything. It may well be that he also felt that he needed their support for him to accomplish his goals (3:39).

The Murder of Ishbosheth (2 Sam. 4:1–12). With Abner dead, Ishbosheth's kingdom fell apart. Two men murdered him as he slept. They cut off his head and carried their gory trophy to David at Hebron. David reacted as he had to the report of Saul's death—he had the murderers executed.

DAVID: KING OVER ALL ISRAEL (993–961 B.C.E.)

David Makes Jerusalem His Capital (2 Sam. 5:1–10)

David ruled another five and one-half years from Hebron (5:1–5), before he captured Jerusalem. This heavily fortified Jebusite city, according to tradition, was built on the site where Abraham attempted to sacrifice Isaac (Gen. 22). The invaders got into the city by entering a tunnel that carried the waters of a spring under its walls. A shaft was cut down to the tunnel so that people could reach the water without going outside the walls. David's men got inside the city and then opened the gate so others could come in.

The choice of Jerusalem was one of a number of shrewd political moves that David made. While he was still a fugitive from Saul, David drew people to him who were unhappy with Saul. He also was careful to present himself as champion and protector of the common folk of Judah. In addition, he wooed the village chiefs with presents when he took spoils in battle (1 Sam. 30:26–31).

David never raised his hand against Saul. Even when opportunists tried to gain his favor by claiming to have killed Saul and Ishbosheth, David had acted correctly—he had put the admitted murderers to death.

The choice of Jerusalem as capital was a good move because it was a neutral site. It never had been held permanently by Israel and thus belonged to no tribe. To have made Hebron, a city of Judah, the permanent capital would have stirred up considerable resentment, especially from the Ephraim, Judah's rival for first place among the tribes.

More importantly, David appeared as a man of integrity, whose dedication to the LORD, the God of Israel, was without question. His leadership fulfilled the ideal of the possession of the land promised to the patriarchs. David's success was so impressive that it caused the covenant at Sinai to fade into the background. It was replaced with the concept of the covenant with David, which said that David's descendants would sit on the throne of Israel into the ages to come.

The Task Ahead (2 Sam. 5:11–25)

After mentioning (1) David's alliance with Hiram, king of Tyre, who furnished builders and materials for David's projects (5:11–12), and (2) David's wives and children (5:13–16), the narrator turns to the Philistine threat, the first major problem that faced David when he became king. How he dealt with the Philistines would determine his success as king over all Israel. Saul's lack of success against the Philistines had been his chief failure.

The Philistines did not wait long to test David. Twice they attacked Israel in the Rephaim Valley, and David, after consulting the LORD, defeated them both times (5:17–25).

Bringing the Ark of the Covenant to Jerusalem (2 Sam. 6:1–23)

The ark, the sacred symbol of the LORD's presence with Israel, had been kept in a private home for over twenty years. David was determined to bring it to Jerusalem. The first attempt ended in tragedy when Uzzah, one of the men who was moving it by cart, died when he touched the ark. The text says, "and God smote him because he reached out his hand to the ark" (6:7). The awe of the holy object caused an immediate halt to David's plan for three months (6:1–11).

During the three-month's period, Obed-edom (in whose house the ark was kept) had evidence of God's blessing on him. David concluded it would be safe to try again to move the ark. This time, a sacrifice was made after the ark was moved only six steps. David played the role of priest, wearing the priestly garment, and dancing before the ark as it was brought into the city (6:12–17).

Michal, who had been returned against her will to David's harem as a condition to the covenant with Abner (3:13) watched the events from her window. The next time she saw David, she told him he had acted like a dirty old man. David argued that he was dancing to honor the LORD. Because of her criticism (6:16–23), she was demoted in the harem.

No Temple Building for David (2 Sam. 7:1–29)

After David's palace was complete, the question arose about building a temple to the LORD where the ark could be housed permanently. At first, Nathan the prophet, who functioned as David's spiritual advisor, encouraged him. Later, however, he told David that he had had a vision that stated: (1) The LORD had always dwelt in the tabernacle from the Exodus until the present time (7:4–7); (2) the LORD had made David what he was (7:8–11); and (3) future rulers of Israel would be David's descendants (7:12–17). David praised the LORD and prayed that the promise spoken by Nathan would be fulfilled (7:18–29).

David's Military Success (2 Sam. 8:1–18)

Israel controlled more territory during David's reign than at any other time in its history. Beginning with the defeat of the Philistines, David led his armies to conquer the territory east of the Jordan (8:2, 12–14); north to the upper reaches of the Euphrates River, including all of Syria (8:3–11); and south to the borders of Egypt (8:15–18).

He ruled his kingdom well. One reason for this may have been that when he captured Jerusalem, he captured people who had been trained by Egypt to run the government. Instead of killing them, he put them to work organizing and running his empire.[2]

THE COURT HISTORY OF DAVID

Second Samuel 9:1–20:26 and 1 Kings 1, 2 contain what is said to be one of the finest pieces of literature that has survived from ancient times. Its author seems to have had a first-hand knowledge of the inner workings of David's court. This enabled him to give an unusually frank picture of the king and his family problems. The literature could be called "David's Watergate tapes" because of the kinds of things it reveals about Israel's greatest king.

David's Kindness to Jonathan's Son (2 Sam. 9:1–13)

David's loyalty to Jonathan caused him to make Mephibosheth, Jonathan's son, a ward of the state.

The War Against the Ammonites (2 Sam. 10:1–9)

Because of a covenant David seems to have made with the Ammonite king during his outlaw days, David sent messengers to the new king of Ammon, offering to continue the covenant relationship. The king was suspicious (10:1–5), however, and disgraced David's representatives. A war resulted, with the Ammonites asking the Syrians to help them. It was all in vain because David's armies, led by Joab, defeated them.

The King's Roving Eyes: David and Bathsheba (2 Sam. 11:1–12:25)

During the Ammonite wars, David stopped going to battle with his men. There may have been two reasons for this: (1) With the enlarged kingdom, David probably felt that he had to pay more attention to matters of government. (2) His advisors may have insisted that he no longer go to battle with them, since, had he been killed, it would have been an irreplaceable loss to the kingdom. In any case, he stayed home (11:1).

During this time, as he was taking a stroll on his roof in the evening, he saw a beautiful woman taking a bath. Shortly thereafter, Bathsheba made a command appearance in the palace, with the result that she became pregnant with David's child (11:2–5).

What followed is a vivid example of how a deeply religious man can be so concerned with protecting his image that he can forget his religious principles. First, David tried by various means to make it possible for Bathsheba's husband, Uriah, to believe that he was the father-to-be. But Uriah, a loyal soldier in David's army, would not cooperate. He felt it was unpatriotic to enjoy the pleasures of wife and home while his friends were still fighting. Finally, in desperation, David sent Uriah back to the battle, carrying a secret order to Joab to put him in the front lines so he would be killed (11:6–21). Soon, the word came back that Uriah indeed was dead. After a proper period of mourning, Bathsheba entered the king's harem (11:22–27).

David must have breathed a sigh of relief, but it was not for long. Nathan, prophet and spiritual advisor to the king, confronted David with what he had done. In that confrontation, some of the character of the king was revealed. Instead of banishing or even killing Nathan for his audacity, David faced his guilt and admitted his wrong (12:1–15).

From the time of its birth, the baby was ill and David mourned. When told of the baby's death, David, having prayed for the child to live, ceased mourning

(12:16–23). Not too long afterward, a second child, Solomon, was born (12:24–25). After Solomon's birth, David returned to battle against the Ammonites and defeated them (12:26–31).

Trouble in the King's House (2 Sam. 13:1–39)

David's moral failures, coupled with his failure to control his children, brought a bitter harvest. Absalom and Tamar belonged to one of David's wives, while Amnon was the son of another wife. Amnon fell in love with his beautiful half-sister, but there seemed to be no way he could marry her. At the suggestion of a cousin, the lovesick Amnon persuaded David to send Tamar to his house to cook for him while he pretended to be ill. While she was there, he raped her. After he had gotten what he wanted, he refused to marry her (13:1–19). This meant that Tamar would never be able to marry, since virginity was considered to be essential for marriage. David took no action against Amnon for his abuse of Tamar.

Two years later, after all seemed to be forgottten, Absalom invited Amnon to a party. Under orders from Absalom, his servants waited until Amnon was drunk and then stabbed him to death. Absalom, with Joab's help, fled to his mother's homeland of Geshur (13:3) where he stayed for two years (3:20–39).[3]

The Widow's Tale (2 Sam. 14:1–24)

Joab, knowing that David wanted an excuse to let Absalom come back home, took an old woman from Tekoa to David. She told him a sad story of her two sons. According to this story, one of the widow's sons had murdered the other. Her relatives were ready to kill the surviving son to avenge the death of the dead son. Since this would leave no living male to carry on the family name, she was appealing to the king for protection for the murderer. David ruled that the need for an heir to carry his father's name was more important than punishment for the murderer.[4]

When David had so ruled, the grieving mother suddenly turned and rebuked David for not allowing Absalom to come home. David immediately was suspicious that Joab had planned the performance of the "widow." Even so, he commanded Joab to bring Absalom home, but on the condition that he not be allowed to see David (14:18–24).

Absalom, the Troublemaker (2 Sam. 14:25–15:6)

Absalom was not content with being allowed to return to Jerusalem. He asked Joab to come to see him, but twice Joab refused. To get Joab's attention, he set Joab's barley field on fire. Joab then agreed to persuade David to allow Absalom to return to court. David agreed (14:25–33).

Then Absalom began a systematic campaign to undermine his father. He would stand at the palace gate and when a man came to bring a problem before the king, Absalom would call him aside. He then would tell the man that it was a waste of time to try to see the king, even though his complaint was a just one. Absalom would then assure the man that should *he* be king, he would give justice. He would allow no man to give the traditional bow of respect, but would warmly embrace him like a brother.

> Thus Absalom did to every Israelite who came to the king for judgment; so Absalom stole the hearts of the people of Israel (15:6).

Absalom's Rebellion (2 Sam. 15:7–17:23)

After four years, Absalom made his move. He sent word to his supporters to gather at Hebron, David's first capital. He told David he was going to celebrate a feast and received David's blessing on the trip. Once there, however, he had himself proclaimed king. Among those who joined him was Ahithophel, one of David's court advisors (15:7–12).

On hearing the news, David chose to run away rather than to fight his own son. He made plans to leave Jerusalem. He instructed ten of his wives to stay behind to take care of his house, but all his servants and his personal bodyguards went with him. Most of them were foreigners who were more loyal to David than to the nation of Israel. Typical of this was Ittai, a Philistine from Gath (15:13–23).

David was not without eyes and ears in Jerusalem, however. Zadok and Abiathar started to take the ark of the covenant with David, but he sent them back and told them to stay in Jerusalem. Hushai, one of David's counselors also agreed to be a spy in Absalom's camp. Among the three of them, they managed to keep David informed of Absalom's moves (15:24–37).

Leaving Jerusalem, David went across the Kidron Valley, which separates the eastern boundary of the city from the Mount of Olives (15:30). As he crossed the mountain, he was joined by Ziba, the servant of Mephibosheth (Jonathan's son), who brought an offering of food and drink, and donkeys for David and his household to ride. Mephibosheth had gone over to Absalom's side (16:1–4).

Further on, he was roundly cursed and stoned by Shimei, a supporter of Saul's family. When one of his men offered to kill Shimei, David kept him from doing so. Instead, he continued on toward the Jordan River (16:5–14).

Meanwhile, Absalom entered Jerusalem. Hushai greeted Absalom and convinced him that he had deserted David. One of Absalom's first acts was to have sexual relations with one of David's concubines in full view of the people. This was meant to show that he had taken over his father's kingdom (16:15–23).

Conflicting advice was given to Absalom by Hushai and Ahithophel. Ahithophel advised immediate pursuit of David, but Hushai suggested that they wait. He suggested, furthermore, that Absalom could prove his leadership ability to the people by personally leading the pursuit (17:1–14). Absalom took Hushai's advice. When he did so, Hushai got word to Zadok and Abiathar, who, after some difficulty, managed to inform David (17:15–22). In the meantime, when Ahithophel saw that Absalom would no longer listen to him, he commited suicide (17:23).

Crushing the Rebellion (2 Sam. 17:24–19:8)

David stopped when he reached Mahanaim in Transjordan. Mahanaim was located near Penuel, where Jacob was said to have wrestled with the angel (Gen. 32:22–32). Loyal followers in the area brought necessary supplies (17:24–29).

In preparation for the battle, David split his army into three parts, putting a commander over each. David wanted to lead, but his commanders refused to let him go. As they left, David asked that they "deal gently" with Absalom (18:1–5).

The battle raged in the forest of Ephraim. A patrol spotted Absalom and gave chase. As Absalom's mule ran under an oak, Absalom was caught by the hair in a tree branch and left hanging. When Joab heard, he came and ordered his men to kill Absalom. When they refused, Joab personally killed him, had his body thrown into a pit, and covered it with stones (18:6–18).

When the messengers brought the news to David, he wept loudly, lamenting Absalom's death (18:19–23). When the people heard him lamenting, their shouts over the hard-won victory turned to shamed silence. Joab's power over David was never more vividly illustrated than when he told David that if he wanted the support of those who had saved his life, he had better hush his crying and praise the people for what they had done. "For," he said,

> you have made it clear today that commanders and officers are nothing to you; for I perceive that if Absalom were alive and all of us were dead today, then you would be pleased (19:6).

David arose and did as he was told to do (19:1–8b).

Putting Things Together Again (2 Sam. 8c-43)

As David returned to Jerusalem, those who had supported Absalom either fled or tried to get back into David's good graces. Shimei, for example, who had cursed David as he left, met him and begged forgiveness. David promised not to kill Shimei, but he did not promise that someone else might not do it (19:8c–23).

Mephibosheth, Jonathan's son, came begging; but David divided his property, giving half of it to Ziba, Mephibosheth's servant, who had brought food to David's men (19:24–30). David offered a place of honor to Brazilli, the Gileadite who had also brought supplies to him. Brazilli asked David instead, to give it to his servant (19:31–40).

When he arrived in Jerusalem, the elders of the northern tribes and the elders of Judah got into a dispute over who had the right to bring David back to Jerusalem. The Judeans claimed it was their right by kingship, while the Northerners claimed it was their right by majority rule. The Judeans seem to have won (19:41–43).

Sheba's Rebellion (2 Sam. 20:1–26)

Taking advantage of the friction between the northern tribes and the Judeans, Sheba started another revolt against David, which gained a number of followers. David put Amasa in charge of the army, replacing Joab after he had killed Absalom. Amasa was given orders to put down the rebellion. Before he could get organized, Amasa was murdered by Joab (20:1–10c). Joab took over the army and soon had the rebellion under control (20:10d-26). The effect of this rebellion was to allow Solomon to establish the Israelite monarchy more on the order of the other Eastern kings. In other words, Solomon was a more autocratic ruler than either Saul or David had been.[5]

Odds and Ends (2 Sam. 21:1–24:25)

The last three chapters of 2 Samuel do not fit into the story of the ins and outs of David's court. First, there is the story of a famine that lasted three years. Through prayer, David became convinced that an atrocity that Saul had committed against the Gibeonites (Josh. 9) had not been forgiven by the LORD. He went to the Gibeonites and asked them if there was anything he could do to make things right with them for the harm Saul had done to him. They replied that the only thing he could do was to turn over to them seven of Saul's sons. He did as they asked, and the Gibeonites hanged the men. Rizpah, the mother of two of the victims, kept their bodies from being attacked by birds of prey until only the bones were left. Then David had Saul and Jonathan's bones returned to Jerusalem from Jabesh-Gilead and buried Saul and his sons together.

The point of this story is that the ancient Israelites believed that murder (in this case, Saul's unjust killing of the Gibeonites) had to be punished by the death of the murderer. Since Saul was dead already, his sons had to bear the blame for him. When justice was not done, the whole land suffered. One way that suffering came was through such natural disasters as drought and famine. The only way to bring such natural disasters to an end was to see that justice was done. (21:10–14).

The next block of material mentioned the giants who might be described as the heavyweight champions among the Philistines. The Israelites who defeated them are listed (21:15–22).

Chapters 22 and 23:1–7 are what are known as orphan psalms—that is, psalms found outside the Book of Psalms. Both are said to have come from David, and both are hymns of praise. Following the psalms is a series of episodes describing exploits of David's mighty men, his personal bodyguards, who were fiercely loyal to him. As a matter of fact, David's army was largely a private army, recruited by him and paid by him (28:8–37).

Chapter 24 describes a census by David, probably for the purpose of taxation. Then, as now, the power to tax was the power to control. The LORD was said to have moved David to take the census. First Chronicles 21:1 corrects this by saying that "Satan" caused David to take the census. A plague came. To ease the plague, David bought Araunah's threshing floor on the top of the mountain overlooking Jerusalem. Later, the Temple was built there. The large rock that formed the threshing floor would become a sacred spot for three great religions—Judaism, Christianity, and Islam. When David bought the site and made sacrifices, the plague was lifted (24:1–25).

The Old Order Passes (1 Kings 1:1–2:12)

Like vultures waiting for a sick animal to die in the desert, so David's sons watched his strength slip away. Even a beautiful concubine brought in to give David her warmest attention could not stir him. When that failed, the air began to be filled with plots and counterplots (1:1–4).

After Absalom was killed, Adonijah was David's oldest surviving son. No longer was there a prophet with the power and influence of Samuel who could anoint a man and place him on the throne. David had that power, but he was almost past the stage to use it.

Adonijah, probably sensing that David would not choose him, decided to take matters into his own hands. He enlisted help from powerful people: Joab, the long-time commander of David's army, and Abiathar, the priest who had been with David since his days as a fugitive. Like Absalom, Adonijah had been pampered and spoiled by his father. He invited many important people to a sacrifice and self-coronation, much the way modern politicians invite prospective voters to a barbecue.

He did not invite Nathan, the prophet; Bathsheba, Solomon's mother; Zadok, the priest; Benaiah, the chief of David's bodyguard, nor any of the bodyguards. He especially ignored Solomon, his chief rival for the throne.

Word of Adonijah's planned attempt at a coup set in motion a counterplot by those who supported Solomon. Nathan and Bathsheba plotted together to force the aged king to choose Solomon. Bathsheba was to tell David of Adonijah's plot and then remind him that he had promised the kingship to Solomon. Nathan would then come in and confirm what Bathsheba had said.

The plan worked to perfection. Nathan confirmed Bathsheba's news and questioned whether David had encouraged Adonijah to have himself proclaimed king. David had Bathsheba called back and swore a solemn oath to her that Solomon would succeed him. There was great irony in her parting words, "May my lord King David live forever!" She did not mean it! (1:11–31).

Immediate action was taken to ensure that David's wishes were carried out. Solomon was placed on David's mule—an animal that no person but the king could ride—and was taken to the Gihon Spring. He was accompanied by Nathan, Zadok, Benaiah, and David's bodyguards. There he was proclaimed king. Afterward he was led through the streets of Jerusalem, where the people, seeing that he was David's choice, filled the streets shouting, "Long live King Solomon!" (1:32–40).

Meanwhile, back at Adonijah's party, people began to wonder what all that noise in uptown Jerusalem was about. A messenger came running in. When he told what was happening, all Adonijah's guests suddenly remembered that they had business elsewhere. Adonijah, fearing that Solomon would have him killed, went to the great altar where sacrifices were made and remained there. The altar was a sacred place and, supposedly, one would be safe from punishment for any crime as long as he did not leave the sacred area. Solomon demanded and got a pledge of loyalty from Adonijah. In return, he promised to let Adonijah live unless some "wickedness" be found in him. Solomon, of course, would determine what that "wickedness" was (1:41–53).

Soon afterward, David gave instructions to Solomon about what he should do when David died. After instructing him about spiritual matters (2:1–4), David turned to more practical matters. First, he gave instructions about Joab, who had been David's general and hatchet man, and whose atrocities David either had been unable or unwilling to control. Joab was to be executed. Next, Solomon was urged to treat Brazilli of Gilead kindly for his help to David during Absalom's rebellion. Shimei's fate was left to Solomon's discretion, but the strong implication was that Shimei was to die. David said nothing about Abiathar. When David died, Solomon became the first Israelite king to succeed his father (2:5–12).

An Evaluation of David

David's accomplishments as king caused him to be ranked with Moses in importance in Israelite tradition. While it is true that there were no major challenges to his rule from Egypt, Asia Minor, or Mesopotamia, the fact that he could take a rather disorganized and divided people and achieve what he did in the short span of forty years marked the man as a genius in military organization and administrative skill. While Solomon's kingdom would be more spectacular in its display of wealth and power, it was only because David's conquests were complete. Solomon had a period of peace in which to develop the kingdom economically.

Beyond the period of the united monarchy, David's influence was felt in three areas. First, in his choice of Jerusalem as his capital, he gave the world its most revered city. To Jew and Christian alike, it would become the earthly version of God's heavenly city. That is why the writer of the New Testament Book of Revelation spoke of the ideal age as beginning when "the holy city, the new Jerusalem," would come down from heaven to earth (Rev. 21:2). Because the Dome of the Rock supposedly is built over the site from which Mohammed ascended to heaven on his white horse, for Muslims, it ranks second only to Mecca in its importance.

Now, some three thousand years later, Jews, Christians, and Muslims make their way to a city whose influence far outweighs any importance it should have.

Many cities are larger; more influential economically; have more to offer in culture, education, and the arts; but none has about it the special quality and drawing power that Jerusalem has.

Secondly, the monarchy, referred to biblically as the "house of David," was established. Until recent years, no known contemporary references to the Davidic monarchy had been discovered by archaeologists. As a result, some scholars have argued from this silence that the Davidic rule was a figment of the biblical writer's imagination. Now the phrase, "house of David," has been discovered at Tell Dan in northern Israel.[6]

The Davidic monarchy would last for more than four hundred years, but its influence would extend even further. Part of its longevity lay in the conviction that the LORD made a covenant with David, saying that his descendants would rule over

Photo by Zev Radovan.

Figure 7–2.   This inscription, found at Tell Dan in northern Israel, was part of a victory stele or column erected by an Aramean (Syrian) ruler to brag about his success in a battle against "the house of David."

Israel. That covenant replaced the Sinai covenant in the thinking of the average Israelite, especially the Judeans. Essentially, a covenant based on moral demands was replaced by one that primarily emphasized family continuity in the monarchy. Following David's time, when a covenant was mentioned, it was assumed that the reference was to the covenant with David.

When the monarchy ended with the Babylonian exile, the hope for its restoration lived on, especially as it was and had been proclaimed by the great prophets (Isa. 9, 11; Mic. 5:2–4). In the midst of the postexilic period, the hope for the ideal king who exemplified the best qualities of David grew into the doctrine of God's Anointed One, the Messiah. Jesus' disciples saw him as the fulfillment of that ideal, while Jewish interpreters continued to look for the new David who would deliver his persecuted people.

In the third place, David left his mark on the poetic literature of Israel. How many of the psalms he wrote is subject to vigorous debate. That he wrote some of them seems certain enough for him to be looked upon as the father of Israelite hymns. The psalms are different from other biblical literature because they are people's deepest emotions addressed to God. Since David is represented as a deeply emotional man, it is fitting that he would be connected with the most emotional literary form in the Old Testament.

Overall, Israelite kingship differed from that of other Near Eastern societies. Both in Egypt and in Babylonia, the king was regarded as divine, though somewhat more so in Egypt where the king was worshiped as a god. In Israel, there was a strong belief that the LORD was king, while the earthly king was the LORD's representative but was still human. This is why, especially during the early monarchy, the prophets dared to call the kings to account if they did not follow the LORD's will (cf. Nathan and David; Elijah and Ahab). It also is illustrated by the fact that Samuel, in his role as prophet, could choose David as king and have him accepted by the people.[7]

SOLOMON: RICHES, WISDOM, AND FOOLISHNESS (961–922 B.C.E.)

If Saul was a judge who tried to be king and David was an empire builder, then Solomon introduced Israel to the rule of a typical oriental despot.

Getting Rid of Potential Rivals (I Kings 2:13–46)

Solomon moved quickly to consolidate his power. Where David had nothing directly to do with the elimination of anyone who might have been his rival, Solomon had no qualms about dealing with his enemies. Adonijah was his first victim. When Adonijah asked Bathsheba to persuade Solomon to let him have Abishag, David's last concubine, for his wife, Solomon found the wickedness in Adonijah that he had been looking for as an excuse to kill him. The request Adonijah made actually was an insult. David's harem became Solomon's responsibility on David's death, even though they probably were not viewed as Solomon's wives, since his own mother was in the group. Adonijah's request was his own death warrant (2:13–25).

Dealing with Abiathar was a more delicate matter. Not only was he a priest, but he had been David's chief northern priest in tandem with Zadok, the chief priest from Judah. His execution most certainly would alienate the northern tribes at a time when Solomon could ill afford to lose their support. By exiling Abiathar to Anathoth, Solomon still offended the northerners somewhat, but not to the extent of losing their support. The prophet Jeremiah probably was a descendant of Abiathar (2:26–27).[8]

Solomon probably considered Joab as his most dangerous rival. Even though he was old, Joab was a cunning and ruthless man who had managed to hold power in the army even when David tried to get rid of him. But his luck had run out. Solomon was just as ruthless, or more so. He ordered Joab's execution. When Joab fled to the sanctuary for refuge and refused to come out, Solomon defied the taboo

Figure 7–3. "Joab fled to the tent of the LORD and grasped the horns of the altar" (1 Kings 2:28). The "horns of the altar," as illustrated by this tenth-century B.C.E. limestone altar from Megiddo, were supposed to keep a fugitive safe as long as he clung to them. This did not hold true in Joab's case.

Courtesy of the Israel Department of Antiquities and Museums.

against killing anyone in the sanctuary. He ordered Joab killed, even as he held on to the horns of the sacred altar. His executioner, Benaiah, the son of Jehoida, took Joab's place as general over the armies of Israel (2:28–35).

The last to be dealt with was Shimei, who was placed under a form of house arrest whereby he was not supposed to leave the city of Jerusalem. Shimei observed the rules for three years, but when one of his slaves ran away, Shimei went after him. Solomon had not forgotten—Shimei died (2:36–46).

Solomon, the Religious Man (I Kings 3:1–28; 4:29–34)

The Israelite historian, in his evaluation of Solomon as a religious man, could not be quite as complimentary as he was about David. Perhaps he was hinting at one of the obstacles to Solomon's devotion to the LORD when he mentions his Egyptian wife. She and other of his wives influenced him to worship pagan gods.

In describing a prayer Solomon prayed, the narrator tells of the LORD appearing in a dream and telling him to ask what he should be given. Instead of asking for great riches, Solomon asked for wisdom to govern his people. The LORD, in turn, promised both wisdom and riches (3:1–15).

An illustration of Solomon's wisdom is the famous story of the two women who claimed the same child. After the women had argued before him, he ordered the child cut into two pieces, one piece to be given to each woman. One woman agreed, but the true mother asked Solomon to spare the child and to give it to the other woman. Solomon awarded the child to its true mother (3:16–28).

A summary statement concerning Solomon's wisdom describes Solomon as wiser than all the eastern wise men. He was a speaker and collector of proverbs, a zoologist and a biologist, and a marvel to all who heard him (4:29–34). The queen of Sheba came from North Africa (Ethiopia) to marvel at his wisdom. Ethiopian tradition has it that she carried away more than wisdom, since later Ethiopian rulers were called in part, "The Lion of Judah" (1 Kings 10:1–13)![9]

Solomon, the Organizer (I Kings 4:1–28)

In organizing the kingdom, Solomon seems to have had two purposes in mind: (1) to divide the land as evenly as possible to provide for the systematic support of his elaborate court and for other taxation purposes, and (2) to break down the old tribal distinctions by paying little or no attention to tribal lines when dividing the country into tax districts. In his first purpose, he succeeded—in the second, he failed.

Solomon, the Builder (I Kings 5:1–7:51)

While David built an empire by conquest, Solomon covered it with buildings. Of all the building projects carried on by Solomon, the Temple at Jerusalem ranked first in importance for the Israelite historian.

Preparations for Building the Temple (I Kings 5:1–18). To build as Solomon was said to have done takes skilled workmen and quality materials, neither of which was abundant in Israel. The one thing that Israel had in abundance was stone, but it lacked the forests to supply the wood needed.

To supply the needed materials and skilled workmen, Solomon turned to David's ally, Hiram, king of Tyre and Phoenicia. Hiram agreed to supply cedar and cypress wood, as well as skilled workmen, to carry out the building of the Temple and the palace complex in Jerusalem. In turn, Solomon agreed to supply food to Hiram. Solomon also furnished Israelites to do the labor of cutting the wood and in quarrying stone in Israel. Israelite men had to work without pay for the state, one month out of every three.

The Temple Is Built (1 Kings 6:1–38; 7:15–51). Like Jerusalem itself, the Temple—first built by Solomon, then destroyed, then rebuilt again in the postexilic period, and a third time by Herod the Great—has managed to seize the imaginations of countless people for nearly three thousand years. Its remains, except for portions of the wall that supported the platform on which it was built, are under an area containing two Islamic mosques—the Dome of the Rock and the el Asqa Mosque. As a result, archaeological work on the Temple Mount is forbidden.

By taking the biblical description, however, and by comparing it with similar temples found in Israel and Phoenicia, a fairly accurate idea of the Temple's appearance can be gained. One such building was a Canaanite temple found at Hazor in northern Israel. It had the three-room plan used in the Jerusalem Temple. A later temple, from the period of the Israelite monarchy, was found at Arad, south of Jerusalem. In addition, a horned altar, such as is mentioned in the Old Testament, was found at Beersheba (1 Kings 1:50–2:28).

First Kings 6:1 says that the Temple was built 480 years after Israel left Egypt. This poses a problem in chronology since it does not agree with other evidence for the date of the exodus. One possible explanation is that the figure 480 represents twelve generations. Biblical writers figured a generation as forty years, while today, twenty-five years equals a generation. If this were the case, twelve times twenty-five equals three hundred years, which would place the exodus at about 1300 B.C.E.

According to all descriptions, both biblical and archaelological, the Temple was divided into three parts: (1) a porch or vestibule, fifteen feet deep and thirty feet wide; (2) the Holy Place, sixty feet long and thirty feet wide; and (3) the Holy of Holies, which was a perfect cube—thirty feet long, thirty feet wide, and thirty feet high. The interior height of the rest of the building was forty-five feet. Along the outside of the building were three levels of rooms, used for storage and other purposes. The interior of the building was decorated with elaborate carved woodwork. Gold also was used extensively in decorating the interior (6:1–36).

The Holy Place contained three principal items: the altar for incense, the seven-branched lampstand, and the table for the sacred bread (shew bread or bread of the presence). In later times the lampstand became a seven-branched candlestick called the *menorah*.

Biblical Illustrator Illustration/Bill Latta.

Figure 7–4. "Solomon began to build the house of the LORD" (1 Kings 6:1). Like temples in other ancient cities of the Mediterranean area, Solomon's Temple stood on the highest point overlooking the city. This is an artist's conception of the Temple.

The Holy of Holies originally contained the sacred box, the ark of the covenant. At either end of the room stood a winged creature, fifteen feet high. It was carved from olive wood and plated with gold. It probably had both human and animal features, designed to represent all living creatures giving praise to the LORD, whose dwelling place was the Holy of Holies. Once a year, on the solemn Day of Atonement (*Yom Kippur*), the high priest would enter the Holy of Holies. Even he had to undergo an elaborate ceremony of cleansing before he could enter the room. His purpose was to bring before the LORD the sins of the people so they might be forgiven. Thus the Holy of Holies represented for Israel the meeting place between God and humankind.

In the Temple courtyard stood the great altar made of uncut stones upon which the sacrifices were made. Two huge bronze columns, named Jachin and Boaz, stood to the north and south of the entrance of the Temple. Their meaning and purpose are unknown (7:15–22). An elaborate bronze bowl resting on a base made from twelve bronze bulls also stood in the courtyard. It held about ten thousand gallons of water and may have been a reminder of the watery chaos mentioned in the creation story and of how God overcame it to create the world (7:23–26).

All the furnishings and equipment for the Temple were made by the Phoenicians. It should not be surprising, then, that the descriptions given in the Bible match things found in Phoenician temples. The major difference seems to be that Israel's Temple contained no image of Deity, while Phoenician temples contained many such images (7:27–51).[10]

The Dedication of the Temple (1 Kings 8:1–66). After years of labor, the Temple was finished. The first act of Solomon was to have the ark of the covenant moved into its permanent home, the Holy of Holies. It was moved with elaborate precautions, and with many sacrifices being offered (8:1–13).

The address and prayer of Solomon (8:14–53) emphasized the importance of the covenant with David and the building of the Temple as carrying out Solomon's responsibility in the light of that covenant (8:14–26).

The prayer was a plea for the LORD to keep the Divine side of the covenant. First Kings 8:27–30 is particularly important because it emphasizes what many Israelites forgot in later years—namely that the LORD did not dwell only in the Temple in Jerusalem. No mere building could hold the LORD. The prayer lists the situation that would give rise to prayer: (1) sin against one another; (2) defeat in war because of sin; (3) drought; (4) famine caused by pestilence, mildew, or locusts; (5) foreigners who came to the Temple to worship; (6) holy war; and (7) sin against God. With each there was a plea for forgiveness based on the choice of Israel as God's people (8:31–53).

In this section, then, the principle of the covenant was in operation. God, who gave the covenant, though not required to do so, was self-obligated to Israel because of Divine mercy. An Israelite could call on God to exercise mercy on his behalf when he came to God in repentance. One could not expect forgiveness without a proper attitude. This theme is repeated by the great prophets and is prominent in the book of Deuteronomy.

After the people were led in praise to the LORD, to conclude the dedicatory services, elaborate festivities were observed. The seven-day feast, held at the time of the feast of Tabernacles, sent away all those who came—proud, happy, and filled with roast beef and mutton (8:54–66).

The LORD Appears to Solomon Again (1 Kings 9:1–9). After the dedication of the Temple, the LORD appeared to Solomon. The promise of the continuance of David's line was made, but it was to be based on faithfulness to the LORD. If Solomon and those who followed him turned away from the LORD, judgment would come upon Israel.

Solomon's Other Building Projects (1 Kings 7:1–12; 9:10–28; 10:14–29). Solomon spent even more time building an elaborate system of palaces and government buildings. Thirteen years were spent in building his palace, which had several sections: (1) the House of the Forest of Lebanon, built almost entirely of cedar; (2) the Hall of Pillars; (3) the Hall of the Throne, where justice was administered; (4) Solomon's house; and (5) the house of his Egyptian wife.

He carried on other extensive building programs, including projects in Jerusalem, Gezer, Hazor, and Megiddo. At the latter three, identical city gates have been found. This would seem to indicate that the same architect planned and constructed all three. Each of these cities shows indications of other building programs during Solomon's time. Elaborate shafts were constructed to enable the people to reach the water supply. At Megiddo, for instance, stone steps led down into the shaft to a tunnel. This tunnel led to a water source outside the city wall.[11]

Another building project consisted of a fleet of merchant ships, based in the Gulf of Aqaba at Ezion-Geber. Here the gulf reaches its northernmost point. Hiram of Tyre furnished the vital know-how, as well as sailors to operate the fleet (9:26–28). The Phoenicians were the supreme sailors of the ancient world, while Israel, with no suitable ports, developed little interest in the sea, except in Solomon's time. The trade probably was with countries along the coast of Africa and the Arabian Peninusla.

Solomon's building projects were costly in more ways than one. For one thing, they cost him part of his empire. For all the work he had done, Hiram demanded payment in the form of territorial grants. Though Solomon gave him twelve cities in the Plain of Acre, Hiram was unhappy still. The name *Cabul*, possibly meaning "that is nothing" was given to the region. Even then, Hiram had to pay him for the region. The remains of a fortress dating to the time has been found. It seems to have served as the administrative center for the area, whose local products—wine, olive oil, and cereals—were collected and stored. That these cities belonged to the northern tribes probably did nothing to increase Solomon's popularity there (9:10–14).[12]

The cost in money was great also. Solomon got money from various sources, the most obvious of which was taxes. But that was not enough. He would also have collected tariffs from caravans that used the international highways, the *Via Maris* and the King's Highway. Another source of income was international trade. Among other things, Solomon traded horses and chariots. He seems to have been the middleman in the trade between Egypt and the Asian and Mesopotamian states. An elaborate description of Solomon's luxuries (10:14–29) helps us to understand why so much money was needed in addition to the cost of his building programs.[13]

The Seeds of Destruction (I Kings 9:15–23; 11:1–43)

The greatest cost of maintaining Solomon's elaborate kingship was in human freedom. That cost eventually would destroy the united monarchy. Slavery made the building projects possible. It is said that "Solomon conscripted forced labor out of all Israel" (5:13) and that the non-Israelite population was put into slavery to carry on the building projects (9:15, 20–23). In so doing, he sowed the seeds of social unrest that eventually would erupt in rebellion. It is said that the Israelites were "the soldiers, . . . his officials, his commanders, his captains, and the commanders of his chariotry and cavalry" (9:22). While it says that "of the Israelites Solomon made no slaves," they did have to give one month out of every three in free labor for the state.[14]

Another destructive force was Solomon's large harem. Composed of more than one thousand women, the harem functioned primarily as a status symbol. Just as a wealthy man today may collect expensive automobiles as a way of showing off his wealth, so some kings collected beautiful women. With the women, many of whom were married to Solomon to symbolize a covenant relationship with a foreign ruler, came the various deities they worshiped. Solomon's tolerance of foreign gods did not sit well with devout Israelites, especially when he built altars for foreign gods and even participated in worshiping them, in defiance to the LORD's commands (11:1–13).

Solomon's last years saw the seeds of destruction begin to take root and grow. People on the fringes of his empire began to rebel and break away. First, it was Edom, led by Hadad, a member of its royal house who had escaped to Egypt when David conquered his country (11:14–22). Soon, Rezon, a Syrian leader, took control of Damascus (11:23–25).

More serious than either of these were stirrings of rebellion within Israel itself. The old rivalry between Ephraim and Judah had been suppressed during David's and Solomon's time, but it still survived. With it was the belief that the LORD through a prophet should designate a leader, not a dying king who passed on the kingdom to his son. Solomon, on the other hand, seems not to have had a prophetic advisor in his court such as Nathan had been to David. Solomon most certainly would have encouraged the idea that the LORD's covenant with David was more important than the idea that a prophet should choose the future king.

The charismatic figure around whom the dissidents rallied was Jeroboam, an Ephraimite. He had been in charge of all Solomon's forced labor. A prophet who also was a northerner, Ahijah the Shilonite, met Jeroboam one day. Taking a cloak, he tore it into twelve pieces to symbolize that an emergency existed. Ten of the pieces he gave to Jeroboam, telling him he was chosen to be leader over ten tribes, leaving only two to Solomon's house. Ahijah said that the LORD was bringing judgment upon Solomon for following foreign gods (11:26–39).

Ahijah was the first independent prophet who led an attempt to overthrow an existing ruler who had become intolerable to the people.[15]

Word came to Solomon of Jeroboam's disloyalty. Fortunately for Jeroboam, he was able to escape to Egypt before Solomon could have him arrested. There he found refuge. Shishak, the new pharaoh of Egypt, seems to have encouraged and protected Jeroboam as he had other rebels and fugitives from Solomon (11:40).

The End of Solomon's Reign (1 Kings 11:41–43)

After forty years of magnificence, Solomon died. He had acquired wealth, built buildings, and gained fame for his wisdom. It was during Solomon's time, furthermore, that Israelite literature began to flourish. Widsom literature undoubtedly was

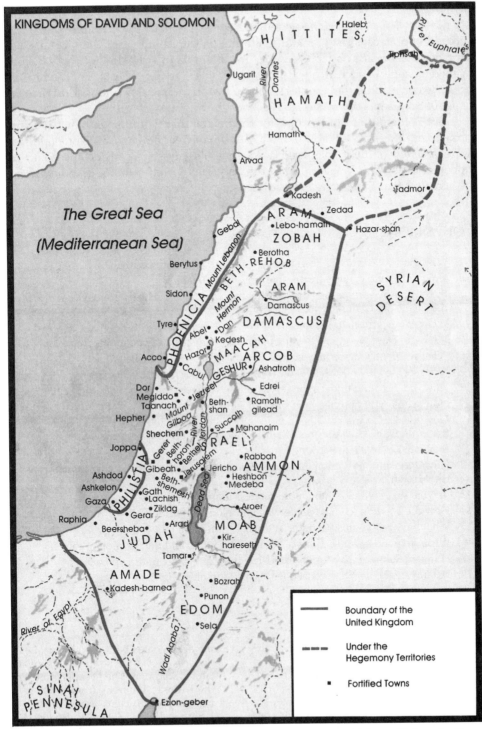

Artwork by Margaret Jordan Brown © Mercer University Press.

Figure 7–5. David's kingdom and the United Monarchy.

rooted in Solomon's reign, making him the patron saint of Israelite wisdom. The long period of peace possibly saw the first attempts to write down Israel's history. A good example of such an attempt may have been the Court History of David. Others have conjectured that the stories of the Egyptian oppression took form then because of Solomon's oppression.[16]

But Solomon also lit the fuse for the bombs that would soon blow the kingdom apart. Excessive taxation, denial of human freedom, and religious apostasy were but a few of the problems left for Solomon's egotistical son and successor, Rehoboam, to solve. Rehoboam, unfortunately, was so self-centered that he did not even realize that there were any problems.

STUDY QUESTIONS

1. Why did David react as he did to the deaths of Saul and Jonathan?
2. How did David eventually become king over all Israel?
3. By the time he became king over all Israel, what actions did he take or have taken to allay the suspicions of the supporters of Saul?
4. What made Jerusalem the logical choice for the capital?
5. What did David's actions toward Uriah and Bathsheba say about his character?
6. What were the long-term effects of David's affair with Bathsheba?
7. What seemed to be Nathan's role in David's court?
8. How did Absalom undermine David, and what were the results of his rebellion?
9. How would you describe Joab's relationship to David?
10. How did David indicate that Solomon was his choice to succeed him as king rather than Adonijah? How did this differ from how Saul and David were chosen?
11. Evaluate David's reign as king.
12. How was Solomon's reign more like that of other Eastern kings rather than like his father's reign.
13. In what ways was Solomon more ruthless than David?
14. How did David's reign pave the way for Solomon's success?
15. What were Solomon's strengths and weaknesses as a king?
16. What were the major sections of Solomon's Temple and the function of each?
17. How did Solomon pay for his extensive and expensive building projects?
18. What were the negative consequences of Solomon's reign?

ENDNOTES

1. Certain scholars tend to minimize the biblical picture of David and Solomon and their accomplishments. Their arguments are based largely on the scarcity of extrabiblical evidence. In keeping with this book's emphasis on the contents of the Bible, it will continue to emphasize its depiction of David and Solomon. For an excellent summary of the arguments about the historical evidences, see Gary Knoppers, "The Vanishing Solomon: The Disappearance of the United Monarchy from the Recent Histories of Ancient Israel," *JBL* 116, 1(Spring, 1997), 19–44. See also Hershel Shanks, "The Biblical Minimalists: Expunging Ancient Israel's Past," *BR* XIII, 3 (June 1997), 32–39, 50–52.

2. For an elaboration of this theory, see George E. Mendenhall, "The Monarchy, *INT* XXIX, 2 (April, 1975), 155–170.

3. On the location of Geshur, see Moshe Kochavi, et al., "Rediscovered! The Land of Geshur," *BAR* XVIII, 4 (July/August, 1992), 30–44, 84.

4. For a fuller discussion, see John H. Tullock, *Blood-Vengeance Among the Israelites in the Light of Its Near-Eastern Background* (Ann Arbor: University Microfilms, 1966), 44.

5. So argues Ranier Albertz, *A History of Israelite Religion* I, 123.

6. "David Found at Dan," *BAR* XX, 2 (March/April, 1994), 26–39. It seems to commemorate a victory over the kings of both Israel and Judah. See also André Lamaire, "House of David Restored in Moabite Inscription," *BAR* XX, 3 (May/June, 1994), 30–37, who suggests that the Moabite Stone also refers to the "house of David."

7. Carol Stuart Grizzard and Marvin E. Tate, "Kingship," *MDB* 490–491.

8. Richard Elliott Friedman, *Who Wrote the Bible?*, 44.

9. For a different view as to the location of Sheba, see Stephen D. Ricks, "Sheba, Queen of," *ABD* V, 1170–71.

10. For what is known about Solomon's Temple, see Victor Hurowitz, "Inside Solomon's Temple," *BR* X, 2 (April, 1994), 24–37, 50.

11. G. Ernest Wright, *Biblical Archaeology*, 2nd ed. (Philadelphia: Westminster, 1960), 129ff. On the city gate and the Hazor water system, see Yadin, *Hazor*, 187–247. It has excellent drawings, plus black and white photographs.

12. Zvi Gal, "Cabul: A Royal Gift Found," *BAR* XIX, 2 (March/April, 1993), 39–44, 84.

13. Alan R. Millard, "Does the Bible Exaggerate Solomon's Golden Wealth?" *BAR* XV, 3 (May/June, 1989), 20–24.

14. Ranier Albertz, *A History of Israelite Religion* I, 140ff.

15. Ibid, 141.

16. Ibid, 141ff.

Chapter 8 🌿

ISRAEL BECOMES TWO

The History of the Northern Kingdom

An American company that specializes in wrecking buildings advertises that it can tear one down in a minute's time without breaking the glass in nearby buildings. By studying its structure, the company's experts can place at strategic places explosives, which, when detonated in proper sequence, will reduce the building to one huge pile of rubble. The nation of Israel was not destroyed by experts, but experts could not have done a better job of destruction than Solomon's successor did!

Method of Approach

One problem in studying the divided monarchy is how to approach it. The Bible combines the histories of the two kingdoms so as to compare the beginning of one king's reign with that of his counterpart in the other kingdom. Because this is somewhat confusing to the reader, in this discussion their histories will be divided as follows: This chapter will discuss the history of the Northern Kingdom (Israel) from the breakup of the united monarchy to the fall of Samaria in 721 B.C.E. Chapter 9 will deal with the history of the southern kingdom (Judah) from the breakup through the reign of Hezekiah. Chapter 10 will continue the history of Judah through the seventh century up to the fall of Jerusalem and the beginning of the Babylonian exile (586 B.C.E.). The prophets of Israel will be introduced at the appropriate places.[1]

The Problem of Chronology

If one reads several books of the Old Testament, one may find different dates for the same person or event. The reason is that biblical calendars, unlike modern calendars, followed no universally agreed-on starting point. Today, the calendars of the Western world use the birth of Jesus as the starting point. Before the coming of Christ, every nation had a different way of figuring dates. For the Israelites, time was figured from the beginning of a king's reign. Thus a given event was said to have occurred "in the eighth year of King Hezekiah." How do we know when the eighth year of King Hezekiah was by our way of reckoning time?

It is necessary to pinpoint a few dates in the history of Israel and calculate from those key dates. Fortunately, the Assyrians and Babylonians kept accurate calendars based on the rule of their kings. The king's reign always began on New Year's Day. Their method was to name each year after a different court official to keep it separate. In addition, important events were recorded for each year. For scholars, the most important events used for dating are eclipses, the mention of contacts with the Israelite kingdoms, and the mention of specific Israelite rulers. As a result, at least two key dates, 853 B.C.E. and 605 B.C.E., can be established. The first was the Battle of Qarqar, involving the troops of Ahab, king of Israel. The mention of an eclipse within a few years of this battle is important because, if one know where it occurs, an eclipse can be dated with precision. Qarqar is not mentioned in the Old Testament, but Ahab is; so the time of his reign can be pinpointed. The same is true of the Battle of Carchemish in 605 B.C.E. The records mention Jehoiakim, king of Judah. An eclipse again was the vital clue to the date.

This does not solve all the problems, but it helps. The Israelites were not careful about giving the length of a king's reign. For instance, Uzziah was said to have reigned fifty-two years. Yet, when he got leprosy, his son Jotham came to the throne as his co-regent and reigned for sixteen years. In reality, the total time was somewhere between fifty-two and fifty-six years, depending on the date of Uzziah's death. This creates difficulties for one working on chronologies and is the major reason why dates vary from one scholar's scheme to another. Most authors pick what seems to be the best chronology and stay with it.

THE DIVISION OF THE KINGDOM (922–783 B.C.E.)

Rehoboam's Folly (I Kings 12:1–19)

Trouble was not long in coming. Solomon was powerful enough to keep things under control as long as he lived, but his successor, Rehoboam, lacked the sound judgment needed to deal with the problems he inherited from his father.

After a coronation in Jerusalem, Rehoboam went to the old northern shrine at Shechem for another coronation by the northern tribes. The people appeared before him and asked relief for the harsh requirements laid on them by Solomon. Rehoboam, instead of taking the advice of his senior counselors to lighten their burdens, listened to his younger friends. His arrogant answer was that if they thought things had been harsh under Solomon, they had not seen anything harsh (12:1–15).

The northern tribes, led by Jeroboam, revolted. Rehoboam tried to put down the rebellion by sending his labor foreman to threaten the people. They killed him by stoning, and Rehoboam barely escaped in his chariot. Thereafter, the kingdoms would be known as Israel and Judah.

Jeroboam (I, 922–901 B.C.E.) Becomes King of Israel (I Kings 12:20–24)

Jeroboam was installed as king of the northern tribes, leaving only the tribe of Judah and perhaps the tribe of Benjamin under Rehoboam's control (12:20). Rehoboam raised an army to take back the northern territory, but a prophet named Shemaiah warned that such an attempt would be futile.

Jeroboam got the better part of the kingdom by almost any standard. Israel, stronger economically, had a larger population, controlled the major roads, and had the best and most productive land. Its greatest weakness was the instability of its government. No consistent way had developed for making the transition from the rule of one king to another. Israel's material assets also made it more attractive to outside powers, to whom Israel was accessible by its roads.

Judah, on the other hand, had the poorest land and the smallest population. It was isolated. This made it less attractive to invaders. Its greatest assets were Jerusalem, with its already-rich traditions, and the Davidic monarchy, which assured stability in government.

Jeroboam's Reign (I Kings 12:25–14:20)

While reading the history of the divided kingdom, one must be aware of certain things. For one thing, the writers were from Judah and admired David. Since Israel opposed the Davidic monarchy and the Davidic covenant, the historians had negative feelings about anything connected with the Northern Kingdom. For another thing, Jerusalem (to the Deuteronomic historians) was the only place where true worship could be carried on. When Jeroboam led the revolt and set up worship centers at Dan and Bethel, he chose golden calves to replace the ark of the covenant as the symbol of the LORD's throne. For this reason, Jeroboam became the devil incarnate to the religious men of Judah. All who followed Jeroboam were put in the same category.

By choosing calves as symbols of the throne of God, he chose the symbol of Hadad, the chief god of the Baal religion (12:25–33). This brought down on him the wrath of the prophets. A Judean prophet came to Bethel and pronounced the LORD's judgment upon it (13:1–3). Jeroboam tried to punish the prophet, but paralysis struck him and caused him to back down. Then he offered to pay the prophet, but the prophet refused (13:4–10).

On his way back to Judah, the prophet was stopped by another prophet who invited him in for a meal. The Judean refused, saying that the LORD told him not to eat in Israel. The Israelite persuaded him to do so by telling him he had a message from the LORD that he should eat. While they were eating, the Israelite told the Judean that he would be killed for disobeying the LORD. When he died, the Israelite buried him and commanded that he, too, should be buried in the same tomb (13:11–32).

As further evidence of the LORD's displeasure with Jeroboam, the prophet Ahijah told Jeroboam's wife that their son Abijah would die. He said, furthermore, that Jeroboam's dynasty would be replaced. All this is an indication of the important roles that prophets played in relation to the kings of both Israel and Judah. When Jeroboam died, he was succeeded by Nadab, another of his sons (13:33–14:20).

Woodfin Camp & Associates.

Figure 8–1. "So the king . . . made two calves of gold . . . and he set one in Bethel" (1 Kings 12:28–29). Tell Bethel, some ten miles north of Jerusalem, was where Jeroboam I set up a shrine to keep Israelites from going to Jerusalem to worship.

The Parade of Kings in Israel (I Kings 15:25–16:20)

After the death of Jeroboam, Israelite kings came and went with surprising rapidity. Before taking the kingship, the only anointing many of the kings received was a personal anointing of greed and a lust for power. The following is a summary of this turbulent time:

King	Length of reign	Fate
Nadab	(901–900)	Murdered by Baasha
Baasha	(900–877)	Died naturally
Elah	(877–876)	Murdered by Zimri
Zimri	(876–7 days)	Suicide provoked by Omri

THE DYNASTY OF OMRI (I, 876–842 B.C.E.)

Israel and Her Neighbors

Israel and Judah had been fortunate to survive the first fifty years following the collapse of the united monarchy in 922 B.C.E. The key to their survival came from the outside, since Egypt was powerless and no one state had achieved dominance in Mesopotamia. For a brief time, it seemed the quiet period would end when Assyria, led by Asshur-nasirpal (884–860 B.C.E.) rose to power and pushed all the way to the Mediterranean. His conquests probably did not reach as far south as Israel, nor were they permanent. He set a standard for cruel treatment of captives that other Assyrian rulers tried to emulate. In one inscription he said of his captives:

> I flayed as many nobles as had rebelled against me [and] draped their skins over the pile [of corpses]; . . . some I erected on stakes on the pile. . . . I flayed many right through my land [and] draped their skins over the walls.[2]

Because of such cruelties, the Assyrians were the most dreaded conquerors in the ancient Near East.

The more immediate problem for Israel was its relationship with Syria (called Aram in the Hebrew text). Ben-Hadad, whose reign extended from about 884 to 842 B.C.E., was strong enough to be a constant problem to Omri and his son Ahab. As a result, the two small countries alternated between being at war and being allies. When no one else threatened them, they fought each other. But whenever a threat arose from Assyria, they joined forces for mutual protection.

Omri also renewed with Phoenicia the old alliance that had been so profitable for both David and Solomon. To seal the covenant, Omri's son Ahab was married to Jezebel, the daughter of the king of Tyre. This marriage would have far-reaching effects upon Israelite society and religion.

Israel's relations with Judah changed for the better during the Omrid dynasty. The two kingdoms became allies, with Israel being the dominant party. To symbolize the union between the two kingdoms, Athaliah, who probably was Ahab's daughter (2 Kings 8:18, 26), was married to Jehoram of Judah.

The Influence of Omri (I Kings 16:21–28)

Omri (I, 876–869 B.C.E.), after overcoming brief opposition from another contender named Tibni, moved quickly to organize his kingdom along the lines of the Davidic and Solomonic kingdoms. He renewed old alliances, began building programs (which Ahab extended), and moved the capital from Tirzah to the hill of Samaria.

This latter accomplishment (1 Kings 16:23–24) showed something of Omri's sense of judgment. From a military standpoint, the hill of Shemer on which Omri and Ahab built Samaria was an excellent city site. A century later, it would take the Assyrian army several years to capture it.

By Omri's time, water was no longer the problem it had been, since in the tenth century the Israelites had developed the cistern. A cistern was an underground jug dug into the rock and plastered with lime to keep it from leaking. During the rainy season, runoff water was channeled into the cisterns to be stored for the dry months.

The ruins of Omri's and Ahab's palace have been found at Samaria. The exceptionally fine masonry work enclosed an area 582 feet long by 424 feet wide. The palace, which Ahab built for Jezebel was 89 feet by 79 feet. In this palace were found many ivory pieces, fitting the description of 1 Kings 22:39 as "the ivory house that he built." During the Omri-Ahab years, extensive building programs were carried on at other cities, including Megiddo.[3] Omri's power and influence can also be seen in the fact that many years after his death, Israel was known in Assyrian records as "the land of Omri." The Moabite Stone (found in 1868) also speaks of how Moab was conquered by Omri and lists the annual tribute or bribe the Moabites had to pay to Israel. Mesha, the king of Moab who erected the stone, threw off Israelite control during Ahab's wars with Syria.[4]

Despite his achievements, the biblical writer only mentions the fact that Omri built Samaria and that "he did more evil than all who were before him" (1 Kings 16:25–28).

The Reign of Ahab (I, 869–850 B.C.E.), (I Kings 16:29–22:4)

Introduction (1 Kings 16:29–34). As far as the biblical writer was concerned, the news about Ahab was bad—first, last, and always. He was worse than his father, Omri (16:30). He married Jezebel, an ardent worshiper of the Canaanite god

Richard T. Nowitz.

Figure 8–2.   [Omri] fortified the hill, and called the city that he built,
Samaria" (1 Kings 16:24). The ruins of the Omri-Ahab
complex at Samaria reveal unusually fine contruction
for that time. Ivory decorations were discovered in the
excavations.

Baal, and he worshiped her gods. He also built altars to Baal and made an idol to
represent Asherah, Baal's mistress. The implication is that he gave approval to
human sacrifice as part of worship (16:31–34).

Aside from the Bible, Ahab, in purely secular terms, was a much more impressive ruler. As excavations at Megiddo, Samaria, and now at Dor on the coastal
plain attest, Ahab was a prodigious builder, "the greatest of the builder kings between Solomon and Herod." What once were thought to be Solomon's stables at
Megiddo are now credited to Ahab. In the military realm, he was able to supply two
thousand war chariots for the western alliance against Shalmaneser III at the battle of Qarqar.[5]

The Canaanite Fertility Religion.   One of Israel's major problems from the
day it entered Palestine was what to do about the Canaanite culture and religion.
The harsh demands for a holy war were one attempt to deal with the problem. Israel's leaders were intelligent enough to know that the sexually oriented religion
of the Canaanites would make the more demanding requirements of the worship
of the LORD harder to live by. For this reason, the uncompromising demands of the
holy war, if carried out, would eliminate not only the religious shrines but all who
taught the religion.

But while holy war may have been practiced occasionally, it was not on a large scale. Israel failed to conquer the land completely. Instead, the Canaanites were absorbed into the population, even when Canaanite lands were taken. With the Canaanites came their culture and religion.

Imagine what it would be like to be Sam Israelite, who comes from the desert fringe, where his principal occupation has been that of a shepherd. Suddenly, he finds himself in possession of a house and land of his own. He is now a farmer. He plants his crops, but they fail. He has a Canaanite neighbor who plants his crops and they produce abundantly.

He goes to his neighbor, Joe Canaanite, and says, "Say, Joe, how is it that your barley looks so much better than mine?"

Joe answers, "Why, Sam, the problem with your crops is that you worship the wrong god. Your god was OK when it came to warfare, but he is just not experienced at growing crops. Come with me tomorrow to the Shrine of Hadad. We are having our Spring fertility dance and, man, are those temple girls beauties. After all, Baal really knows how to make that barley grow!" It is not hard to imagine what many Israelite men would do in that case.

It was this religion that Jezebel was so ardently promoting in Israel. She also donated money to it. In the court alone there were 450 prophets of Baal and 400 prophets of Asherah (1 Kings 18:19). Baalism threatened to sweep over the land, but one man—the prophet Elijah—stemmed the tide.

Elijah Among the Prophets.   Elijah was the first prophet who could be ranked with the great prophets. In later Jewish tradition, he became the symbol of the ideal prophet as Moses was the symbol of the ideal lawgiver (Luke 9:30, 33). Before he is discussed, it might be well to look at the whole idea of prophecy as it was practiced in Israel and Judah in the time of the Hebrew kingdoms. (In this discussion, the term *Israel* will apply to all the people, north and south, not just those of the Northern Kingdom).

Israel was not alone in having prophets. Balaam (Num. 22:1–24:25) was not an Israelite, as both the Bible and a recently found inscription show.[6] Mari, a city in northern Mesopotamia, had prophets who gave oracles (sayings) in much the same manner that the Israelite prophets did.[7] Furthermore, as later discussions will show, not all Israelite prophets were admirable men. Some simply were "yes" men to the kings. But the true prophets of Israel were men who were in a class by themselves.

Three Hebrew terms are used to describe the prophets. Two of them, *ro'eh* and *hozeh*, are translated "seer." The third word is *navi'*, which probably meant "one who speaks for another." Thus Aaron was the *navi'* for Moses since he was the one who spoke for Moses (Exod. 7:1). "Seer" was a term used earlier to describe the prophets, but by the time of the great prophets (eighth to sixth centuries B.C.E.) it was a somewhat derogatory term.

Two other descriptive but nonbiblical terms applied to the prophets were *ecstatic* and *diviner*. Ecstatics were prophets whose prophecy came as part of a psychological experience, such as a trance or highly emotional state. This was what was meant when Saul was described as being among the prophets (1 Sam. 10:10–13). Ecstatic prophets did strange things and had strange experiences.

Figure 8–3. "Ahab took as his wife Jezebel . . . and went and served Baal, and worshiped him" (1 Kings 16:31). Baal was the god of the storm, and thus the god of fertility, since water was essential for the growth of crops. This stele (stone monument) of Baal, which is from the nineteenth or eighteenth century B.C.E., is from Ras Shamra. It shows the god holding a bolt of lightning.

Courtesy of Art Resource.

Diviners, on the other hand, read the signs of nature—the pattern of the clouds, the patterns of the intestines of a bird or animal—in short, the equivalent of reading palms or tea leaves today. None of the great prophets were diviners in this sense of the word, but a number of them (especially Ezekiel) did have some characteristics of the ecstatics.

These characteristics marked Israel's prophets as spiritual giants:

1. They were God-moved men whose message was, "Thus says the LORD."
2. They were courageous men, unafraid to deliver their message regardless of the personal danger involved.
3. They were honest men, always concerned with the truth.

4. They were moral men who preached a message that demanded the highest in moral living from their hearers.
5. They were compassionate men, sensitive to the cry of the oppressed.
6. They were sensitive men, sensitive to what was happening in the world around them and convinced that the LORD was in control of what was happening.

Not all who claimed to be prophets were true prophets. Not all true prophets made the headlines so they could appear in the Bible. Some undoubtedly died in obscurity. None of the true prophets enjoyed great popularity, even though some of them were counselors to kings. Some prophets lived together in a communal society, such as Elisha's "sons of the prophets." Some were on the payroll of the court as Ahab's prophets were (1 Kings 22). Isaiah was a royal counselor, whether invited to be or not (Isa. 7:3–9). Others were loners like Elijah, fiercely independent and critical of the established order.

Two other matters need to be mentioned. For one thing, the prophets were primarily concerned with their own time and what was about to happen to their people. Their message has meaning for today because they were applying divine principles to human problems. This is still the task of religion. In the second place, time was the sure test of the validity of a prophet's message. Many times it was very difficult to distinguish between contradictory messages of two prophets. Naturally, the people preferred the word of the prophet with the more positive message. The same problem is with us today.

Elijah Confronts Ahab (1 Kings 17:1–24). While there is no book in the Bible that bears Elijah's name, he is given more space in the Deuteronomist's history than any other prophet, including Isaiah and Jeremiah.

Elijah was a mysterious person. He would appear, give an oracle (pronouncement), and disappear. He was a prophet of doom and a man who could be both courageous and cowardly. His first confrontation was with Ahab. He appeared before Ahab to tell him there would be a three-year drought in Israel. The point was that Baal, whom worshipers claimed could bring rain, was to be challenged at his own game (17:1). Elijah finished his immediate task and returned to the eastern side of the Jordan, where he was in familiar territory and safe from Ahab's clutches (17:2–5). When the drought began to devastate the Transjordan, Elijah, at the LORD's command, went to Phoenicia, where he stayed with a widow and her son. The presence of the man of God in her home brought prosperity to her and restored her son to life after he died (17:8–24).

The Contest on Carmel (1 Kings 18:1–46). Things were bad in Israel—so bad, in fact, that the king himself went out looking for water for the royal animals. Accompanying Ahab was Obadiah. Unknown to Ahab and Jezebel, during a purge by Jezebel, Obadiah had been responsible for saving one hundred prophets of the LORD (18:1–6).

When Obadiah and Ahab separated to increase their chances of finding water, Obadiah met Elijah. Elijah asked Obadiah to tell Ahab that he wanted to see him. Obadiah was afraid that if they did, Elijah would disappear again. Finally, he was convinced and agreed to do as Elijah asked (18:7–16).

King and prophet confronted each other, each accusing the other of being a "troubler of Israel." Then Elijah issued a challenge: Bring the people and all the Baal prophets to Mt. Carmel for a test of strength (18:17–19).

Ahab took up the challenge and did as Elijah proposed. Mt. Carmel was an ancient worship site, a mountain that juts out into the Mediterranean Sea on Palestine's northern coast. Its height causes clouds blowing in from the sea to release their moisture, so that the vegetation stays green longer there than in any other place in Israel. The sure sign of severe drought was when the vegetation on top of Mt. Carmel withered (Amos 1:2). Thus, it was a favorite shrine for Baal worshipers. Like Moses' challenge to pharaoh by the Nile, Elijah was issuing a challenge from the LORD to play the contest on Baal's home court (18:20).

The people gathered. Elijah challenged them to follow either Baal or the LORD. Then he challenged the 450 Baal prophets to prepare a sacrifice. They were to call on Baal to ignite the fire since he was the god of storm and fire (lightning). Elijah would do the same thing and would call on the LORD. The god who answered by fire would be the winner. The people agreed and pledged to follow the god whose power was revealed (18:21–24).

The Baalites prepared their sacrifice and began a day-long ritual, designed to evoke Baal's response. Doing a sort of limping dance, they circled the altar crying, "O Baal, answer us!" Noon came, but there was no response from Baal. Elijah made sarcastic remarks and suggested that they were not crying loud enough, that Baal was meditating, relieving himself, traveling, or perhaps just sleeping. The frenzy among the prophets increased. They cut themselves, hoping the flowing of blood would cause the falling of rain. "But there was no voice, no answer, no response" (18:25–29). The rain did not come. Baal had failed.

When evening came, the exhausted Baalites gave up their futile efforts. Elijah went into action! He built an altar, prepared the sacrificial bull (which, ironically, was the symbol of Baal), and then soaked everything thoroughly with water. Elijah's prayer was simple:

> O LORD, God of Abraham, Isaac, and Israel, let it be known this day that you are the God in Israel, that I am your servant, and that I have done all these things at your bidding. Answer me, O LORD, answer me, so that this people may know that you, O LORD, are God, and that you have turned their hearts back. Then the fire of the LORD fell (18:36–38).

What happened on Mt. Carmel? Some say lightning, others say the water contained petroleum or gas. What happened really defies explanation, but it was a vital moment in the history of a people. The LORD had beaten Baal at his own game by bringing rain when Baal could not. Elijah took a practical approach to limiting the power of Baalism. He called upon the people, who seized the Baal prophets and killed them, even as Jezebel had killed the prophets of the LORD. Elijah did not stop Baalism completely; but he dealt it such a severe setback that it, at least, did not envelop Judah as much as it had Israel (18:30–40).

When the rains came, Ahab had to ride furiously to get down the mountain. Elijah showed his ability as a distance runner by outrunning Ahab's chariot to Jezreel, some seventeen miles away. It was just a warm-up for his encounter with Jezebel (18:41–46).

An Angry Woman and a Scared Prophet (1 Kings 19:1–21).   Courageous Elijah soon became cowardly Elijah when Jezebel heard what they had done to her prophets. She sent him word that when she got her hands on him, it would be the end of him. Elijah decided it was time for him to beat a hasty retreat.

Being an experienced runner, he lost no time in putting distance between himself and Jezebel. His servant could not keep up, so Elijah left him at Beersheba and continued southward toward Sinai. In the wilderness, where he stopped to rest, he prayed to the LORD to take his life. Instead, he awoke to find food. After eating, he continued his journey (19: 1–8).

Arriving at Horeb (Sinai), Elijah rested in a cave. While he was there, the LORD appeared (theophany) with an accusing question: "What are you doing here, Elijah?" (19:9). Instead of answering the question, Elijah complained that he was the only faithful servant of the LORD left. Told to go stand on the mountain, he experienced wind, earthquake, and fire, but the LORD did not appear in any of the natural phenomena. Instead, in the quietness following the tumult, a still, small voice asked the same accusing question: "What are you doing here, Elijah?" (19:13). Elijah gave the same whining excuse (19:14). The answer came back, "Get up and get busy. There are 7000 people in Israel who are still faithful" (19:9–18). On Elijah's return, he found a new disciple named Elisha(19:19–21).

Ahab and Ben-hadad[8] (1 Kings 20:1–43).   The most dangerous enemy Ahab had was Ben-hadad of Syria. Warfare between the two kingdoms was frequent, each side winning some and losing some. Ben-hadad laid siege to Samaria and took tribute, as well as Ahab's wives and children. Ahab, on the advice of an unknown prophet, launched a surprise attack and routed the Syrians. Later, in a battle at Aphek in Transjordan near the Sea of Galilee, Israel defeated Syria and took Ben-hadad prisoner. He pleaded for his life and agreed to grant Ahab business concessions in Damascus. Ahab agreed to let Ben-hadad go. The unknown prophet rebuked the king for freeing Ben-hadad to fight again. The prophet had seen the war as a holy war in which Ben-hadad should have been killed (20:1–43).

Ahab, Naboth, and Elijah (1 Kings 21:1–29).   Naboth's story illustrates the changes that were taking place in Israel. While on the surface, Ahab's offer to buy his land, cultivated as a vineyard, seems fair, Naboth's refusal to sell illustrates the strong sense of responsibility that Naboth had to preserve the family inheritance for his children. It was a legacy to be passed on from generation to generation.

When Naboth refused, Ahab went home and sulked. Jezebel found out the cause of his unhappiness and set about to get Ahab what he wanted (21:1–7).

Skillfully using the law to the advantage of the royal house, she bribed the village elders to call a meeting of the group, of which Naboth probably was a member. Then, she hired two of the most dishonest witnesses that money could buy to swear that they had heard Naboth curse God and the king. Two witnesses were required by the law to prove any charge (Deut. 17:6). The penalty for blasphemy (cursing God) was death by stoning. After Naboth was accused, tried, and convicted, the sentence was carried out (21:8–14). To compound the tragedy, Naboth's supposed crime also made his sons liable to the death penalty, thus effectively eliminating any heirs for the property within his family (2 Kings 9:26).

The story of Naboth's vineyard illustrates two important matters: (1) the role of the prophet as the conscience of the nation, and (2) the transition of Israelite society from a nation of small, independent landowners to one where most of the land was owned by a few wealthy men. This left the rest of the population more or less at their mercy.

The last obstacle out of the way, Ahab took over Naboth's land. When he went to inspect it, however, the first person he saw was Elijah. Elijah pronounced the LORD's judgment upon Ahab and his family, and more specifically, upon Jezebel. He said she would be eaten by dogs. This was the most disgraceful thing that could happen to a person. Ahab repented, but it only stayed the execution for a little while (21:15–29).

Two Kings and a Courageous Prophet (1 Kings 22:1–40). Before the incident described here, an important historical event had taken place. In 853 B.C.E., at Qarqar on the Orontes River in northwestern Syria, Shalmaneser III of Assyria fought against an alliance of western kings, including Ahab of Israel and Ben-hadad of Syria. They, along with other small kingdoms, patched up their differences long enough to face a common enemy. A measure of Ahab's prosperity can be seen in the fact that he furnished two thousand war chariots, half of the total chariots used by the western alliance. The importance of this battle lies in the fact that it can be dated precisely, and thus is an invaluable aid in dating events in the Old Testament.[9]

Three years later (850), Ahab and Ben-hadad were ready to go at it again. The bone of contention was Ramoth-Gilead, a border city in Transjordan. Ahab (I) called on Jehoshaphat (J) to go to battle with him to recapture Ramoth-Gilead (22:1–4).

After assembling his troops and making it obvious what he was about to do, Ahab took Jehoshaphat's advice and consulted his four hundred court prophets. They saw what the king wanted to do, and since he fed and clothed them, they were not about to contradict his wishes. So, with one accord the four hundred told Ahab to go to battle and the LORD would give him victory. Jehoshaphat could not accept that much agreement and asked if there was another prophet. Ahab replied that there was one, Micaiah ben Imlah, but that he was a negative thinker who was always predicting doom (25:5–12).

At Jehoshaphat's urging, Micaiah was called. When he seemed to agree with the four hundred, Ahab was suspicious. Then Micaiah gave an oracle predicting the death of the king. He told of being in the heavenly council (a way of emphasizing that the message was the LORD's, not his) and hearing the LORD say he would cause Ahab's prophets to lie to him (22:13–23).[10]

Ahab accepted the advice he wanted to accept and went to war. He left orders for Micaiah to be jailed and fed bread and water until he returned. Micaiah's last word was that if Ahab returned, the LORD had not spoken by him (22:24–28).

Ahab died in the battle, bleeding to death from a chance shot by a Syrian archer. When they returned his body to Samaria, harlots washed themselves in the water made bloody from washing his chariot. The water presumably gave them special appeal. The fate of Micaiah is unknown (22:29–40).

Ahaziah (I, 850–849 B.C.E.), Elijah, and Elisha (1 Kings 22:51–2 Kings 2:25). The only reason Ahaziah rated any notice was that he was consulting a pagan god about an injury he had received. When Elijah heard of it, he sent word to Ahaziah that he would die. When Ahaziah sent soldiers to arrest Elijah, they met disaster. Finally, he pleaded for Elijah to come. When Elijah went, he simply repeated his judgment—that Ahaziah would die because he consulted a pagan god (2 Kings 1:1–18).

Shortly afterward, Elisha, Elijah's assistant, was told by a group of prophets that Elijah was going to be taken away in a whirlwind. Elisha did not want to accept this prophecy. When it happened, Elijah's cloak was left for Elisha, symbolizing his role as Elijah's successor. Other prophets saw Elisha as Elijah's successor and joined with him, making him their mentor. Unlike Elijah, who was a very private person, Elisha was a more public figure and political activist. As a result, many miracle stories were told about him (2:1–25).

Jehoram (Joram) of Israel (849–842 B.C.E.) (2 Kings 3:1–27). The relation of Mesha of Moab to Israel was that of vassal, described in the Moabite Stone. During the Israelite-Syrian wars, he broke away. Jehoram (I) and Jehoshaphat (J) went on an expedition against Mesha. When they saw him sacrifice his son to his pagan god, they were horrified and turned back.

Stories about Elisha (2 Kings 4:1–9:14)

Numerous stories grew out of Elisha's ministry. Like Elijah, he was said to have helped a poor widow (4:1–7). His prayer to the LORD was credited with making fruitful a barren woman who had befriended him. Later, he restored her child to life when it died (4:8–37). He was said to have made poisonous stew safe to eat and to have multiplied loaves of bread (4:38–44).

One of the most famous stories is about the healing of Naaman, a Syrian army commander, of leprosy. Naaman had heard of Elisha through an Israelite slave girl. When Naaman came to Elisha, he offered to pay for the cure. Elisha refused but instructed Naaman to wash seven times in the Jordan River. When the leprosy disappeared, he tried again to pay Elisha, but the payment was refused. Then Gehazi,

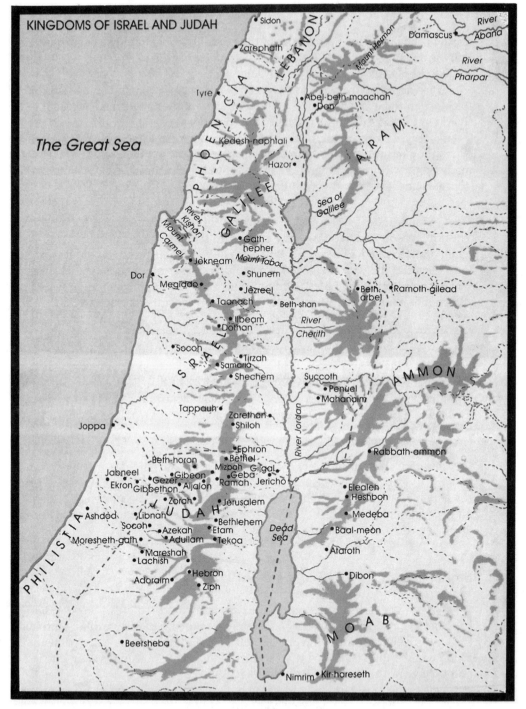

KINGDOMS OF ISRAEL AND JUDAH

The Great Sea

Sidon
Zarephath
Tyre
Kedesh-naphtali
Hazor
LEBANON
Mount Hermon
Damascus
River Abana
River Pharpar
ARAM
Abel-beth-maachah
Dan
Sea of Galilee
GALILEE
River Kishon
Mount Carmel
Jokneam
Gath-hepher
Mount Tabor
Shunem
Dor
Megiddo
Jezreel
Taanach
Beth-shan
Beth-arbel
Ramoth-gilead
Ibleam
Dothan
River Cherith
Socoh
Tirzah
Samaria
Shechem
Succoth
Penuel
Mahanaim
AMMON
ISRAEL
Tappauh
Zarethan
Shiloh
Joppa
River Jordan
Ephron
Bethel
Beth-horon
Mizpah Gilgal
Jabneel
Gibeon
Geba
Rabbath-ammon
Gezer
Ramah Jericho
Ekron
Gibbethon
Aijalon
Zorah
Jerusalem
Elealeh
Heshbon
PHILISTIA
Ashdod
Libnah
Bethlehem
Medeba
Socoh
Azekah
Etam
Dead Sea
Baal-meon
Moresheth-gath
Adullam
Tekoa
JUDAH
Mareshah
Lachish
Ataroth
Hebron
Adoraim
Ziph
Dibon
Beersheba
MOAB
Nimrim
Kir-hareseth

Artwork by Margaret Jordan Brown © Mercer University Press.

Figure 8–4. Israel and Judah—850 B.C.E.

Elisha's servant, saw a chance for some easy money. He followed Naaman, and, telling him that Elisha had changed his mind, took Naaman's money. When Elisha found out what Gehazi had done, he cursed him with Naaman's leprosy (5:1–27).

When Ben-hadad, king of Syria, tried to attack Israel, Elisha warned the Israelites and frustrated Ben-hadad's plans. Ben-hadad gave orders for Elisha's capture, but they failed (6:8–23). Then Ben-hadad attacked Samaria and laid siege to it. Food became so scarce that the people resorted to cannibalism. Because Elisha had provoked the king (probably Jehoram), he was blamed for the problems in Samaria, causing Jehoram to seek to arrest him. When the men came to Elisha's house, he told them that food would be plentiful by the next day. Having been frightened by noises of what they thought was an army about to attack them, the Syrian army fled during the night. Four Israelite lepers found their abandoned camp and brought the news to the city (6:24–7:20). The supplies left by the Syrians fell to the Samaritans, fulfilling the prophet's prediction.

The final mention of Elisha shows him as a political activist. Called by the ill Ben-hadad of Syria to predict whether he would die, Elisha confirmed that he would, sending word by the messenger Hazael, and telling him that Hazael would be king in his place. Hazael returned to Ben-hadad and made Elisha's prediction come true—he smothered Ben-hadad and seized the throne (8:7–15).

In the meantime, Judah also had a king named Jehoram (849–842 B.C.E.) who managed to lose control of Edom. He married Athaliah, Ahab's daughter. When he died, their son Ahaziah (J, 842 B.C.E.) succeeded him. Ahaziah died that year (8:16–29). Jehoram of Israel (Joram) was killed in a battle that same year by Jehu, a chariot commander in his army. Jehoram's death and Ahaziah's death were the direct result of an action of Elisha. He chose Jehu to be king of Israel and commissioned him to destroy the family of Ahab. Jehu's army unit supported him and proclaimed him king (9:1–13).

JEHU TO JEROBOAM II (842–746 B.C.E.)

The century from 842 to 746 B.C.E. began with a violent purge and ended with the Northern Kingdom's most glorious days, under Jeroboam II. Although the Assyrians flourished for a short time and forced Israel's kings to pay tribute, their last serious threat came from Adad-nirari II. He destroyed Syrian power in 802, but he was unable to follow up his advantage. Syria and Assyria both were weak for the next fifty years.[11]

Bloody Jehu (I, 842–815 B.C.E.) (2 Kings 9:1–10:34)

After Jehu was anointed king (9:1–13), he immediately set out to establish his power. King Jehoram (Joram) of Israel was recovering at Jezreel from wounds received in the Syrian war. King Ahaziah of Judah was visiting him. Jehu met the two kings at Naboth's vineyard. Jehoram (I) was killed immediately by an arrow through his heart. Ahaziah (J) was chased down and shot. He managed to get to Megiddo before he died (9:14–29).

Going on to Jezrel, Jehu came to the house of Ahab's wife, Jezebel, and had her thrown out of a second-story window into the street. When soldiers came by later to pick up the body, all but her hands had been eaten by dogs (9:30–37). Then Jehu systematically slaughtered all the relatives of Ahab, as well as his close advisers. Ironically, if the reference to Jehu as "the son of Omri" on the Black Obelisk of Shalmaneser III of Assyria is correct, Jehu was killing members of his own family![12] In addition, he killed relatives of the Judean king who had come north to visit (10:1–17). Pretending he was a Baal worshiper, he called a meeting of Baal worshipers. When they gathered together, they too were slaughtered (10:8–31).

What Jehu did was the equivalent of a new president's taking office and all the former president's family, all his advisers, and all government workers killed. It also had the same effects that such a purge would have on the government of the United States—Jehu's new government was very unskilled. Later on, Hosea, an eighth century prophet of Israel, would condemn the bloodthirstiness of Jehu. Jehu lost territory to Syria (10:32–36) and paid tribute to Shalmaneser III of Assyria in 841 B.C.E.

Two Israelite Kings and the Death of Elisha (2 Kings 13:1–25).

The next two Israelite kings were not particularly distinguished. Jehoahaz (I, 815–801 B.C.E.) was reduced by the Syrians to a military weakling. His successor, Jehoash (I, 801–786 B.C.E.) had a bit more success than his father, since the Assyrians had virtually destroyed Syria in 801. It was during his reign that Elisha died (13:1–25).

Jeroboam II (I, 786–746 B.C.E.) (2 Kings 14:23–29)

Israel's last burst of prosperity came during the reign of Jeroboam II, who combined with Uzziah of Judah (J, 783–742 B.C.E.) to extend the limits of the Hebrew kingdoms to those achieved during the days of David and Solomon. Such prosperity was made possible by two things: (1) Assyria's knockout blow to Syria in 801 B.C.E., combined with Assyria's own fifty-year weakness after that event, and (2) the talents of Jeroboam as a military leader and civil administrator. Uzziah of Judah seems to have been equally talented. While condemning his religious failures, the narrator speaks volumes in one verse about Jeroboam:

> He restored the border of Israel from Lebo-hamath as far as the Sea of the Arabah, according to the word of the LORD, the God of Israel, which he spoke by his servant Jonah son of Amatti, the prophet, who was from Gath-hepher (14:25).

Even the Syrian capital of Damascus came under Israelite control.

Courtesy of the British Museum. Drawn by Buford Winfrey.

Figure 8–5. "The time that Jehu reigned over Israel in Samaria was twenty-eight years" (2 Kings 10:36). Jehu's reign began in a bloodbath and ended in submission. "Jehu, son of Omri," is shown in an artist's representation of a panel of the Black Obelisk on display in the British Museum. He is paying tribute to Shalmaneser III of Assyria.

ISRAEL'S EIGHTH-CENTURY PROPHETS: AMOS AND HOSEA

In the Israelite kingdoms, between the mid-eighth century and 500 B.C.E., there arose a remarkable group of men whose words furnished a large portion of the text of the Hebrew Bible. The eighth-century prophets were the first of a series of remarkable relgious leaders who appeared over the known world, including Buddha, Zoroaster, and Confucius. Why this unique phenomenon should have arisen in eighth-century Israel has defied explanation by historians, but one scholar has pointed out three striking characteristics of these remarkable men: (1) where previous prophets had addressed their messages primarily to kings, these men spoke to the people as a whole; (2) beginning with Amos, the prophet's messages were concerned with applying divine principles to society, not just to royal and political failures; and (3) for the first time, these spoken messages called "oracles" were written down. The writing probably was done by disciples of the prophets, who memorized the oracles and then later committed them to writing (Isaiah 8:16). The collection of these oracles resulted in the books of the prophets. Even though the prophets were unpopular in their own day, later generations realized the truth of what they said and preserved it.[13]

Two of the prophets, Amos and Hosea, preached in Israel in its last days. Amos brought to bear the viewpoint of an outsider, while Hosea revealed the heartbreak of a native who saw his beloved country sliding toward the brink of destruction.

The Principles of Hebrew Poetry

Before discussing the prophets whose messages become books in the Old Testament, it is necessary to look at a major vehicle for those messages—namely, poetry.

While certain portions of the Old Testament are spoken of as "poetic literature" (Psalms and Song of Solomon, for example), poetry is not confined to books listed under that category. The books of the prophets contain large amounts of poetry, and so it is appropriate to discuss the nature of Hebrew poetry at this point. What follows is a brief look at the mechanical aspects of Hebrew poetry.

Parallelism

Hebrew poetry, unlike English poetry, was not as concerned with rhyme as it was with the balancing of ideas within a line. Each line of Hebrew poetry had at least two parts, but rarely were there more than three. As a general rule, when a line of Hebrew poetry is translated into English, each part forms a separate line in English. Each part contains an idea. The other parts of the line either repeat it in a slightly different manner, state a contrary or opposite idea, or add to the original idea. This way of relating ideas to each other is called *parallelism*. While there are many types of parallelism, three basic types discovered by a scholar named Lowth will be discussed here.

Synonymous Parallelism.   In synonymous parallelism, the idea in the first part of the line is more or less duplicated in the second part of the line, using different language. Some examples are:

> A good name is to be chosen
>   rather than great riches,
> and favor is better than silver or gold (Prov. 22:1).

> For the righteous will never be moved;
>   they will be remembered forever (Ps. 112:6)

> He raises the poor from the dust,
>   and lifts the needy from the ash heap (Ps. 113:7).

Antithetical Parallelism.   In antithetical parallelism, the idea in the second part of the line is the opposite of the idea in the first part. Proverbs 10 to 14 contain many examples of antithetical parallelism:

> A wise child loves discipline,
>   but a scoffer does not listen to rebuke (Prov. 13:1).

> The righteous know the needs of their animals,
>   but the mercy of the wicked is cruel (Prov. 12:10).

Formal, or Synthetic Parallelism. Formal parallelism actually is not parallel at all; the second part of the line adds to the idea of the first part of the line.

> Come and hear, all of you who fear God,
>> and I will tell you what he has done for me (Ps. 66:16)

> So I looked upon you in the sanctuary,
>> beholding your power and glory (Ps. 63:2).

Growing out of Lowth's work, other types of parallelism—such as emblematic, which involves comparisons; stairlike, in which the second part repeats part of the first idea and adds to it; and introverted, which extends over several lines—can also be found. They will not be discussed in detail here, however.

Lowth's conclusions have been modified over the years, especially in the recent past. Now, the emphasis in the second or third part is seen as intensifying or elaborating on the idea expressed in the first part. As one scholar puts it, "If something is broken in the first verset [part], it is smashed or shattered in the second verset."[14]

Meter

Meter has to do with the rhythm of poetry. Hebrew poetry had a strong emphasis on rhythm, thus making it easy to remember. Each part of the line has either 2 or 3 strong accents or beats, and on rare occasions 4. If the line has 2 parts and each part has 3 strong beats, the rhythm is 3:3. This is the most common rhythm. If the poet wanted to express quickness, often he would use 2 strong beats for each part of the line. The meter then would be 2:2. Sadness was expressed by an uneven number of beats—3 in the first part and 2 in the second part. This meter is called *qinah*, which means dirge or sad song. The Book of Lamentations was written almost exclusively in this meter. Finally, if there are three part lines, the meter could be 3:3:3 or 2:2:2.

It is not always easy to tell from English translations what the meter is in Hebrew poetry. Only by a knowledge of the Hebrew language itself can one know for certain what it is. As a general rule, however, the nouns and verbs (except forms of the verb "to be") indicate where the strong accents are.

Amos: The Shepherd from Tekoa

The Times. Amos preached in Israel after Jeroboam II had completed his wars of conquest. The nation was riding the crest of a superficial prosperity. There was a merchant class, whose motto must have been "Buyer, beware!" Short-weight, shoddy merchandise, and inflated prices were the rule and not the exception. The small farmer was cheated when the merchants bought his surplus grain. They used oversized measures when buying and weighed out the farmer's money on rigged scales. When they, in turn, sold grain to common people, they used a substandard

Richard T. Nowitz.

Figure 8–6.   "Amos, who was among the shepherds of Tekoa" . . .
(Amos 1:1). In this barren, rocky country, Amos heard
God's call to "Go, prophesy to my people Israel!"
(Amos 7:15).

measure and charged an inflated price. The grain, furthermore, was rotten and full
of trash. The demand of the law: "Love your neighbor as yourself" (Lev. 19:18) was
forgotten in their greed for gain.

Religion was very popular. The shrines were filled with worshipers, and feast
days were numerous. The king had his personal shrine at Bethel. Sacrifices were offered in abundance, and many people even slept near the altar at night to demonstrate their devotion to the LORD. But for all their religiosity, it had little effect on
dealings in the marketplace.

Society was divided into the haves and have-nots. The rich were getting richer, and the poor were becoming poorer. The rich man cared nothing about the poor
man. Harsh debt laws permitted the rich not only to take a man's property if he
could not pay his debt, but also members of his family could be enslaved. If the
poor man starved to death, it would just decrease the surplus population.[15]

While all was tranquil on the domestic scene, things were beginning to change
on the international front. Within a few years from the time Amos appeared at
Bethel, Assyria would rouse itself and begin a westward march that would crush
the small western kingdoms, including Israel.

The Man.   There has been much discussion about Amos. After all, he was the first prophet whose words became an Old Testament book. Nothing is known about his family or whether he even had one. He was a Judean, a native of Tekoa, a small village about twelve miles south of Jerusalem in the hill country.

He was a shepherd. Much of the debate about Amos is over the Hebrew term used to describe him, since it is not the usual word for shepherd. The only other time the word is used in the Hebrew Bible was in 2 Kings 3:4, where Mesha, king of Moab, was described as a "sheep breeder" (Amos 1:1). Amos also described himself as a "dresser of sycamore trees" (7:14). The sycamore was a kind of low-quality fig used for food for cattle and poor people. To "dress a sycamore tree" seemed to involve pinching or puncturing its fruit to hasten its ripening. The sycamore did not grow at Tekoa, so Amos had to go either to Jericho or westward to the Shepelah (foothills) to do that job.

Opposite conclusions have been drawn from these known facts about Amos. Either, (1) he was a poor man who had to have two jobs to make a living; or, (2) he owned flocks and lands that others looked after, freeing him to take wool from his flocks to Bethel and Samaria, where there were more traders and prices would be better.

Whatever the truth was, he did go north, and what he saw provoked his imagination. He was a passionate believer in the LORD, the God of Israel. What he saw taking place in the cities of Israel did not agree with what he knew of the requirements of the covenant the LORD made with his people at Sinai. He went to preach, not because he wanted to, but because he felt compelled by the LORD:

"The LORD *took* me . . . and the LORD said to me, '*Go*, prophesy to my people Israel'" (7:15) [emphasis added].

The Book.   While the Book of Amos, as it stands, probably was put in its final form during the Babylonian exile, the messages were spoken sometime near 760 B.C.E., but not later than 750 B.C.E.

The introduction (Amos 1:1–2).   After an introduction that is somewhat standard for the prophets, the theme of the book, "the LORD roars from Zion," emphasizes the source of the prophet's message.

Look what the neighbors are doing (Amos 1:3–2:5).   Amos's sermon started out by painting a lurid picture of the sins of Israel's neighbors. Syria had committed unspeakable atrocities in war by tearing captives to pieces under iron threshing sledges (1:3–5); the Philistines were slave traders (1:6–8); the Phoenicians also traded in slaves and were covenant breakers (1:9–11); Edom had maintained an undying hatred for Israel (1:11–12); the Ammonites had mercilessly ripped open the stomachs of pregnant women (1:13–15); Moab had desecrated the bones of the Edomite king (2:1–3); and Judah had rejected the law of the LORD (2:4–5). Each section opens with "For three transgressions of———and for four, I will not revoke the punishment," and ends with "I will send a fire. . . ."

You are even worse, Israel (Amos 2:6–16).   While Amos charged Israel's neighbors with one major sin, the charges against Israel were many. The rich enslaved the poor for the least of debts (2:6). They pushed the poor man down at every opportunity (2:7a). Father and son patronized the same prostitute at the shrine where the LORD supposedly was worshiped (2:7b). In violation of Israelite law, they took a man's only garment and kept it overnight (Deut 24:13) with the excuse that they needed it for religious purposes (2:8a). The priest and their friends used religious funds to buy wine for drinking parties (2:8b).

They did these things despite the LORD's blessing upon them (2:9–11). In fact, they went even further. They demanded that the prophets not prophesy and tried to get Nazirites to violate their vows not to drink wine (2:12). Because of these sins, judgment would be swift and certain (2:13–16).

Hear this word (Amos 3:1–5:17).   These chapters contain three sections, introduced by the phrase, "Hear this word." In Chapter 3 the theme is "privilege brings responsibility." The reason for the severity of Israel's punishment was that it had been blessed more than any other people by being chosen by the LORD (3:1–2). As a result, the LORD God was bringing a judgment that would destroy shrine and altar, winter house and summer house (3:3–15).

Chapter 4 was directed to the women of Samaria. Amos compared them to the fat, sleek cows of the pastures of Bashan. They, like their husbands, were greedy drunkards concerned only with their own desires. When the invader comes, instead of being given an honorable burial, their dead bodies would be speared with hooks and dragged through the broken city walls to be cast out for the animals to devour (4:1–3).

Religion had become sin because it was false worship (4:4–5). The LORD had warned the people by famine (4:6), drought (4:7–8), blight and locusts (4:9), war (4:10), and natural catastrophe (4:11); but none of these had turned them back to the LORD. Thus judgment was certain (4:12). In 4:13 there is a hymn to the power of the LORD:

> For lo, the one who forms the mountains, creates the wind,
> reveals his thoughts to mortals,
> makes the morning darkness, and treads on the heights
> of the earth—
> the LORD, the God of hosts, is his name.

The prophet set before Israel the alternatives in 5:1–17—death or life. He sang a funeral song in the limping, halting rhythm of the dirge:

> Fallen no more to rise
> is the maiden Israel;
> forsaken on her land,
> with no one to raise her up (5:2).

Its only hope for life was to seek the L ORD, for life could be found in him (5:4,6,14). Otherwise, judgment would be so severe that farmers would have to be pressed into service as wailers since there would not be enough professional wailers to meet the need (5:16–17).

The day of the L ORD is upon you (Amos 5:18–27).   In some of the most vivid imagery found in prophetic literature, Amos described the day of the L ORD. In popular thought, the day of the L ORD was to be a day of triumph and celebration when the L ORD would give Israel victory over its enemies (5:18). Not so, said Amos. It would be a day of:

> darkness, not light;
>> as if someone fled from a lion,
>> and was met by a bear;
> or went into the house and
>> rested a hand against the wall,
>> and was bitten by a snake.

The Israelite's religious services were such farces that they had no effect on the way people lived. The only thing that could satisfy the L ORD was to

Photograph by John H. Tullock.

Figure 8–7.   "Hate evil, and love good, and establish justice in the gate" (Amos 5:15). The city gate, shown in the plan of the gate at Megiddo, was the courthouse in ancient Israel. The city elders met in the alcoves to conduct the business of the city, which included trials.

> let justice roll down like waters,
> and righteousness like an ever-flowing stream (5:24).

This verse sums up the major theme of the preaching of Amos—that a righteous God demanded righteous living to accompany sincere worship. Right living involved giving every man his due. When viewed from the standpoint of mercy, justice can have an almost negative quality; mercy means that personal merit does not come into consideration. So the rich men of Israel preferred mercy. The poor, however, looked at justice as a positive quality. They had never rated high on the scale of human values. When a person suffering injustice achieves justice it is a blessing.

Amos also raised the question of the value of sacrifice (5:25). What he seemed to say was that what was wrong with the system was not sacrifice so much as it was the sacrificer. A wrong attitude changes worship of any kind into blasphemy.

Woe to the wealthy (6:1–14).   Amos saw pride and self-indulgence as major problems in Israel. Because of the nation's military successes, its leaders pictured themselves as the great leaders of the world. But the LORD had brought down other nations, so Israel should not think that it could not fall (6:1–3).

The upper classes spent time in drunken carousing, bragging on their greatness, and caring nothing for their fellow Israelites. The term Amos used to describe their rites, *marzeah,* may have involved ceremonies memorializing the dead and most likely included sexual orgies performed in the name of worship. They were celebrating while their ship was sinking, unaware of the danger around them (6:4–7). Because of their pride, judgment was inevitable.[16]

The visions of Amos (7:1–9:14).   The visions of the prophets were a major part of the prophetic experiences. Five visions are described in the Book of Amos: (1) the locust plague; (2) the judgment by fire; (3) the plumb line; (4) the basket of summer fruit; and (5) the LORD by the altar.

What was the nature of these visions? The visions of Amos—as well as those of later prophets, especially Isaiah, Jeremiah, and Ezekiel—seemed to begin with some ordinary circumstance of the prophet's life. But in a particular situation the ordinary event took on extraordinary meaning and significance for the prophet. He drew from it a lesson that had an application to the situation with which he was dealing. This could mean that the prophet never went through any trancelike state or extreme emotional condition as the ecstatics did. Rather, it may well be that the vision was played out in a sort of "glorified" imagination. Ezekiel's visions by the River Chebar (Ezek 1) would seem to be the exception to this. Even so, those visions, strange as they were, began when Ezekiel observed the approach of a thunderstorm (Ezek. 1:4).

The first two visions of Amos were different from the other three. They threatened judgment, but when the prophet pleaded for the people, judgment was suspended (7:1–6). With the vision of the plumb line, there was no suspension of judgment—it was inevitable. These visions may say something of the stages of Amos' thinking about Israel. For a time, he had hope. As time went by, however, he became convinced that there was no hope—judgment had to come.

The account of the visions is interrupted by a prose description of a confrontation between Amos and Amaziah, the head priest of the king's shrine at Bethel. Amos was told to go back to Judah and mind his own business. Amos replied, in effect, that he was minding the LORD's business and that Amaziah would not escape the judgment, even though he was a religious leader (7:10–17).

The fourth vision (8:1–3) contains a pun or play on words. Written Hebrew words contained only consonants. The consonants for "summer fruit" and "the end" are *qts*, though the two words respectively are *qayits* and *qets*. So when Amos was asked, "What do you see?" he replied, "A basket of *qayits* (summer fruit)." The LORD said, "The *qets* has come upon my people Israel." This word of judgment formed the text for a sermon of judgment on those who could not worship because they were thinking of how they could cheat their neighbors in the market when the religious holiday was over. For such people, judgment would include famine for those who were gluttons. Furthermore, there would be a famine of the word of the LORD when people wanted most to hear it (8:4–14).

The final vision spoke of judgment coming upon the religious shrine. Amos probably saw a priest standing by the altar and that scene led to the vision of the LORD standing by the altar calling for judgment (9:1). No matter how men tried to escape, there would be, in the words of the spiritual, "No hiding place down here" (9:2–4). Following another hymn (9:5–6) comes one of the most remarkable statements in the book:

> "Are you not like the Ethiopians to me
>   O people of Israel?" says the LORD.
> "Did I not bring Israel up from the land of Egypt,
>   and the Philistines from Caphtor and the Arameans from Kir?" (9:7).

This question attacked a commonly held view among the Israelites—that the LORD was their God alone and was not concerned with any other people. Other people had their own gods. A conflict between two nations meant a conflict between the respective deities of those nations. But, both here and in the opening words of judgment on Israel's neighbors, Amos was saying that the LORD, the God of Israel, was God of all nations. Because of that, the LORD was concerned not only about the Israelites but about other peoples as well.

A better day (Amos 9:10–15).   The Book of Amos ends with a hopeful note that may have been added by a Judean editor during the dark days of the Babylonian Exile (9:11–15). By that time, the judgments spoken of by Amos were a reality, and the role of the prophets had changed from pronouncing doom to holding out hope for the future. None of the earlier prophets, however, had seen God's judgment as the complete destruction of the people. Instead, they saw it as a means whereby the nation would be cleansed of its corruption and purified for a new and better day.

Amos: A Summary.
Why was Amos important?

1. He was the first of the so-called writing prophets, although the writing probably was done by later disciples.
2. He represented what was best in the prophetic tradition—courage, honesty, compassion, and the ability to see the inevitable result of the things that were wrong in Israelite society.
3. The ideas he preached were these:
    a. The LORD, the God of Israel is the God who is concerned with all people.
    b. The LORD is a righteous, highly moral deity who demands right living by those who worship him.
    c. No person who is right with the LORD will treat others like a thing to be abused.
    d. The inevitable result of the abuse of privilege will be judgment. Though people may be unjust, the LORD of all the earth will see that justice is done.

Hosea: The Prophet with the Broken Heart

Amos had preached during the days of Israel's glory, but now those days were over. When Jeroboam died in 746 B.C.E., the government that had seen forty years of stability and progress fell apart like a sand castle before the ocean waves. The causes were both internal and external. As Amos had seen the internal rottenness which had created a situation that made it impossible for the kingdom to last much longer, Hosea was the witness to the disintegration of the kingdom brought on by that rottenness. If that was not enough, the giant who had been sleeping between the Tigris and Euphrates Rivers woke up hungry and began to look in all directions for victims to gobble up. The nightmare the prophets had been talking about was on its way to becoming a frightening reality.

The Rise of Assyria.   The Mesopotamian state Assyria had overrun the small West Asian countries before, but it had not been able to maintain its hold on them. Now it had a new and vigorous king, Tiglath-pileser III (745–727 B.C.E.). He had an empire as his goal, and he set out to get it. His armies went in all directions, conquering as they went. He first conquered his neighbors, the Babylonians, and took the name *Pulu* (or *Pul* as the Old Testament calls him). More important to this story, he moved westward in 743, invading the Syrian city-states. It seems that Uzziah of Judah led the opposition to Tiglath-pileser but was unable to deter him. By 738 the northern Syrian states were paying heavy tribute to him.

But money was not the only price Tiglath-pileser demanded of his victims. Determined to crush rebellion before it started, he had a policy of taking all the survivors in the upper levels of society, along with the skilled workers, and moving them to other parts of his empire. This was particularly true in Galilee where resistance had been strong. There the land was left barren. In other areas where resistance had been less severe, the land was repopulated by bringing in peoples from other captured lands. This policy was also followed by the next king, Sargon II, who even incorporated Israelite troops into his army.

Of the original population, only the poor people, the elderly, and the sick were left behind—none of whom were able to provide leadership for a rebellion.[17]

Israel (745–721 B.C.E.)

The parade of kings in Israel (2 Kings 15:8–26).   After Jeroboam's death, if one became king in Israel, it was almost a sure guarantee that he would be murdered. Had there been an insurance company to insure the lives of king, it almost certainly would have been bankrupted.

King	Length of reign	Fate
Zechariah	(746–745)	Murdered by Shallum
Shallum	(745—1 month)	Murdered by Menahem
Menahem	(745–738)	Became Assyrian vassal
Pekahiah	(738–737)	Murdered by Pekah

Pekah (I), Jotham (J), Ahaz (J), and the Syro-Ephraimitic War (2 Kings 15:27–16:20; see also Isa. 7:1–25).   In the beginning of the reign of Pekah (I, 737–732 B.C.E.), the Assyrians struck the northern region of Israel (later known as Galilee). Pekah probably had failed to pay the required money into the Assyrian treasury. At the same time, Jotham (J, 742?–735 B.C.E.) was ruling in Judah, having been coregent with Uzziah for many years. A coregent was one who carried out the king's duties when the king was unable to perform them.

Jotham was succeeded by Ahaz (J, 735–715 B.C.E.), his son. Pekah, smarting under the Assyrian rule, tried to stir up a rebellion against Assyria. In that action, he was supported by Rezin, king of Syria. When Ahaz refused to join, Pekah and Rezin threatened to invade Judah and put their own man on the throne.

An attack was made in 734, but as the prophet Isaiah had told Ahaz it would be (Isa.7:1–25), it was unsuccessful. Ahaz, however, put more trust in Assyria's armed might than he did in the prophet's promises. He carrried a huge bribe to Tiglath-pileser to buy his favor. Ahaz went out of his way to prove his loyalty to Tiglath, even to the extent of setting up in the Temple court a bronze altar to the chief Assyrian deity. In addition, he commanded that regular sacrifices be made to the deity (16:1–20).[18]

Meanwhile, back in Israel, disaster was developing. Tiglath probably needed no encouragement from Ahaz to invade. In 734, he followed the international highway southward, knocking out Philistine cities that were also involved in the rebellion. Then, he reduced Israel to a few square miles of territory in the central hill country surrounding Samaria. In 732, he destroyed Damascus, killed Rezin, and added Syria to his empire (16:9).

Hoshea (I, 732–722/21 B.C.E.) Israel's last king (2 Kings 17:1–41). Hoshea, like most of his immediate predecessors, became king by murder. Pekah became his victim in 732. Hoshea played the role of the obedient servant to Assyria for a time, but when Tiglath-pileser died in 727, Hoshea got ideas about rebellion. The change of kings always was a time of testing, since major empires like Assyria also had those who coveted the kingship enough to murder for it. The vassal states hoped for a power struggle, thus giving them an opportunity to regain their freedom from the overlords, who were beset with internal problems.

Hoshea had chosen a broken stick to lean on when he appealed to Egypt for help. Egypt was like an aged man who had been living on a starvation diet. It could hardly support itself, much less offer help in a rebellion against Assyria. Shalmaneser V (726–722 B.C.E.) of Assyria struck Samaria in 725 and set up a siege of the city. That siege showed that Omri had chosen well when he moved the capital to Samaria. It took the armies of Assyria three years finally to capture it in 722/21 (17:1–6).

With the fall of Samaria, the kingdom of Israel disappeared, never to rise again. The biblical writers saw the LORD at work in its downfall, just as the prophets Amos and Hosea saw its inevitable ruin. The narrators named Jeroboam I as the chief culprit. He had brought about the division of the kingdom and had introduced the golden calves as objects of worship (17:7–23).

Assyria's policy of switching populations among its vassal states was continued in the Northern Kingdom by Shalmaneser and Sargon II . That action would produce a mixed race of people known in later times as the Samaritans. That result came about when the new inhabitants intermarried with the poor people who had been left in the land. The mixing of cultures included a mixing of religions. This mixed religion would be looked down upon with contempt by later Jews because they felt the true worship of the LORD had been corrupted (17:24–41).

The Man. Unlike Amos, who came from outside Israel to pronounce judgment, Hosea was a native of the Northern Kingdom. While his judgments were as severe as those of Amos, they were spoken with tearful pleading instead of a tone of righteous indignation. The Book of Hosea is one of the most difficult Old Testament books to translate from Hebrew. This has led some to suggest the reason as being the highly emotional nature of the prophet.

Hosea had enough reasons to make him emotional. Not only was his nation in a mess, but his marriage was also. His marital problems were used to present a unique view of the LORD's relationship to Israel. Prophets, like ministers today, could not resist the temptation to use their families as sermon illustrations!

The Book. Since the first three chapters of the book deal with Hosea's relations to his wife and family, his life can be discussed as part of the discussion of the book.

Marriage and the family (Hos. 1:1–2:1). The introductory verse suggests that the time of Hosea was after 750 B.C.E. to the downfall of Israel in 722/21 B.C.E.

On the LORD's command, Hosea married Gomer, the daughter of Diblaim:

Courtesy of *Biblical Archaeologist.* Drawn by Valerie M. Fargo.

Figure 8–8.   "Pul [Tiglath-pileser III] the king of Assyria came against the land" (2 Kings 15:19). Ancient kings were more interested in booty than in territory. Assyria wanted both. In the drawing, officials of Tiglath-pileser III are recording spoils after a victory—sheep, goats, cattle, prisoners. The reign of Tiglath-pileser III, Central Palace at Nimrud, eighth century B.C.E.

> Go, take for yourself a wife of whoredom and have children of whoredom, for the land commits great whoredom by forsaking the LORD (1:2).

Did the LORD actually command his prophet to marry a common prostitute? This question has been answered in several ways:

1. The LORD actually commanded Hosea to marry a prostitute, which he did.
2. Gomer was not a prostitute physically. Instead, she was a Baal worshiper and, as such, was spiritually unfaithful. Whether she was physically unfaithful is unimportant.
3. Gomer was a virgin when Hosea married her, but she became unfaithful after marriage. Later, when he looked back upon the experience, he realized that she already had such tendencies when he married her.
4. The whole story is an allegory, which has no real relationship to Gomer's morals.

The first three possibilities are the ones most often advanced. The fourth is usually rejected on the grounds that, if it were not true, no self-respecting prophet would tell such a story about his wife. If he did, he surely would have trouble at home!

Hosea's children not only had to bear the burden of their mother's disgraceful conduct, but their names became a part of their father's sermon illustrations. The first-born, Jezreel, reflected Hosea's opinion of Jehu's bloody purge which had been commissioned by the prophet Elisha. Since Jeroboam was of the Jehu dynasty, Hosea saw the LORD's judgment coming upon Israel because of Jehu's indiscriminate slaughter of people (1:3–5).

The second child was a daughter, Lo-ruamah, or "Not pitied." This meant that judgment would come upon the sinful nation and no pity would be shown by the conquerors (1:6–7).

The third child's name may have a double meaning. It was a son named Lo-ammi, or "Not my people." Primarily, the name was meant to say that Israel could no longer claim to be the LORD's people. It may also reflect Hosea's suspicions about his wife's indiscretions by saying, "This one is not mine!" (1:8–9).

In 1:10–2:1, the prophet spoke a word of hope that the day would come when the message of the children's names would be changed. In that day, instead of the LORD saying to Israel, "You are not my people," they would be called "sons of the living God." Lack of pity would give way to pity, and Jezreel would be a place of joy, not destruction.

Unfaithful wife—unfaithful people (Hos. 2:2–23). In an oracle calling for his children to plead with their mother to change her ways, Hosea compared his relations with Gomer to the LORD's relations to Israel. As Gomer had followed her lovers and had been unfaithful to Hosea, so Israel had gone after the Baal cult and had forsaken the LORD. Israel praised Baal for making the land fruitful, when, in reality, it was the LORD who had brought fertility to the land. The LORD would punish Israel, therefore, for her unfaithfulness (2:2–13).

But punishment was not all. Once Israel had been punished, she would be wooed by the LORD as she had when she came from Egypt to the wilderness, in hopes of bringing back the love of her youthful days. Again, a play on the names of Hosea's children was used to emphasize the LORD's hope for his people (2:14–23).

The purchase (Hos. 3:1–5). Whereas Chapter 1 tells Hosea and Gomer's story in the third person, Chapter 3 tells how the story ended in the words of the prophet himself. Few details are given, but it can be assumed that, because she had been abandoned by her lovers, Gomer probably was being sold as a slave. Hosea bought her for the price of a slave—fifteen shekels of silver and about ten bushels of barley. He did not restore her immediately to the place of a wife, however. She had to undergo a period of probation before that could happen. In like manner, the LORD would do this for Israel. She, too, would be bought back, but not without penalty on her part (3:1–5).

Judgment Must Come, But There Is Hope (Hos. 4:1–14:9)

1. The LORD's lawsuit (Hos.4:1–3). The prophets often used the language of the court to give their message of judgment. This is usually indicated in English translations by the terms *controversy* or *contention*. This is not just an argument—it is a legal charge. Three key terms stand out in the accusation in 4:1: "There is no *faithfulness*, or *loyalty* or *knowledge of God* in the land." The lack of these three qualities was the basis for all the other failures of the people. Faithfulness meant carrying out the promises that were made. Loyalty had about it the sense of "steadfast love" since the Hebrew word used here is most often translated in that way. It was a sense of compassion that had depth and meaning. Knowledge referred to an intimate, personal kind of knowing, such as was shared by husband and wife, and the word was used for this kind of relationship. These terms recur frequently in the oracles of Hosea and are the key to understanding the book.

The lack of these qualities had caused

Swearing, lying, and murder, and stealing and adultery break out; bloodshed follows bloodshed (4:2).

2. The guilt of the religious leaders (Hos. 4:4–10). The first ones indicted in the LORD's lawsuit were the priests and prophets. They were dispensers of the knowledge of God so vital to the survival of the people. As a result of their failure, the people were being destroyed because of their lack of knowledge (4:4–6).

Religious prosperity had brought increased sin. More priests and prophets meant more leaders to lead the people astray, since the people followed their leaders. The LORD's priests had led the people to the worship of Baal (4:7–10).

3. The harlotry of the people (Hos. 4:11–5:2). Baalism had the people in its grip. They worshiped the wooden poles, phallic symbols of Baal. The young women of Israel, married and unmarried, became involved in the sexual rites at the shrines (4:11–13) with the knowledge and approval of the men in the family (4:14). As a result, worship at the traditional shrines was a mockery. They paid no attention to the LORD and stubbornly went on their way (4:15–19). False leaders had brought them to destruction and punishment (5:1–2).

4. The result of idolatry (Hos. 5:3–7). Israel had become so mired in the muck of Baal worship that the people could no longer find their way back to the LORD. Even though they might seek the LORD, it would be in vain. The LORD had withdrawn from them because of their sin.

5. War on the horizon (Hos. 5:8–14). Another device of the prophet was to speak of the approach of an invading army, announcing its progress from town to town (5:8). Judah and Ephraim, the two strongest tribes, symbolized for Hosea the two kingdoms. They sought the aid of the great powers when they were in trouble, but they ignored the LORD, who would turn from healer to destroyer. The only hope was that their suffering would bring them to their senses (5:9–14).

6. False repentance (Hos. 5:15–7:2).   Even though Israel repented, it was a false repentance. It had no more permanence than a fog in the morning (5:15–6:4). The key verse in Hosea follows:

> For I desire steadfast love and not sacrifice,
>   the knowledge of God, rather than burnt offerings (6:6).

As was true with Amos, Hosea's understanding of the LORD's demands was that acts of worship within themselves were not enough to please him. Sacrifice as an attempt to bribe the LORD was useless, for the LORD would not be bribed. Only a commitment of love whose endurance was based on knowing and doing what the LORD demanded was satisfactory.

Instead of steadfast love and the knowledge of God, Israel's worship was a flagrant violation of everything good. At every shrine, sin was multiplied. At Adam, the covenant was broken; at Gilead, there was bloodshed; even the priests at Shechem were murderers, and harlotry was the accepted thing (6:7–10). Every time the LORD would bless Ephraim, there was more evidence of corruption uncovered (6:11–7:2).

7. Anarchy in the country (Hos. 7:3–7).   This passage reflects the period when the kings came and went in rapid succession. There were plots and counterplots in the palace, and one king had hardly taken the throne when he was murdered and another took his place. Hosea compares the plotting to an oven filled with hot coals ready to burst into flame when they get sufficient oxygen (7:3–7).

8. Ephraim is a half-baked cake (Hos. 7:8–16).   Here, Hosea shows his mastery of figures of speech. Bakers had to turn the flat, thin pieces of bread for them to cook properly. Israel was like a cake unfit to eat—left unturned, it burned on one side and was doughy on the other. Again, Israel was like a dove, a bird easily snared in a net. So Israel had fallen into the trap of its powerful enemies by trying to play the game of international politics. In religion, the people turned to Baal, even though the LORD was the one to whom they owed their blessings (7:8–16).

9. False worship and false friends (8:1–14).   The enemy was hovering over Israel like a bird of prey. The kings it had chosen were not the LORD's choice. The idols the people worshiped were false gods. They have sown "the wind and they shall reap the whirlwind" (8:7). The friends they had tried to buy were false. The numerous altars they had built were for sinning, not for worshiping. They sacrificed so as to gorge themselves on meat, not for truly worshiping the LORD. Israel and Judah both faced the LORD's judgment (8:1–14).

10. *The judgment to come (Hos. 9:1–17).*   Because Israel had forsaken its God and had been a harlot for Baal, Egypt and Assyria would destroy it (9:1–3). All worship would end and would be replaced by mourning. The days of punishment had arrived. Even the prophet, who was supposed to be the LORD's spokesman, was listened to no longer. The people called him a fool and tried to destroy him. But God would bring judgment upon them (9:4–9).

Israel had once been faithful. When it entered Canaan, however, it took up Baal worship. Now barrenness would afflict Israel. "No birth, no pregnancy, no conception" would be the rule (9:11). Baal could not make Israel fertile. Even when she did give birth, the children would die in infancy or be slaughtered by the invaders (9:10–17).

11. *Increased altars—increased sin (Hos. 10:1–8).*   Like a grapevine heavy with grapes, Israel was filled with places of worship, but these would be destroyed (10:1–2). The people were liars, making covenants with no intention of keeping them. Their major concern was to preserve their licentious worship, but it would be destroyed by the armies of Assyria (10:3–6). There would be no place to hide when judgment came (10:7–8).

12. *Judgment must come (Hos. 10:9–15).*   Hosea refers to the atrocity of the Benjaminites at Gibeah (Judg. 19) as the kind of sin that was still present in Israel. The LORD was pleading with them to sow good things—righteousness and steadfast love—and seek him (10:9–12). Instead, they were sowing iniquity and reaping injustice. They were trusting in military power and not in the LORD. They would have war, but they would suffer destruction instead of enjoying victory (10:13–15).

13. *The LORD still loves Israel (Hos. 11:1–11).*   Despite its sins, the LORD still loved Israel.

> When Israel was a child, I loved him,
>   and out of Egypt I called my son.
> The more I called them,
>   the more they went from me;
>   . . . .
> Yet it was I who taught Ephraim to walk,
>   I took them up in my arms;
>   but they did not know that I healed them.
> I drew them with cords of human kindness,
>   with bands of love (11:1–4)

Despite the LORD's love, Israel turned away. Now, it faced judgment at the hand of Assyria. Those people who escaped Assyria's clutches would flee to Egypt (11:5–6). But this was not what the LORD wanted:

> How can I give you up, O Ephraim?
> How can I hand you over, O Israel?

> How can I make you like Admah?
>   How can I treat you like Zeboiim?
> My heart recoils within me,
>   my compassion grows warm and tender.
> I will not execute my fierce anger,
>   I will not again destroy Ephraim:
> for I am God and no mortal,
>   the Holy One in your midst,
>   and I will not come in wrath (11:8–9).

Hosea had hope for the survival of the nation despite the fact that it had to go through judgment. This applied to the people as a whole, including Judah (11:10–12).

14. Judgment must come (Hos. 12:1–13:16). Judgment had to come. The people had sinned too much to avoid it. From Jacob's deception to the prophet's day, the record was one of sin and broken promises (12:1–6). There was cheating in the marketplace (12:7–9); there was no attention paid to the warnings of the prophets— they were all to no avail. Even though a prophet (Moses) brought them out of Egypt, the people turned away (12:10–14). Idols were made in abundance, and sin was piled on top of sin (13:1–2). Because of this, the nation would vanish like the morning mist, or like the chaff of wheat before the wind (13:3).

The Lord who wanted to be Israel's savior, had to be its destroyer instead. Like the beast of prey when it is provoked, he would destroy Israel. No king could save them, for kings, too, would be destroyed (13:4–11). Only the Lord had power to defeat even death and the power of Sheol (the grave). But, because of Ephraim's sin, it would not be done (13:12–16).

15. A plea to return (Hos. 14:1–8). Hosea made one last plea to the people to put their trust in the Lord and not in Assyria. Only the Lord could heal them of their wickedness. Only the Lord would be to them like water to thirsty plants; like a tree under whose shade they could dwell.

16. A wisdom saying (Hos. 14:9). Hosea closes with a word of wisdom:

> Those who are wise understand these things;
>   those who are discerning know them.
> For the ways of the Lord are right,
>   and the upright walk in them,
>   but transgressors stumble in them.

17. Summary on Hosea. Like Amos, Hosea was a prophet of judgment; but he emphasized that the Lord still loved Israel. The chief architects of Israel's downfall were the religious leaders. They were supposed to be experts in the knowledge of God, but they were leading the people to worship Baal. Instead of lives marked by compassion and concern for their fellowman, most of the Israelites were selfish, corrupt, and immoral. While the remnant idea of the later prophets was not a part of Hosea's theology, it was strongly implied in his emphasis on the LORD's love for the people and the suggestion that there would be those who would survive the judgment. After all, the ultimate goal of God's judgment is the redemption of Israel.

The Death of the Northern Kingdom.   When the Assyrians, led by Sargon II, finally were able to break down Israel's last remaining stronghold, Samaria, in 722/21 B.C.E., the Northern Kingdom died. While some think Sargon's brother, Shalmaneser actually was the one who did it (2 Kings 17:1–6; 18:9–12), Sargon took the credit and boasted that he removed 27,290 captives to other locations and, in turn, repopulated the city with captives from other territories that he had captured. Judah escaped because King Ahaz had bet on the Assyrians rather than casting his lot with the alliance between Syria and Israel.[19]

STUDY QUESTIONS

1. What two dates are pivotal for the development of chronologies for the Old Testament and how are they determined?
2. How does Hebrew poetry differ from English poetry?
3. Know the function of parallelism and be able to identify the three major types.
4. What is the importance of meter? What is *Qinah?*
5. What factors contributed to the negative reaction of the Northern tribes to Rehoboam?
6. What advantages and disadvantages did Jeroboam have as he began his rule over the Northern Kingdom (Israel)?
7. Why was Israel called the "the land of Omri" for many years after that king's short reign?
8. Why was Omri able to make Samaria his capital and what were its advantages?
9. Why did Baalism apeal to the Israelites so strongly?
10. What characteristics did all of Israel's great prophets have in common?
11. How were the great prophets concerned about the future?
12. What were the issues in Elijah's contest with Baal's prophets on Mount Carmel?
13. Why did Ahab handle Elijah differently from the way Jezebel dealt with him?
14. What changes in Israelite society does the story of Naboth reflect?
15. What is the importance of Micaiah ben Imlah?
16. Compare the ministries of Elijah and Elisha.
17. In what ways did Jehu's purge of the house of Omri contribute to the instability of Israel?
18. What international conditions made it possible for Israel and Judah to flourish during the reigns of Jereboam II and Uzziah?
19. How would a secular historian rate Jeroboam II?
20. In what three important ways did the prophets of eighth-century Israel differ from previous Israelite prophets?
21. What kinds of conditions gave rise to the ministry of Amos?
22. What do the oracles against the nations (Amos 1:3–2:5) say about Amos' doctrine of God?
23. What were the major themes of the preaching of Amos?
24. Know the five visions of Amos and their possible meanings.
25. Assess the importance of Amos as a prophet.
26. Why should Hosea's attitude toward Israel differ from that of Amos'?

27. Identify: (a) Tiglath-pileser III; (b)Sargon II; (c) Pekah; (d) Hoshea.
28. Would the LORD really command a prophet such as Hosea to marry a harlot?
29. How did Hosea relate his marriage problems to his message for Israel?
30. What is the significance of the names of Hosea's children?
31. How did Hosea make use of legal terms and forms to present his case against Israel?
32. What did Hosea mean by "knowledge" and "steadfast love" (6:6)?
33. Terms to know: *navi'*, *marzeah*, ecstatic, diviner, oracle, vision.

ENDNOTES

1. To help students keep the kings and their countries straight, (I) will follow the names of Israel's kings, and (J) will follow the names of Judah's where there might be confusion.
2. Albert Kirk Grayson, *Assyrian Royal Inscriptions*, Part 2 (Wiesbaden, Germany: Otto Harrassowitz, 1976), 124, quoted by Erika Bleibtreu, "Grisly Assyrian Record of Torture and Death," *BAR* XVII, 1 (January/February, 1991), 57.
3. Gaalyah Cornfeld and David Noel Freedman, eds., *Archaeology of the Bible: Book by Book* (New York: Harper & Row, 1976), 119–121. See also Martin Noth, *The History of Israel*, 2nd ed. (New York: Harper & Row, 1960), 231.
4. J. B. Pritchard, ed., *ANE*, 209.
5. Ephraim Stern, "The Masters of Dor—Part 2: How Bad Was Ahab?" *BAR* XIX, 2 (March/April, 1993), 18–29. See also Rainer Albertz, *The History of Israelite Religion*, I, 149.
6. Jo Ann Hackett, "Deir 'Alla, Tell: Texts," *ABD*, 129–130, is an up-to-date discussion of this important discovery.
7. Jean-Marie Durand, "Mari (Texts)," Jennifer L. Davis, trans., *ABD* IV, 529–538.
8. On the threat of Syria to the Israelite kingdoms, see Noth, *The History of Israel*, 240–241.
9. Yohanan Aharoni and Michael Avi-Yonah, *MBA*, rev. ed., 81.
10. Walter Brueggemann, *Theology of the Old Testament: Testimony, Dispute, Advocacy* (Minneapolis: Fortress Press, 1997), 628–632, gives an extended discussion on the "heavenly council" and the idea of authoritative utterance.
11. Bright, *A History of Israel*, 255ff. gives the details.
12. Tammi Schneider, "Did King Jehu Kill His Own Family?" *BAR* XXI, 1 (January/February, 1995), 26–33, 80 presents a sound argument for such an interpretation.
13. For a more detailed look at Israel in this period, see Philip J. King, "The Great Eighth Century," *BR* V, 4 (August, 1989), 22–33, 44. See also Albertz, *A History of Israelite Religion* I, 159ff.
14. Robert Alter, "The Characteristics of Ancient Hebrew Poetry," in *The Literary Guide to the Bible*, Robert Alter and Frank Kermode, eds.(Cambridge: Belknap Press, 1987), 615. See also an excellent brief discussion of the characteristics of Hebrew poetry in *NOAB* in *NRSV* (New York: Oxford University Press, 1991), 392–400 in the supplementary section on "Modern Approaches to the Bible."
15. Albertz, *op. cit.*, 160.
16. Philip J. King, "Using Archaeology to Interpret a Biblical Text: The Marzeah Amos Denounces," *BAR* XV, 4 (July/August, 1988), 34–44. Also Eleanor Ferris Beach, "The Samaria Ivories, Marzeah, and Biblical Text," *BA* 56, 2 (June, 1993), 96 (inset).
17. On the attraction that the western lands had to the Mesopotamian rulers, see Noth, *A History of Israel*, 253–254, and on population deportations, see K. Lawson Younger, Jr., "The Deportations of the Israelites, " *JBL* 117, No. 2 (Summer 1998), 201–227.
18. Bright, *A History of Israel*, 274ff.
19. John C. H. Laughlin, "Sargon," *MDB*, 797.

Chapter 9 🦢

JUDAH

Rehoboam to Hezekiah (922–687 B.C.E.)

No rivalry in human relationships can be more devastating than sibling rivalry. To live in the shadow of a more accomplished or more attractive brother or sister can be depressing, to say the least. Judah lived in the shadow of Israel throughout the period of the divided kingdom. Yet, it was Judah that survived—in part, at least, because its lack of material assets and its out-of-the-way location made it less attractive than its more strategically located and materially wealthy sister kingdom.

JUDAH AFTER THE BREAKUP

Rehoboam's Reign (1 Kings 14:21–31)

Rehoboam (J, 922–915 B.C.E.) had a notably unsuccessful reign. Not only did he have to deal with the revolt of the northern tribes, but he also had a war on his southern border. Shishak of Egypt had dreams of reviving the glory of the Egyptian empire. To do that, he had to control Palestine and its vital highways. He attacked in the south, penetrating the hill country and the coastal plain. He extended his conquests all the way northward to Megiddo, as both Egyptian records and an inscription found at Megiddo attest. Jerusalem, as well as a number of cities in the hill country, came under attack. This forced Rehoboam to pay an enormous bribe to keep Shishak from destroying the city (14:21–28).[1] At his death, Rehoboam was succeeded by his son Abijam (14:29–31).

Abijam and Asa of Judah (I Kings 15:1–24)

Abijam's reign (915–913 B.C.E.) was negative and short. According to 2 Chronicles, he enjoyed considerable military success over Jeroboam. He captured Bethel, Jeshanah, and Ephron. This pushed Israel's front lines back some six to eight miles in places (2 Chron. 13:1–22; 1 Kings 15:1–8).

His brother Asa (J, 913–873 B.C.E.) had one of the longest reigns of any king of Judah. He was credited with at least a halfway attempt to abolish pagan religions, but he did not go so far as to get rid of local worship centers. The historians gave him an "A" for his personal religious attitudes.

The war with Israel continued during Asa's reign. Baasha of Israel was able to move within five miles of Jerusalem, where he fortified Ramah, a town on the main road through the hills. In desperation, Asa sent an expensive bribe to Ben-hadad, the king of Syria, to persuade him to attack Israel. Ben-hadad obliged Asa, invading the northern and eastern territories of Israel, capturing a number of cities, including Dan and Hazor. This forced Baasha (I) to retreat. Asa took advantage of the retreat to use the materials in the fortifications at Ramah to fortify Mizpeh and Geba. In recent years, evidence of the fortifications have been found by archaeologists (15:9–24).[2] Second Chronicles 14:9–15 tells of another military attack on Judah by Zerah the Egyptian, but Asa was successful in defeating his armies.

Jehoshaphat (J, 873–849 B.C.E.), a Good King (I Kings 22:41–50)

With the coming of Ahab to the throne of Israel, relations between the two states took a more positive tone. Jehoshaphat and Ahab formed an alliance, confirming it with the marriage of Jehoshaphat's son Jehoram and Ahab's daughter Athaliah (2 Kings 8:18,26). They united to fight their old nemesis, Syria. The disastrous results of this war were foretold by Micaiah ben Imlah (1 Kings 22).[3]

After the incident involving Micaiah, Jeshoshaphat's reign is summarized briefly. For the most part, his was a positive rule that rooted out corrupt religious practices, made peace with Israel, took control of Edom, and tried to reestablish sea trade through Ezion-geber. He was succeeded by Jehoram (J, 849–842 B.C.E.).

JEHU'S PURGE AND JUDAH (849–783 B.C.E.)

Jehoram (849–842 B.C.E) and Ahaziah (J, 842 B.C.E.) (2 Kings 9:16–29; 10:1–17)

From 849–842, both states had kings named Jehoram, although Israel's king is sometimes called Joram. Neither king was notable. Judah's king Jehoram escaped the Jehu uprising by dying before it took place, but his son and successor, Ahaziah, was not so fortunate. Both he and Jehoram (Joram) of Israel were Jehu's victims (2 Kings 9:16–29). In addition, those of Ahaziah's relatives who were so unfortunate as to be in Israel during the uprising also became Jehu's victims (2 Kings 10:1–17).

Athaliah (J, 842–837 B.C.E.) (2 Kings 11:1–21)

The only woman to rule either kingdom was Athaliah of Judah, the mother of Ahaziah, whom Jehu had killed. She seized power and started a purge of her own, but failed to kill prince Joash, a small boy who was hidden by his aunt. Eventually, Jehoiada, the chief priest, led a coup that overthrew Athaliah and put seven-year-old Joash on the throne.

Joash (J, 837–800 B.C.E.), the Boy King (2 Kings 12:1–21)

Joash's long reign was peaceful except for an attack by Syria led by Hazael. Hazael was bribed to withdraw, using monies that Joash had collected to repair the temple, along with any other money he could find.

Amaziah (J, 800–783 B.C.E.) (2 Kings 14:1–22)

Amaziah came to the throne after his father Joash had been assassinated. This in itself was a testimony to the stability of Judah's government since the succession to the throne of the Davidic line could survive even attempted coups. Warfare between Israel and Judah broke out once more. It resulted in Amaziah's (J) capture by the army of Jehoash (I).

Uzziah (J, 783–742 (?) B.C.E.) (2 Kings 15:1–7; 2 Chron. 26:1–23)

Uzziah is given no more notice in 2 Kings than Jeroboam (I). Yet he also brought to his kingdom unparalleled prosperity. In the Chronicler's history, his accomplishments are more fully told: (1) He conquered the Philistine territory and once more established Judah's control of the vital coastal highway. (2) He pushed back the Ammonites and the Arabs of Transjordan and in the Negev to the traditional borders of Egypt. (3) He fortified Jerusalem and cities in the Negev, as well as in the footlhills of Judah and the coastal plain. (4) He promoted agriculture. (5) He modernized his army, equipping it with the latest weapons (2 Chron. 26:1–15).

During his reign, he became a leper. The Chronicler blamed the disease on Uzziah's pride, which caused him to try to assume the priestly role. When he became angry because of the priests' opposition, "a leprous disease broke out on his forehead, in the presence of the priests in the house of the LORD " (2 Chron. 26:19). A leper was segregated from all public contact. This meant that even though Uzziah was still called the king, his son Jotham, as coregent, carried on his duties as king until Uzziah died in 742 B.C.E. Some, however, would date his death at 735, the same year Jotham died.

JUDAH DURING ISRAEL'S LAST DAYS

When Tiglath-pileser III came to the throne, Judah had ideas of rebellion, but soon decided that such was not the wisest course of action. In 743 B.C.E., Judah under Uzziah had led a coalition of western states in opposition to Assyria, but it was unsuccessful in its attempts to stop Tiglath-pileser III. When Ahaz (J, 735–715 B.C.E.) came to the throne, he faced a more immediate threat from Israel, led by Pekah, and Syria, whose king was Rezin. These two kings tried to persuade Ahaz to join in opposing Tiglath. Unlike his grandfather Uzziah, however, he chose to join Assyria rather than to fight it. He therefore appealed to Assyria to help against the threats by his neighbors. Tiglath-pileser III readily obliged, taking tribute from Ahaz and quickly subduing Syria and Israel.

THE EIGHTH-CENTURY PROPHETS FROM JUDAH

Just as Amos and Hosea had preached the word of the LORD in Israel, so Isaiah and Micah were prophets in Judah. These remarkable men undoubtedly knew of each other since they came from such a limited area. None of their writings, however, and none of the historical books give any indication of this fact, except for one oracle common to both (Isa. 2:2–4; Mic. 4:1–3). Each was unique, and each in his ministry emphasized the important issues of the day. Isaiah, a native of Jerusalem with access to the royal court, viewed things on an international scale. Micah, in contrast, was limited in his vision to the Israelite kingdoms and was a rural conservative. Both men were sensitive to the cries of the poor and downtrodden. They believed that the true man of God could not ignore the cries of the oppressed. Religion that made no difference in one's sensitivity to his fellow Israelite was an insult to the LORD.

ISAIAH AND THE KINGS OF JUDAH

Just as Israel was going to its grave, Judah was about to be blessed with Hezekiah (715–687/86 B.C.E.), one of its best kings. The prophet Isaiah served as his wise and respected counselor. Previously, Isaiah had advised Hezekiah's father, Ahaz, but Ahaz did not welcome Isaiah's advice.

Isaiah and Ahaz (Isa. 6:1–8:21)

Isaiah was a man of Jerusalem, obviously from the upper classes of society. Some have even suggested that he might have been related to the royal family. In any case, he seemed to have an access to the royal court that few people enjoyed.

He was a family man with a wife and at least two, and perhaps three, sons. His wife is referred to as the prophetess (Isa. 8:3). This may mean that she, too, functioned as a prophet, or it simply may mean that she was Mrs. Prophet Isaiah.

The Call of the Prophet (Isa. 6:1–13). Isaiah's call came in the year of King Uzziah's death. The young Isaiah was in the Temple, possibly watching the pomp and pageantry surrounding the coronation of Jotham, Uzziah's son. The king was supposed to be God's representative on earth. But Isaiah saw more than the earthly representative of God—instead, it was the LORD sitting on the throne. In his vision, the LORD was flanked by two bright six-winged creatures called "seraphs" *NRSV* or "flaming creatures" (Today's English Version: hereafter, *TEV*), who called out,

> Holy, holy, holy is the LORD of hosts;
> the whole earth is full of his glory (6:3)

The formula, "Holy, holy, holy" was the Hebrew way of saying, "the most holy" or "holiest of all," since repeating the adjective took the place of the comparative and superlative degrees (holy, holier, holiest). This was not a reference to the Trinity (Father, Son, and Holy Spirit) since such as idea was unknown in Isaiah's day (6:1–3).

The Temple foundations shook under Isaiah's feet, and smoke rising from the altar gave an eerie appearance. The vision of the holy God overwhelmed the young man with a sense of sin and guilt. In his spiritual agony, he cried out in a confession of sins: "Woe is me! I am lost" (6:4–5).

In his vision, he saw one of the flying creatures take a fiery coal from the altar and touch his lips, symbolic of the cleansing power of the LORD in forgiveness. Then he heard a call, "Whom shall I send and who will go for us?" Isaiah's response was, "Here am I; send me!" (6:6–8).

Then he was given a strange commission: he was told to go preach to people who would pay no attention to him. When he questioned how long he was to preach, he was told to preach until the land lay desolate, stripped of its inhabitants. Only a remnant would remain. In short, Isaiah was called to be faithful, not successful (6:9–13).

This chapter contains two unique features of Isaiah's preaching. Like the other prophets, before and afterward, he would be a prophet of judgment and doom. But among the things that were different about his preaching were the ideas concerning the holiness of God and the righteous remnant of Israel.[4] The importance and meaning of these ideas will be discussed later.

Isaiah and Ahaz: The Syro-Ephraimitic War (734–732 B.C.E.) (Isa. 7:1–8:21).
The first appearance of Isaiah as a prophet is described in Chapter 7. Isaiah and his
son Shear-jashub met Ahaz in Jerusalem. The son was taken along because his name
represented a part of his father's message. The name was symbolic of Isaiah's doctrine of the remnant. It meant, "A remnant shall return." As such, it reflected a hopeful theme in Isaiah's preaching (7:1–4). (Even prophets couldn't resist using their
family members for illustrations!)

Ahaz was troubled by the threat of Syria and Israel. Isaiah gave him a message from the LORD to ignore the threats. Instead, he counseled, "Take heed, be
quiet, do not fear," for the little tyrants threatening him would soon vanish. The
prophet showed his contempt for King Pekah (I) by referring to him only as the
"son of Remaliah (7:5–9).

Isaiah challenged Ahaz to ask for a sign from the LORD that what he was saying was true (7:11). Ahaz refused to do so (7:12). Isaiah then said that the LORD
would give a sign anyway. That sign was that a young woman would have a child
whose name would be Immanuel. The name meant, "God with us" (7:14). It was in
keeping with the earlier promise to Ahaz that what he needed to do was to trust in
the LORD, not in Assyria.

Isaiah 7:14 is one of the most controversial passages in Scripture. Following
the basic principle of biblical interpretation which says a verse should never be interpreted apart from its surroundings or context, the verse said that a woman who
was then pregnant would bear a child a few months from that time. Before the child
was capable of making its own decisions (7:15, *TEV*), Judah's persecutors would be
gone (7:10–16).

This interpretation is not accepted by many Christians because they see the
passage as a direct reference to the virgin birth of Jesus Christ. This view is based
on the King James Version, which translates, "Behold, a virgin shall conceive, and
shall bear a son, and shall call his name Immanuel." Thus it is seen as a messianic
prophecy. In support of this view, Matthew 1:23 is cited. It quotes Isaiah 7:14 to
support the teaching concerning the virgin birth of Jesus.

The Hebrew word translated "virgin" (King James Version: hereafter *KJV*), or
"young woman" (*NRSV*), is not a technical term for a morally upright, unmarried
young woman. Rather, it is a more general term that describes all young women,
married or unmarried. In that sense, it is a neutral word. It has nothing to say about
the young woman's character. This is why modern versions of the Old Testament
translate the word as "young woman" (*NRSV* and *TEV,* for example). The Gospel
of Matthew followed the Greek text of the Old Testament, not the Hebrew text. The
Greek text has the technical word for "virgin." Matthew quoted the only Bible he
had (which was the Greek Old Testament, or *LXX,* the Septuagint version) to rein-
force his doctrine that Jesus was born of a virgin.

To summarize, Isaiah said a child would be born to a young married woman
in his day and the child would be named Immanuel ("God with us"). That would
be a sign to a stubborn king that he needed to trust in the LORD's power, not in the
power of the Assyrian army. Many hundreds of years later, a new child was born

to a virgin girl in a cave in Bethlehem. As the child grew, people began to realize that in him they sensed the presence of God among them. When the writer of Matthew's Gospel was searching the Jewish Scriptures (the *LXX*), he read Isaiah 7:14. In the ancient promise of Isaiah to Ahaz, he sensed a deeper and more meaningful fulfillment of the passage in the life of Jesus of Nazareth. He truly was Immanuel, "God with us." To that writer, the old promise had been filled in a new and magnificent way.

Who was the original child? Some believe that it was Ahaz's son, Hezekiah, who would become one of Judah's most devout and able kings. Another possibility was that the child was Isaiah's own son. This would seem to find support in the fact that the two other children mentioned in this passage (7:1–8:15) are Isaiah's children.[5]

Ahaz ignored the warnings, even though Isaiah continued to issue them. Isaiah named another son by the ominous name, Maher-shalal-hash-baz. (Someone has suggested that he was nicknamed "Hash" because his name was so long!) The name means, "Quick loot, fast plunder" (*TEV*) and describes the greed and destructiveness of the Assyrians. Isaiah told Ahaz that if he refused the LORD's peaceful waters, he would find himself floundering in the Assyrian flood (8:1–4). The reference to the waters of Shiloah ("peaceful waters") probably referred to the waters of an irrigation stream that ran along the edge of the Kidron Valley, while "the River" was the Tigris-Euphrates, and by extension, the Assyrians who came from that region (8:5–8).

Finally, because the people would not listen to him, a frustrated Isaiah told his disciples to record what he had said. If the people were more interested in listening to fortune-tellers than to the word of the LORD, then that was their responsibility (8:16–21).

Isaiah and Hezekiah
(2 Kings 18:1–20:21; Isa. 20:1–6; Isa. 36:1–39:8)

Isaiah found a more receptive ear in Hezekiah (715–687/86 B.C.E.), who succeeded his father Ahaz. Isaiah was Hezekiah's friend and counselor in at least two major crises during his reign—the Ashdod Rebellion and Sennacherib's invasion.

Hezekiah's Reform and the Ashdod Rebellion (2 Kings 18:1–12; Isa. 20:1–6). Hezekiah came to the throne when Assyria's attention was diverted from the western states. Given a bit of breathing room, he set out to bring about a reform in the religious practices in Judah. He moved vigorously to destroy the pagan altars built by his father and destroyed shrines where Baal worship still persisted. One such place where an altar probably was destroyed was at Arad, south of Jerusalem in the Negev region, where a temple had existed since early in Judah's history. The altar was destroyed either in Hezekiah's reform or in a later reform by Josiah. Similarly, the remains of an altar were found at Beersheba, where the stone was reused as building material.[6] Hezekiah even destroyed the bronze serpent made by Moses that was kept in the Temple as a reminder of Israel's days in the wilderness. It had become an object of worship, with people burning incense to it as if it were divine. The evaluation of Hezekiah was that

> He trusted in the LORD, the God of Israel; so that there was no one like him among all the kings of Judah after him, or among those before him (2 Kings 18:5).

He slightly enlarged his kingdom, especially at the expense of the Philistines. For a short period of time, he also refused to pay tribute to the Assyrians (18:1–12).

Soon Assyria was on the prowl again. In 714, the people of Ashdod, a Philistine city, tried to lead a rebellion against the Assyrians. Egypt, which, for a change, had a strong king, encouraged the rebellion because the Assyrian power was too close to its borders. Hezekiah was invited to join the leaders of the other small western states.

Isaiah advised Hezekiah to steer clear of the fight. To emphasize the gravity of what he said, Isaiah walked about Jerusalem naked and barefoot for three years. This was to stress what could happen to Judah if Hezekiah was foolish enough to oppose the Assyrians. While such an action would seem strange to us today, Isaiah was portraying an all-to-familiar sight to the Judeans—naked captives of war being paraded through the streets (Isa. 20:1–6).

Sennacherib's Invasion (2 Kings 18:13–19:36; 20:12–19).   Hezekiah seems to have stayed out of the rebellion that was crushed in 711. But trouble would not stay away for long. Near the end of Sargon's life, revolt flared again in the Assyrian empire. Bablyon, under Merodach-baladan, led the revolt. Egypt stirred up the western states, including Judah, hoping to regain a foothold for itself in Palestine. The descriptions in 2 Kings 20:6–19 of envoys from Merodach-baladan who came to Hezekiah from Babylon may represent an attempt to persuade Hezekiah to join the revolt. Isaiah protested that dealings with Babylon would bring troubles in the future.[7]

Hezekiah was drawn to the conflict like a moth to a flame and with much the same results. Expecting an invasion by Sennacherib (704–681 B.C.E.), he set about strengthening the defenses of Jerusalem. Among other things, to insure a safe water supply, he had a tunnel dug from the Gihon Spring in the Kidron Valley to a pool inside the city. The source of the spring was then covered so the enemy could not find it. In New Testament times, the pool into which it flowed was known as the Pool of Siloam. The tunnel, which still exists, is more than 1700 feet long and represents an unusual feat of engineering for such an early time. In the tunnel an inscription describing how it was dug was found by accident by a young Arab boy who was wading through it. It is still possible to go through the tunnel today.[8]

One water tunnel was not enough to stop Sennacherib. In 701, he attacked the coast and the land east of the Jordan, taking forty-seven Judean cities and, in his words, shutting Hezekiah up in Jerusalem "like a bird in a cage." Hezekiah emptied his treasury, the Temple treasury, and even stripped the gold decorations from the Temple to pay Sennacherib off (2 Kings 18:13–16; Isa. 36:1).

Yet a different picture of Sennacherib's success is presented in 2 Kings 18:17–19:37. After threats were made by Sennacherib's officers about what the Assyrians would do to the city (2 Kings 18:17–37; Isa. 36:2–22), Hezekiah consulted Isaiah. Isaiah assured him that Sennacherib would withdraw and would be killed in his own country (2 Kings 19:1–7; Isa. 37:1–7).

In the meantime, when the Egyptian King Tirhakah threatened Sennacherib's southern flank, Sennacherib withdrew long enough to put down the threat. When that was finished, he returned to renew his seige of Jerusalem. Once again, he sent threatening letters to Hezekiah (2 Kings 19:8–13). Hezekiah once more went to the Temple to pray, and Isaiah, as spokesman for the LORD, brought the answer to that prayer. He reassured Hezekiah that Jerusalem would not fall. In fact, he said that not one arrow would be shot into Jerusalem nor any seige mound be built around it. He repeated the prediction that Sennacherib would return home and be murdered (2 Kings 18:13–16; Isa. 37:8–35).

Some think that there were two invasions by Sennacherib. The main reasons given are as follows:

1. The account in Kings says Hezekiah submitted and paid a heavy tribute to Sennacherib (2 Kings 18:13–16).
2. Yet, Isaiah said that Sennacherib would not take Jerusalem nor would he even lay seige to it (2 Kings 19:32–34; Isa. 37:33–35).
3. Second Kings 19:9 says that "King Tirhakah of Ethiopia" opposed Sennacherib. But according to Egyptian records, Tirhakah became coregent of Ethiopia (Egypt) only in 690/89 B.C.E., and did not become king until 685/84 B.C.E. He probably was no more than ten years old in 701.

Some simply say that the differences can be accounted for by realizing that the biblical account and Sennacherib's account are told from two different points of view. Others are led to conclude that there were two invasions by Sennacherib. The first, in 701, devastated Judah, causing Hezekiah to pay heavy tribute. The second, coming around 690/89, was the one where Isaiah made the prediction that Sennacherib would never take Jerusalem. Second Kings (18:17 and following) would describe that invasion. Sennacherib started to attack Jerusalem, only to be drawn away by Tirhakah's threat. After taking care of that, he came back, only to meet disaster in the form of a devastating plague that struck his army. As the historian writes:

> That very night the angel of the LORD set out and struck down one hundred eighty-five thousand in the camp of the Assyrians; when morning dawned, they were all dead bodies (19:35; Isa. 37:36).

Later, Sennacherib was murdered by his own sons (19:36–37; Isa. 37:37–38).[9]

One other narrative (other than the visit by the Babylonian representatives, which probably preceded the Sennacherib invasion) concerns Isaiah and Hezekiah. Hezekiah was ill. The prophet came and told him he would die. Hezekiah prayed,

Courtesy of the Israeli Department of Antiquities and Museums.

Figure 9–1. "[Hezekiah] rebelled against the king of Assyria and would not serve him" (2 Kings 18:7). Hezekiah had this tunnel, which brought water from the Gihon Spring into Jerusalem, dug as a defensive measure.

requesting that he be permitted to live longer. Isaiah then returned and said that Hezekiah would live another fifteen years. As a sign that he would recover, the shadow of the sundial was to go back ten steps (Isa. 38:1–8).

The Book of Isaiah

The book that bears Isaiah's name was one of the scrolls of the prophets in the Jewish scriptures: Isaiah, Jeremiah, Ezekiel, and the Twelve (the minor prophets). Isaiah has two major divisions: 1–39 and 40–66.

The Book: Its Background. There are two major views about the authorship and unity of the book. Those who argue for a single author hold the following:

1. The oldest form of the book, the Dead Sea Scrolls manuscript, has the entire sixty-six chapters, much as it stands today.
2. The primary emphasis in prophecy was on prediction. God enabled the prophets to see what would happen hundreds of years in the future.
3. The author of the whole book, therefore, was Isaiah of Jerusalem in the eighth century B.C.E.

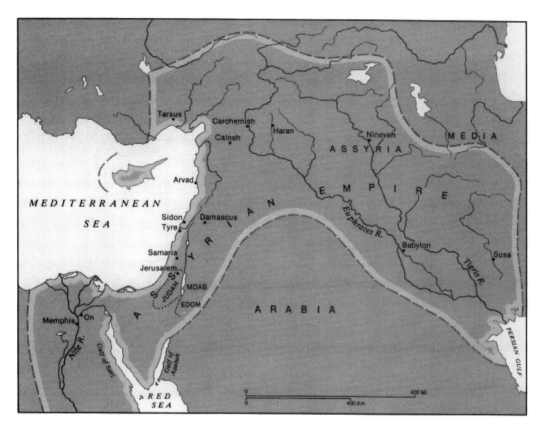

Figure 9–2. The Assyrian Empire.

Those who argue for more than one author make the following points:

1. The prophets primarily were spokesmen for their own time. The future they were most concerned with was the immediate future.
2. Isaiah 1–39 and 40–66 are different in a number of ways:
   a. They differ in historical background: 1–39 was set in an eighth-century background, while 40–66 was set in the Babylonian exile.
   b. They differ in style: 1–39 is narrative and typical prophetic oracles, while 40–66 is very elaborate poetry.
   c. They differ in their view of God: 1–39 speaks of the holiness of God, while 40–66 speaks of God as Creator.
   d. They differ in speaking of God's representative: 1–39 speaks of the Messiah, while 40–66 speaks of the Suffering Servant.

On this basis, those who hold to a multiple authorship see the work of at least two different prophets in the Book of Isaiah, the second of whom looked upon himself as a disciple of Isaiah of Jerusalem, even though one hundred years separated the two men.

While there is disagreement about the authorship of the book, most of those who study it will agree that 40–66 reflect an exilic background. For that reason, those chapters will be discussed in the historical context of the Babylonian exile and the years immediately following it.

The Book: Its Contents.　How was this or any other prophetic book formed? The prophet furnished much of the basic materials (oracles), but did he influence the present form of the book? Isaiah 8:16 contains his admonition to his disciples to "bind up the testimony, seal the teaching among my disciples."

It is more likely that the prophet's immediate followers or his more "distant" disciples, later admirers who saw themselves as heirs of the Isaiah tradition, shaped the book by contributing biographical materials, as well as oracles that they saw furthering the themes of Isaiah of Jerusalem. The most striking example of the latter would be the oracles of Isaiah 40–66. Just as the mantle of Elijah fell on Elisha, so the mantle of Isaiah fell on his unknown disciples. A similar situation involved Jeremiah and his scribe Baruch, who undoubtedly was responsible in large measure not only for the shaping of the Book of Jeremiah, but also much of what is to be found in it (see Jeremiah 36).

Oracles concerning Judah and the Messiah (Isa. 1:1–5:23; 8:22–12:6).

1. Hear, O heavens (1:1–9)
2. Luxurious religion (1:10–23)
3. There is hope (1:24–31)
4. There's a great day coming (2:1–5)
5. The day of the LORD (2:6–22)
6. Trouble in Jerusalem (3:1–15)
7. Those Jerusalem women (3:16–4:1)
8. The righteous remnant (4:2–6)
9. The LORD's love song (5:1–7)
10. Woe! woe! woe! (5:8–23)
11. The LORD's messiah (8:22–9:7; 11:1–9)
12. Miscellaneous oracles (9:8–10:4; 5:24b–30; 10:5–19; 10:27b–34; 11:10–16)
13. Words of hope and joy (10:20–27a; 12:1–6)

Chapters 1 to 12 of Isaiah reflect the changing historical situations and the prophet's reactions to those changes. There seems to be no pattern by which they are arranged except for certain catch words that sometimes cause two oracles to be thrown together. For instance, Isaiah 1:9 mentions Sodom and Gomorrah, using those cities to show the devastation that has come to the cities of Judah because of the sins of the people. The oracle, which begins in 1:2, is an oracle lamenting Israel's unfaithfulness:

Your country lies desolate,
　your cities are burned with fire;

> in your very presence
>> aliens devour your land;
>> it is desolate, as overthrown by foreigners (1:7).

Such a description fits well into the context of Sennacherib's invasion of Judah in 701 B.C.E., when he captured city after city and laid seige to Jerusalem. The prophet's only consolation is that

> if the LORD of hosts
>> had not left us a few survivors,
> we should have been like Sodom,
>> and become like Gomorrah (1:9).

The oracle that follows this one also mentions Sodom and Gomorrah, yet the historical situation is radically different. The people are so prosperous that they bring "multitudes of sacrifices" (1:11). Their worship is not lacking in quantity—instead, it is woefully lacking in quality. In this case, Sodom and Gomorrah are examples of decadence, not of destruction. Hands spread in prayerful supplication condemn the worshiper because "your hands are full of blood" (1:15).

Another vivid oracle deals with the humiliation of the upper-class women of Jerusalem who

> walk with outstretched necks,
>> glancing wantonly with their eyes,
>
> . . . .
> Instead of perfume there will be a stench
>
> . . . .
> instead of beauty, shame (3:16, 24).

A series of oracles in 5:8–23 catalogs the sins of a prosperous society: covetousness (5:8–10); drunkenness (5:11–12); failure to know the LORD (5:13–17); cynicism (5:18–19); glorifying evil instead of right (5:20); conceit (5:21); and judges who accept bribes (5:22–23).

One of the most unusual oracles is the Song of the Vineyard (5:1–7). It is in the form of a wedding song, but Isaiah used it to develop an allegory about Israel and Judah. A farmer plants the finest grapes after carefully preparing the soil. But, to his despair and disgust, what he thought were fine grapes, actually were wild sour grapes, worthless for his purposes. In anger, he destroys the vineyard. The meaning of the allegory is then explained:

> For the vineyard of the LORD of hosts
>> is the house of Israel,
> and the people of Judah
>> are his pleasant planting;
> he expected justice,
>> but saw bloodshed;
> righteousness,
>> but heard a cry! (5:7)

Is there hope?   Isaiah did not view the situation as hopeless. The people must turn to the LORD in true repentance by ceasing to do evil and learning to do good, meaning specifically:

> seek justice,
>   rescue the oppressed,
> defend the orphan,
>   plead for the widow (1:17).
>   . . . .
> if you are willing and obedient,
>   you shall eat the good of the land;
> but if you refuse and rebel,
>   you shall be devoured by the sword;
> for the mouth of the LORD has spoken (1:19–20).

Or again,

> Zion shall be redeemed by justice,
>   and those in her who repent by righteousness.
> But rebels and sinners shall be destroyed together,
>   and those who forsake the LORD shall be consumed (1:27–28).

Isaiah and the Messiah.   Messianic oracles arose in times when things looked hopeless for the people. As such, they had both a backward and a forward look. A prophet looked back at those good qualities of David that made him a great king. Then he looked forward to a time in the future when a new David would come to bring prosperity and blessings to the people.

Did Isaiah of Jerusalem speak such oracles? There are those who would see all such oracles as coming from the exilic or postexilic period after the monarchy had ceased to exist. Yet there were times when the ruling monarch was so bad that there would be little reason why such hopes would not have been aroused in the minds of devout Israelites.

Two such oracles hold a prominent place in Isaiah 1–12. The first of these (9:2–7) would fit well into the early years of Isaiah's ministry. The Assyrian hordes had overrun the Northern Kingdom, while at the same time making Ahaz pay a terrible price for the safety of his kingdom. Such a time would make anyone long for the blessings of peace. The occasion for the oracle may have been the birth of a royal child.[11]

Ahaz's rejection of Isaiah's advice on other occasions gave no basis for hope for a sensible policy from Ahaz. Thus he may well be the one who yearned for a leader who would be called "Wonderful Counselor, Mighty God, Everlasting Father, Prince of Peace," whose kingdom would be one where justice and righteousness would be the hallmarks. When no contemporary king arose who fulfilled this dream, its projection to a future time was not difficult.

The other oracle in this category is found in 11:1–9. Some would argue that since reference is made of " a shoot . . . from the stump of Jesse" (11:1), this oracle comes from a time when the monarchy no longer exists. While this certainly is a persuasive argument for such a view, the figure of the stump appeared in the call vision (6:13). Since the figure of speech is not strange to Isaiah, this oracle could well be from him. Whatever the case, whether from Isaiah or a later disciple, the ideal ruler will be one who will possess

the spirit of wisdom and understanding,
the spirit of counsel and might,
the spirit of knowledge and the fear of the LORD (11:2).

Oracles against foreign nations (Isa. 13:1–23:18).

1. Against Babylon (13:1–14:23)
2. Against Assyria (14:24–27)
3. Against Philistia (14:28–32)
4. Against Moab (15:1–16:14)
5. Against Damascus (Syria) and Israel (Ephraim) (17:1–6)
6. Against idols (17:7–14)
7. Against Egypt (18:1–20:6)
8. Against Babylon again (21:1–10)
9. Against Dumah (Edom) (21:11–12)
10. Against Arabia (21:13–17)
11. Against Jerusalem (22:1–14)
12. Against Shebna (22:15–25)
13. Against Tyre (23:1–18)

Beginning with Amos, such a collection of oracles is a common feature in prophetic literature. These oracles were directed against those nations that in one way or another offended the prophet's sense of justice, particularly regarding that nation's attitude toward Israel.

In the Book of Isaiah, there is a greater variety of oracles than in other books. Other materials have been introduced which at first glance would seem to be out of place. For example, in Isaiah 20 is the story of Isaiah's symbolic action to protest Hezekiah's possible involvement in the Ashdod rebellion. Since Egypt was one of the instigators of this rebellion, this probably explains its inclusion here.

Less easy to understand is an oracle directed against an individual, Shebna, an official in Hezekiah's court. There the answer may lie in the suggestion that he may have been a promoter of the same rebellion, an action which Isaiah strongly opposed.

The two oracles against Babylon (13:1–14:23) may well be from Isaiah's later disciples. One's view of the relationship of Isaiah and such disciples is the crucial point in this conclusion. If one takes what seems to be clear historical references—the overall assumption that Babylon is the dominant world power; the reference to the rise of the Medes (13:17); and the oracles against the king of Babylon (14:3–23)—the conclusion could be reached that these oracles came from the sixth century B.C.E. If, on the other hand, one assumes that the prophet's primary function was long-range prediction, a different conclusion would be reached as to the source of these two oracles.

The oracle against the king of Babylon (14:2–23) is a good example of a biblical passage that often is misinterpreted. This is a dirge directed against a tyrant who has exalted himself against God (14:13–14). Now he will be brought down to the "depths of the pit" (death) and his power will vanish (14:15). That such tyrants are satanic in their abuse of power does not justify interpreting this passage as describing the fall of Satan. To do so is to *eisegete* (read a meaning into a passage), rather than to *exegete* (let the passage say what it says).

Not all these oracles were *against* foreign nations. In the Moab oracle (15:1–16:14), the prophet urges the people to give refuge to fugitives from Moab, even though he does regard Moab's troubles as a just punishment (16:6–7).

Egypt was a major object in Isaiah's foreign oracles (18:1–20:6). It was pressuring Hezekiah to rebel against the Assyrians. The prophet constantly warned the king to avoid such entanglements, advice that Hezekiah heeded in 714–711 (the Ashdod rebellion). Later, however, Hezekiah would not be so wise, thus provoking Sennacherib's 701 invasion.

The Isaiah apocalypse (Isa. 24:1–27:13).

1. Destruction is coming (24:1–13)
2. Praise the LORD (24:14–16a)
3. Judgment will be universal (24:16b—23)
4. Praise to the triumphant LORD (25:1–12)
5. A psalm of praise (26:1–19)
6. The LORD comes in judgment (26:20–27:1)
7. The deliverance of Israel (27:2–13)

The chapters are called apocalyptic literature because they share some characteristics with such books as Daniel and Revelation. Apocalyptic literature differed from prophetic literature in a number of ways:

1. It aimed at encouraging the faithful of the LORD's people in a time of trouble instead of telling sinners among the LORD's people that judgment was coming.
2. It usually was written first and read later instead of being spoken first and then written later.
3. It used unusual imagery and numbers in a sort of code, which the readers for whom it was intended understood but which outsiders could not understand.
4. It spoke of God being directly involved in conflict with the earthly enemy. This differed from the common Old Testament idea of God working through human and natural means.
5. It was concerned with the triumph of God over the forces of evil in the universe. This was a cosmic struggle.
6. The author usually was anonymous since he did the work under the name of a famous person.

While these oracles are not truly apocalyptic, they do represent a transition between prophetic and apocalyptic literature. Like apocalyptic literature, they speak of the earth and the universe being in turmoil, while they alternate prophetic words of judgment with apocalyptic words of comfort for the faithful. The LORD is at work in the universe to bring deliverance to the faithful.

The authorship of this material usually is assigned to a later time. The first oracle depicts the earth in turmoil:

> The earth lies polluted
>   under its inhabitants;
>   . . . .
> Therefore a curse devours the earth
>   and its inhabitants suffer for their
>   guilt (24:5, 6).

Yet the words of judgment are balanced by words of praise (24:14–16a) and promise (25:1–5). The righteous will be preserved in the midst of judgment (26:1–19). This section closes with the promise of a return of the exiles (27:12–13).

Oracles from various times (Isa. 28:1–35:10).

1. The drunkards of Ephraim (28:1–13)
2. The leaders of Jerusalem (28:14–22)
3. The parable of the farmer (28:23–29)
4. Judah's future (29:1–8)
5. Spiritual stupidity (29:9–24)
6. Do not trust Egypt—trust the LORD (30:1–17)
7. The LORD will be gracious to the faithful (30:18–26)
8. Assyria will fall (30:27–33)
9. Trust the LORD—not Egypt (31:1–3)
10. Sennacherib cannot harm you (31:4–9)
11. Justice will prevail (32:1–8)
12. Be warned, foolish women (32:9–20)
13. Prayer and praise (33:1–6)
14. Bad times but the LORD still cares (33:7–16)
15. The glorious future (33:17–24)
16. The LORD's vengeance (34:1–17)
17. Joy for Zion (35:1–10)

This final group of oracles from Isaiah 1–39 is varied in time and context. For example, Isaiah 28:14–22 lambasts cynical leaders who have "made a covenant with death" (28:15b) and thus expect it to pass them by. Instead, they will find they are not immune to God's wrath (28:17–22).

The prophet's indignation over Hezekiah's flirtation with the Egyptians won him no ribbons for popularity (30:8–11). His feelings were aptly expressed in a scathing oracle in 30:1–7. He points out that

> Egypt's help is worthless and empty,
> > therefore I have called her,
> > "Rahab who sits still" (30:7).

Instead, Hezekiah is admonished to remember that

> In returning and rest you shall be saved;
> > in quietness and trust shall be your strength (30:15).

Failure to give heed will result in Judah being left:

> like a flagstaff on top of a mountain,
> > like a signal on a hill (30:17).

On the other hand, since they have themes that sound like Isaiah 40–66, the oracles in chapters 34 and 35 usually are assigned to the period of the exile. The subject of 34:1–17 is the LORD's warfare against the nations that oppose him. The LORD is spoken of as a dread warrior whose sword "is sated with blood . . . is gorged with fat" (34:6). The expression "the day of the LORD's vengeance" (34:8) was used in primitive justice, and meant "the day when the LORD sets things right." Vengeance, in the biblical sense, meant "bringing back to even keel things that were uneven" or "balancing what was unbalanced" (34:1–8).

Edom was used as an example of those nations who opposed the LORD, and thus opposed Judah. There seems to have been a particularly strong hatred between the Edomites and Israel, because Edom took every opportunity to strike at Israel when she was weak. Thus the LORD's enemies will be left as desolate as Edom (34:9–17).

The other side of the coin of the LORD's judgment upon the nations would be the restoration and prosperity of Israel in the land. This is why vengeance and salvation are mentioned together in 35:4:

> Say to those who are of a fearful heart,
> > . . . .
> "Here is your God,
> > He will come with vengeance,
> with terrible recompense.
> > He will come and save you."

As a result,

> the ransomed of the LORD shall return,
> > and come to Zion with singing;
> everlasting joy shall be upon their heads;
> > they shall obtain joy and gladness,
> and sorrow and sighing shall flee away (35:10).

The final chapters, 36 to 39, were discussed under "Isaiah and Hezekiah," earlier in this chapter.

Summary on Isaiah.   As we have seen, Isaiah 1–39 contains a wide variety of materials, some of which may not be from Isaiah of Jerusalem. There is also much in the book that sounds like the other prophets. Like the other eighth century B.C.E. prophets, Isaiah was a prophet of judgment. Isaiah's prophecy, however, had four distinct ideas which are:

1. The holiness of God.   Holiness has about it the idea of separation, of difference, or of distinction. Some speak of God's "otherness." For Isaiah, God's holiness or difference from man is, among other things, a moral difference. God is a moral being who demanded morality on the part of the worshiper (6:3).

2. A quiet, confident faith.   In addition to being holy, God is trustworthy. Isaiah's advice to both Ahaz and Hezekiah in times of crisis was to trust God, not military power (7:4, 15; 30:15).

3. A righteous remnant.   Judgment was sure to come on Israel, but its purpose was not to destroy but to purify the nation. A small group of holy people would survive who would form the basis of a new and righteous society (7:3; 10:20–23).

4. The Messiah.   The new age would be ruled by the ideal David. Isaiah may have hoped that Hezekiah would fulfill this dream, but later interpreters looked into the future for the LORD's Chosen One (9:2–7; 11:1–9).

MICAH: THE COUNTRY PREACHER

While Isaiah was counselor to the kings of Judah, a prophet from the country village of Moresheth-gath in the Philistine territory was also preaching the word of the LORD.

The Book

. The small book that bears Micah's name falls into four parts: oracles against Jerusalem (1:1–3:12); a new day for Israel (4:1–5:15); oracles against Israel (6:1–7:7); and Israel restored (7:8–20).

Oracles against Jerusalem (Micah 1:1–3:12).   Micah preached before the Northern Kingdom had fallen, so part of his preaching was directed toward Samaria and its sins. But the main use of Samaria and its sins was to say that Jerusalem was just like it. Just as the LORD's judgment was coming on Samaria, so it would come on Jerusalem (1:1–9).

Micah, like the other prophets, enjoyed using puns. In a series of puns in Hebrew which are not easily translated into English, he described the destruction of the small cities in the path of the invaders (1:10–16).

Micah reserved his most scathing comments for the upper classes of society. He accused them of lying awake, plotting to steal from the common man (2:1–5). They tried to stop the prophets of the LORD from prophesying the truth, prefering that a prophet would

> go about uttering empty falsehoods,
>   saying, "I will preach to you of wine and strong drink,"
> such a one would be the preacher for this people! (2:11)

The oracle was softened by a later addition which spoke of the righteous remnant (2:12–13).

Particularly biting was an oracle about the leaders of Judah. They hated good and loved evil. They were like cannibals,

> who tear the skin off my people,
>   and the flesh off their bones;
> who eat the flesh of my people,
>   flay their skin off them,
> break their bones in pieces,
>   and chop them up like meat in a kettle,
> like flesh in a caldron (3:2–3).

The LORD would not hear them on the day of judgment (3:1–4).

Prophets, too, felt the lash of Micah's tongue, especially those prophets who curried the favor of the rich. They would be disgraced, but the true prophet would be vindicated (3:5–7). Micah, of course, considered himself to be a true prophet:

> But as for me, I am filled with power,
>   with the spirit of the LORD,
>   and with justice and might,
> to declare to Jacob his transgression
>   and to Israel his sin (3:8).

Where Isaiah had said Jerusalem would not fall to the armies of Sennacherib in 701 B.C.E., Micah had no such faith in the future. The sins of the city's leaders were sure to bring doom. He foresaw a day when Zion would "be plowed like a field" and Jerusalem's hills would be covered with trees instead of houses (3:9–12).

A New Day Will Come (Micah 4:1–5:15).   In startling contrast to Chapters 1 through 3, this section of Micah speaks of restoration and a glorious future, leading many interpreters to say another prophet of a later time was responsible for it. The first passage (4:1–3), in particular, has questions raised about it because it also appears in Isaiah 2:2–4. It speaks of a time of universal peace when all nations would come to worship the LORD, the God of Israel. It would be a time when weapons of war would be turned into instruments of peace and safety (4:1–5). The crippled and rejected peoples of the earth would receive special attention from the LORD (4:6–8).

The next oracle speaks of the Babylonian exile and how the LORD will rescue his people from it. Under the LORD's plans, Israel would triumph over her enemies and live by the LORD's will. The present condition, however, was an enemy siege (4:9–5:1).

One of Micah's most famous sayings was the Bethlehem oracle (5:2–6). Since the messianic concept was connected with the Davidic monarchy, it would be quite natual to expect the birth of the future king to be connected to David's city, Bethlehem. This was quoted in the New Testament as a messianic prophecy (Matt. 2:6).

The remainder of Chapter 5 deals with the defeat of the Assyrian army and the restoration of the remnant of Jacob, who will be scattered "like dew from the LORD." The remnant would be purified from its worship of idols (5:7–15).

Oracles against Israel (Micah 6:1–7:7).   If only one sermon from Micah had survived, Micah 6:1–8 would be sufficient to rank him among the great prophets of Israel. In this oracle, he managed to sum up the important point of the message of each of the three other eighth-century prophets.

The oracle is a classic example of the use of court language by the prophet to present the LORD's case against Israel. The essentials of a trial are present:

1. The court is called to order (6:1–2).   The LORD, who is judge, jury, and prosecuting attorney, calls on the mountains and hills to be spectators at the trial and announces that the court is in session.

2. The indictment and the evidence is presented (6:3–5).   The indictment is presented in a series of questions (6:3) charging the people with being tired of the LORD. The LORD's past dealings with Israel are recalled to show that Israel has no right to complain.

3. The defense pleads its case (6:6–7).   Protesting their innocence, the people ask, "What more can we do? Does the LORD require more offerings?" If so, they would be willing to sacrifice even their first-born children.

4. The verdict is delivered (6:8).   What the defense had said was that whatever bribe the LORD demanded, the people would pay. But that was the heart of the matter. Material offerings, even first-born children, were meaningless when that was all that was offered.

> He has told you, O mortal, what is good;
>   and what does the LORD require of you
> but to do justice, and to love kindness,
>   and to walk humbly with your God? (6:8)

In this verse, Micah sets forth Amos' theme of justice; Hosea's theme of love (kindness); and Isaiah's theme of the quiet, confident walk with God.

Following this oracle, Micah spoke against cheating in the marketplace and oppression of the poor by the rich. These sins would bring the LORD's judgment in the form of famine and desolation (6:9–16). The LORD lamented the fact that good men had perished and that the ungodly seemed to be everywhere, ready to murder at every opportunity. Bribery was rampant; no one could be trusted; and children were disobedient to parents. In such an evil time, the only hope was to look to the LORD for salvation (7:1–7).

Israel's Triumph over Her Enemies (Micah.7:8–20).   Israel would not always be under the enemy's heel. The time would come when the LORD would deliver Israel and the enemy would be destroyed (7:8–10). The nations that despised Israel would be drawn to her (7:11–13).

Micah 7:14 is a prayer to the LORD as a shepherd to his flock; a response from the LORD follows in 7:15–17, promising a repeat of the marvels of the Exodus days. The nations would be subject to Israel instead of the reverse being true.

Finally, the book closes with a short psalm of praise to God:

> He will again have compassion upon us;
>   he will tread our iniquities under foot.
> You will cast all our sins into the depths of the sea.
> You will show faithfulness to Jacob,
>   and unswerving loyalty to Abraham,
> as you have sworn to our ancestors
>   from the days of old (7:19–20).

SUMMARY ON THE EIGHTH-CENTURY PROPHETS

The prophets of the eighth century in Israel and Judah—Amos, Hosea, Isaiah, and Micah—represent a remarkable flowering of religious genius. The only previous Israelite prophet who could compare with them was Elijah. What they called for was not something new, however, but for the reestablishment of the old values of the Sinai covenant.

Their favorite watchword was "return." They called for a return to a wholehearted commitment to "knowing the LORD" and a return to the principles of justice in dealing with one another, tempered by a sense of mercy and compassion.

STUDY QUESTIONS

1. What kept Rehoboam from enforcing his will over the northern tribes?
2. What happened to bring an end to the hostilities between Israel and Judah?
3. Who was Athaliah?
4. What was Uzziah able to accomplish?
5. What role did Ahaz play in the eventual downfall of Israel?
6. How did Judah manage to survive the Assyrian invasions that destroyed Israel and Syria in the later part of the eighth century (745–721 B.C.E.)?
7. What was the nature of Isaiah's call to be a prophet?
8. What was Isaiah's relationship to Ahaz? to Hezekiah?

9. Do you think Isaiah's advice to Ahaz in the Syro-Ephraimitic crisis was sound? Explain your answer.
10. What was the significance of the names Isaiah and his wife gave their children?
11. Why do you think Isaiah advised Hezekiah as he did concerning the Ashdod rebellion?
12. How did Hezekiah prepare for a possible invasion by the Assyrians during Sennacherib's reign?
13. What possible physical evidence has been found to confirm Hezekiah's reform?
14. Discuss the theory that Sennacherib invaded Judah twice.
15. What are the aguments for and against the unity of the book of Isaiah?
16. Know the distinct teachings of Isaiah 1–39 and one passage to support each.
17. Compare Isaiah's attitude toward Jerusalem to that of Micah.
18. What did Micah see as the evils of Israelite society?
19. Show how Micah 6:1–8 reflects the procedures of an ancient law court.

ENDNOTES

1. See J. Maxwell Miller and John H. Hayes, *A History of Ancient Israel and Judah* (Philadelphia: Westminster Press, 1986), 245–246, on Shishak's invasion.
2. On the military movements of Israel and Judah, see Johanan Aharoni and Michael Avi-Yonah, *MBA*, 122–123. For a description of the fortress, see G. Ernest Wright, *Biblical Archaeology,* 2nd ed., 151 ff.
3. See page 176f.
4. From now on Israel will be used in the older sense of all the Hebrew people, not just those of the northern portion of the country.
5. For a fuller discussion of the proposed identities of both mother and child, see John H. Hayes and Stuart A. Irvine, *Isaiah: The Eighth-Century Prophet, His Times and His Teaching* (Nashville: Abingdon Press, 1987), 135f.
6. Ze'ev Herzog, Miriam Aharoni, and Anson F. Rainey, "Arad—An Ancient Israelite Fortress with a Temple to Yahweh," *BAR* (March/April, 1987) reprinted in "The Best of *BAR*," I, Hershel Shanks and Dan P. Cole, eds. (Washington: Biblical Archaelogy Society, 1990), 203–224. See also Albertz, *The History of Israelite Religion,* trans. John Bowden (Louisville: Westminster/ John Knox, 1994, 180ff.

7. On Hezekiah's role in the rebellion against Sennacherib, see Noth, *A History of Israel,* 265–267.
8. Dan Gill, "How They Met," *BAR XX,* 4 (July/August), 22–33. In the same issue of *BAR*, see also, Simon B. Parker, "Siloam Inscription Memorializes Engineering Achievement," 36–38.
9. John Bright, *A History of Israel,* 3rd ed., 298–309, has an extended discussion of this problem. Noth, *The History of Israel,* 268ff., sees only one invasion, which left Hezekiah as an Assyrian vassal.
10. As far as the writer of this text is concerned, the point at issue in this statement for either view is not God's ability to do what he willed with the prophet. The central question then was, "What *did* God do?" not "What *could* God do?" I believe that the prophets spoke primarily about their own times and circumstances.
11. For a discussion of this possibility see Sigmund Mowinckel, *He That Cometh,* (Nashville: Abingdon Press, 1954), 104f. For a differing interpretation, see John H. Hayes and Stuart A. Irvine, *Isaiah: The Eighth Century Prophet,* 180ff.

Chapter 10 🌿

JUDAH

Manasseh to Zedekiah and the Exile

Judah's last century started badly with the reign of Manasseh, saw some of the nation's best days under Josiah, and ended with the death of Judah under Zedekiah. One hundred years after the death of Hezekiah, the nations died in the flames of Jerusalem; but the remnant survived on the banks of the Tigris and Euphrates Rivers.

THE INTERNATIONAL SITUATION

The rivalry between Assyria and Egypt continued and, as usual, Judah was caught in the middle. After Sennacherib's murder by two of his sons, a third son, Esarhadon (680–669 B.C.E.) became king and proved to be more than able to bring his vast empire under control. Babylon was the first victim. Egypt was soon to follow in 671. Asshur-banapal, Essarhadon's son and successor, had to deal twice with a rebellion in Egypt. It finally was smashed when the ancient capital of Thebes, located in southern Egypt, was captured in 663. Egypt was left in a weakened state for a period of time.

THE SITUATION IN JUDAH

Bad Days Under Manasseh (2 Kings 21:1–18; 2 Chron. 33:1–20)

Israel's historians had little good to say about Manasseh. Both the Bible and Assyrian records indicate that he was a puppet king. Second Chronicles 33:10–13 tells how he once was bound with chains and taken before an Assyrian king at Babylon.[1]

His reign saw a rebirth of Baal worship in Judah. He rebuilt the high places, where he set up altars to the Canaanite fertility gods and goddesses. He also built altars in the Temple area for the worship of the star deities ("the host of heaven"), also showing Assyrian influence. He practiced human sacrifice, even burning his own son on an altar to a pagan god, and he encouraged the practices of black magic and fortune-telling. Those who opposed him were severely persecuted:

> Manasseh shed very much innocent blood, until he had filled Jerusalem from one end to another (2 Kings 21:16).

Josiah, the Boy King (2 Kings 22:1–23:30)

When Amon (642–640 B.C.E.) tried to continue the policies of his father Manasseh, he signed his own death warrant. After ruling two years, he was assassinated. His eight-year old son, Josiah, was put on the throne in his place.

Josiah's Early Years.   Josiah (640–609 B.C.E.) came to the throne at a time when Assyria was fading as a world power. Egypt was still weak, and Babylon had not yet become a threat to the western states. Since he was only eight years old, the government actually was controlled by the high priest, who was the chief religious official of the kingdom (2 Kings 22:1–2).

First attempts at reform (2 Chron. 34:1–7).   Hilkiah, the high priest, influenced Josiah to take strong action early in his reign to destroy the pagan religions that Manasseh had so ardently promoted. This activity extended even into the cities of the old Northern Kingdom. This seems to have begun in 627 B.C.E., the year that Asshur-banapal, the last strong Assyrian king, died.[2]

The Prophet Zephaniah (Zeph. 1:1–3:20)

1. His life.   Before Josiah's reform had made too much headway, the prophet Zephaniah seems to have been active. Little is known about Zephaniah except that his ancestry was traced back to Hezekiah. It probably is safe to assume that this was

King Hezekiah. This would mean that Zephaniah was related to the royal family. Although he preached during Josiah's reign (1:1), the nature of his preaching would indicate that his ministry took in the early years of Josiah, perhaps from 640 to 630.

2. The book. The major idea in the book of Zephaniah is the day of the LORD, which indicates that the traditions about Amos had had significant influence on him. Many of the phrases in Zephaniah's description of the day of the LORD are almost direct quotes from Amos, especially Amos 5:18–20 and 8:9–14.

a. The LORD's sweeping judgment (Zeph. 1:2–6). The LORD's judgment would devastate land and sea. The special object of that judgment would be Judah's idols and those who worshipped them—the Baalites; the worshipers of the heavenly bodies; the followers of Milcom, an Ammonite deity; and any others who had turned from the LORD.

b. The high and the mighty of Jerusalem (Zeph. 1:7–13). Judgment would begin at the top, where responsibility was the greatest. It was Judah's leaders who had led the people astray, and judgment would reach even to the royal family itself. Among the pagan practices they observed was the custom of leaping over the threshold or doorsill because they believed a demon lived there. If one stepped on it, evil would result. The custom of carrying the bride over the threshold may have had its origin in a similar belief (1:7–9).

From the palace, the judgment would sweep on through the city, where the merchants hawked their wares. The LORD is pictured as going though the city with a lamp, searching every nook and cranny, trying to find the cynical men of Judah who had said that he would not do anything to them. They were compared to wine that had become thick and useless because the lees—small sandlike particles— settled to the bottom of the wineskins as the wine aged (1:10–13).

c. The great day of the LORD (Zeph. 1:14–18). In tones like Amos, Zephaniah described the day of the LORD that was rapidly approaching. It would be a day of wrath,

> a day of distress and anguish,
> a day of ruin and devastation,
>   a day of darkness and gloom,
> a day of clouds and thick darkness,
>   a day of trumpet blast and battle cry
> against the fortified cities
>   and against the lofty battlements (1:15–16).

d. Hope for the righteous (Zeph. 2:1–3). Zephaniah did see hope for the humble people of the land, who would come to the LORD and "seek righteouness" and "seek humility."

Figure 10–1. The kingdom of Judah—seventh century B.C.E.

e. Devastation on the nations (Zeph. 2:4–15).   As was common among the prophets, Zephaniah did not see the day of the LORD's judgment as being limited to Judah. Judgment would come as well on Judah's enemies, for they too were rebels against the LORD. The Philistines (2:4–7), Moab and Ammon (2:8–11), Ethiopia (Egypt) (2:12), and Assyria (2:13–15) would know the wrath of the LORD. Of Assyria, he said:

> Herds shall lie down in it,
>   . . . .
> the owl shall hoot at the window,
>   the raven croak on the threshhold;
>   for its cedarwork will be laid bare.
>   . . . .
> What a desolation it has become,
>   a lair for wild animals!
> Everyone who passes by it
>   hisses and shakes the fist (2:14–15).

f. Woe to Jerusalem (Zeph. 3:1–7).   Having pronounced the LORD's judgment on Judah's enemies, Zephaniah once more turned to Jerusalem and her officials. He compared her officials to beasts of prey (the lion and the wolf). Her prophets were immoral men, disgraces to the name of the One whom they claimed to represent. The LORD alone was concerned with justice. There was no responsible human representative to see that it was done.

g. A better day is coming (Zeph. 3:8–13).   The net effect of the LORD's judgment would be to cleanse the earth. The defiled speech that began with man's rebellion at the Tower of Babel would be purified when the people were brought back to the land (3:8–10). Sins would be forgiven, and pride would be no more. In its place, the people would be humble and lowly, teachable and truthful (3:11–13).

h. Jerusalem shall be restored (Zeph. 3:14–20).   The climax of the new day would be the restoration of Jerusalem. Judgment would achieve its purpose of cleansing the nation. When the people were once more gathered in the land, days of mourning would become festival days.

Changes under Josiah (2 Kings 22:3–23:27)[3]

Finding the scroll (2 Kings 22:3–20).   If the chief priest hoped to shape the young king's thinking to cause a return to the basic religious foundations of the nation, he did a good job. Efforts at reform may have begun as early as 630 B.C.E. and gained intensity as the years passed.

In 622, an important event took place. On instructions from Josiah, a major cleansing of the Temple began under the direction of Hilkiah, the chief priest (22:3–7). In the process of cleaning out the building, a scroll containing a version of the Law of Moses was found. The manuscript was taken to the king's secretary, Shaphan, who in turn reported its discovery to the king (22:8–10).

When the scroll was read to Josiah, he was greatly upset and tore his clothes in despair. He immediately gave orders that Huldah, a prophetess, should be consulted as to the course of action that should be taken (22:11–13). The oracle that Huldah gave spoke of the LORD's displeasure at idol worship in Judah, but it promised that Josiah would prosper because of his pentitent attitude (22:14–20).

Covenant renewal and religious reform (2 Kings 23:1–17).   When Josiah received word of Huldah's oracle, he led the people in a ceremony of covenant renewal (23:1–3). But he went further than just pledging to keep the law of the LORD; he applied the law in practical ways to the situation. Josiah's actions, based on the law that had been discovered, have led scholars to conclude that the scroll was the major part of what is known today as the Book of Deuteronomy. Thus they refer to Josiah's reform as the Deuteronomic reformation.

His first major step was an attempt to rid the land of pagan cults. In Jerusalem, many altars to pagan deities had been erected in Manasseh's time. These were destroyed, along with various images that were part of the worship. Extending the purge further, orders were given that not only were the altars in Judah to be destroyed, but also the altars in northern cities, such as Bethel. To rid the land of their influence, those who were priests at the pagan shrines were slain.

Next, Josiah ordered the celebration of a great passover, reminding the people of the LORD's mighty acts in bringing them out of the land of Egypt (23:21–23). This reminder of the LORD's covenant with Moses was a call for revival of the old-time religion that had, for the most part, been forgotten, replaced by the emphasis on the covenant with David. So impressive were the passover services that the historian said of them:

> No such passover had been kept since the days of the judges who judged Israel, or during the days of the kings of Israel or the kings of Judah (23:22).

A most important aspect of the reform was the gathering of all the priests of the LORD in Jerusalem for the purpose of centralizing of all worship services in the Jerusalem Temple. This was to assure that the worship would be kept pure, not mixed with elements of pagan worship. While this was a noble idea, one major result of the action would prove fatal to the whole reform. Out of the centralizing of worship developed the ideas that: (1) the Temple was the LORD's dwelling place; (2) the LORD would never permit his dwelling to be destroyed; and (3) since the Temple was located in Jerusalem, Jerusalem would never be destroyed, since the LORD lived there in the Temple. The conclusion that Jerusalem was safe from all attack, furthermore, seemed to be supported by Isaiah's words, spoken during the days of Sennacherib's invasions, to the effect that Jerusalem was protected by the LORD (Isa. 37:33–35; 2 Kings 19:32–34).

Meanwhile, in the Rest of the World.   Josiah had been able to operate so freely because Assyria was so weak that it was on the verge of being completely eliminated from the international scene. The beginning of the end came when the

Photograph by John H. Tullock.

Figure 10–2.   "King Josiah went to meet him; but when Pharaoh
Neco met him at Megiddo, he killed him" (2 Kings
23:29). Josiah lost his life on this famous battlefield,
called the Plain of Megiddo or Esdralon, when he tried
to block Egypt's invasion of the Babylonian Empire.

Babylonians gained their independence and joined the Medes in an attack on Assyria. The Egyptians came to the aid of Assyria, but it was a case of too little—too late. In 614, the Medes captured Asshur, Assyria's early capital. In 612, the combined forces of the Medes and Babylonians captured and destroyed Nineveh. The final blows came with the fall of Haran and the failure of an attempt by the Assyrians to recapture it. The giant was dead.[4]

The Death of Josiah (2 Kings 23:28–30; 2 Chron. 35:2–27).   Josiah, the most capable of the Judean kings, died a tragic death on the famous battlefield of Megiddo. Pharaoh Neco of Egypt was pushing northward along the coastal highway to try to stop the advance of the Medo-Babyloniah armies at Carchemish. For some unknown reason, Josiah chose to try to stop Neco; but he only succeeded in getting himself killed. The year was 609. His death would set in motion a chain of events that would lead to the death of the nation itself.[5]

TWO PROPHETS AND KING JEHOIAKIM

Of the two prophets, Habakkuk and Nahum, only Habakkuk was directly concerned with the fate of Judah, while Nahum concerned himself with the destruction of Nineveh, the capital of Assyria.

Nahum: Prophet of the LORD's Vengeance on Nineveh

Almost nothing is known of Nahum. He is called *Nahum of Elkosh* in 1:1. Speculation about the location of Elkosh suggest it was either in Judah, the Galilee region, or Mesopotamia. The name of the city of Capernaum, famous in the New Testament, literally means "village of Na(h)um." This probably is the basis of believing Elkosh was located in Galilee. The only thing that could be said with certainty about Nahum was that he hated the Assyrians. The book dates from about 612 B.C.E. It mentions the plunder of Thebes (Nah. 3:8), which took place in 663, and thus it could not be earlier than that date. Since Nineveh was destroyed in 612, that would seem to be the latest year one should date the book.

The LORD is a Jealous God (Nah. 1:1–11).   The book starts with an ancient poem of the LORD as an avenging God. It is an acrostic—that is, different letters of the alphabet start each line. Since not all the letters of the Hebrew alphabet are used, it is an incomplete acrostic. The poem may be original with Nahum, or he may be quoting it from some other source.

The LORD punishes those who have set themselves against him (1:2–3a), using the forces of nature to carry out the judgment (1:3b–5). No one can endure the wrath of the LORD, for

> He will make a full end to his adversaries,
>   and will pursue his enemies into darkness (1:8).

Behind this idea of the LORD as the avenger is the basic idea that the LORD is the God of justice, the one who can set things right in the universe. The LORD's enemies are those who would destroy the principle of justice in the earth, but things will be set right. The LORD's vengeance is directed toward punishing the guilty and righting things that have been made wrong.

You Are Doomed, Nineveh (Nah. 1:12–3:19).   In what is probably the most powerful poetry in the Bible, Nahum describes the fate of Nineveh, the capital of the hated Assyrian Empire. There is little that is positive in the poem except the words of assurance to Judah in 1:12–13 and 1:15, where Judah was told that it would be delivered from the Assyrian threats. Between these words of assurance were words of doom for Assyria (1:14).

In vivid language, Nahum described the fall of the doomed city. First came the warning of the approaching armies (2:1), followed by a description of the invaders.

The scarlet-clad soldiers were accompanied by the gleaming metal war chariots that flashed like torches under the dazzling Mesopotamian sun (2:3–4). The defenders of the city were caught unprepared for the attack. They rushed about in confusion, trying to organize the defense; but it was all in vain (2:5). The invaders were already inside the city walls, even in the king's palace, carrying off the queen. To describe the fall of the city, the poet used the image of a dam breaking, releasing the waters of a pool (2:6–8). As a result:

> Devastation, desolation, and destruction!
>   Hearts faint and knees tremble,
> all loins quake, all faces grow pale! (2:10)

In another powerful poem (3:1–19), one hears the sound of the pounding horse's hooves and the rumble of chariots on cobblestone streets (3:1–3). Nineveh was like a harlot who had lost her allure, who now would be stripped naked and assaulted with manure. She was now viewed with contempt (3:4–7).

Nineveh was no better than other great cities that had fallen, such as Thebes, the ancient capital of Egypt. No matter how strong Nineveh's defenses might be, nor how large her population, she was doomed. Her unceasing evil would soon end, and she would be wiped from the face of the earth (3:8–19).

The Reigns of Jehoiakim and Jehoiachin (2 Kings 23:31–24:17)

Josiah's death brought radical changes in Judah. The reign of his son Jehoahaz (609 B.C.E.), who had succeeded him, was cut short by Pharaoh Neco of Egypt. Once more Judah was put under a foreign overlord. Jehoahaz was imprisoned and died in Egypt (23:31–34).

In his place, the Egyptians made his brother Eliakim king. When Eliakim became king, his name was changed to Jehoiakim (23:34). Among some peoples, the king always took a new name when he became ruler. Such may have been the case in Israel, but this is the only direct evidence of it.

Jehoiakim (609–597 B.C.E.) paid heavy tribute to the Egyptians the first few years of his reign. That did not keep him from spending rather extravagantly for his own comfort, however. At Beth-kerem, just south of Jerusalem, he had an elaborate palace built, which was to draw the fire of the prophet Jeremiah:

> Woe to him who builds his house by unrighteousness,
>   and his upper rooms by injustice;
> who makes his neighbors work for nothing,
>   and does not give them their wages;
> who says, "I will build myself a spacious house
>   with large upper rooms,"
> and who cuts out windows for it,
>   paneling it with cedar,

and painting it with vermilion.
Are you a king because you compete in cedar? (22:13–15a)

The remains of his palace have been found, and some of the stones still have traces of the bright red paint.[6]

Jehoiakim's loyalties changed in 605 when the Babylonian army defeated Egypt at the battle of Carchemish in northern Mesopotamia. The only thing that kept the Babylonians from sweeping southward through Palestine was the death of Nabopolassar, the ruler of Babylon. He was succeeded by Nebuchadnezzar, who demanded and got Jehoiakim's submission with the resulting money payment.

Hosea's earlier description of Israel as a "silly dove" (Hos. 7:11), flitting first to one great power and then the other, was an apt description of Jehoiakim. By 601, he had switched his loyalties back to Egypt. The Babylonians, having seized control of the Coastal Plain by 602, fought a battle with Pharaoh Neco's forces in 601. Both sides suffered heavy losses, causing Nebuchadnezzar to withdraw from Palestine for a time to lick his wounds. Jehoiakim quickly switched his allegiance to Egypt. It was a fatal mistake.

In 598, the Babylonians invaded Judah with force. It was a convenient time for Jehoiakim to die, and he did—either from natural causes or by assassination (2 Kings 24:1–6). His son Jehoiachin (597 B.C.E.) succeeded him, coming to the throne just in time to be captured when the city fell in 597. Several thousand people—including the king, his mother, many of Jerusalem's leading citizens, and an enormous amount of booty—were taken to Babylon. Most of the people, among them a priest named Ezekiel, were settled in villages along a large irrigation canal called the River Chebar (Ezek. 1:1). Babylonian records describe the event and speak of the spoils of the victory. Jehoiachin would remain a captive until 560, when he was released and made a ward of the Babylonian royal court (2 Kings 25:27–30).

Habakkuk: The Philosopher Prophet

If philosophers are people who ask important questions, then Habakkuk must be called a philosopher. While most prophets said, "Thus says the LORD," or "thus the LORD is about to do," Habakkuk said, "Why, LORD, are you about to do what you are about to do?"

The Man. Nothing personal is known about Habakkuk. Unlike other prophets, no mention is made of his family or birthplace. Other than a brief mention in a book of the Apocrypha, no other mention is made of him in any Jewish religious literature. What can be learned of him has to come from the way he approached his work as the LORD's spokesman.

The Book. Set in the time when the Babylonians were threatening to overrun Judah, Habakkuk raised some searching questions about the meaning of God's activity in the events of his day, the period from about 609 to 597 B.C.E. The writers of the Dead Sea Scrolls interpreted the prophet's words as bearing directly on their own situation (165 B.C.E.–70 C.E.). A commentary on Habakkuk 1–2 interprets the reference to the Chaldeans as meaning the Romans.

The book falls naturally into three sections: 1:1–2:5, Habakkuk's questions; 2:6–20, woes; and 3:1–19, a psalm entitled "Habakkuk's prayer."

Habakkuk's questions (Hab. 1:1–2:5). The first question was this: "LORD, how long must this flouting of your will go on?" Who was flouting the LORD's will? Was it the people of Judah? Or was it the Babylonians? He probably was referring to the situation in Judah that developed after Josiah's death.

The answer to the question came: The Chaldeans (Babylonians) were being sent to punish the Judeans for disobeying the will of the LORD (1:5–11).

That answer shocked Habakkuk and brought forth a second question: "LORD, how can you punish us with people who are more unrighteous than we are?" After all, the Babylonians were cruel and merciless pagans who were catching small nations in their nets as fishermen catch fish (1:12–17).

Since the answer did not come immediately, the prophet mounted a watchtower to see what the LORD would do (2:1). Then the answer came: The LORD did things in his own good time. The man who would survive and live was the man who was faithful to the LORD. The great Christian Apostle Paul quoted Habakkuk 2:4 in his letter to the Galatians (3:11): "The just shall live by faith." Later, in the sixteenth century C.E., this verse was instrumental in setting Martin Luther on his way to the beginning of the Protestant Reformation.

"Woe to him" (Hab. 2:6–20). The woes, a common feature of prophetic oracles, are directed toward five groups: (1) Woe to him whose greed drove him to plunder to get riches; (2) woe to the violent man; (3) woe to the bloody man; (4) woe to the drunkard; and (5) woe to the idol maker.

Habakkuk's prayer (Hab. 3:1–19). The psalm has the name of a tune by which it was to be sung, indicating that it was used in the worship services of the Temple. It was used to praise the LORD's mighty works (3:1–15). The exodus events are described in highly figurative language:

> The mountain saw you, and writhed:
> a torrent of water swept by;
> . . . .
> In fury you trod the earth,
> in anger you trampled nations.
> . . . .
> You trampled the sea with your horses,
> churning the mighty waters (3:10, 12, 15).

The psalmist was overcome by what he had seen of the LORD's activity and waited expectantly for what he would do to the invaders (3:16). This caused him to rejoice, even though all else failed around him, for

God, the LORD is my strength;
    he makes my feet like the feet of the deer,
    and makes me tread upon the heights (3:19).

JEREMIAH, ZEDEKIAH, AND THE LAST DAYS OF JUDAH

To have to preach about people's sins and shortcomings made the lot of the prophet a hard one. But to have to advocate surrender to the hated enemy and to be called a traitor was the fate of Jeremiah, the last great prophet of the days of the Israelite kings.

Jeremiah's Early Life and Call (Jer. 1:1–19)

Jeremiah was from a priestly family who lived in Anathoth. It was the village where Abiathar, David's friend, who supported Adonijah as David's successor, had been exiled. Jeremiah probably was a descendant of Abiathar.

He preached during the reigns of Josiah, Jehoiakim, and Zedekiah and continued until he was taken by a group of rebels in 582 to Egypt, where he died.

The Call (Jer. 1:1–19).   The traditional date for the call of Jeremiah as a prophet is 626 B.C.E. This is based on Jer. 1:2, which says, "To whom the word of the LORD came in the days of Josiah . . . in the thirteenth year of his reign." A problem arises with the 626 date when Jeremiah mentions a threat of a northern enemy against Palestine (1:13–19).

Advocates of the 626 date believe that Jeremiah's "foe from the north" was the Scythians, a people about whom little is known. They were from east of the Persian Gulf and were one of the peoples who gave Assyria increasing problems as its empire declined. If they did invade the West, as the Greek historian Herodotus says, it would have been about the time that Jeremiah was called. There is little hard evidence, however, that such an invasion took place.[7]

The more realistic threat from the north was the Babylonians. For this reason, some interpreters would date Jeremiah's call in 616, rather than 626. These interpreters argue that Babylonians were the real "foe from the north." As to the dating in "the thirteenth year of Josiah," it is explained as a scribal mistake that should read "the twenty-third year of Josiah." This argument does not convince many scholars, however, with the result that most still date Jeremiah's call in 626 B.C.E.

Jeremiah's ministry compares to that of Isaiah's in length, especially if his call came in 626. It extended over part or all of the reigns of five kings, as well as the rule of Gedeliah, the governor of the Babylonian province that included Judah. His influence, both positive and negative, extended across all lines of society and even across national boundaries. In the call, several interesting features appear:

1. He felt that the LORD had destined him to be a prophet even before he was born (1:5ab).
2. He was called to minister over national boundaries (1:5c).
3. He was still quite young when he became conscious of his call (1:6). His protest that he "was only a youth" probably means he was still in his teens.
4. The LORD assured Jeremiah that he would be with him and take care of him (1:7–8).
5. Jeremiah was called to be a prophet to the nations. His message, while one of judgment, would lead to a positive result (1:9–10).

Two visions were part of the call of Jeremiah: the vision of the almond tree and the vision of the boiling pot. As with the visions of Amos, Jeremiah's visions involved ordinary things that took on a deep spiritual meaning.

The vision of the almond tree (1:11–12) involves a pun, as did Amos' vision of the summer fruit. The noun *shaqed* in Hebrew meant "almond tree," while the verb "to watch" was *shoqed*. Jeremiah said, "I see a rod of almond (*shaqed*). The LORD answered, "You have seen well, for I am watching (*shoqed*) over my word to perform it" (1:12). The point was that the LORD would perform as promised. The almond tree would remind Jeremiah of that assurance.

The vision of the boiling pot probably came when Jeremiah saw someone spill a pot of hot water. As he watched the water sweep along the twigs and pebbles before it, the message came that a foe from the north would sweep over the land and sweep away its inhabitants (1:13–15). Jeremiah was told to preach that judgment courageously in the face of all opposition (1:16–19).

His Early Ministry.   What did Jeremiah think of the reform under Josiah? This is one of the mysteries surrounding the book of Jeremiah. Little is said of Jeremiah's relations to Josiah, either in the Book of Jeremiah or in the history in 2 Kings. Whether Jeremiah preached at all during Josiah's reign is uncertain, although some would assign the oracles in chapters 2 to 6 to that period.[8] If that is so, he had a rather low estimate of the value of the reform movement. His personal evaluation of Josiah appears in 22:15–16, where he compares Josiah and Jehoiakim:

> Are you a king because you compete in cedar?
> Did not your father eat and drink
>   and do justice and righteousness?
> Then it was well with him.
> He judged the cause of the poor and needy;
>   then it was well.
> Is not this to know me?
>   says the LORD.[9]

The Book.   Another mystery about Jeremiah relates to the arrangement of the book that bears his name. In Chapter 36, there is a description of the writing of what probably was the first edition of the book. Jeremiah hired a scribe named Baruch to write down all the oracles that he had given to that date (605 B.C.E.). When Baruch did so, he was instructed by Jeremiah to read them in the Temple. At that time, for some unknown reason, Jeremiah was barred from the Temple (36:1–8). When the scroll was read, it caused quite a reaction. Officials of King Jehoiakim's court who were still friendly to Jeremiah thought it should be taken to the king. When Jehoiakim heard it, he burned it, a sheet at a time. Jeremiah then redictated the scroll, adding a number of oracles to it (36:9–32). That edition may be Chapters 1 to 25, since Chapter 26 starts a second version of a story found in Chapter 7.

The mystery about the book is that it is as if someone had each chapter on a single sheet, threw them down the stairs, and then arranged them in the order in which they were picked up. There seems to be little purpose in the way the book is arranged. For this reason, the dated prose sections will be discussed in chronological order as nearly as possible. Then the oracles will be discussed as they appear.

Jeremiah and Jehoiakim

If Jeremiah admired Josiah, his admiration did not carry over to his son, Jehoiakim. From the beginning of Jehoiakim's reign, Jeremiah was in big trouble.

The Temple Sermon (Jer. 7:1–15; 26:1–24). In the year 609, Jehoiakim was placed on the throne of Judah by Pharaoh Neco of Egypt. In that same year, Jeremiah appeared in the Temple during a festival to preach a scathing sermon. Its theme was as follows:

> Amend your ways and your doings, and let me dwell with you in this place. Do not trust in these deceptive words: "This is the temple of the LORD, the temple of the LORD, the temple of the LORD" (7:3–4).

Versions of this sermon appear in both Jeremiah 7 and 26. Chapter 7 contains a fuller version of the sermon. It attacked the popular notion that the LORD would not permit Jerusalem to be destroyed because the Temple was located there. Instead, the people's only hope was a return to the great moral principles of the Sinai Covenant. If the people did not change their ways, Jerusalem's fate would be the same as Shiloh's, one of Israel's earliest shrines. It had been destroyed by the Philistines in 1050 B.C.E. (7:5–15; 26:2–6).

If Jeremiah hoped to move the people to action, he was not disappointed. The action, however, was directed toward him. He was seized and threatened with death (26:7–9). Word got to the community leaders about the commotion in the Temple. Jeremiah was saved from lynching, but he was put on trial for his life on the charge of blasphemy—that is, cursing the Temple, which was the LORD's dwelling place. This meant that he was cursing the LORD.

A formal trial followed. First, the evidence against Jeremiah was presented (26:10–11). Then, Jeremiah spoke in his own defense. He admitted saying what he had said and even repeated the essentials of his sermon (26:12–13). Having done that, he threw himself on the mercy of the court, but not without warning it that if he were put to death, an innocent man would be dying (26:14–15). When the verdict came, Jeremiah was declared "not guilty." The judges cited Micah 3:12, where Micah had also predicted Jerusalem's destruction. They pointed out that Hezekiah did not put Micah to death, therefore Jeremiah should be freed (26:16–19).

Another prophet, Uriah, who made a similar prophecy, was not so fortunate. He fled to Egypt, but Jehoiakim brought him back and put him to death (26:20–23). Jeremiah still had powerful friends who protected him (26:24).

Jeremiah's Conflict with Jehoiakim.   By 605, Jeremiah was in trouble with Jehoiakim. In a symbolic action that involved burying a linen waistcloth on the banks of the Euphrates River, he criticized Jehoiakim for submitting to the Babylonians. When he dug it up later, it was soiled. Judah's relations to Babylon would cause her to be as soiled and as useless as the waistcloth (13:1–11).

Another action that aroused Jehoiakim's ire came when Jeremiah and a group of his supporters went to the Valley of Hinnom. There Jehoiakim had set up altars to Baal and had practiced child sacrifice. Jeremiah condemned the pagan cults. He smashed a flask to symbolize how the LORD would smash Jerusalem and its inhabitants for following false gods (19:1–15).

Jeremiah was arrested by Pashhur, a Temple official. He was beaten and placed in stocks for public ridicule. When he was released the next day, Jeremiah denounced Pashhur and repeated his warning, with a private word of judgment for Pashhur (20:1–6). This may have been the action by Jeremiah that resulted in his being barred from the Temple. This would have been the time when Baruch became his secretary and wrote the first edition of his book.[10]

Finally Jeremiah warned Jehoiakim that Babylon would come and destroy Judah. This warning may have come after the battle of Carchemish in 605, or it could have been a warning that preceded the Babylonian invasion of 598, which led to the first fall of Jerusalem. In any case, Jeremiah saw it as the certain judgment on Jerusalem for the people's failure to follow the law of the LORD (25:1–14).

Jeremiah and Jehoiachin

Jehoiachin's reign (598–597 B.C.E.) was so brief that Jeremiah said little about him. In an oracle in 22:24–30, he spoke of Jehoiachin (whom he called Coniah) as being like "a despised broken pot." He was to be considered childless since none of his children would ever succeed him as king of Judah (22:30).

Jeremiah and Zedekiah

Jeremiah's and Zedekiah's relationship was most unusual. When Jerusalem fell in 597, Zedekiah was put on the throne by the Babylonians. He was the son of Josiah and thus the uncle of the previous king. The Babylonians seem not to have deported all the leadership in 597, but seem to have left those they thought would be loyal to them. Their loyalty was short-lived! Soon there was a powerful group that was pressuring Zedekiah to declare his independence from Babylon or to switch his loyalties to Egypt. A group of "righteous ones," probably led by some of the prophets, kept insisting that the LORD had permitted the exile only as a temporary punishment. It would end in a year or so with a dramatic deliverance of the people. Zedekiah seems to have responded to whichever group was exerting the most pressure. He respected Jeremiah enough to ask him for advice, but he was too weak to carry out the advice he received.

The Vision of the Figs (Jer. 24:1–10). Jeremiah's opinion of the exiles, as compared to those left in the land, is shown by the vision of the figs. To steal some lines from a nursery rhyme, the figs could be described as follows:

> The basket that was good was very, very good,
>   but the one that was bad was horrid.

For Jeremiah, the good figs represented those taken into exile; but the bad figs were those who had been left behind.

True and False Prophets: The Sign of the Yoke (Jer. 27:1–28:17). Pressure began to mount on Zedekiah to break away from Babylon as soon as Nebuchadnezzar, the Babylonian king, lessened the pressure on the city after its capture. Two things had led to this situation: (1) A revolt in Babylon involving some of Nebuchadnezzar's army. Some of the Jews who were in exile may also have been involved. (2) The accession of a new king, Psammethicus II (594–589 B.C.E.), to the throne of Egypt. He and his successor, Hophra (589–570 B.C.E.), both encouraged rebellion against Babylon.[11] The court prophets encouraged Judah to join the revolt, preaching that the LORD was about to deliver the exiles and bring them home. Those who opposed them were branded as traitors and unbelievers.

Jeremiah aroused the ire of the superpatriots by consistently insisting that Judah's only hope of survival lay in being loyal subjects of Nebuchadnezzar. To emphasize his point, he made a wooden yoke like that used to hitch oxen to a plow and wore it on his neck. This object lesson was to emphasize the wisdom of Judah's wearing the yoke of Babylon (27:1–22).

Hananiah, a leader of the superpatriots and a prophet from Gibeon, grabbed Jeremiah's wooden yoke and broke it. The LORD, he said, had broken Babylon's yoke and would return the exiles to the land in two years. Jeconiah (Jehoiachin), furthermore, would be restored to his rightful place as king (28:1–4; 10–11).

Jeremiah replied that he hoped Hananiah was right, but that the real proof would rest on whether his words came true (28:5–9). Later, Jeremiah came back with yoke bars made of iron. He told Hananiah that not only would Babylon's yoke not be broken, but that Hananiah himself would die (28:12–16).

In that same year, in the seventh month, Hananiah died (28:17).

The Letter to the Exiles (Jer. 29:1–32). About 593, to help defuse the situation in Babylon and to help the exiles get a better hold on reality, Jeremiah wrote a letter. He made four major points:

1. Live as normally as possible. Do those things that would be done if you were at home and the country were at peace (29:4–6).

2. Be good citizens. What is good for Babylon is good for the exiles, for "in its welfare you will find your welfare" (29:7).
3. Pay no attention to the superpatriots and false prophets. They are just trying to deceive you. The LORD did not send them (29:8–9).
4. When the time is right, the LORD will bring you home (29:10–14). This is the meaning of the phrase *when seventy years are completed for Babylon.* In the same connection, Ezekiel would use forty years as his symbol for a complete period (Ezek. 4:6).

Jeremiah specifically named two prophets who were stirring up trouble—Ahab and Zedekiah. Nebuchadnezzar would soon snuff out their lives, for they were nothing but liars and deceivers (29:15–23). He had a further word to say to Shemaiah, who had written to Zephaniah, a Jerusalem priest, telling him to arrest Jeremiah and put him in the stocks. Zephaniah was Jeremiah's friend, however, and shared the letter with him. When he heard it, Jeremiah predicted the doom of Shemaiah (29:24–32).

The Babylonian Invasion (Jer. 34:1–7).   Zedekiah's rebellion brought a disaster. Jeremiah warned him that his only hope for a peaceful death with a proper burial was to surrender to Nebuchadnezzar, the king of Babylonia. By early 588, all the other cities of Judah had fallen, except Jerusalem, Lachish, and Azekah (34:1–7). The Lachish letters, found in the ruins of that city a few years ago, describe the desperate situation. As a significant passage from one of the letters says:

> We are watching for the signals of Lachish, according to all the indications which my lord has given, for we cannot see Azekah.[12]

This letter, written to the commander of the garrison at Lachish, indicated that Azekah had fallen and it would only be a matter of time until Jerusalem and Lachish would fall also. There may also be a reference to Uriah, the prophet mentioned in Jeremiah 26:20–24, or a reference to Jeremiah himself in the letters, but this is uncertain.

False Dealings with the Slaves (Jer. 34:8–22).   The situation became so desperate in Jerusalem that Zedekiah was willing to do almost anything to improve it. One of the things he did was to persuade the people to free all their Israelite slaves. Such people usually were slaves because they were unable to pay debts they owed. The law provided, however, that such would never be held in bondage for more than six years against their will (Exod. 21:1–6; Deut. 15:12–18). It seems that by Jeremiah's time, this was largely being ignored. Zedekiah thus was reviving an ancient religious practice, thereby invoking divine favor. From a practical standpoint, the freed slaves would be more likely to fight for the city if free. Then, too, the owners would no longer be responsible for feeding them in a time when food was becoming increasingly scarce.

Scarcely had the action been taken when it was withdrawn and the freed people were once more enslaved. The probable cause for this reversal was the lifting of the siege of Jerusalem when the Egyptians marched out to oppose the Babylonians. Feeling that the threat was removed from the city, the wealthy men seized their former slaves and enslaved them again. Jeremiah warned that because of their dishonesty, the LORD would grant a release to them of "liberty to the sword, to pestilence and to famine" (34:17). The destruction of the city and its leaders was a foregone conclusion (34:11–22).

Jeremiah in Prison (37:6–21). Jeremiah warned Zedekiah that the Babylonian withdrawal was temporary (37:6–10). While the siege was lifted, Jeremiah sought to leave the city for a trip to Anathoth to inspect some property. Thinking that he was deserting to the Babylonians, an overzealous guard arrested him and brought him before the city leaders. They had him beaten and thrown into the dungeon (37:11–15).

Finally, Zedekiah ordered that Jeremiah be brought out secretly so he could consult with him. When he asked Jeremiah if there was any word from the LORD, Jeremiah told him that there was—the same word of judgment that he had pronounced before. Then Jeremiah, weakened by the prison experience, begged Zedekiah not to put him back in the dungeon. Zedekiah protected him for a time and saw that he got what food was available (37:16–21). This probably is the time when Jeremiah buys some ancestral property from his cousin Hanamel, since both 32:2 and 37:21 speak of Jeremiah being imprisoned in the "court of the guard."

Purchasing the Field at Anathoth (Jer. 32:1–44). The LORD told Jeremiah that his cousin Hanamel wanted to sell a field at Anathoth and that he was to buy it. Hanamel was following the law of redemption of property. That law provided that if any property were for sale, it had to be offered to one's nearest kin—brothers, uncles, and then cousins, in that order (Num. 27:9–11).

When Hanamel came, Jeremiah bought the property and received a proper deed for it. The deed consisted of two copies, one that was kept sealed and another that could be opened for public inspection (32:1–15).[13] Hanamel's purpose in selling the field was to get money that could be more easily held if the city fell. On the other hand, Jeremiah purchased the field to show his confidence that people would survive the coming exile and would once more live in the land (32:16–44). In that sense, it was carrying out the positive aspect of his call "to build and to plant." It illustrates quite vividly the prophetic view of judgment as redemptive and cleansing rather than annihilating—completely wiping out the people.

Meanwhile, the siege tightened and, as the food supply sank lower and lower, other conditions within the city worsened. Lamentations 4 describes in gruesome detail the effects of the food shortage: the dry shriveled skin of people who once were sleek and healthy (Lam. 4:8); mothers resorting to cannibalism, eating their own children (Lam. 4:10); and the danger of walking in the streets for fear of being killed for food (Lam. 4:18).

Zedekiah's Last Warning (Jer. 38:1–28).   Jeremiah's enemies were persistent, to say the least. When they found Zedekiah had rescued Jeremiah from the dungeon, they pressured Zedekiah to turn the prophet over to them. Again, Zedekiah yielded, and once more Jeremiah was in the hands of his enemies.

The next place he found himself was in a cistern. Cisterns are underground containers for water, hewn out of the rock. They varied in size from those that would hold a few thousand gallons of water to others that would hold tremendous amounts of water. Jeremiah was thrown into a small cistern partially filled with mud that had been washed in. Jeremiah sank into the mire, and had he not been rescued by one of Zedekiah's servants, he probably would have died there (38:1–13).

Once again, Jeremiah came before Zedekiah. Once again, Zedekiah asked the prophet if there was any message for him from the LORD. Once again, Jeremiah told Zedekiah that his only hope was to surrender to the Babylonians. Otherwise, death and destruction awaited him and the inhabitants of Jerusalem (38:14–23). But in contrast to their previous meeting, when Jeremiah pleaded for his life (37:20), Zedekiah was now pleading with Jeremiah not to let the leaders know Zedekiah had consulted him. If he did so, the leaders would kill Jeremiah. He assured Zedekiah that he would only tell them that he was pleading for his life. In exchange, Zedekiah kept him in prison in the royal quarters (38:24–28).

And Then There Were None: Jerusalem Falls (Jer. 39:1–10; 52:1–34; 2 Kings 25:1–21).   Famine, pestilence, and the Babylonian army finally prevailed. Jerusalem fell, probably in the year 587 B.C.E., although some date the fall in 586. Ancient armies won more battles by patiently waiting for their enemy to starve than they did by direct assault. For almost two years, Nebuchadnezzar's army had cut off the inhabitants of Jerusalem from any source of food other than what had been stored in the city. Since there was no room within the city walls to grow food, the people inevitably faced the choices of surrender or starvation if the siege could not be lifted by other means. While the Babylonians had battering rams to break down the walls, Jerusalem had strong fortifications that enabled her to hold out until starvation and disease took its toll on the defenders of the city (39:1–2).

Zedekiah, realizing that further resistance was futile, fled the city at night. He was captured near Jericho, however, and carried before Nebuchadnezzar at Riblah of Hamath in the northern part of Syria. He was condemned to watch the slaughter of his sons and his chief officials. Then his own eyes were punched out and he was taken to Babylon as prisoner (39:3–7).

Meanwhile, Jerusalem was burned—including the palace complex and the Temple. The walls were broken down, and most of the talented people among the population were taken to Babylon. The Babylonians sought to ensure the loyalty of the poor people by giving them land (39:8–10).

The Fate of Jeremiah (Jer. 39:11–40:6).   Jeremiah, still in prison as a result of his problems during the siege, was brought out and released. At first, it seems he had been included among those to be taken to Babylon. Later, when given the

Photograph by David Rogers.

Figure 10–3.   "King Nebuchadnezzar of Babylon and all his army came against Jerusalem and besieged it; in the eleventh year of Zedekiah, in the fourth month, on the ninth day of the month, a breach was made in the city" (Jer. 39:1–2). These are ruins of a seventh century B.C.E. wall that was destroyed by the Babylonian invaders.

choice of remaining in the land, he chose to do so. He was put into the custody of Gedaliah, an official of Zedekiah's court who had been appointed governor by the Babylonians.

After the Fall (Jer. 40:7–44:30)

The murder of Gedaliah (2 Kings 25:22–26; Jer. 40:7–41:18).   The land was in ruins. The dreams of independence were shattered, and the people were left beaten and disillusioned. The Babylonians appointed Gedaliah as governor over the Babylonian province of which Judah was now a part. The seat of government was moved to Mizpah, as Jerusalem was only a heap of blackened rubble (Jer. 40:7–8).

Gedaliah urged the people to serve the Babylonians (Chaldeans) and to gather what food they could from the vines and trees. People who had fled to Transjordan returned to their homes when they heard that the land was once more at peace. Fortunately for them, the fruit crops were abundant. (40:9–12).

Unfortunately, at the urging of the Ammonite king Baalis,[14] Ishmael, who claimed descent from David, plotted against Gedaliah. Although warned of the plot, Gedaliah ignored it, to his own downfall. In 582, Ishmael killed not only Gedaliah but also a large number of Jews and a contingent of Chaldean soldiers. Among those he attacked were eighty men from Shechem, Shiloh, and Samaria who seemingly had come to the site of the ruined Temple to offer sacrifice on that sacred spot. This would indicate that even though the Temple was destroyed, worship of a sort was still carried on there. Ishmael killed all but ten of the worshipers. They bought their lives with promises of food for Ishmael and his men. Ishmael also took captive the remaining inhabitants of Mizpah (41:1–10).

Johanan, a leader who had supported Gedaliah, soon raised a force to fight Ishmael. When the fight came, many of the people from Mizpah whom Ishmael had taken captive fled to join Johanan. Ishmael beat a hasty retreat to the other side of the Jordan (41:11–18).

The flight to Egypt. Johanan, fearing that he would be blamed for Gedaliah's death, fled to Egypt. Jeremiah tried to persuade him not to do it, but Johanan did not heed Jeremiah's advice. Instead, Jeremiah was forced to go along (42:1–43:7). The last words of Jeremiah were predictions of doom for Egypt and for those who had fled to it for protection. Only Baruch, Jeremiah's faithful disciple, would escape with his life (43:8–45:5). As far as is known, Jeremiah died in Egypt.

The Oracles of Jeremiah

The oracles of Jeremiah are scattered throughout the book. Those found in chapters 2 to 6, 8 to 20, 30 to 31, and 46 to 52 will be examined, emphasizing prominent themes found in them.

Early and Mixed Oracles

Early oracles (Jer. 2:1–6:30).

1. Remembering better days (2:1–3)
2. Israel has been unfaithful (2:4–37)
3. Repent, O Israel (3:1–4:4)
4. Beware the foe from the north (4:5–31)
5. Judah is hopelessly immoral (5:1–6:30)

Mixed oracles (Jer. 8:4–10:25).

1. The people have shown incredible stupidity (8:4–17)
2. The heartsick prophet (8:18–9:1)
3. Beware of your neighbor's tongue (9:2–9)
4. Cry for Zion (9:10–22)

5. The glory in serving the LORD (9:23–26)
6. Idols and those who make them (10:1–25)

These two groups of oracles are discussed together because they share some common themes.

Israel, the unfaithful wife.   In the oracles of Jeremiah, one hears echoes from earlier prophets, especially Hosea. In 2:2–3, Jeremiah introduces the bride figure:

> I remember the devotion of your youth,
>   your love as a bride,
> how you followed in the wilderness,
>   in a land not sown (2:2).

He continues this theme in a oracle found in 3:1, where he asks whether a woman, once divorced and remarried, can return to her original husband. Israel has known many lovers and wants to return to the LORD (3:1), but she has so polluted herself with Baalism that the land is filled "with your vile harlotry" (3:2). Still the LORD pleads for the people to return (3:12, 14, 22; 4:1).

The worship of idols.   The prophet was perplexed over the people's fascination with idols. Idols, as such, were not seen as being actual gods; rather, the deity was thought to be present in an image that was properly clothed and cared for.[15] How the people could be drawn away from the living LORD mystified the prophet:

> What wrong did your ancestors find in me
>   that they went far from me
> and went after worthless things,
>   and became worthless themselves? (2:5)
>
> Has a nation changed its gods,
>   even though they are no gods? (2:11)
>   . . . .
> for my people have committed two evils;
>   they have forsaken me,
> the fountain of living waters,
>   and dug out cisterns for themselves,
>   cracked cisterns
> that can hold no water (2:13).

Jeremiah's most extended polemic against idols is found in 10:1–25. He observes:

> Their idols are like scarecrows in a
>   cucumber field,
> and they cannot speak;
> they have to be carried
>   for they cannot walk.
> Do not be afraid of them,
>   for they cannot do evil,
>   nor is it in them to do good (10:5).

The foe from the north.   A much discussed theme from Jeremiah deals with oracles about a "foe from the north." In addition to the initial vision of the boiling pot (1:13–19), the prophet also takes up the subject in other oracles. A series of such oracles is to be found in Jeremiah 4:5–31. Some of the prophet's most vivid language is used to describe this threat:

> Blow the trumpet through the land;
>> shout aloud and say,
> "Gather together, and let us go
>> into the fortified cities!"
>>> . . . .
> for I am bringing evil from the north,
>> and a great destruction (4:5,6).

Later in the chapter, the devastation is described:

> I looked on the earth, and lo, it was
>> waste and void:
> and to the heavens, and they
>> had no light.
> I looked on the mountains, and lo
>> they were quaking,
> and all the hills moved to and fro.
>>> . . . .
> I looked, and lo, the fruitful land
>> was a desert,
> and all its cities were laid in ruins
>> before the LORD, before his fierce anger (4:23–26).

The prophet's responsibility.   Jeremiah, like others of the prophets, was particularly disturbed by those religious leaders, both priest and prophet, whose main concern was to curry favor with the rich and powerful. He speaks of those who

> have treated the wound of my people
>> carelessly,
> saying, "Peace, peace,"
>> when there is no peace.
> They acted shamefully, they
>> committed abomination;
> yet they are not ashamed,
>> they did not know how to blush (6:14–15; 8:11–12).

The responsible prophet would warn the people of the dangers they faced (28:8). Jeremiah was a realist who tested the people the way an assayer would test ore to determine its metal content (6:27–30).

The Confessions and Other Oracles (Jer. 11:1–20:18)

1. The broken covenant (11:1–17)
2. The first confession: Save me from my enemies (11:18–12:6)

3. The LORD's lament (12:7–13)
4. The fate of Judah's neighbors (12:14–17)
5. The spoiled loincloth (13:1–11)
6. The wine jar (13:12–14)
7. The fate of Judah and the shame of Jerusalem (13:15–17)
8. Oracles during a drought (14:1–16)
9. The certainty of calamity (14:17–15:9)
10. The second confesssion: Why do you treat me this way, LORD (15:10–21)
11. No wife for Jeremiah (16:1–9)
12. Mixed oracles (16:10–17:4)
13. The proverbs of Jeremiah (17:5–13)
14. The third confession: Heal me, LORD (17:14–18)
15. A trip to the potter's house (18:1–17)
16. The fourth confession: Let them have it, LORD! (18:18–23)
17. The message of the shattered flask (19:1–20:6)
18. The fifth confession: You have made a fool out of me, LORD (20:7–13)
19. The sixth confession: Why was I ever born, LORD? (20:14–18)

The prophet's frustrations: The denial of family life.   The primary personal aim of every normal Israelite male was to marry and to have children. In preexilic times, a doctrine of life after death had not developed. As a result, a man thought of living beyond this life in terms of living through his children. If he did not marry, then he could not legitimately carry out this basic desire. Or, if his marriage produced no children, the desire was frustrated. This was why barren women were portrayed in the Old Testament as being persons who put forth great efforts to become pregnant.[16] The fact that the man might be the one who was to blame seems never to have entered their thinking.

Jeremiah was told not to marry because it would only mean tragedy to him. Any wife and children he would have would die in the wars fought over Jerusalem. He would be better off without any family than to have his family destroyed by the war (16:1–4). In addition, he was to avoid the normal social functions. He was to avoid funerals, parties, and weddings—three of the chief social functions of his day (16:5–9).

The prophet's frustrations: The confessions: One of the unique features of the Book of Jeremiah is a series of oracles called "the confessions of Jeremiah." They are found in 11:18–12:6; 15:10–21; 17:14–18; 18:18–23; 20:7–13; and 20:14–18. These confessions give us a window to Jeremiah's inner struggles as he tries to carry out his prophetic ministry. Because of their importance, they will be discussed individually.

The first confession: Save me from those who would kill me, O LORD! (11:18–12:6). The first confession follows a sermon in which Jeremiah spoke of being told to pronounce judgment upon those who refused to follow the covenant. He was told, furthermore, not to even pray for them because of the vileness of their sins (11:1–17).

Such sermons did not earn Jeremiah the "Favorite Prophet of the Year" award from the board of trustees of the Jerusalem Temple. Instead of repentance, their reaction was threats of violence. When Jeremiah heard of their threats, he did not say, "O LORD, forgive them," either. Instead, he asked for the LORD to protect him from those who would kill him (11:18–20).

To make matters worse, Jeremiah was told that the leaders among the plotters were his own kinfolk, "the men of Anathoth" (11:21). Again, he pleaded for the LORD to come to his rescue. He could not understand how such wicked men could prosper (12:1–4).

The answer was not encouraging. The LORD said, in effect: "Jeremiah, if you think things are bad now, just cheer up—they will get much worse!" (12:5–6).

The second confession: Why do you treat me this way, LORD? (15:10–21).   Following another oracle that continues the theme of Judah's doom, Jeremiah's second confession begins. In words that echo Job's lament (Job 3:1–10), Jeremiah bemoaned his fate. Nothing he did pleased men, even though he had pleaded with the LORD on their behalf. The assurance came to him that the doom of the sinners was certain (15:10–14).

Jeremiah recalled the circumstances of his call to be a prophet:

> Your words were found and I ate them,
>   and your words became to me a joy
>   and the delight of my heart;
> for I am called by your name,
>   O LORD, God of hosts (15:16).

He had shunned the society of others, especially places of merrymaking, because he was so moved with indignation over the conditions in the country. But that had only brought him pain. Like a wet-weather spring that promised water all year long but dried up when the rains ceased, the LORD had deceived him (15:15–18).

After that outburst, a word of assurance came to Jeremiah. If he would faithfully preach the LORD's words, he would still have enemies; but they would not overcome him. The LORD would be with him to deliver him out of the hands of those who would harm him (15:19–21).

The third confession: Heal me, O Lord (17:14–18).   This confession was a prayer for healing and salvation. Jeremiah's enemies were cynics who would not believe him. He declared that he had not prayed for disaster for his enemies. If he had not before, he did then. He called for them to be destroyed with "double destruction!" (17:18).

The fourth confession: Let them have it, LORD! (18:18–23).   This confession is introduced by a report of the plots against Jeremiah. What is of particular interest is the mention of the three major classes of religious leaders—the priests, the wise men, and the prophets. This is one of the few places where the "wise men" are classed with the priests and prophets as leaders of the religious community. The wise men were particularly concerned with the practical matters of how to get along in human society. Their major interest was the day-to-day existence of humanity (18:18).

Jeremiah's enemies ganged up to counteract anything he said about them. They decided to "bring charges against him." In desperation, the prophet turned to the LORD to plead his case once again. Reminding the LORD how he had pleaded for those who were abusing him, Jeremiah appealed for justice for himself. In a scathing tirade against his enemies, he asked that the worst of calamities should befall them and their families because of their plots against him (18:19–23).

The fifth confession: You have made a fool of me, Lord (20:7–13).   This confession reflects the prophet's increasing sense of frustration as he tried to minister to the people of Jerusalem. The LORD had deceived him into being a prophet with promises of his presence. But the life of a prophet, even with the LORD's presence, was more than Jeremiah had bargained for. He got so tired of preaching about violence and destruction that he determined that he would quit. Instead, the urge from the LORD was so strong that he found himself preaching again in spite of his resolutions not to do so. Since even his closest friends were trying to destroy him, he did not need enemies (20:7–10).

Suddenly, his mood shifted. As he realized that the LORD would take care of his enemies, his complaints changed to praise (20:11–13).

The sixth confession: Why was I ever born, LORD? (20:14–18). The final confession probes the depths of the prophet's misery. Like Job (Job 3), he curses the day he was born: "Why did I come forth from the womb to see toil and sorrow and spend my days in shame?" (20:18).

The significance of Jeremiah's confessions.   In the confessions, the agony of Jeremiah's inner struggles are revealed. Here was an honest man whose faith in the justice of God led him to put aside all pretense in his prayers. He survived those horrible times because he was able to purge himself of his inner conflicts through prayer to the One whom he experienced as the personal LORD.

The prophet as optimist: The parable of the potter (18:1–7).   While this incident ends with a rather negative conclusion, it does have a positive premise, namely, that at the time the prophet spoke, the situation for Judah was not hopeless. Were the people willing to submit to the LORD's direction, salvation was still possible. Their stubbornness, however, negated that hope.

The prophet as optimist: The oracles of consolation (30:1–32:40).   These oracles expressed the positive side of Jeremiah's call to prophesy. Judgment on Judah was not the final act of God. It was a cleansing fire, designed to burn away the impurities. The LORD would restore the purified people to the land (30:1–3).

While there are oracles that emphasize the restoration, the most noted passage in this section is 31:23–40 and the incident involving the purchase of the field.[17]

As the LORD had watched over the people (1:12) to "pluck up and break down, to overthrow, destroy, and bring evil" (31:28; see also 1:10), so the LORD would now "watch over them to build and to plant" (31:28). In the earlier times, the emphasis had been upon how the sins of one affected his whole family, so much so that a common proverb said, "The parents have eaten sour grapes and the children's teeth are set on edge" (31:29). This would no longer be so. The responsibility for acts of sin rested upon the one who commited them.

This concept of individual responsibility introduced by Jeremiah was one of his distinct contributions to biblical theology. Ezekiel would take the same idea and expand on it (Ezek. 18, 33).

An idea growing out of Jeremiah's teaching about individual responsibility was the new covenant (31:31–34). The old covenant had been written on stone tablets and, more often than not, had failed to make the transition from written principle to living practice. The principles had not become personal guidelines for life. Jeremiah looked for a day when the LORD's law would be the normal way of life. Each person would "know the LORD" and live by that knowledge.

Jeremiah illustrated the LORD's relationship to Israel by comparing it to the fixed order of nature (31:35–37). Jerusalem would be rebuilt and become the LORD's sacred city again (31:38–40).

Oracles against Foreign Nations (Jer. 46:1–51:64).   The section on oracles against foreign nations was standard for many of the prophets.[18] Many of Jeremiah's oracles were specifically dated to a time and situation, whereas other prophet's oracles were less specific as to their date.

1. Against Egypt (46:2–28)
2. Against Philistia (47:1–7)
3. Against Moab (48:1–47)
4. Against Ammon (49:1–6)
5. Against Edom (49:7–22)
6. Against Syria (49:23–27)
7. Against Kedar and Hazor (49:28–33)
8. Against Elam (49:34–39)
9. Against Babylon (50:1–51:64)

Of these oracles, comment will be given for only a select group.

Against Egypt (46:2–28).   These two oracles, the first of which was dated in 605, taunted Egypt because of its defeat at Carchemish in Northern Mesopotamia by the armies of Nebuchadnezzar of Babylon. Jeremiah saw it as a day when the LORD brought a well-deserved punishment to Egypt. No amount of medicine would heal its wounds (46:2–12).

The second oracle referred to one of the times when Babylon met Egypt on its own territory. This was either in 605 or in 601, when Jehoiakim switched his loyalties to Egypt after the two armies fought to a standstill. Jeremiah foresaw the eventual destruction of Egypt by the Mesopotamian power (46:13–26). The LORD's people would survive, even though they had to face judgment for their sins (46:27–28).

Against Philistia (47:1–7).   This brief oracle describes the march of invading armies down the coast, isolating the Phoenician cites of Tyre and Sidon, then moving down the coastal highway to knock out the main Philistine cities of Gaza and Ashkelon.

Against Moab (48:1–47).   To read the oracle against Moab with real understanding, one needs a Bible atlas with detailed maps. It was a travelogue of Moabite territory, listing most, if not all, its major cities. Though it speaks of Moab's destruction, it ends on a promise of restoration to Moab "in the latter days." This reflected the fact that the Moabites and Israelites were not so antagonistic toward each other as Israel had been with others of its neighbors. The story of Ruth, told to support the claim that David had a Moabite grandmother, gave an indication of the friendly relations between the two peoples.

Against Babylon (50:1–52:64).   The oracles of Jeremiah are concluded with a series of oracles against Babylon since it was Israel's chief foreign enemy. There was a constant shifting of persons spoken of in these oracles. The oracles began with the LORD announcing to the nations that Babylon has been taken (50:2–4). The people of Judah would return to the LORD, asking the way to Zion (50:4–5). They had been like lost sheep, attacked by wild animals (50:6–7).

The LORD addressed the people and told them to flee from the land of the Chaldeans (Babylon), for invaders were coming who would destroy everything in their path (50:8–10). Babylon was told that her doom was sure. She would be hissed at by all who passed her (50:11–13). Her enemies were invited to attack her, for they would be carrying out the LORD 's vengeance against her (50:14–16).

Attention was then shifted to Israel. Israel was compared to a sheep hunted by lions. Assyria, then Babylon, had attacked Israel. Now the tables would be turned. Israel would be restored as Babylon was destroyed (50:17–20).

There follow a series of oracles describing the destruction of Babylon. The hammer that had broken many was now broken (50:21–28). The archers were summoned to bend their bows at it. Fire would burn its cities (50:29–32); the LORD would redeem Israel, but the sword would devour Babylon (50:33–38); unrest would upset its inhabitants (50:39–40). As it had come from the north to devastate Palestine, so a northern foe would devastate it. Its king would be helpless, for the enemy would be like a lion in a sheepfold (50:41–46).

Jeremiah 51 continues on the theme of Babylon's destruction. It would be winnowed as a farmer winnowed grain (51:1–7), and no balm could heal its great wounds (51:8–10). The enemy was summoned to prepare its weapons and to mount an assault against the city, for the LORD had promised victory (51:11–14).

In the midst of the oracles of doom, there is a hymnlike section describing the LORD's power in nature. In contrast to that power, the idol was the powerless product of stupid men. It could not compare to the God of Jacob (51:15–19). In 51:20–23, there is the oracle of the hammer. Babylon had been a hammer by which the LORD had meted out punishment to those who had sinned against him. Now, however, the destroyer would be destroyed. The LORD summoned the nations to make war against it, to make it a land of desolation and waste (51:24–33). What Nebuchadnezzar had done to Jerusalem would be done to Babylon (51:34–37). It would be like a land awash with the waves of the sea (51:38–44). Judah was warned to flee, for the LORD's wrath would be poured out on the land (51:45–46). Babylon's fall would come because of what it had done to Israel (51:47–51). The LORD, the God of justice, would see to it that Babylon was laid waste (51:52–58).

According to 51:50–64, Jeremiah wrote on a scroll all the oracles against Babylon. He sent it to Babylon by Seraiah, the quartermaster of Zedekiah's court. Seraiah was told to read the oracles in Babylon. Having done that, he was to tie a stone to the scroll and throw it into the Euphrates. Just as the scroll would sink in the river, so Babylon would sink—to rise no more.

The Importance of Jeremiah 52.   This chapter, which briefly summarizes Zedekiah's reign (52:1–3a), is concerned mainly with details of Jerusalem's capture by the Babylonians. After duplicating 39:1–12, additional details are given. The fact that the Babylonians took some of the poor people as captives is unusual, since such people usually were passed over (52:15). The final note about King Jehoiachin (52:31–34), found also in 2 Kings 25:27–30, lets it be known that the Book of Jeremiah did not reach its final form until later than 560, the year that Jehoiachin was released from prison. Actual records of the allowances given for the king and his family have been found.

Evaluation of Jeremiah

Jeremiah was a man of unusual courage. While he was not without supporters in Jerusalem during the dark days of Judah's decline, it required great fortitude to say what he felt necessary in face of the strong opposition among the powerful men of Jerusalem. The full effect of what he said was realized only as the exiles looked back at what had happened and realized how right Jeremiah had been. Their appreciation of what he had said helped them to make a more realistic evaluation of their situation and adjust to it.

Was he more than this? Strong arguments have been advanced recently that Jeremiah, aided by Baruch, was responsible for writing the Deuteronomic History, or at least an edition ending with 2 Kings 23. Should this be true, Jeremiah would have been responsible for a major portion of the Old Testament, comparable to Paul's contribution to the New Testament.[19]

STUDY QUESTIONS

1. How did Manasseh's reign differ from that of his father Hezekiah?
2. Describe the reform that took place in Josiah's time. Why is it called the Deuteronomic reform?

3. What were the advantages and disadvantages of centralizing all worship in Jerusalem?
4. How did Zephaniah's ministry reflect the influence of Amos?
5. What great international events were taking place in the last years of Josiah's reign?
6. How does one deal with the attitude of hatred expressed in the book of Nahum?
7. How did the policies of Jehoiakim differ from those of his father Josiah?
8. Why is Habakkuk called the "first Jewish philosopher"?
9. What is unusual about Jeremiah's call to be a prophet?
10. What was the meaning of the two visions associated with Jeremiah's call?
11. Why are Chapters 1 to 25 referred to as the "first edition" of Jeremiah?
12. How did Jeremiah compare Josiah and Jehoiakim?
13. What was the Temple Sermon and what were its results?
14. Describe Jeremiah's dealing with King Zedekiah.
15. What advice did Jeremiah give the exiles and why did he feel it necessary to give such advice?
16. How did Jeremiah show his faith in the future of the nation?
17. Why was Jeremiah considered a traitor by many of the people of Jerusalem?
18. What happened to Jeremiah when Jerusalem fell?
19. Identify: (a) Baruch; (b) the New Covenant; (c) 597 B.C.E.; 587/86 B.C.E.
20. What theme in his book shows Hosea's influence on Jeremiah?
21. What are the possible identities of the "foe from the north" and why?
22. What were some of the factors in Jeremiah's sense of frustration?
23. What do the "confessions" reveal about Jeremiah?
24. Describe the kind of person you think Jeremiah was.

ENDNOTES

1. John Bright, *A History of Israel*, 3rd ed., 311, suggests that Manasseh was accused of taking part in the revolt. The Chronicler saw it as punishment for his sins.
2. Ibid., 313–316, gives the details of Assyria's decline. See also Martin Noth, *The History of Israel*, 2nd ed., 269–271.
3. The traditional date for the beginning of the prophet Jeremiah's ministry is 626 B.C.E. However, since the major portion of his ministry followed the reign of Josiah, discussion will be reserved until the reigns of Jehoiakim, Jehoiachin, and Zedekiah.
4. For details, see Bright, *A History of Israel*, 316ff.
5. Noth, *The History of Israel*, 278, discusses possible reasons for Josiah's challenge to Neco.
6. See Gaalyah Cornfeld and David Noel Freedman, eds., *Archaeology of the Bible: Book by Book*, 171ff.

7. Bright, *A History of Israel*, 315.
8. See notes on Jeremiah in *NOAB, NRSV.*
9. On Jeremiah's evaluation of Josiah in this passage, see Walter Brueggemann, *Theology of the Old Testament: Testimony, Dispute, Advocacy* (Minneapolis: Fortress Press, 1997), 613.
10. See page 236f.
11. Bright, *A History of Israel*, 329ff.
12. J. B. Pritchard, *ANET*, 213.
13. Such deeds were found in recent years among the Bar Kochba letters. Yigael Yadin, *Bar Kochba: The Rediscovery of the Legendary Hero of the Second Jewish Revolt Against Rome* (New York: Random House, 1971), 229ff.
14. The official seal of "Milkom'ur, servant of Baalyasha (Baalis)" has been found, confirming the historicity of this Ammonite king. See Larry G. Herr, "Whatever Became of the Ammonites?" *BAR* XIX, 6 (November/ December, 1993), 33f.

15. Philip J. King, "Jeremiah's Polemic Against Idols: What Archaeology Can Teach Us," *BR* X, 6 (December, 1994), 23–29.

16. Read again the story of Rachel and Leah in the Jacob stories for an example of this (Genesis 30:1–24).

17. See page 241.

18. See Amos 1–2; Isaiah 13–23; Ezekiel 25–32; Zephaniah 2:4–15.

19. For a statement of this position, see Richard Elliott Friedman, *Who Wrote the Bible?*, 101–135.

Chapter 11 ❧

THE EXILE

Judah's Dark Night of the Soul

The land lay in ruins. Cities that once had been alive with people now were blackened piles of rubble. Fields that once had produced abundant crops of life-sustaining foods now lay idle, overgrown with weeds. Jerusalem, the once proud capital city of David and Solomon, was wrecked. Its houses, from the hovels of the poor to the palaces of its kings, were burned to the ground; its massive walls were filled with gaping holes; and the Temple, the building that popular religion was sure would be the magic charm to protect the city, was just another heap of rubble. And the people who had given life to the city were gone. Many were dead in the city's ruins; others were exiles in neighboring lands. Those of the upper echelons of society who had survived, for the most part, had been carried to Babylon as prisoners of war. Most of those left behind were poor farmers and shepherds, men incapable of leading any kind of revolt against the powerful armies of Babylon.

AFTER THE FALL

The fall of Jerusalem was a shattering blow to the people, who were convinced that the presence of the Temple would protect the city. The giddy optimism of a few years before was replaced by an air of gloom and despair. Nowhere was that spirit reflected more starkly than in the Book of Lamentations.

Lamentations: Funeral Songs for a Dead City

This book, which is only five chapters long, is made up of five poems that mourn the fall of Jerusalem. Chapters 1, 2, and 4, especially, are written in such vivid language that they must have come from the pen of an eyewitness to the horrors described. Chapters 3 and 5 may well have come from the same author, but probably they were written later when the author had the opportunity to reflect on what had happened.

Characteristics of the Book. There are two distinct characteristics to the poems. First, they are all in what is called *qinah*, or dirge, rhythm. To understand this, one must remember a bit about Hebrew poetry. Hebrew was based on the principle of parallelism. To have parallelism, each line of poetry had to have at least two or more parts. What was said in the first part of the line was more or less answered or intensified in the second part of the line. Generally speaking, in English translation a verse in English is one part of a line in Hebrew. For instance, Lamentations 5:20 says:

> Why have you forgotten us completely?
> Why have you forsaken us these many days?

What was said in the first part of the line was repeated in the second part of the line (the second line in English).

Rhythm also was vital in Hebrew poetry. Each part of the line had certain stresses or strong verbs. As a general rule, no part of the line had less than two or more than three stresses in it. In *qinah* there were three stresses in the first part of the line and two stresses in the second part of the line, creating a 3:2 rhythm. This 3:2, or *qinah*, rhythm was used for dirges (funeral songs) or laments over calamities that had occured.

A second feature of the poems is that all of them are written as acrostics. An acrostic was formed by starting successive lines of poetry with the letters of the alphabet, or the letters of a word. For example, early Christians used the fish as a symbol because they could form an acrostic on the Greek word for fish (*ichthus*) as a confession of faith:

Ieosous (Jesus)
Christos (Christ)
Theou (God)
Uiou (Son)
Soter (Savior)

Lamentations is a series of alphabetic acrostics using the letters of the Hebrew alphabet. Since the Hebrew alphabet has twenty-two letters, Chapters 1, 2, 4, and 5 have twenty-two verses each, while Chapter 3 has sixty-six, or three times twenty-two verses.

Contents of the Book. The mood of the book is set by a cry of anguish in the first word. The English *how* translates a Hebrew expression of woe:

> *How* lonely sits the city
>   that once was full of people!
> How like a widow she has become,
>   she that was great among the nations!
> She that was a princess among the provinces
>   has become a vassal.

Jerusalem, the abandoned widow (1:1–22).   Jerusalem was like a widow, weeping bitterly, because she has been deserted by all who loved her (1:2). Her people carried away (1:3–6), all she has left are her memories of past glory. The victim of her enemies, she is filthy and soiled (1:7–10). Hunger stalked the land. Because of her sin, the LORD's blessing has been withdrawn from her (1:11–13).

Those sins had become a yoke on Jerusalem's neck. Its best soldiers had been helpless before the power of the invader. Mocked and despised by its neighbors and with no comforters, Jerusalem wept. (1:14–17). Yet the LORD had been just because Jerusalem had been disobedient. Its allies had refused its pleas for help. Only now, with death and destruction everywhere, was there sorrow for sins commited. Its enemies taunted it because of its condition. The poem ends with a plea for the enemy to be punished in the same measure that Jerusalem has suffered (1:18–22).

The punishment of Jerusalem (Lam. 2:1–22).   The second lament falls more easily into natural divisions. Lamentations 2:1–9 describes the destruction of the land and city; 2:10–12 describes the emotional and physical effects of the siege; 2:13–19 was an address to Jerusalem reminding it of the causes of its condition; and 2:20–22 was a prayer to the LORD to be aware of what was happening to the city.

1. The destruction of the land (2:1–9).   The Temple, the LORD's dwelling place, was abandoned. The LORD had gone through the land, destroying without mercy both villages and cities. Forts and palaces alike were in ruins. The Temple was smashed—the services were ended. The strong walls that protected Jerusalem were broken down. The gates where justice was dispensed and where the ebb and flow of humanity was seen as it entered the city were buried in the rubble of the walls.

2. The effect on the people (2:10–12).   Old men sat in an unbelieving daze, while young girls bowed to the ground in sorrow. The author had wept until he could weep no more. Famine stalked the city so that hungry children fell like wounded men, while others died in their mother's arms.

3. O Jerusalem, how can I comfort you? (2:13–19).   Jerusalem's condition was hopeless. It had let itself be deceived by lying prophets. Now, people passed by and poked fun at its condition. Its enemies sneered at it. The LORD's patience had run its course, and destruction had come. The poet called for Jerusalem's walls to cry out to the LORD for mercy for its children, who were "starving to death on every street corner" (2:19 *TEV*).

4. LORD, look what you are doing (2:20–22).   The poet pleaded with the LORD to look at the suffering. Mothers were becoming cannibals, eating their own children. Priest and prophet, young and old, were being slaughtered everywhere. Jerusalem's enemies were having a "carnival of terror" (2:22 *TEV*) at its expense.

A personal lament, advice about God's righteousness and mercy, and a prayer for help against the enemy (3:1–66).   This poem is two things. First, it actually is a combination of three poems, each with a different purpose. Second, they appear here as one triple alphabetic acrostic; that is, instead of each line starting with a different letter of the alphabet, here each set of three lines starts with a different letter of the alphabet.

1. A lament about life (3:1–24).   The poet had known suffering. He had been quite ill or injured, having come close to death (3:1–5). He had cried to God, but there seemed to be no answer. Instead, like Job, because God's arrows had pierced his body, he felt that God had used him for target practice. He had been pushed down into the dirt so many times he had lost hope (3:6–18).

Yet, in the depth of his bitterness, he remembered an important thing:

> The steadfast love of the LORD never ceases,
>   his mercies never come to an end;
> they are new every morning;
>   great is your faithfulness.
> "The LORD is my portion," says my soul,
>   "therefore I will hope in him" (3:22–24).

2. The importance of trusting God (3:25–51).   As if to answer and to add to the positive note found in the last stanza of the previous psalm, this poem speaks of the importance of patience. That it was a different poem can be seen in the shift from the singular to the plural in the use of the personal pronouns.

The goodness of the LORD was to all who trusted him. Patience should be practiced, therefore, in whatever situation life brought. The LORD might permit sorrow and pain, but he took no pleasure in doing so. He was aware of what was happening to everyone. His will would be carried out. The people should admit their sin. The calamities that had come upon them caused the poet sorrow, especially for what had happened to the women of the city.

3. *Rescued from my enemies (3:52–66).*   This was a combination of a lament and a thanksgiving. The poet spoke of his treatment by his enemies. He cried to the LORD and was assured that he would be rescued. The LORD's word came true. The poet prayed then for punishment for the enemy.

Conditions during the siege of Jerusalem (4:1–22).   The horrors of the siege of Jerusalem are nowhere more vividly portrayed than in this chapter. The holy objects of the Temple were scattered in the streets and people were smashed like clay pots. Those who survived lost all sense of humanity in their wild urge to live. Children starved to death because adults would not share food with them. The upper classes, always the healthier people in the population because of a better diet, starved like the poor. Those who died by the sword were the fortunate ones. Things were so bad that mothers boiled and ate their own children (4:1–10).

The LORD's wrath rained down on the city with such violence that Jerusalem's neighbors were shocked. None of them believed that Jerusalem could be conquered. Prophets and priest who had misled the people were now shunned as though they were lepers. The city's leaders were ignored instead of being honored (4:11–16).

The survivors kept looking for help, but none came. It was not safe to walk in the streets; if a person fell, he could be eaten! (4:17–19).

The end came. Those who tried to flee were chased down. The king, trying to escape the city, was captured. The Edomites, Judah's neighbors to the southeast, taunted the victims, increasing the natural hatred the two peoples had for each other. Judah's punishment was complete (4:20–22).

Restore us, O LORD (5:1–22).   The people were under the oppressor's heel. Taken from their land, they were like motherless children. Everything they got had a price on it, even the water they drank. The punishment for their sin was upon them. The famine produced diseases that had brought raging fevers; their women were abused physically by the invading soldiers; oppression was the rule and not the exception. Joy had turned into mourning (5:1–18).

The LORD was their only hope. The only question was whether or not they had been completely rejected (5:19–22).

The Fate of the Survivors

Not everyone who survived the war was taken to Babylon. As had been noted previously, a number of people, including Jeremiah, were left in the land under the governorship of Gedaliah. When Gedaliah was murdered in 582, those who were his supporters fled to Egypt, thinking they would be blamed for the murder. They, and others who went to Egypt from time to time, would become the basis of a strong Jewish community in later centuries.

In Judah, the remaining population has been estimated by some to have been as low as twenty thousand, less than one-tenth of what it had been in the days of the eighth-century prophets.

Of those taken to Babylon in three deportations (597, 587 and 582), the grand total probably was less than five thousand. This suggests two possibilities: (1) a large number of people died in the Assyrian and Babylonian wars; and (2) not as many upper-class Judahites were taken to Babylon as was once thought.[1]

WITH THE EXILES IN BABYLON

The Babylonian Exile had a profound effect upon the future of the people who had been known as the Israelites. It affected every area of their lives, from how they were to live in relation to their God, to how they were to live in relation to their fellow human beings.

There Were Some Changes Made

The people who went into exile in Babylon survived not only as individuals but also as an identifiable group of people. Their religion, though tested in the fires of war and surrender, also survived. But there were some important changes that took place.

A New Name.   Since the survivors of the Babylonian wars were principally from the tribe of Judah, from that time forth they have been known as Jews, a short form for Judahites.

A New Way of Life.   While some of the people had lived in cities and were merchants, the majority of the survivors basically were rural people, dependent upon pastoral and agricultural occupations for a living. After the exile, the Jews were predominately an urban people, living in cities and making a living in various commercial enterprises.

A New Language.   The people who went into exile spoke Hebrew; those who returned spoke Aramaic, the language of the Babylonians. Aramaic was the most widely spoken language in the Near East. It was similar to Hebrew, so that the change was not a difficult one to make. Hebrew continued to be used to some extent, especially in religious services.[2]

A New Way of Worship.   Exile brought separation from the Temple and its system of sacrifices. Devout Jews, however, found that the LORD was with them, even in a foreign land. Whether the synagogue was founded in the period from

586 to 538 cannot be determined with certainty. Undoubtedly, the conditions that led to its founding were present in the exile. Services of prayer, praise, and reading of sacred writings surely must have been carried on. From the worship services, it was only a short step to the formal structure that made up synagogue worship.

A New Emphasis on the Traditions of Israel. The exile brought the threat of the loss of the sacred traditions of Israel. Since many of them were unwritten, it was a matter of urgency that they be committed to writing before those who knew them died. Many of those who possessed such traditions in their memories had perished already in the siege of Jerusalem. The exile must have been a time of unusual literary activity. That at least the final materials were added to Israel's history which had been preserved in 1, 2 Samuel and 1, 2 Kings (the so-called Deuteronomic History) can be seen from the account of the release of King Jehoiachin from prison in 560 (2 Kings 25:27–30). Writing down the traditions became a project of the priests during the exile, especially since they had no sacrifices to offer. It would continue for many years.[3]

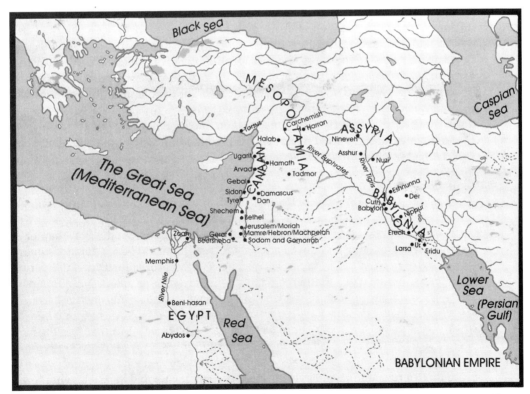

Artwork by Margaret Jordan Brown © Mercer University Press.

Figure 11–1. The Babylonian Empire—sixth century B.C.E.

A New Emphasis on Theology.   The Israelites who went into exile were not true believers in one God alone (monotheists). Evidence suggests that the devotees of popular religion, while paying lip service to the worship of the LORD, (the God of Israel), actually were worshipers of numerous gods (polytheists). Or at least they believed that other gods existed, even though they only worshiped one God (henotheists). The Jews who returned from the exile were devout monotheists, so much so that they wanted nothing to do with the people of the old northern territories who still considered themselves to be worshipers of the God of Israel. Their religion had incorporated too many foreign elements to please the Jews. Because of this, there would be increasing friction between the two groups.

The Prophet of the Transition: Ezekiel

Jeremiah had done his part to prepare the people for the exile, as well as to help those who were in exile to take a realistic view of their situation. Even so, religiously, the exile was a shock, as the Book of Lamentations so vividly illustrates. The inevitable question, "Why did it happen to us?" must have been asked of the religious leaders in the exilic community. Some wanted to believe the pious predictions of the false prophets that the exile would be ended soon, when the LORD would bring about a miraculous overthrow of the Babylonians. In line with that belief, indications are that a number of people plotted to overthrow the government and were executed.[4] It was to counter such false optimism that Jeremiah's letter to the exiles had been written (Jer. 29). Others of the community undoubtedly were not willing to accept any explanations and gave up any idea of God. For a third group, two prophets made sense and enabled them to survive the exile with a more mature faith founded in a deeper understanding of the LORD, the God of Israel. Ezekiel was the first of these prophets.

Ezekiel, the Man.   Ezekiel was a priest before he became a prophet (Ezek. 1:3). His father was Buzi, about whom nothing is known. We know Ezekiel was married, since Ezek. 24:15–18 tells of the death of his wife. From the first chapter of his book, it is evident that he was a most unusual man. He had bizarre visionary experiences, he acted out many of his messages to the people instead of delivering them orally, and he had a mathematician's delight in precise detail. A modern psychiatrist would have a field day trying to figure what made him function.

He had been taken to Babylon in the deportation of 597. At that time he was still a priest. In 593, he experienced a call of the LORD to be a prophet. For the next twenty years or so he carried out that responsibility.

All his ministry was among the exiles, doing in Babylon what Jeremiah was trying to do in Jerusalem—that is, (1) trying to prepare the people for the inevitable fall of Jerusalem, and (2) trying to put a damper on the false hopes for an immediate return to Palestine, which some of the prophets were promoting. Once Jerusalem fell in 587/86, however, Ezekiel became a prophet of hope, trying to prepare the people for their return to the land. He laid out a blueprint for a restored Temple and worship system.

The Book of Ezekiel. In the past ninety years, studies of Ezekiel have come almost full circle. Early in the century, the book was widely viewed as a unity. Then, a series of challenges to this consensus arose, some of which were rather extreme. Today, the conviction is that Ezekiel had a major hand in shaping the present form of the book, notwithstanding the aid and influence of his disciples. The result is a book with the most precisely dated oracles of any of the major prophets. It falls naturally into three major divisions: Chapters 1 to 24—oracles against Jerusalem; Chapters 25 to 32—oracles against foreign nations; and Chapters 33 to 48—oracles of restoration.

Oracles Against Jerusalem (Ezek. 1–24)

1. The call of Ezekiel (1:1–3:27). The call of Ezekiel was similar to that of earlier prophets, such as Isaiah and Jeremiah, that visions were associated with it. It was different in the nature and extent of the visions.

a. The prophet called (1:1–28). Ezekiel was by the River Chebar, which actually was a major irrigation canal on the Euphrates River (1:1).[5] The young priest probably was in a meditative mood when the darks clouds of an approaching thunderstorm caught his attention (1:4). The mention of "brightness around it," "fire flashing forth continually," and the reference to "gleaming amber" (1:4), all suggest a particularly violent thunderstorm with much lightning and possible hail associated with it. Up to that point, Ezekiel's description would fit any violent summer storm.

From then on, the storm forms the backdrop for an astounding vision, which for Ezekiel seems to be normal. Unlike Amos, who saw messages from the LORD in ordinary events, Ezekiel saw extraordinary sights that became bearers of the divine message.

First, there were the creatures of the vision. They had four faces, four wings, and the legs of bovine animals with hooves like calves (1:5–7). Under the wings were human arms and hands. The faces were those of an eagle, an ox, a lion, and a man. The eagle suggested mobility, the ox suggested strength, the lion suggested lordliness, and the human face suggested intelligence. The number four denotes that the power of God is effective to the four corners of the earth.[6] Their wings permitted them to fly in any direction without turning around. Fire (lightning?) was in the midst of the creatures, symbolic of the cleansing power of the LORD (1:11–14).

The creatures were accompanied by wheels arranged somewhat like a gyroscope. In other words, there were two wheels, one of which was arranged at a 90° angle from the other. Or, they were like a ball with quarter sections cut out except for a small band of material. This permitted them to roll in any of the four major directions (1:15–17). The eyes that decorated the rims were suggestive of the all-knowingness or *omniscience* of God. Wherever the living creatures went, so did the wheels (1:18–21).

Above the creatures—symbols of all living creation at the service of the LORD—and the wheels, Ezekiel saw a vision of the LORD sitting on a throne, just as Isaiah did (Isa. 6). The creatures covered their bodies with two wings in the LORD's presence (1:22–23; see Isa. 6:2). As they flew, the sound of the wings was like the thunder of the storm. When they came into the LORD's presence, they stopped flying (1:24–25).

The prophet-to-be saw the LORD from the waist down. The upper part of the body was obscured by fire, the brightness of which reminded him of the rainbow that followed the storm (1:26–28). "This was the appearance of the glory of the LORD" (1:28). The word "glory" as used here might also be translated as the "overwhelming presence" of the LORD.

What the first chapter describes is basically the same thing Isaiah describes—that is, a theophany or appearance of the LORD to the one who was being called. Behind all the elaborate symbolism was the prophet's basic conviction that the LORD who had called him to be a prophet was master of the universe, not just master of a narrow little strip of land called Palestine. As such, the LORD could be anywhere, even among the forlorn exiles by the River Chebar in Babylon.

b. The prophet commissioned (2:1–3:37). Ezekiel, who had fallen on his face when he realized he was in the LORD's presence, was commanded to stand on his feet. He was addressed as "son of man": ("O mortal" *NRSV*) which, for Ezekiel, emphasized the difference between himself and the exalted LORD (2:1–3). "I am sending you" expresses a standard type of formula that appeared in prophetic calls (cf. Jeremiah 1:7).[7] He was given a five-fold commission:

(1). As a prophet to a rebellious people (2:1–3:3). They were an "impudent and stubborn" people (2:4), but he was not to let that stop him from doing his job. In an action symbolizing the receiving of the LORD's message of lamentation, mourning, and woe, Ezekiel ate a papyrus scroll that tasted sweet as honey. He would enjoy speaking the LORD's message.

(2). As a prophet to a stubborn people (3:4–9). Although the word was sweet to Ezekiel, it would be distasteful to those to whom it would be preached. Their failure to understand would not be a language difference, but because of a lack of willingness to hear.

(3). As a prophet to the exiles (3:10–15). Ezekiel's mission was directed specifically to the people who were in exile, more specifically to the exiles at Tel-abib (from which the modern Israeli city of Tel-aviv derives its name) on the Chebar canal. He went there and sat silently in the midst of the community for seven days.

(4). *As a watchmen for the house of Israel (3:16–21).* The emphasis in this commission laid the responsibility upon Ezekiel to carry out his call as a prophet. Like Isaiah, he was called to be faithful whether or not he was successful (Isa. 6:11–13).

(5). *As a portrayer of the* LORD's *judgment (3:22–27).* Ezekiel, more than any other prophet, was the master of symbolic action. By such pantomimes, he acted out what was about to happen rather than describing with words the LORD's impending judgment. As part of this phase of his ministry, he was to remain silent until the LORD told him to speak.

2. *The prophet in action (4:1–5:17).* Almost immediately, it seems, Ezekiel began to prophesy by pantomime.

a. *Let's play war. (4:1–3).* First, he played war. Using a large sun-dried brick as a symbol for Jerusalem, he set up miniature camps and siege lines around it, built dirt ramps up to it, and made miniature battering rams as if to knock down the imaginary walls. He took a small piece of iron to make a movable shield such as was used by attacking armies as they tried to get near city walls to attack them. Then he enthusiastically played war.

b. *The long rest (4:4–8).* Next, Ezekiel was commanded to lie on his side for 390 days as a sign of the length of Israel's punishment. For Judah's punishment, he was to lie on his side for forty days. While each day was to indicate a year's exile, the significance of the numbers is not explained further. The period of 390 years may simply indicate that Israel's exile would go on indefinitely; forty years would seem to indicate for Ezekiel what seventy years represented for Jeremiah—a symbol of the completion of the LORD's time. When things were right, the exiles would return.

c. *Food is scarce! (4:9–17).* A third action involved the mixing of various grains, beans, and peas to make flour for bread. Under ordinary circumstances such a thing was not done; but when a siege was on, one ate anything available. The command to cook the food over dried human manure was too much for Ezekiel's priestly instincts. When he pleaded for an exception, the LORD permitted using dried cow manure for the cooking fires. All this demonstrated the extreme conditions that existed during the siege of Jerusalem.

d. *The prophet's haircut (5:1–17).* A man's hair was his pride. The prophet got a lesson in humility when he was told to cut his hair like a captive of war. Then he took the hair from his shorn head and divided it into three parts. A third was burned, a third was chopped to pieces with the sword, and a third was scattered to the wind. A few hairs left clinging to his garments were divided in the same manner. Then the symbolism of this action was explained. Like the prophet's hair, so the inhabitants of Jerusalem would be divided:

One-third of you shall die of pestilence or be consumed by famine among you; one-third shall fall by the sword around you; and one-third I will scatter to every wind and I will unsheathe the sword after them (5:12).

Athough the LORD had made Jerusalem the center of the universe, she was doomed (5:5).

3. The prophet preaching (6:1–7:27).   A spoken sermon follows the descriptions of the pantomimed sermons. Its title might be "Judgment on the Mountains." The sermon was directed against the mountains where the Baal cults had their worship centers. The sermon had four parts, each closed by the refrain, "I am the LORD." The first division was spoken to the mountains as if they were living persons, describing how the pagan altars, designed to celebrate life and fertility, would be the scene of death and barrenness (6:1–7).

The second part spoke of the scattering of the people into foreign lands. They would remember how they had grieved the LORD and would realize that his threats had not been in vain (6:8–10).

The third division called for mourning to take place because men would die of pestilence and famine. When corpses were found on the altars, the high hills, and every place they worshiped god; when the land was made desolate—then "they shall know that I am the LORD" (6:11–14). The sermon closes with oracles of doom for the land (7:1–27).

4. Heresy in the Temple (8:1–11:25).

a. Those abominable idols (8:1–18; 11:1–21). Pages have been written about the visions of Ezekiel found in Chapters 8 to 11. One of the major questions relates to whether they were really visions or whether Ezekiel actually was present in Jerusalem to witness the things he described. Travel back and forth to Jerusalem from Babylon was not unknown. Ezekiel's intimate knowledge of the Temple, growing out of his training as a priest, however, would explain his detailed descriptions. His powers of discernment and previous visionary experiences, furthermore, would seem to argue for these being visions on the order of extrasensory perception.

As Ezekiel described it, he was transported to Jerusalem by a hand that held him by a lock of hair. He was brought in vision to the northern gateway of the inner court, where there seemed to be some sort of pagan image. Immediately, he was aware of the overpowering presence of the God of Israel (8:1–4).

After having the pagan image and the ceremonies pointed out to him (8:5–6), he was shown a hole in the wall. Following instructions , he dug into the hole and found a door. Entering the door, he saw seventy of Judah's leaders, led by a Temple official, worshiping pictures of animals drawn on the walls (8:7–13). They may have been evidence of the worship of Egyptian deities.[8]

Going to the north gate of the Temple, there Ezekiel found women weeping for Tammuz, the Babylonian god of vegetation (8:14–15).[9] Next, he went to the east side of the Temple, where he found twenty-five men worshiping the rising sun. Thus in the house where the LORD alone was to be worshiped, all sorts of services to pagan gods were being carried on (8:16–18). Jerusalem's doom was certain:

> Therefore I will act in my wrath; my eye will not spare, nor will I have pity; and though they cry in my hearing with a loud voice, I will not listen to them (8:18).

This passage seems to be continued in 11:1–21. There specific people who were leaders in the worship of pagan deities are named. In his vision, Ezekiel saw one of them, Pelatiah, the son of Benaiah, die. The hope for a righteous remnant was mentioned, along with certain judgment for the sinners of Jerusalem.

b. Marked for destruction (9:1–11). The LORD called for the executioners to make ready. Six men, prepared to act as the LORD's executioners, stepped up with their weapons ready. A seventh man with a writing case was with them (9:1–2). The LORD instructed the seventh man to go through the city and to put a mark on the foreheads of those who were disturbed by the abominations that were being practiced in the Temple. They were the righteous who would survive the siege. This was in keeping with a commonly held theological view that the righteous would enjoy blessings and a long life, while sinners would die young. Ezekiel would have said that those who died during the siege were sinners (9:3–4).

Once the righteous were marked, the executioners were ordered to do their job. As Ezekiel experienced this vision, he, like Amos, prayed to the LORD, asking him if he was going to destroy all the people. The LORD answered that the guilty would not be spared. The scribe reported that he had done his job (9:5–11).

c. No more glory in the Temple (10:1–22; 11:22–25). When Ezekiel looked, he saw a repeat of the vision by the River Chebar with the LORD on the throne, the winged creatures (now called "cherubim"), and the wheels. The LORD commanded the scribe to take fire from among the cherubim, which was done. The fire was scattered over the city to burn it (10:1–8).

In 11:22–25, the glory of the LORD (the overpowering presence) left the Temple, accompanied by the cherubim and the wheels. This was Ezekiel's way of saying to the exiles that the Temple and Jerusalem could no longer claim the LORD's protective presence. Thus the vision ended. The time was 592, only five years before Jerusalem was destroyed.

5. In action again (12:1–20). In an activity closely related to this word about the withdrawal of the presence of the LORD from Jerusalem, Ezekiel acted out before the people what would happen to the survivors in Jerusalem. Like one who was going into exile, he gathered up his portable possessions . He dug through the mud wall of his house at night and crawled through the hole, taking his baggage with him (12:1–7). He was then instructed to tell the people that his action symbolized what

King Zedekiah was attempting to do to escape from Jerusalem. Zedekiah would not be successful, however. He would be captured, blinded, and taken to Babylon as a captive (12:8–16).

Ezekiel then drank water and ate, quaking and trembling like one who was mortally afraid. This would be the condition of the people in Jerusalem as they awaited the fall of the land (12:17–21).

6. Hard words for false prophets and unfaithful people (12:21–14:23).

a. The LORD will vindicate Ezekiel (12:21–28). Some people made fun of Ezekiel, saying that he kept predicting doom, but it never came. He was told to warn the people that judgment no longer would be delayed. His words were not for the sweet by-and-by; they were about a harsh here-and-now (12:21–28).

b. The fate of false prophets (13:1–16). The prophets of popular religion were not concerned with the LORD's message. Instead, they were busy thinking up messages that would soothe the people and cause them to react favorably to the messenger. Instead of building a wall of truth behind which Israel could be secure, they had built a faulty wall. Then they covered their mistakes with whitewash. When the flood of judgment came, the whitewash would not hold the wall together. So the prophets who kept on crying peace when war was unavoidable would be destroyed like the faulty wall.

c. The fate of fickle women (13:17–23). Ezekiel condemned women " who sew bands on all wrists, and make veils for all persons of every height" (13:18). This referred to some sort of witchcraft or magical practice that was condemned in Israel in the time of the early monarchy (1 Sam. 28:3). They had led righteous people astray. As a consequence, judgment upon them would be severe. Ezekiel closes the oracle with a favorite theme: "Then you will know that I am the LORD" (13:20–23).

d. The fate of idol worshipers (14:1–23). When certain leaders of the people came to Ezekiel, it was revealed to him that they were idol worshipers. The LORD would not permit such a person to have a correct message through the prophet because of that person's false worship (14:1–5). The only hope for the idol worshiper was to repent and put away his idols. Idol worshipers would be cut off even if they tried to appear righteous by consulting a prophet. Both the idol worshiper and the prophet he consulted would be false and would face the LORD's judgment (14:6–11).

Such unfaithfulness would condemn the land. Even if Noah, Daniel, and Job still lived in the land, their righteousness would only save them, but not others (14:12–20). (This idea of individual responsibility was further discussed by Ezekiel in Chapters 18 and 33.) Jerusalem was about to face four severe acts of judgment—"sword, famine, wild animals, and pestilence, to cut off humans and animals from it" (14:21). Any survivors would testify that the LORD's action was just (14:22–23).

7. The prophet and his allegories (15:1–17:24). Ezekiel was particularly fond of allegories—stories where some actual person or event is represented by a symbol.

a. Jerusalem, the grapevine (15:1–8). Here, Jerusalem was represented by a grapevine. The grapevine's main function is as a fruit-bearing plant. Since its wood is useless as lumber, it can only be burned. So Jerusalem was like a dead grapevine, ready to be burned.

b. Jerusalem, the faithless wife (16:1–63). Next, Jerusalem was like an unfaithful wife. Ezekiel suggested that the racial background of the Jews was mixed: "Your father was an Amorite and your mother was a Hittite." The LORD found her (the people of Israel) when she had been abandoned to die at birth, and he brought her up. When she was a grown woman, he wooed her and won her as his bride. He gave her all the luxuries that a beautiful woman desired (16:1–4).

Unfortunately, she became a harlot, selling her favors to anyone who passed by. She gave to others the blessing the LORD (her husband) had given her. She even sacrificed her children to her lovers. Egypt and Assyria had been her lovers, but she had been so lustful that she had paid them to take her favors instead of them paying her (16:15–34).

Her days were numbered. She would be stripped naked before the world and held up to shame. Her land and possessions would be given to others. She would be cut to pieces by the swords of those who had patronized her (16:35–43). Samaria and Sodom had been her sisters. They had been bad, but not nearly so bad as Jerusalem. She had used Sodom as a byword in the days when things had been going well for her. Now Jerusalem would be like Sodom (16:44–58).

The LORD would restore Jerusalem. The very act of restoration would cause her to blush in shame when she remembered how she had acted in the past (16:59–63).

c. The great eagles (17:1–24). This allegory of the eagles concerned the royal house of Judah and its attempts to play one power off against another. The first eagle represented Babylon, who took Jehoiachin to Babylon and set Zedekiah in his place. But Zedekiah—instead of doing as the Babylonians wanted, and in so doing, preserving the lives of the people—sent envoys to Egypt (the second eagle). The result would be the destruction of the kingdom and Zedekiah's deportation. This allegory applied to the intrigues that led to the second Babylonian invasion of Palestine in 589.

8. The soul that sins shall die (18:1–32). One of the new features of Ezekiel's theology was his doctrine of individual responsibility. The dominant view in Israel was the idea of corporate responsibility. In this view, the emphasis was on the group rather than the individual. Out of it grew the concept that a child could suffer for the parents' sins or vice versa. This was expressed in a common proverb: "The parents have eaten sour grapes, and the children's teeth are set on edge." It was also enshrined in the law in Exodus 20:5, where it is said that the children would be punished "for the iniquity of the parents, to the third and the fourth generation." Now things had changed. The new rule was this: "The person who sins shall die" (18:1–4).

The remainder of the chapter was spent in illustrating that basic point. A righteous man who kept the covenant provisions would live. If he had a son who broke every law in the book (of the covenant), the son would die for his sins, but the father would be blameless (18:5–13).

The reverse of that situation was also true. The righteous son of a covenant-breaking father would live, but the unrighteous father would die for his own sins. If the sinner turned to righteousness or the righteous man turned to sin, he who turned to righteousness would gain life while he who turned to wrong would lose it. Some were saying that the LORD was not doing right, but they were the ones who were wrong. The LORD was the judge, who preferred to give life rather than death. What they must do was to turn from their sins so the LORD could give them life (18:14–32).

9. Two poetic allegories (19:1–14).   Reverting to the allegory form again, Ezekiel combined it with the lament, or dirge, rhythm. The allegory was of a lion with two cubs which she raised in proper '"lion fashion" to adulthood. One (Jehoahaz, Josiah's successor) was captured and taken to Egypt. The second was either Jehoiachin (598–597), or Zedekiah (597–587/86), who both were taken as prisoners to Babylon (19:1–9).

10. Three sermons (20:1–22:31).

a. The will of God (20:1–49).   In 590, some of the community leaders came to Ezekiel to ask him what the LORD's will was for the people. Undoubtedly, this was a perplexing question since they had been getting advice from the other prophets of the community. This contradicted the advice given by Ezekiel and by Jeremiah in his letter to the exiles (Jer. 29). In answer to their questions, they were reminded of the long and sordid history of disobedience of their forefathers. Time after time, the LORD had affirmed and reaffirmed the covenant to be their God and to lead them to a good life on the condition that they put aside other gods and worship the LORD only. They had violated this covenant and gone after other gods in Egypt. Yet, the LORD had delivered them (20:7–9).

Both in the desert and in the land that the LORD had promised to give them, they had been given the LORD's laws and the sabbath as the sign of the covenant (20:10–29). Yet they turned to the worship of other gods. The LORD was disgusted with such behavior. Yet, the present generation was commiting the same sins that their fathers had commited, in their desire to be like "the nations" (20:30–32).

The LORD was determined to weed out the sinners from among the people. Only the righteous would be allowed to return to Palestine. If they were going to serve idols, they had better do it while they could. Such would not be allowed when the return came about. They would worship the LORD only. The LORD was acting to protect his honor. For that reason, the people's wickedness would not be dealt with as severely as it deserved (20:33–44).

The sermon ends with a short oracle about a fire in the south. Judah (the southern kingdom) would be devoured by a northern fire. Instructed to deliver this warning, the prophet protested having to speak in riddles (20:45–49).

b. The sword of the LORD *(21:1–32).* The sense of urgency that frequently appeared in Jeremiah's prophecies as Judah's end neared can also be seen in these oracles on the sword. As one of the common weapons of war, the sword symbolized death and destruction. The LORD is spoken of as drawing a sword to kill the people of Jerusalem (21:1–4). The prophet was told to groan and to cry out in despair. When the people asked why he was groaning, he was to give them the news of what was to happen. The news was about a sword, sharpened and polished for the battle, ready to slaughter whoever got in the way (21:5–13). The prophet was to act as a soldier, using his sword in battle to bring home the truth of his message (20:14–17).

The prophet then was told to draw a map, portraying the roads from Mesopotamia to the west. There was a fork in the road—the west fork leading to Jerusalem and the east fork leading to Rabbah, the capital of Ammon. The king of Babylon was described as standing at the fork, consulting his gods about which city to strike. Taking a handful of arrows, he shook them and threw them down. He hoped the pattern they made would give an indication of which road he would take. By means of divination or casting lots, he consulted his gods and examined an animal's liver, another mode of divination. The arrows pointed to Jerusalem (21:18–22).

This would shock the people of Jerusalem, who had made treaties with Babylon but had forgotten how they sinned against the LORD. They were guilty, and Babylon was the sword of the LORD's righteous anger. The rulers would be exiled, and the land would be given to the poor. Ruin! ruin! This would be the fate of Jerusalem (21:23–27).

Although the Ammonites had been spared, they had no reason to gloat. Their day was coming. The sword and the fire would destroy them in their own land (21:28–32).

c. The sins of Jerusalem (22:1–3). This sermon contains a laundry list of the sins of Jerusalem. The commandment said, "You shall not murder," but they were murderers (22:1–4a). The commandment said, "You shall make no graven images," but they worshiped idols (22:4b). The commandment said, "Honor your father and mother," but they dishonored their parents (22:7a). The commandment said, "You shall not steal," but they stole from foreigners, widows, and orphans (22:7b). The commandment said, "Remember the sabbath," but they did not keep the sabbath and they desecrated holy things (22:8). The commandment said, "You shall not lie," but now they faced the death penalty for lying about one another (22:9a). The commandment said, "You shall not commit adultery." Not only had they commited adultery, they also had commited incest (sexual relations with a relative) (22:9b–11). Beyond the Ten Commandments, they loaned money at interest and took bribes to murder. They had forgotten the LORD (22:1–12).

Those sinners would not go unpunished. They would be scattered among the nations as evidence that the LORD was the ruler (22:13–16). Ezekiel compared what would happen to the people to refining metal. The impure metal is put into a hot furnace, where the heat is used to separate the pure metal from the waste or slag. The people of Jerusalem would be refined in the fires of the exile as sinners would be separated out for destruction (22:17–22; cf. Jer. 6:27–30).

The major problem was the leaders of the land: the upper classes, the priests, and the prophets. They were like voracious animals, seizing by force things that were not theirs. The priests had become so materially minded that spiritual things were meaningless to them. The rulers had become thieves, while the prophets had become purveyors of false oracles. The people, too, had followed the examples of their leaders. They were extortioners and robbers. The LORD had looked for someone to stem the tide of corruption, but he had found no one. Judgment was certain (22:23–31).

11. Those wild, wild sisters (23:1–49).   In this allegory Samaria and Jerusalem are represented as two sisters, Oholah and Oholibah. Together they represented all of the Israelite people, both north and south. They had already been guilty of sexual immorality in Egypt. Just as the prophet Hosea took Gomer as his wife, they, too, had become the LORD's wives, despite their previous records of sexual looseness. Children were born, but the sisters would not stay away from other men. First, it had been Egypt and Assyria. Oholah (Samaria) became a victim of Assyria, who had disgraced her and then killed her (23:1–10).

Oholibah (Jerusalem) was even wilder. She cavorted with Assyria and Babylon. She especially was attracted to the Babylonian officials. But, as was generally the rule, they abused her so much that she sought other lovers. She became even more immoral as she offered herself to any who would take her (23:11–21).

Her former lovers, the Babylonians, would be her executioners. Their well-equipped armies would pour down the northern invasion routes and rape the land. She would be handed over to people who hated her. Soon her fate would be like that of her sister Oholah (Samaria) (23:22–35).

The oracles close with a restatement of what had been said previously and with the theme, "You shall know that I am the LORD God" (23:36–39).

12. The rusty pot (24:1–14).   The allegory of the rusty pot was dated in January, 588, as Nebuchadnezzar's army laid siege to Jerusalem. Ezekiel was using this figure to say that Jerusalem's "goose was cooked"—that is, its fate was sealed. Because of the bloody atrocities they had committed that had gone unpunished, Jerusalem's inhabitants would be destroyed. The reference to blood poured out on a rock (24:7) comes from the idea that one's life was in the blood. If blood was shed, as in a murder, the victim usually was left unburied. The ancients believed that the spilled blood cried out to God for the murderer to be punished. Blood poured on a rock would be especially conspicuous since it would stain the rock, and thus would be hard to wash out.

The rusty pot spoke of the filthiness of Israel's sin. The only way to get rid of it was to burn it out, so the destruction of Jerusalem was part of the cleansing process (24:1–14).

13. The prophet's wife dies (24:15–27; 33:21–22). Ezekiel's final oracle of doom was the most difficult of all. It was an acted oracle. He was told that his wife would die, and that when she did, instead of following the usual customs of wailing, going without a turban, going barefoot, having the mouth covered, and eating only "the bread of mourners" (24:17), he was to act as if nothing had happened (24:15–18).

After his wife's death, the people asked the reason for his strange and unconventional behavior. He told them, as instructed, that the news of Jerusalem's fall would soon reach them. When it did, they were to take no special note of it. Instead, they were to go on with life as usual. As Ezekiel had done when his wife died, so they were to do when Jerusalem died (24:19–24).

Ezekiel was told that when a fugitive came to bring the news of Jerusalem's fall, a new phase of his ministry would begin (24:25–27). The sequel of this passage appears in Ezekiel 33:21–22. In January, 586[10], a messenger arrived in Babylon, bringing news of Jerusalem's fall. Ezekiel had been silent since the evening before, but when the news came, he began to proclaim a new message.

Oracles against Foreign Nations (25:1–32:32) As was standard, at least among the more prominent prophets, Ezekiel had a fairly long section on oracles against foreign nations. At times his arrangement of oracles suggests the influence of the Amos traditions, about which Ezekiel undoubtedly knew. His oracles were confined to nations immediately surrounding Israel, and to Egypt. Notably absent were oracles against Babylon and Syria. Syria probably was omitted since it had long since ceased to be a threat to Judah. Only selected oracles will receive comment.

1. A roll call of the neighbors 25:1–17
2. Many words against Tyre and the Phoenicians (26:1–28:19)
3. A short word about Sidon (28:20–23)
4. Blessings on you, Israel (28:24–26)
5. The fall of Egypt (29:1–32:32)
   a. The Egyptian crocodile (29:1–16)
   b. Egypt is given to Nebuchadnezzar (29:17–21)
   c. Egypt is doomed (30:1–19)
   d. Oracles against the pharaoh (30:20–32:32)

1. Many words against Tyre and the Phoenicians (26:1–28:19). Ezekiel had a multitude of oracles against Tyre. The Phoenicians, for whom Tyre was the most representative city, had played an important role in the history of the Israelite people.

Although the fact is not mentioned in biblical history, the Phoenicians had a vital impact on the language and thought of the Hebrews. During the Israelite monarchy, furthermore, Tyre was an important ally of the Israelites. For David and Solomon, as well as for Omri and Ahab at a later time, the Phoenicians furnished building materials and expert help to carry out the huge building programs of those kings. They also furnished a sea arm for those Israelite kingdoms. Since Israel had no suitable ports, their alliance with the Phoenicians served Israel well. Throughout most of their histories, the Phoenician and Israelite kingdoms were united by covenants. There is no mention of any military activity between the two peoples.

Despite their previous history of peaceful relations, Ezekiel said that Tyre had tried to profit from Jerusalem's troubles. As a result, they would feel the hand of judgment and "They will know that I am the LORD" (26:1–6). Nebuchadnezzar would besiege the city for thirteen years. Finally, its surrender to him would bring an end to Phoenician life. It would eventually be joined to the mainland by a causeway built by Alexander the Great in his conquest of the city in 333 B.C.E. It continued to exist as an important city down into the New Testament era.[11]

Ezekiel saw the LORD's punishment for Tyre growing out of its gloating over Jerusalem's fall (26:2). He went on to describe in vivid detail what would happen to the city and especially to cities on the coast around Tyre. All this was to demonstrate the LORD's power (26:7–21).

Chapter 27 was a lament or funeral song for Tyre. A description of its ships, the vehicles of commerce that made it a great trading center, is found in 27:1–9. Its armies were mercenaries, soldiers hired from other nations (27:10–11). A directory of goods, services, and clients gives an insight into the wide range of Tyre's merchant ships (27:12–24). A funeral song would be sung, while shocked mourners would stare in disbelief at the fate of the great merchant city (27:25–36).

Ezekiel then turned his attention to the king of Tyre. The king was pictured as being puffed with pride, ripe for the calamity that was about to befall him (28:1–10). No matter how rich and handsome he was, his evil conduct would be his undoing. He would be hurled to the ground and his city destroyed (28:11–19).

2. *The fall of Egypt (29:1–32:32).*   These chapters contain a number of oracles about Egypt, dating from 587 to 571.

a. The Egyptian crocodile (29:1–16).   Egypt was like a giant crocodile, lying in the Nile River and waiting for a victim to come within its range. The LORD was going to take a large hook and catch the crocodile. Then it would be thrown, covered with fishes, into the desert to die (29:1–6a).

Israel had gone to Egypt for support, but it was attacked instead. The LORD was going to make Egypt a wasteland because of the way Israel had been treated. Its people would be scattered, and only a weak kingdom would continue to exist there (29:6b-16).

b. Egypt is given to Nebuchadnezzar (29:17–21).   This oracle, dated 571, was the last dated oracle of the prophet. Nebuchadnezzar had laid siege to Tyre in 585. After thirteen years, Tyre surrendered, but it was a hollow victory for Nebuchadnezzar, since what he gained was not worth the cost.[12] Ezekiel, whose earlier oracles had spoken of the devastation that was coming upon Tyre at Nebuchadnezzar's hand (26:17–21), spoke this oracle that recognized the realities of the situation regarding Tyre. Nebuchadnezzar's army had fought hard, so much so that "every head was made bald and every shoulder was rubbed bare" (29:18). Since he had failed at Tyre, he was given Egypt as his pay for hard work against Tyre (29:20). Nebuchadnezzar took advantage of a change of kings to invade Egypt in 568, but what he did is uncertain since records of the action have been lost. During the last days of Babylon, there was peace between Babylon and Egypt.[13]

   c. Egypt is doomed (30:1–19). Continuing the theme of Nebuchadnezzar's conquest of Egypt, Ezekiel compares it to the "day of the LORD" (Amos 5:18). Egypt and all her allies would fall (30:1–9). Nebuchadnezzar was about to carry off all of Egypt's wealth and devastate the land (30:10–12). Along with the other destruction would come the destruction of Egypt's idols. Its strong cities would no longer protect it. From one end of the land to the other, devastation would come (30:13–19).

   d. Oracles against the pharaoh (30:20–32:32). Turning from the land in general, the oracles were directed toward the ruler of Egypt, Pharaoh Apries, otherwise known as Hophra (589–570). In 587, Ezekiel said that the LORD would weaken the king of Egypt ("break his arms," 30:22) and strenghen the king of Babylon (30:20–26).

   In an allegory of the cedar tree, Pharaoh Hophra was compared to a cedar in Lebanon. In that country, cedars grew to magnificent size, making the country famous for that particular kind of wood. In the allegory, one particular tree outgrew all the rest because it had more water (the Nile River). It was so big that it towered over the other trees. Even the trees of the garden of Eden could not match it (31:1–9).

   But the woodcutter came (Babylon). The tree was cut down and left. Its valuable wood became nothing more than a brush pile where the birds nested. That would be the pharaoh's fate. He would die and go to Sheol (the grave), where all men went. Hophra was assassinated in 570 (31:10–18).[14]

   A lament was sung for Pharaoh Hophra (32:1–16). He had been a lion among the nations, but God would throw a net over him and cast him to the ground. His body would become food for the birds. Babylon would come with the sword and make the land of Egypt desolate.

   The prophet pictured Egypt in the grave with the other nations that had perished—Assyria, Elam, Meshech and Tubal, Edom and the Sidonians. The pharaoh might not like it, but that would be his end (32:17–32).

   Hope for a Better Day (33:1–48:35) From Chapter 33 on, the oracles of Ezekiel were directed toward encouraging the people to plan for the future, when they would be restored to the land of Palestine. Chapters 33 to 39 deal with oracles of restoration, while 40 to 48 deal with rebuilding the Temple and the restoration of worship.

Oracles of Restoration (33:1–39:29)

1. The watchman's responsibility (33:1–20). This oracle took a principle and illustrated it by a number of examples. The principle was that a watchman bore the responsibility to warn the community of danger. If he did his job well and the community failed to heed his warning, then the community as a whole bore the blame for whatever happened. If, however, the watchman failed to be alert and to warn the community of imminent danger, when they had to suffer because of his failure the watchman also shared in the suffering (33:1–6).

So it was with people and their sins. If the prophet warned them, then only the people were responsible for their sins. If the prophet failed to warn them, then the prophet had to share the responsibility (33:7–20; see also Chapter 18).

2. Oracle against the inhabitants of the land (33:23–39). The people who had been left in the land had claimed the abandoned properties for themselves. But that would not be so because they had sinned by continuing to act in the way they had before the exiles had been taken away.

3. They don't believe you, Ezekiel (33:30–33). The people were listening to Ezekiel, but they took him no more seriously than they would an entertainer who sang songs to them.

4. The responsibility of shepherds (34:1–31). Shepherds who enjoyed all the benefits derived from their flocks but failed to take care of them soon would lose them. So it was with the spiritual shepherds of Israel. In looking out for themselves first, they had lost their flocks (34:1–10).

In contrast, the LORD would go out and search for the lost sheep until they were found. He would bring them back and care for them—caring for the sick, separating the good from the bad, and protecting the poor and mistreated from the strong who would oppress them. A Davidic king would be restored to the throne, and Jerusalem would prosper once more. By this they would know the LORD (34:11–31).

5. You are going to get it, Edom (35:1–15). This sounds like a misplaced oracle against a foreign nation. At the least, it indicates the depth of the feeling of antagonism that existed between the Israelites and the Edomites. This especially was true after the Edomites seemed to have taken advantage of Judah during the Babylonian war. Edom was accused of saying that it would rule Judah and Israel (35:10), but the LORD would see that Edom was left desolate (35:15).

6. Blessings on you, Israel (36:1–38). This really is a continuation of the oracle against Edom. The nations surrounding Israel had made fun of it in its time of calamity. The situation was about to change, however. Israel would prosper while they would be humiliated. Israel's cities would be rebuilt when the people returned to Palestine. The land had devoured them before, but that would no longer be so (36:1–15).

When Israel had lived in Palestine before the exile, they had defiled it. They had disgraced the name of God. What the LORD was about to do then was for the sake of the Divine name and reputation. The implication of this was that it was an act of grace toward Israel, something it did not really deserve:

> A new heart I will give you, and a new spirit I will put within you; and I will remove from your body the heart of stone and give you a heart of flesh. I will put my spirit within you, and make you follow my statutes and be careful to observe my ordinances. . . . you shall be my people and I will be your God (36:26–28).

7. *O dry bones, hear the word of the LORD (37:1–14).* The most famous of Ezekiel's visions perhaps was the vision of the dry bones. The prophet, either physically or in a vision, was taken to a battlefield. The corpses of the slain had been left to rot in the sun or to be devoured by animals. As a result, bones were scattered everywhere. The prophet was commanded to preach to the bleached bones. As he preached, the bones came together. In the words of the spiritual:

> The toe bone connected to the foot bone;
> The foot bone connected to the ankle bone;
> The ankle bone connected to the leg bone . . .

When the bones were connected into a skeleton, the prophet was told:

> Prophesy to the breath (*ruach*) . . . and say to the breath (*ruach*) . . . Come from the four winds (*ruachoth*), O breath (*ruach*), and breathe upon these slain (37:9).

As can be seen by the words in the parentheses, there is a play on words (pun) here. The point of the whole oracle was to continue to express the idea that the Jews would be restored. The nation that was dead and scattered, like the bones, would be brought alive again by the LORD's action.

8. *The two shall be one (37:15–28).* The prophet was told to take two sticks and to write the word Judah on one and Israel on the other. Then he was to hold them in his hand as though they were one. His action would symbolize the reunion of the two parts of the nation under one king.

9. *The LORD and Gog of Magog (38:1–39:29).* With these oracles, Ezekiel moves into the realm of the apocalyptic. Instead of judgment on Israel for its sins, the LORD promises to intervene from heaven to overthrow the forces of evil arrayed against Israel. While not all the elements of the apocalyptic are present here, these oracles carry out the major theme of the triumph of the LORD over those who would destroy Israel.[15]

Attempts have been made to identify Gog of Magog (38:2) with some ruler of Ezekiel's time. The best that can be said is that with our present knowledge, no satisfactory identification can be made. This has led to numerous attempts over the centuries to identify Gog with rulers of various nations by those who see these oracles purely in a futuristic sense, with unfortunate results.

Perhaps the best that can be said is that Gog was representative of those forces that have opposed, and will continue to oppose, the LORD's rule in the world. This would seem to be supported by the fact that the descriptions of Israel (whom Gog was to invade) was an idealized description that had not existed before Ezekiel's time, nor has it since. Ezekiel expected it in the near future.

The invasion would be the signal for the LORD to intervene by unleashing the forces of nature against Gog—"Then they shall know that I am the LORD" (38:23). The devastation of the armies of Gog would be so great that Israel would be burning abandoned weapons (those with wooden handles) as firewood, thus saving their own trees (an early form of recycling?). As they attempt to clean up the land, it would take them seven months to bury all of Gog's dead soldiers (39:1–20).

That Ezekiel was talking about something in the near future would seem to be indicated by the closing part of the oracle, where once again he spoke of Israel's restoration to the land. This would be done to show the LORD's holiness—"Then they shall know that I am the LORD" (39:21–29).

The Restoration of the Temple (40:1–48:35)   The remainder of the Book of Ezekiel deals with the rebuilding of the Temple and its related buildings, along with the altar for sacrifices (40:1–43:37); the priests (44:1–31); the division of the country (45:1–8); the prince's lands and the rules of conduct (45:9–46:18); the priest's quarters (46:19–24); the Temple foundations (47:1–12); the division of the land (47:13–48:29); and the names of the gates of Jerusalem (48:30–35).

This interest in priestly things was in keeping with Ezekiel's interest in the priesthood. He of all the prophets would be the most likely to try to put into practical activities the principles preached by the prophets. For him, this would not only include social action but also worship activity.

The Temple would continue to be the center of such worship activity in the restored community. Thus the vision of the Temple, with details of its dimensions, would be of interest to Ezekiel. He, a former priest, would be receptive to such a vision (40:1–42:20).

As he envisioned the overpowering presence of the LORD leaving the Temple (11:22–25), so he envisioned its return to the restored community and the rebuilt Temple. It was to be a new day when the people with new hearts of flesh would be obedient to the LORD's commands (30:26), would be ashamed of their old ways, and would serve the LORD alone in faithfulness (43:1–12).

The responsibility of priestly service would be limited to those priests who were the descendants of Zadok. All other Levites would serve as helpers, but, because of their unfaithfulness, they would not be allowed to serve as priests (44:10–31).

Special lands were to be set aside for the LORD, including the area around the Temple (45:1–6). The ruler, now called the prince instead of king, was also alloted certain territory, but he was given severe warnings about his conduct toward the people (45:7–9). Instructions were given about what the prince was to receive in offerings from the people. He, in turn, was to furnish animals and materials for national offerings in important festivals and other holy days (45:10–46:15).

Among the unusual features of this series of visions was the description of a stream of water flowing from the base of the Temple toward the Jordan Rift and the Dead Sea. The further it flowed, the deeper the stream was. When it reached the Dead Sea, the Dead Sea's stagnant waters came to life with all kinds of animals and fish.

One of the features of the Garden of Eden was that it was well-watered. To people who lived in a dry land, a stream of fresh water was priceless. For Ezekiel in his idealized vision of the restored land, the "LORD in his holy Temple" would be the source of life for a land and a people who had been to the grave of exile, but had returned from the dead. Even the Dead Sea would come alive in that time (47:1–12).

Ezekiel: A Summary. Ezekiel was a prophet with a number of differences:

1. While he, like Jeremiah, was from a priestly family, Ezekial's priestly background seems to have had more effect upon him than Jeremiah's had upon himself.
2. The visions of Ezekiel were much more elaborate and numerous than were those of earlier prophets. As such, he was a connecting link between the prophets and the later apocalyptic writers.
3. He made extensive use of allegory as a teaching device.
4. He made a major contribution, with Jeremiah, to prophetic thought in his teaching of individual responsibility.
5. Perhaps his most important contribution was to give meaning to Jewish religious life after the calamity of 587/86 B.C.E. His work served as a bridge between the preexilic religion of Israel and later Judaism.

Courtesy of Ewing Galloway.

Figure 11–2. The ruins of the Ishtar Gate suggest the magnificence of Babylon at the height of its power.

THE END HAS COME FOR BABYLON

The Babylonian (Chaldean) Empire was like a shooting star. It flashed across the heavens briefly and then burned out.

The Decline of Babylon

When Nebuchadnezzar died in 562, Babylon began to die. His successor Evil-Merodach (562–560) released King Jehoiachin of Judah from prison (2 Kings 25:27–30), but Evil-Merodach died in the same year. Other kings came to the throne with Nabonidus (556–539) being the final one. He aroused great antagonism by trying to make major changes in the national religion. Nabonidus was interested in excavating and exploring ruins and abandoned temples—a sixth century B.C.E. archaeologist! He left the running of the kingdom to his son Belshazzar. He even refused to come to Babylon for the New Year's Festival, the chief religious festival of the year and one in which the king played a leading role. This brought major unrest among the people just as a new power was rising in the East.

Cyrus the Persian

Babylon's most dangerous rival was Media. When a revolt led by the Persian king Cyrus broke out in the Median empire, Nabonidus may have supported it. But Cyrus rapidly became a dangerous rival to be reckoned with. By 550, Media was under his control. He defeated an alliance of Egypt, Babylon, and Lydia by conquering Lydia in 546 and Babylon in 539, and penetrating all the way to the Egyptian frontier by 538.[16]

THE EXILE'S GREAT UNKNOWN PROPHET

Cyrus was to be the instrument of Israel's restoration to the land. The very fact that the people were sent back home was an unusual action by an unusual leader. A prophet in exile saw Cyrus as the LORD's instrument to bring about his aim to restore Israel to its land. He, along with Ezekiel, helped the people to adjust to their situation.

The Man

In a discussion of Isaiah of Jerusalem,[17] the arguments are advanced for the belief that the Book of Isaiah was the product of the ministry of more than one prophet. Many dispute such a theory, but it also has an equal number of strong advocates. An acceptance of a multiple authorship is assumed here. As a result, the prophet will be referred to as Deutero-Isaiah (Second Isaiah).

Even when one assumes that there was at least one other prophet whose work is found in the Book of Isaiah, little can be said about him. The Second Isaiah was among the exiles, as was Ezekiel. He obviously was an admirer and probably considered himself a disciple of Isaiah of Jerusalem, even though one hundred years separated them.

Much can be said about his work, for he, along with Ezekiel, gave the Jews reasons still to believe in their God. Without their work, the religion of Israel would have had difficulty surviving. They gave the devout Jews reason for their devotion.

The Book

The book, in reality, is not a separate book as the Old Testament now stands; it is Chapters 40 to 66 of the Book of Isaiah. It falls naturally into two parts: 40 to 55 and 56 to 66. The first is set in Babylon; the second seems to be set in the restored community of Jerusalem.

Comfort to Israel (Isa. 40–55)

The prophet's call (40:1–11).   The keynote of Isaiah 40–55 was reassurance to a nation that had been trampled underfoot by Babylon, reviled and scoffed at by her neighbors, and exiled in a distant land. Rebuke enough had been flung at them. The LORD, through the prophet, sent a word of comfort:

> Speak tenderly to Jerusalem,
>   and cry to her
> that she has served her term,
>   that her penalty is paid,
> that she has received from the LORD's hand
>   double for all her sins (40:2).

Such a condition could have existed only after the fall of Jerusalem. Only then could it be said, "She has received from the LORD's hand double (punishment) for all her sins" (40:2).

A dialogue follows the opening lines. It would seem to be the prophet's unique way of describing the LORD's call to him. He was told to be like a king's herald, going through the land announcing the king's imminent appearance. He was to see that the bumps in the road were smoothed down and that the holes were filled in. The LORD's overpowering presence was about to make itself known in the midst of the people as they would be led in a new exodus back to Palestine (40:3–5).

A command came to "cry," or preach. When the prophet-to-be asked what the nature of his message would be, he was told to proclaim that, like the grass and the flower, everything would pass away except the enduring word of God (40:6–8).

He was to herald the good tidings to Jerusalem from the high mountains that the LORD was about to return to rule the land with strength, justice, and compassion:

He will feed his flock like a shepherd;
  he will gather the lambs in his arms,
and carry them in his bosom,
  and gently lead the mother sheep (40:11).

In praise of the LORD, the Creator (40:12–32).   The prophet's job was not an easy one. He faced the questons of the cynics who said, "My way is hidden from the LORD, and my right is disregarded by my God" (40:27). They could understand punishment for their sins, but what had happened to them seemed to have gone beyond the punishment due for their sins. The prophet's answer was a magnificent poem on the LORD as Creator.

The poem consisted largely of rhetorical questions—that is, questions whose answers were already known both to the asker and to the one of whom they were asked. By those questions he pointed out that the LORD had created the universe (the waters, the heavens, and the earth). The LORD consulted no one, for the nations were as nothing to him (40:12–17).

The LORD could not be compared to idols, for they were only wooden gods created by a puny man:

Have you not known? Have you not heard?
  Has it not been told you from the beginning?
  Have you not understood from the foundations of the earth?
It is he who sits above the circle of the earth,
  and its inhabitants are like grasshoppers;
who stretches out the heavens like a curtain,
  and spreads them like a tent to live in;
who brings princes to naught,
  and makes the rulers of the earth as nothing (40:21–23).

A king scarcely was seated on his throne before he passed away, and his place was taken by another (40:24).

There was no one to whom the LORD could be compared; he had created the universe, giving each heavenly body its name and placing it in the created order (40:25–26). His people, therefore, had no reason to question his concern for them for:

The LORD is the everlasting God,
  the Creator of the ends of the earth.
He does not faint or grow weary;
  his understanding is unsearchable (40:28d–29).

The LORD gives power to every age—the elderly ("the powerless"), children ("youths"), and those at the peak of their physical strength ("the young"):

those who wait for the LORD
  shall renew their strength,
they shall mount up with wings like eagles,
they shall run and not be weary,
they shall walk and not faint (40:31).

The message is that young children can reach their full potential ("mount up like eagles"); young people can still reach high goals ("run and not be weary"); and the elderly can still have a meaningful life ("walk and not faint") (40:29–31).

The nations on trial (41:1–29). The LORD was calling the nations to judgment, where they would have a chance to defend themselves (41:1). While Cyrus was not named, the prophet described the rapid advances he was making. But Cyrus was the LORD's agent:

> Who has performed and done this,
>   calling the generations from the beginning?
> I, the LORD, am first,
>   and will be with the last (41:4).

The nations were trembling at the news of the Persian advances. The idol makers were trying to encourage one another, hoping their idols would save them. But the LORD had taken Israel from the ends of the earth. Israel was the LORD's servant and could be assured of the LORD's presence and help (42:2–10). Israel's enemies would be put to shame, for the LORD would help Israel triumph over its enemies (41:11–16). The desert, furthermore, would bloom for Israel as evidence that "the hand of the LORD has done this" (41:17–21).

The false gods were challenged, therefore, to submit evidence of their ability to produce results. They could not, of course, since they were nothing. Only the LORD had the power to move nations and men at his command. The coming of Cyrus (still not named) had been announced to Israel. When one looked to the idols for any help, they found nothing (41:22–29).

The Servant Songs

Introduction. One of the unique features of Second Isaiah is the Servant Songs. There are four poems (42:1–4; 49:1–6; 50:4–11; and 52:13–53:12). They are called the Servant Songs because they introduce a figure referred to as the LORD's Servant. Each poem adds more information about the Servant, with the climax coming in 52:13–53:12, where the Servant's trial and death are described.

Numerous questions are raised about the poems, especially in two major areas: (1) What is their relationship to the rest of 40–55? Did they originate separately from 50–55 or as a part of it? (2) Who was the Servant?

As for the first of the questions, whether they originated separately or not, they are so skillfully blended into the rest of the material that they do not seriously interrupt it. The first poem, for example, climaxes the section on the LORD's judgment of the nations. The Servant is portrayed as the instrument of that judgment.

The question of the Servant's identification will be left until the last of the poems is discussed.

The First Servant Song: The Servant's Mission (42:1–4). In this poem, the LORD describes the mission of the Servant, who would "bring justice to the nations" (42:1). Unlike military conquerors, he would do his work quietly, but his gentle manner would not deter him in his object:

> He will not faint or be crushed
> until he has established justice in the earth;
> and the coastlands wait for his teaching (42:4).

I am the LORD your God (42:5–46:13). Oracles in these chapters constantly return to the single theme: "I am the LORD your god." Like the theme notes of a symphony, they recur time and time again. Different subjects are discussed—idols and idol makers, Cyrus, the restoration of Israel—but all come back to the theme.

God created heavens and earth with all of its inhabitants. His Servant had been given to bring light to the people. He alone would do it, for no idol could share his glory (42:5–9).

The prophet broke out in a hymn of praise, calling on the whole creation to praise God for his fight against his foes (42:10–13). In the battle, the people would be helped, even though they were blind to what God was doing for them. Even so, the LORD would keep his promises (42:14–17).

Unfortunately, all that Israel had seen was meaningless to the people. The LORD had wanted to save them, but they had been led from the land. They had been given over to the enemy because they had sinned against the LORD. They had learned nothing from their experience (42:18–25).

Yet the LORD would rescue his people, because they were his.

> When you pass through the waters I will be with you;
> and through the rivers, they shall not overwhelm you;
> when you walk through the fire you shall not be burned,
> and the flame shall not consume you.
> For I am the LORD your God,
> the Holy One of Israel, your Savior (43:2–3ab).

Others would be given in exchange for Israel. A new exodus would take place, bringing the people back to the land; they were the LORD's people, created for his glory (43:1–7).

In using the figure of a trial again, the prophet portrayed God as summoning the nations to demonstrate that he was God above all others. No god was formed before him; none would be formed after him. They were witnesses to that fact. The LORD had saved Israel before any other God came along. He alone could deliver them now (43:8–13).

To prove his power, he was sending an army to conquer Babylon. Many years before, the LORD had led the nation in the first exodus from Egypt. Now a new thing was about to happen—a new exodus was about to take place (43:14–21).

Israel had sinned against God by failing to worship properly. Yet, he would not hold their sins against them. They were challenged to bring witnesses to court to prove that God had wronged them (43:22–28). He had created Israel. Israel was his servant, the people he loved. He would bless them so that they would thrive like plants that had plenty of water. Gradually they would come to recognize that he was the first, the last, the only God (44:1–8).

In contrast to the living God were the idols. In a scathing satire on idols (44:9–20), the prophet concludes that both idols and idol makers are nothing. After all, a man chooses a tree or metal and fashions it with his hand to look like himself. The maker of wooden idols took a tree, burned part of it to cook his food and to warm himself, and then used the other part to make a god to worship. Such a person was stupid! "He feeds on ashes; a deluded mind has led him astray, and he cannot deliver himself and say,'Is not this thing in my right hand a fraud?'" (44:20).

The LORD had swept away Israel's "transgressions like a cloud" (44:21–22). The prophet broke out in song at the prospect of the LORD's redemption of the people. He who was doing this had created heavens and earth, had confounded the wisdom of men, and had promised that Jerusalem would be rebuilt. He was the one, furthermore, who raised up Cyrus the Persian to be his servant who would rebuild Jerusalem (44:21–28).

In an address to Cyrus[18] (45:1–7), the LORD promised to go before him and prepare the way for his conquests. What Cyrus was about to do was for the sake of the LORD's people. He had been chosen as the LORD's servant.

> I call you [Cyrus] by your name,
>   I surname you, though you do not know me.
> I am the LORD, and there is no other;
>   besides me there is no god.
> I arm you, though you do not know me,
>   . . . .
> I form light and create darkness,
>   I make weal and create woe;
>   I the LORD do all these things (45:4–5, 7).

Using a figure from Jeremiah, the prophet pronounces woe on one who strives against his maker, like a pot against the potter (Jer. 18). The created ones cannot question the Creator's actions. The man Cyrus was created to do the LORD's work in freeing Israel. The nations would acknowledge that Israel's God was supreme. He was the Creator, and he spoke the truth. No idol could take his place. The judicial decision must be made, therefore. Who was the Creator? Who is the only true God? Who could save the people? The LORD, the God of Israel. In him alone is salvation, for to him, "every knee shall bow, and every tongue shall swear (45:8–25).

Look at the gods of Babylon. They had to be carried on donkey's backs, because they could not go from place to place, much less create anything! They were dependent on their makers to move them. They could even be captured and carried away. Yet the LORD had cared for Jacob from the beginning; and he would be with them to the end. Could the LORD be compared, then, to a god made of gold by a human craftsman? An idol that had to be carried on men's shoulders? Absolutely not!

> for I am God, and there is no other;
>   I am God, and there is no one like me,
> declaring the end from the beginning
>   and from ancient times things not yet done (46:9–10).

He was the one who would soon deliver Israel (46:1–13).

Sing a sad song for Babylon (47:1–15).   The prophet sang a lament for Babylon. It would be reduced to slavery. Even though the LORD had permitted it to take Israel into exile, it had been proud. It thought it would rule forever, but its end would come (47:1–7). Though it thought it would never be like a childless widow, it would be (47:8–9). It thought it could do evil and no one would know it, but ruin would come quickly (47:10–11). Its sorcerers and wise men who claimed they could save it were like stubble and would fail because they could not deliver it (47:12–15).

You have heard, now see all this (48:1–22).   The prophet sums up in this chapter what he had said in Chapters 40–47. The chapter marks the dividing point in Chapters 40–55. In it the LORD reminded the people that he had revealed the past to them long ago. Now, he was about to reveal new things to them—things they did not know. These things had been kept from Israel because of its previous inclinations toward unfaithfulness. Because of that record, what the LORD was about to do was for his own sake. He would not give his glory to anyone else. It was the LORD who had created the heavens and the earth (48:1–13).

No one would have predicted that Cyrus would have attacked Babylon; yet the LORD had been behind the success of Cyrus. The prophet adds a note of reminder to his audience: "And now the LORD God has sent me and his spirit" (48:16). If the people had followed the LORD:

> Then your prosperity would have been like a river,
>   . . . .
> your offspring would have been like the sand,
>   and your descendants like its grains;
> their name would never be cut off
>   or destroyed from before me (48:18–19).

The oracle ends with the prophet urging the people to begin the new exodus, to shout it to the ends of the earth, "The LORD has redeemed his servant Jacob." He would lead them through the desert, making water flow from the rocks (48:14–22).

The Second Servant Song: The Servant's Responsibility (49:1–6).   The second Servant poem goes further than the first in describing the Servant and his role in the world. Instead of being written in the third person, this poem was written in the first person. In it, the Servant described his call from God. Like Jeremiah, he felt that from birth he had been chosen by the LORD for his role. The LORD spoke of him as being like a secret weapon (49:1–2).

The first suggestion of the Servant's identity is in this oracle: "He said to me, 'You are my servant, Israel, in whom I will be glorified'" (49:3). The Servant protested the he had worked, but his strength was wasted. He realized that the LORD had his reward (49:3–4).

After the identification in verse 3, verses 5 and 6 take away some of the certainty. After restating that he was "formed from the womb to be his servant," the LORD went on to state that one of the Servant's responsibilities would be to bring Jacob and Israel back to the LORD. But that was not a big enough job. The Servant was also given the responsibility of being "a light to the nations," so that the LORD's salvation might "reach to the ends of the earth" (49:4–6).

Because verse 7 also refers to "the servant (slave, *NRSV*) of rulers," some take it also to be a part of the second Servant Song. According to verse 7, the role would be reversed, the kings serving the one who had once been their servant.

The return of the people (49:7–13). This seems, with verse 7, to be a response to the second Servant poem. The reference to "you" would seem to refer to the Servant, who has been helped by the LORD and given "as a covenant to the people." They were called upon to come forth as the LORD would lead them from exile, seeing to their physical needs along the way (49:8–12). The prophet interrupted to sing a song of praise because the LORD comforted the people (49:13).

Zion shall be comforted (49:14–50:3). This is the first of what are sometimes called the "Zion poems," which make up much of Chapters 50 to 55. They deal with the restoration of Jerusalem, frequently called Zion in the Old Testament. This poem begins as a charge by Zion (as though it was a person), claiming that she had been forgotten by the LORD. The response was that the LORD could no more forget Zion than a mother could forget her suckling child (49:15). Indeed, his plans were for her rebuilding, her enemies becoming as ornaments for a bridal dress (49:14–18).

The time would come when the land would not hold the people. Then the people would have to live in other kingdoms simply because there would not be enough room in Palestine. No power, however, could keep the LORD's people captive; the LORD would take the side of Israel in court and win the case. The opponent would be punished by death (49:19–25).

> Then all flesh shall know
> that I am the LORD your Savior,
> and your Redeemer, the Mighty
> One of Jacob (49:26).

Some would think that because the LORD had divorced his bride (Israel), this meant that he could not redeem her again. Such was Israel's law of divorce (Deut. 24:1–4). But he was God, not man. He could forgive sin, and he could redeem what had been put away. After all, creation did his bidding (50:1–3).

The Third Servant Song: The Servant's Submission (50:4–11). The Servant again spoke, as in the second poem. He spoke of his God-given ability to comfort and encourage the weary and downtrodden. He was also open to the teaching that the LORD gave him day by day. But his work aroused opposition. He faced it with courage (50:4–5).

> I gave my back to those who struck me,
>   and my cheeks to those who pulled my beard;
> I did not hide my face
>   from insult and spitting (50:6).

With God's help, he had not been discouraged by the insults and persecution. He depended upon God, who would stand up for him in court. No one could bring a charge against him when the Supreme Judge of all the universe was on his side. His opponents would wear out before they would be successful (50:7–9).

He urged all who feared God to keep up their courage. Those who were trying to plot against others ("lighters of firebrands") would answer to the LORD in the end (50:10–11).

Joy for Jerusalem and beyond (51:1–52:12). Those who were wanting the LORD's salvation only had to be reminded how Abraham had been blessed. When it seemed there was no hope, Isaac, his son and heir, was born. The LORD would bring joy and gladness to Jerusalem. It would become a new garden of Eden (51:1–3).

But that would not be all. The LORD would extend his teaching and his rule to the nations. The heavens would disappear, but the LORD's deliverance would last forever. Thus, the one who was in the right should endure taunts and insults because the LORD's deliverance would be everlasting (51:4–8).

Verses 9 to 11 call for the LORD to wake up and deliver his people as he had done in the Exodus from Egypt. If he would do so, those who were traveling back to Jerusalem would reach it with singing and everlasting joy.

The LORD responded by assuring them that he was the same one who had created the heavens and the earth. Yet they lived in constant fear of the Babylonians, from whom they had been freed. He was the Creator, and Jerusalem's inhabitants were his people whom he would teach and protect (51:12–16).

Jerusalem was called upon to awaken. Its punishment was over for it had experienced the double disaster of war and hunger. The anguish of the last days of Jerusalem would now be visited upon those who had caused them in Jerusalem (51:17–23).

Since Jerusalem's days of sadness and oppression were over, it was to put on its most beautiful garments, for

> How beautiful upon the mountains,
>   are the feet of the messenger who announces peace,
>   who announces salvation,
>   who says to Zion, "Your God reigns" (52:7).

Watchmen, who usually raised their voices in alarm, were to "sing for joy" as they watched "the return of the L ORD to Zion" (52:8). Even the waste places would break forth in singing, for the L ORD had redeemed his people. Then the ends of the earth would see the L ORD's salvation. In preparation for the return, the people were to purify themselves. They did not have to leave Babylon in a hurry. They were not fugitives; instead, they were a people led and guarded by the L ORD (52:1–12).

The Fourth Servant Song: The Servant's Trial and Death (52:13–53:12). With this poem, the Servant Songs reach their climax. Unlike poem 1, where the L ORD was the speaker; poem 2, where the Servant describes his call from the L ORD; and poem 3, where the Servant talks of his initial suffering, poem 4 has at least two different speakers.

The poem is divided into five stanzas of three verses each: 52:13–15; 53:1–3; 53:4–6; 53:7–9; and 53:10–12. In stanza 1, the L ORD speaks about the Servant, while in stanzas 2 through 5, another speaks about the Servant.

1. The appearance of the Servant (52:13–15). The L ORD introduced the Servant as one who had been given a high place, yet his physical appearance was shocking because he had been disfigured. When the kings of the earth saw him, they were astonished. Somehow all of this seems to tie in to the Servant's commission to "be a light to the nations" (49:6).

2. The rejection of the Servant (53:1–3). The things reported about the Servant were unbelieveable, especially since the L ORD's power was said to have been revealed through him. He was like a dried-up, scrubby desert plant.[19] People were not attracted to him, for he really was not compelling in his manner. Indeed, he was hated and shunned—a lonely man who knew great sorrow.

3. The Servant suffering for others (53:4–6). The narrator became personally involved as he described the Servant's suffering for "us." This kind of suffering, in which an innocent person suffers for another, is called "vicarious" suffering. In this section, the personal pronouns "we," "us," and "our" are used ten times to emphasize that the Servant suffered for the narrator and those with him.

> All we like sheep have gone astray;
> we have all turned to our own way,
> and the L ORD has laid on him
> the iniquity of us all (53:6).

4. The death and burial of the Servant (53:7–9). The Servant was like a lamb about to be slaughtered or a sheep about to be sheared. The sheep is not noted for its intelligence. It will stand still and mute as it is being killed. So the Servant offered no defense as he was unjustly condemned to death. He was "cut off from the land of the living." When he died, he was buried along with the wicked (which he was not) and the rich (which he was not).

5. The vindication of the Servant[20] (53:10–12).   The LORD had permitted the Servant's suffering on behalf of the sins of others. The Servant would see his reward because his action would lead to many being counted as righteous. Instead of physical children, he would have children of righteousness—those who owed their right relationship to God to him. Then an astonishing thing would happen. Because of the unselfish act he had done for others, the one who was despised and rejected would be classed with the great and the strong.

6. Who was the Servant?[21]   This is a problem that has intrigued interpreters for centuries. The answers can be divided into two groups: (1) those who identify the Servant in a group or collective sense, and (2) those who identify the Servant as an individual.

Those who argue for the first option point out that the Old Testament frequently spoke of a group as an individual. Thoughout Second Isaiah, as well as the other prophets, all the people of Israel were spoken of as Israel, Jacob, Jerusalem, or Zion. Israel (the nation), furthermore, is identified as the Servant in 49:3, as well as in several other places in Second Isaiah (41:9, 43:10, 44:1). Both Jewish and non-Jewish interpreters argue for Israel as the Servant.

But, even among these interpreters, there is a distinction between those who see the reference to Israel as a whole and others who argue that the remnant (or ideal) Israel is meant. The Servant would not be Israel as it was, but Israel as it ought to be.

Many are convinced that the fourth song indicates that the servant had to be an individual, A number of historical persons have been suggested—Jeremiah, or King Jehoiachin, or even Moses since the prophet speaks of a new exodus.[22]

As there are those who identify the Servant with the ideal Israel, so there are those who identify with an ideal person. Such a person would show Israel the revolutionary idea that through suffering, the door was open to the guilty to repent and enjoy the LORD's salvation.[23]

Christian interpreters, beginning with the early church, have looked upon the Servant as Jesus Christ. There can be little doubt that Jesus interpreted his own life in terms of the Servant, more than he did in terms of the kingly Messiah of Isaiah 9 and 11. When one does this, however, one must realize that, as a Christian, he is looking back into the Servant Songs through Christian eyeglasses. If such a person had been in the position of Second Isaiah, would that person have been so positive in his/her identification? Perhaps the safer estimate is that found in the statement: "The Servant is the climactic figure in the prophetic line, who will proclaim the way of salvation and be himself the medium of salvation."[24]

Israel is assured (54:1–17).   This song of assurance reminds one of the picture of the "lonely widow" of Lamentations 1, who had lost her children but who now was assured that the number of her children would be more than that of others who were married. It was a time to make enlargement plans, for prosperity was just around the corner (54:1–3).

The prophet goes back to the familiar husband-wife figure to speak of how the LORD had gone away from Israel for a while because of her unfaithfulness. But now she had been taken back because of the LORD's great love for her (54:4–8).

It was like Noah's time when God had destroyed the earth. As Noah was promised that the earth would not be destroyed again, so a covenant was made with Israel that "shall not be removed" (54:9–10).

The new Jerusalem would be built, many sons would be born, and enemies would be defeated. Since the LORD made the weapon makers, he would see that no weapon would be made that could destroy Israel (54:11–17).

The great invitation (55:1–13). The climax of Isaiah 40–55 comes in an invitation for all to come and accept the LORD's free banquet. The LORD would make an everlasting covenant, for this banquet would be a covenant-making meal. Israel would call nations that did not know the LORD. They would come to "the LORD your God . . . the Holy One of Israel" (55:1–5). The invitation was to

> Seek the LORD while he may be found,
>   call upon him while he is near,
> let the wicked forsake their way,
>   and the unrighteous their thoughts;
> let them return to the LORD, that
>   he may have mercy on them,
> and to our God, for he will abundantly pardon (55:6–7).

Since God's ways of thinking and doing things are far superior to that of people, his word would accomplish its purpose when it was sent out. Thus Israel would "go out in joy" and "be led back in peace" (55:12). As a sign of the LORD's doings, trees would grow where once only thorns grew (55:8–13).

Oracles of a Restored People (56:1–66:24). These oracles no longer had the unbroken note of comfort found in Isaiah 40–55. Instead, there were mingled notes of comfort and rebuke, suggesting that the ideal conditions and conduct anticipated by the prophet had given way to the harsh realities of living once more in the land. When the exiles returned, they were confronted by at least two major problems: (1) Most of them were not prepared for the barrenness of the land compared to the lush, well-watered valleys along the Tigris and Euphrates Rivers. (2) They encountered the people who had remained (or who had moved in), who (a) looked upon the land as theirs by right of possession, and (b) looked upon themselves as still being true followers of the God of Israel. The returning exiles were not willing to agree on either point, thus setting up a troublesome conflict that would continue for a long time. It is likely that the conflict was intensified by priests from families who stayed behind in Palestine, who still saw themselves as authentic representatives of the LORD, clashing with priests of the Zadokite line who accompanied the returning exiles. Growing out of this conflict would be a rival temple that eventually would be built on Mt. Gilboa in the territory of the old Northern Kingdom. In the postexilic period, the Zadokite priests gained control in Jerusalem.

Was there a third prophet?   The source of this material is in question. Some argue for a third prophet, designated as Trito-Isaiah,[25] while others see these oracles as coming from the same person who was responsible for 40–55. It has been suggested that the differences arise from the fact that 40–55 was a unified composition, while 56–66 consists of spoken oracles that were collected and written down later.[26] The changed circumstances of the returnees and language similarities also would seem to be sufficient to attribute these oracles to Deutero-Isaiah.

An outline of the oracles follows:

1. The LORD's salvation is for all (56:1–8)
2. The beasts and bad leaders (56:9–12)
3. The idol worshipers are back (57:1–13)
4. Peace to all but the wicked (57:14–21)
5. Holy day religion (58:1–14)
6. A call to repentance (59:1–21)
7. Poems about Zion (60:1–62:12)
    a. Jerusalem's glorious future (60:1–22)
    b. Good tidings to the lowly of Zion (61:1–11)
    c. New days and new names for Jerusalem (62:1–12)
8. The day of the LORD's vengeance (63:1–6)
9. A prayer and its answer (63:7–65:25)
10. The final words (66:1–24)

The LORD's salvation is for all (56:1–8).   In the light of a later movement in Judaism known as particularism which rigidly held that the Jews were the only people of the LORD and in keeping with Isaiah 40–55, this oracle, which extended the LORD's salvation and deliverance to such outcasts as eunuchs and foreigners, showed a universal spirit. The eunuch, a man who had been castrated and thus had lost his ability to function sexually, was forbidden in the law to ever be a part of the congregation of Israel. The Book of Deuteronomy required kind treatment for foreigners, but it did not include them in the congregation of Israel. The prophet foresaw, however, a time when even the most extreme outcasts would be received by the LORD on the basis of their faithfulness to him.

Holy day religion (58:1–14).   The LORD could not fault the people for their Temple attendance. They were conscientious in keeping the law, sacrificing, and fasting. But it did not affect their relations with their workers or their neighbors. Kindness and justice did not increase when worship increased. The hungry were still just as hungry, and the naked had no clothes. When the worship was translated into action, then the presence of the LORD would be near (58:1–9). Only then would God's blessing flow like a spring of cold water and the cities be rebuilt. Worship and service were twins—one must accompany the other (58:10–14).

A call to repentance (59:1–21).   This oracle complains about a lack of justice in the land. For this reason, a wall separated God and the people. It was not the LORD's ability to save that had created the situation; rather, it was the people's sin (59:1–13).

> Justice is turned back,
>   and righteousness stands at a distance;
> for truth stumbles in the public square,
>   and uprightness cannot enter (59:14).

God would give justice, both to the just and to the unjust. He would subdue the enemy and redeem his people. His spirit would come upon them and upon their children to follow them (59:15–21).

Poems about Zion (60:1–62:12)

1. Jerusalem's glorious future (60:1–22).   Jerusalem had been in darkness for many years, but now the light of the LORD would once more shine in it as his presence was felt. Its people would return, along with the nations bringing gifts to the LORD from the desert countries and from the Mediterranean countries. Jerusalem would be open to all nations as the Temple would arise in new splendor.

> The sun shall no longer be your light by day,
>   nor for brightness shall the moon
>   give light to you by night,
> but the LORD will be your everlasting light,
>   and your God will be your glory (60:19).

2. Good tidings to the lowly of Zion (61:1–11).   This oracle, made even more famous by Luke's account of Jesus' sermon at Nazareth (Luke 4:16–39), originally was a word of assurance to the poor and oppressed of the land of Palestine. The poor rarely had a champion, one who would protect their rights. The reference to "the day of vengeance of our God" meant the day when God would right those things that were wrong. The mourners would become rejoicers. The nation that had been poor and oppressed would be restored. Those who had mistreated the people would know the sting of justice, while Zion would know the joy of justice. This would come because the LORD loved justice and hated wrong (61:1–9). The oracle ends with a call to praise God (61:10–11).

3. New days and new names for Jerusalem (62:1–12).   Jerusalem's restoration would not only bring a new day but also new names for its changed condition. Before, it had been called "Forsaken" and "Desolate" (62:4), but now it would be called Hephzibah ("my delight is in her") and Beulah ("married"). It would be like a newly married woman.

The responsibility of the city's watchmen would be to remind the LORD of the LORD's obligations to Jerusalem until all that was promised was done. Among those promises was that hunger would no longer be a problem (62:6–9).

Jerusalem was under obligations also to prepare the way for the returning exiles. They, too, would share in the new names, being called "The Holy People, The Redeemed of the LORD," "Sought Out, A City Not Forsaken" (62:10–12).

A prayer and its answer (63:7–65:25).   As a sort of prologue to the prayer that follows, the prophet reminded the people of the LORD's past blessings as opposed to the people's failures. They were reminded once again how the LORD had led the patriarchs in their wanderings and the Hebrews in the Exodus (63:7–14).

The prophet then prayed, addressing the LORD as "our father; our Redeemer from of old" (63:16). He asked for help to keep from erring. He prayed that the LORD would give aid against Israel's enemies. He was unlike any God man had seen. He helped the good and punished evil men. Israel had come to him polluted and he had hidden his face from them (63:15–64:7).

He pleaded that the LORD not be angry, for he was their father. Their land was wilderness, their Temple was burned, and the beautiful places ruined (64:8–12).

In reply, the LORD said he was ready to answer prayer but no one sought him. While he waited, they had rebelled against him by sacrificing to pagan gods. They pretended to be so holy that others could not touch them, but the One who was really holy was angry at their lack of holiness. They would be punished as they deserved. They would not be destroyed, however, for the tribe of Judah would be chosen to receive the LORD's blessings. As examples of these blessings, the Plain of Sharon, formerly unusable to Israel because it was covered with forests, would become a pasture for sheep. The Valley of Achor, symbol of everything bad because of the incident involving Achan (Josh. 7), would be a place of rest for flocks (65:1–11).

Because of the evil they had done, those who were rebellious would be destined for the sword—nothing would turn out right for them. In contrast, the LORD's servants would prosper in everything. The rebellious would be under the curse, while the chosen would know the blessing of the LORD (65:12–16).

An ideal age with a new heaven and a new earth would come to be (this is an apocalyptic idea). Jerusalem and its inhabitants would prosper with long, good lives filled with prosperity and peace (65:17–25).

The wolf and the lamb shall feed together,
　　the lion shall eat straw with the ox;
　　　but the serpent—its food shall be dust!
They shall not hurt or destroy
　　on all my holy mountain, says the LORD (65:25).

The final words (66:1–24). The LORD who had his throne in heaven and earth as his footstool had no need of a house built by people. What the LORD looked for were people who were "humble and contrite in spirit" and who trembled at the LORD's will. Sacrifices made by people who did not do the LORD's will were an insult. Such false religion would be punished (66:1–6).

Even though it did not seem possible, Jerusalem would be reborn because the LORD would do it. Those who loved it could rejoice with it. They could be nourished by it as a mother cared for and fed her children (66:7–12). It would carry them around like a baby on its hip. They would be comforted by the LORD and would prosper like grass in a rainy time.

On the other side of the coin, the LORD would come in judgment upon those who defiled the land with idol worship. The survivors would be scattered to the nations of the world. They would carry the message of what the LORD had done. The people of Israel would be gathered, coming to Jerusalem by every means of transportation. As the new heavens and the new earth would remain, so the people of Israel would remain before the LORD, while the rebels would die (66:13–24).

Summary of Second Isaiah. Some of the major ideas found in Second Isaiah are as follows:

1. The LORD, the God of Israel, is Creator of the universe and the Redeemer of Israel.
2. The LORD was about to bring about a new exodus using Cyrus, the Persian king.
3. Redeemed Israel had a mission to the world as shown through the Suffering Servant. The Servant, variously identified as Israel or as an individual, was to bring God's light to the nations through his suffering.

Summary: Prophets of the Exile

In some ways, the prophets of the exilic period faced the most difficult task of all. They were dealing with people who had been greatly disillusioned by what had befallen them. Those people who had been taken to Babylon were the leaders of the community. They were the ones who were so thoroughly convinced that since God lived in the Temple, Jerusalem could not fall because it enjoyed special protection as God's dwelling place. By telling the truth about what was about to happen to them, Ezekiel helped them, along with Jeremiah, to adjust to the reality of exile. Deutero-Isaiah, whoever he might have been, gave them assurance that they were still the object of the LORD's love and concern, while at the same time giving them the basis for a future hope.

STUDY QUESTIONS

1. What makes the Book of Lamentations distinctive?
2. What does Lamentations tell us about conditions in Jerusalem during the Babylonian siege?
3. What changes did Israel experience as the result of the Babylonian Exile?
4. Compare the work of Ezekiel in exile to that of Jeremiah in Jerusalem.
5. How did the vision associated with Ezekiel's call affect him?
6. What symbolic actions did Ezekiel act out and what was their significance?
7. What symbolized for Ezekiel the inevitable doom of Jerusalem?
8. Compare Ezekiel's view of individual responsibility to that of Jeremiah's.
9. Why did Ezekiel not mourn his wife's death?
10. Name four allegories that Ezekiel used.
11. What was the meaning of Ezekiel's vision in the valley of dry bones?
12. What was the basic message of the Gog of Magog oracles?
13. What is the overall theme of Ezekiel 40–48?
14. How are Ezekiel 11:22–25 and 43:1–4 related to the two divisions in which they appear, 1–24 and 33–48?
15. What happened to the Babylonian Empire?
16. How is Isaiah 40–66 related to Isaiah 1–39?
17. What are the major themes of Isaiah 40–55?
18. What are the Servant Poems?
19. How has the Suffering Servant been identified?
20. How do the oracles in Isaiah 56–66 differ from those in 40–55?
21. Food for thought: What difference would it make if there were three or more prophets who contributed material to the Book of Isaiah?

ENDNOTES

1. On the first point see Bright, *A History of Israel*, 3rd ed., 345; and Noth, *The History of Israel*, 2nd ed., 287–288. On the second point see Hugh G. M. Williamson, "Laments at the Destroyed Temple," *BR* VI, 4 (August, 1990), 12, who discusses recent discoveries that seem to indicate that a number of wealthy Jewish families lived in Jerusalem during the Exile.
2. On the history and sources of the Aramaic language, see Scott C. Layton, "Old Aramaic Inscriptions," Dennis Pardee, ed. *BA* 51, 3 (September, 1988), 172–189.

3. Noth, *The History of Israel*, 292, argues that the Deuteronomic History was written in Palestine, while Richard Elliott Friedman, *Who Wrote the Bible?* 146–149, believes that Jeremiah and Baruch were the author-editors of the work.
4. Bright, *A History of Israel*, 346 (Jeremiah 29:21).
5. Walter Eichrodt, "Ezekiel," *OTL* (London: SCM Press, 1970), 52.
6. Walther Zimmerli, "Ezekiel 1," *HER*, 120.
7. Ibid., 132.
8. See note on Ezekiel 8:10, *NOAB, NRSV*.

9. Pritchard, *ANE*, 76–79.

10. According to *NOAB*, *NRSV* note on Ezekiel 33:21.

11. A. S. Kapelrud, "Tyre," *IDB* IV, 721–723.

12. For a fascinating article on Tyre and Phoenicia, see S. W. Matthews, "The Phoenicians: Sea Lords of Antiquity," *National Geographic* 146 (1978), 149–189.

13. Bright, *A History of Israel*, 352.

14. Ibid.

15. See pages 215–216.

16. For further details, see Bright, *A History of Israel*, 354–355, 361–362; and Noth, *The History of Israel*, 300–302.

17. See pages 210–212.

18. Cyrus is called *Meschiach* (Messiah) according to the *LXX* in 45:1.

19. John L. McKenzie, "Second Isaiah," *AB* 20 (Garden City, NY: Doubleday, 1968), 131.

20. I owe the basic idea for this outline to J. Leo Green, Professor of Old Testament, Southeastern Baptist Theological Seminary.

21. An excellent discussion of this problem can be found in McKenzie, "Second Isaiah," *AB* 20, xxxviii–iv.

22. Ibid., xlvii.

23. Ibid., liv–lv.

24. Ibid., lv.

25. George A. F. Knight, "Isaiah 56–66: The New Israel," *ITC*, xi–xvii argues for such a view.

26. James D. Smart, *History and Theology in Second Isaiah: A Commentary on Isaiah 35, 40–66* (London: Epworth, 1970), 231, makes this argument.

Chapter 12 🕮

THE POSTEXILIC PERIOD

Judah Revived

In Thomas Wolfe's novel *You Can't Go Home Again,* the author spoke of how home could never be what we thought it was. When we try to return, the home we knew is no longer there. Such must have been the experience of the Jews who returned to Palestine in 538 B.C.E. They came with big plans and high hopes, only to see them dashed on the hard rocks of reality.

THE INTERNATIONAL SITUATION (538–522 B.C.E.)

Cyrus the Great

Israel's return to the land was made possible by Cyrus the Great's conquest of Babylon. Nabonidus, the ruler of Babylon, had managed to antagonize a large number of his subjects by his neglect of the kingdom and especially by his neglect of the national religion. When the armies of Cyrus came to Babylon, Nabonidus had already fled. The city, without any resistance, fell like an overripe plum. Many citizens welcomed the conqueror, who promptly declared that Marduk, the chief god of Babylon, had sent him. As his local ruler, Cyrus appointed his son Cambyses. By 538 B.C.E., Cyrus controlled all of western Asia as far as the frontier of Egypt.[1]

The Reign of Cambyses (530–522 B.C.E.)

In 530, Cyrus was killed and his son Cambyses succeeded him. Cambyses conquered Egypt in 525, completing the establishment of an empire that would dominate the Near East for two hundred years.

Darius I (522–486 B.C.E.)

In 522, there was a rebellion in the eastern part of the empire. Cambyses, for some reason, committed suicide. Darius, one of his officers, immediately claimed the throne. He further strengthened his claim by defeating Gaumata, the rebel leader of the eastern provinces. Revolts sprang up like wildfire throughout the empire, with the result that it took Darius two years to gain full control of the throne. By 520, however, he had put down all the rebels and had begun a long and stable reign.[2]

THE RESTORED COMMUNITY

The day the prophets had preached about and that the pious Jews has dreamed about for so long finally came in 538. The Jews were permitted to return to Palestine and to rebuild their Temple, which had lain in ruins for over forty years.

Cyrus' Decree (Ezra 1:1–4)

The restoration was the result of the policies of Cyrus the Great. He reversed the policies of the previous kings who had dominated the Near East. Where they had deported people to help keep down rebellion, Cyrus permitted as many of the exiles as wanted to, to return to their original homes. Where previous kings had tried to destroy such religious shrines as the Temple, Cyrus encouraged subject peoples to rebuild their shrines. He even gave money to subsidize the cost of rebuilding such shrines.

In 538, Cyrus issued a decree that permitted exiled persons to return to their homelands.[3] The Jewish version of that decree is found in Ezra 1:2–4. In it, Cyrus declared that the LORD had given him the responsibility of seeing that the Temple was rebuilt. The returning exiles were to be given help in "silver and gold, with goods and with animals, besides freewill offerings" (1:4). If one reads the biblical version of this decree, it would appear that only the Jews were given such help. It seems, however, that this was the kind of thing Cyrus did for peoples of all religions.

The Returners (Ezra 1:5–2:70)[4]

In the years after 538, several groups of Jews returned to Palestine. The first group was led by Sheshbazzar, "the prince of Judah," who was the son of

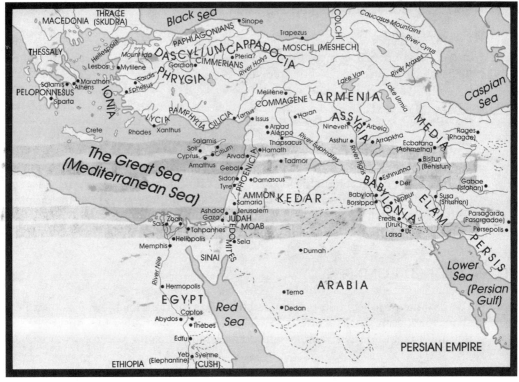

Artwork by Margaret Jordan Brown © Mercer University Press.

Figure 12–1.   The Persian Empire.

Jehoiachin. They carried with them some of the Temple treasures Nebuchadnezzar had taken away. The most Sheshbazzar was able to accomplish was to lay the foundations of the new Temple (Ezra 5:14–16). Then the doldrums seems to have hit the community.

This condition evidently came from several major sources: (1) the harsh realities of coming into a land still bearing many of the marks of the Babylonian conquest; (2) the opposition of the people left in the land, who felt it was theirs by virtue of the fact that they had lived there undisturbed for more than forty years; and (3) the attitudes of the people of the old northern territories, who looked upon themselves as still being faithful to the religion of Israel. The returnees, on the other hand, looked down upon them as heretics.

Since there seems to have been less-than-ideal agricultural conditions in those early years, making a living turned out to be quite a chore. By way of contrast, Babylon, with its well-irrigated fields and busy cities, offered money and food in abundance. Because of their prosperity, conditions were so attractive that many Jews chose to remain there. Babylonian records indicate that some Jews became prominent bankers, businessmen, and high government officials. Some of those who returned to Palestine probably wished at times that they had not done so.

No word is given about the fate of Sheshbazzar. He is mentioned only in scattered references. He may have died or may have been replaced by Zerubbabel, who probably returned with another group of exiles in 520. The spiritual leader was Joshua, who was high priest.

Haggai: Promoter of Temple-Building (Hag. 1:1–2:23). In four oracles dated in the late summer of 520, Haggai challenged the people to get on with the job of rebuilding the Temple.

If you expect the LORD's blessings, then do the LORD's will (1:1–15). In reaction to the people's excuse that the time had not "yet come to rebuild the LORD's house" (1:2), Haggai reminded them that they had not let anything stop them from building their own homes. Yet, despite all efforts to meet their own needs, they still were

Photo by Fon Schofield, Dargan-Carver Library.

Figure 12–2. King Darius I (Ezra 5 and 6) was not noted for his modesty. His exploits were recorded on this monumental inscription at Behistun in the mountains of Northern Mesopotamia (Iran). The trilingual inscription (Old Persian, Akkadian, and Elamite) is especially valuable because it provided Sir Henry Rawlinson with the key to deciphering cuneiform script.

not prosperous. Their efforts in agriculture had brought little produce, and they never seemed to have enough to eat and drink. Inflation also had taken its toll. Haggai's picturesque way of saying it was that "you that earn wages earn wages to put them into a bag with holes" (1:6). They needed to rebuild the Temple if they expected the LORD to bless them. Otherwise, drought would continue to devastate their crops (1:1–15).

There will be a greater Temple than Solomon's (2:1–9).   To encourage the builders, the prophet asked if there was anyone who remembered Solomon's Temple. Since there must have been people present who did, the prophet went on to assure them that, regardless of the unpromising beginnings of the new building, "The latter splendor of this house shall be greater than the former." Such a promise would only be realized many centuries later, when Herod the Great rebuilt the Temple for the second time.

If the Temple is built, you will prosper (2:10–19).   Haggai pointed out once more how poor their lot had been since they returned to Palestine. If they wanted to prosper, the Temple had to be completed.

Zerubbabel, you are the chosen one (2:20–23).   The uproar in the Persian Empire undoubtedly caused Haggai's enthusiasm to outrun his judgment. In reference to the problems of Darius I, Haggai promised that this meant that Israel would be freed and Zerubbabel would be the Messiah.

Zechariah: Man of Visions (Zech. 1:1–8:23).   Zechariah was the second of the prophets who helped stir up the people to work on the Temple. His messages were of a different type from those of Haggai, however. Haggai dealt with bread and butter issues—that is, he saw completing the Temple as a necessary condition for receiving the LORD's blessings in a practical form, such as food, clothing, and an improved standard of living. Only briefly did he mention the possibility of the coming of a messianic age.

Not so with Zechariah. First of all, the form of his messages was radically different. Instead of oracles like those of Haggai and most of the preexilic prophets, he, like Ezekiel, experienced numerous visions. In the second place, those visions dealt almost exclusively with the coming of the messianic age. This means that Zechariah was as much an apocalyptist as he was a prophet. He delivered messages like a prophet; their content was apocalyptic. He preached to encourage the people as they tried to do a hard job in a difficult time. That he and Haggai succeeded in inspiring the people to rebuild their ruined house of worship is a tribute to their faith and perseverance. They were not among the greatest prophets of Israel, but they served a useful function in their own day.

The oracles in Chapters 1 to 8 are to be dated from 520 to 518. Many interpreters believe these chapters contain the genuine materials from Zechariah. Chapters 9 to 14 are also apocalyptic, but the internal historical references indicate that they originated in the Greek period.

Return from your evil ways (1:1–6). Like those of the earlier prophets, this first oracle was a call to repentance: "Return from your evil ways and from your evil deeds" (1:4). From this point on, however, Zechariah's visions, similar to Ezekiel's allegories, follow. The vision is presented and is then followed by an explanation, the meaning of which, unfortunately, is not always clear.

The first vision: The four horsemen (1:7–17). In this vision, a man was seen riding a red horse, accompanied by three others riding red, sorrel, and white horses. They were sent out by the LORD to patrol the earth to check on conditions. The earth was at peace, but Jerusalem still lay in ruins. The LORD promised that the city and the Temple would be rebuilt.

The second vision: The four horns and the four smiths (1:18–21). The horn was used throughout the Old Testament as a symbol of strength and power. In this vision, the four horns stood for the four great powers that had such an influence on the destiny of the Israelite peoples: Assyria, Media and its ally Babylon, plus the Persians. The smiths were metal workers who made the weapons that gave the strong nations their power. Since they could give power, they could also take it away.

The third vision: The man with the measuring line (2:1–5). In modern society such a man would be called a surveyor. He was marking out property lines, a practice only appropriate for land that was about to be occupied. The vision meant that Jerusalem's population would increase so that it would spill over any walls built around the city.

A call to flee from Babylon (2:6–13). Many Jews remained in Babylon. The prophet said that the LORD was going to let Babylon be plundered. Many nations would be drawn to the LORD and his people. Here was a prophet proclaiming the day of the LORD like the popular view in the time of Amos. Zechariah assumed that the Jews' day of judgment was over and their time of glory was about to begin.

The fourth vision: Satan and Joshua (3:1–10). In one of the three places in the Old Testament where Satan was specifically named (the others are 1 Chron. 21:1 and Job 1–2), Satan stood up as an accuser against Joshua.[5] Obviously, there were those who tried to discredit Joshua as high priest since he is pictured as wearing dirty clothes. In the prophet's mind, this was the work of Satan. The LORD knew the truth and changed Joshua's dirty clothes for clean clothes (3:1–5).

Joshua was promised that if he would follow the LORD wholeheartedly, he would "rule my house and have charge of my courts" (3:6). The LORD, furthermore, would bring his servant "the Branch." This probably refers to Zerubbabel. When this happened, "You shall invite each other to come under your vine and your fig tree" (3:10).

The fifth vision: The golden lampstand and the two olive trees (4:1–14). This vision of a gold lampstand with branches for seven lamps represented the presence of God. The lamps were small clay lamps containing olive oil and a string that served as a wick. In later Judaism, the seven-branched lampstand became a seven-branched candlestick. It is called a *menorah* and is still a common Jewish religious symbol. The light of the gold lampstand and the number seven represented attributes of God (4:1–5; 10–14).

On either side were two live trees representing Joshua as spiritual leader and Zerubbabel as the messiah figure. There followed a word of assurance to Zerubbabel that he would be successful in completing the Temple. It would be "not by might or power, but by my Spirit, says the LORD" (4:6).

The sixth vision: The flying scroll (5:1–4).   The flying scroll was a written curse that would afflict thieves and those who took false oaths. The reflects the commonly held belief that a curse had the power within to destroy whatever or whoever it was directed toward. It was not a flying saucer!

The seventh vision: The woman in an ephah (5:5–11).   The ephah was a dry measure similar to a wicker basket. This particular basket had a lead cover on it so the contents could not escape easily. A woman whose name was "Wickedness" was in the basket. Two winged women carried her off to Shinar (Babylon), the sin city of Zechariah's day. This wickedness was removed from the land in preparation for the messianic kingdom.

The eighth vision: The four chariots (6:1–8).   The final vision was of four chariots pulled by red, black, white, and gray horses. They were sent out to the "four winds of heaven," although only three directions were mentioned (north, south, and west). The vision seems to be incomplete since no explanation was given. It undoubtedly had something to do with the announcement of the coming of the messianic kingdom.

Concluding oracles (7:1–8:23).   Zechariah was approached by some northerners who had been observing a fast commemorating the fall of Jerusalem in 587. They asked if they should continue to observe such fasts. Zechariah gave an oracle by which he exhorted them to "put away the fasts which the exile had made necessary, and address themselves, as of old to the virtues and duties of civic life."[6] Like the earlier prophets, he called upon the people to

> Render true judgments, show kindness and mercy to one another, do not oppress the widow, the orphan, the alien, or the poor; and do not devise evil in your hearts against one another (7:9–10).

Failure to live by these principals had brought on the exile in the first place (7:1–14).

In the closing oracle, Zechariah saw Jerusalem restored and prosperous, a city where the elderly could live in peace and children could play in freedom. The exiles in every land would be returned, the Temple would be rebuilt, and the Jews would no longer be the doormat of their enemies (8:1–13).

While the LORD had good purposes in mind for Jerusalem, they were not to forget the basic rules of justice and love toward one another. The fasts once had been for mourning; the fasts of Jerusalem would become feasts of joy and celebration. The nations of the world would be drawn to the Jews, whose LORD had blessed them (8:14–23).

The Effect of Haggai and Zechariah's Work (Ezra 5:1–6:22). The prophets, along with Zerubbabel and Joshua, inspired the people to return to the Temple building with vigor. Trouble would not be long in coming, however. The ruler of the province of which Jerusalem was a part sent someone to investigate what was going on. He found out who was responsible and sent someone to the Persian capital to see if the work had indeed been authorized by Cyrus, as the Jews claimed. When the answer came back, not only was the right to rebuild the Temple confirmed, but also the governor Tattenai was instructed to pay the building costs out of royal revenues. The building was finished and dedicated with joyful ceremonies in the year 515 B.C.E.

THE TIME OF SILENCE

With the completion of the Temple, a curtain was drawn over events in Palestine for more than fifty years. What happened no one knows. Zerubbabel's hopes of bringing in the messianic kingdom most certainly did not come to pass. In fact, his hopes and the efforts of the prophets to promote him as the Jewish ruler may well have had fatal results. The Persians, while remarkably tolerant in their policy toward conquered peoples, were so highly organized that revolt was kept at a minimum. It could be that Zerubbabel was removed because of the hopes that he would be the promised messiah.

EZRA AND NEHEMIAH[7]

With the fading away of Zerubbabel, the messianic hope also faded. When the Jews once more became visible on the stage of history, there was no mention of a king. Instead, the dominant figure in Jewish life was the priest. In the hands of the high priest would come to rest both the chief religious and political powers of the Jewish people.

Ezra the Priest

In the person of Ezra, we meet perhaps the most influential person in the postexilic community. His activities earned him the title "Father of Judaism."

The Date of Ezra. Ezra led a group of immigrants from Babylonia to Jerusalem "in the seventh year of Artaxerxes the king" (Ezra 7:7). Given the dates of Artaxerxes I (465–424), it would seem a simple matter to conclude that Ezra arrived in Jerusalem in 458. But things are not quite that simple; there were two kings named Artaxerxes. Artaxerxes II ruled from 404 to 358. Ezra could have arrived in Jerusalem in 397 instead of 458.

A third date that has been suggested is 428, based on the belief that Ezra came in the thirty-seventh year of Artaxerxes I. This would assume that the word *thirty* has fallen out of the biblical text. There is little evidence to support such an assumption.

Recent evidence has given new support to the first date, 458 B.C.E. One of the major arguments against that date is that Ezra started some important reforms, of which Nehemiah found little evidence when he came in 445. As one scholar has pointed out, however, reformers in biblical history were not noted for their long-lasting success. Good examples were King Hezekiah and King Josiah, both of whose reforms died quickly.[8] It is assumed here, therefore, that Ezra returned in 458, the seventh year of King Artaxerxes I.

The Work of Ezra (Ezra 7:1–10:44; Neh. 8:1–9:37)

The return to Jerusalem (Ezra 7:1–8:36). The picture given of Ezra is that he, like many Jews, had achieved a place of some respect in the Persian Kingdom. This was shown by the fact that not only did King Artaxerxes permit him to gather a group of immigrants to return to Jerusalem, but he also gave a generous amount of money to subsidize the immigrants (7:1–24). Ezra, furthermore, was to "appoint magistrates and judges, who may judge all the people in the province Beyond the River" (7:25).

In Ezra 7:27, the narrative switches to a first-person account of what happened on Ezra's trip to Jerusalem in 458 (7:7–9). First, there was a prayer of thanksgiving for the undertaking (7:27–28). Then, in true priestly fashion, there was a listing of those who made the trip (8:1–14). Finding that there were not sufficient priests, Ezra sent some eloquent and influential men to the Levites to persuade some of them to go along on the trip (8:15–20).

They were successful. After Ezra gave a selected group of the priests responsibility for looking after the money and sacred vessels given for use in the Temple, the pilgrims set out on the long trip to Jerusalem. Finally, they arrived safely. The money and vessels were turned over to the Temple officials for safekeeping. Then the proper calls of respect were paid to the local Persian officials, who were given letters of instruction from Artaxerxes as to their part in aiding Ezra (8:21–36).

Ezra's reforms (Ezra 9:1–10:44).
Ezra did not lose any time making his presence felt in the community of Jerusalem.

1. The problem of foreign wives (Ezra 9:1–10:44). Discovering that many of the Jews, including priests, had married non-Jewish women, like the holy men of old Ezra tore his clothes, pulled his hair, and went into a state of mourning (9:1–5).

At the time of the evening sacrifice, he prayed an eloquent prayer of confession about this condition, which for him represented a great sin by the people (9:6–15). By the time his prayer was ended, he was joined by many others who also were confessing that they had sinned by marrying non-Jewish women. In the emotion of the moment, they made a covenant that they would divorce all non-Jewish wives. Ezra swore all the Levites and others present to do as they had promised (10:1–5).

After a night of prayer and fasting, Ezra called a meeting within three days of all Jews at Jerusalem. To impress on the people the importance of being present, any person who failed to appear would lose his property. Needless to say, a large crowd was present, even though a heavy rain was falling. It was decided that a council of leading men would be set up to deal with the matter. The council was formed. Those who had married non-Jewish women divorced them and sent them away, along with any children born to them (10:6–44).

2. The renewing of the covenant (Neh. 8:1–9:38). Again, Ezra called the people together. The purpose was a ceremony of covenant renewal, recalling an ancient custom going back to the years following Israel's covenant at Sinai (Josh. 24). First, there was the reading of the Torah, or Law. By this time, that probably included essentially what we know as the Pentateuch today (Gen.–Deut.). As Ezra read the law, it had to be put into the language of the people, which now was Aramaic, not Hebrew. This, then, was the first recorded attempt to paraphrase the Scriptures (8:1–8).

The Aramaic paraphrase in later years was known as the Targums. They included Torah (Gen–Deut.), the Prophets (Josh. through 2 Kings, Isa., Jer., Ezek., and the Twelve), and the Writings (except for Daniel and Ezra–Nehemiah).

While reading the law, it was discovered that the seventh month (when this was taking place) was also the time for the celebration of the Feast of Tabernacles or Booths. The people went into the hills, cut tree limbs, and built shelters. They lived in the shelters for seven days to remind them of Israel's wilderness years. During those days they spent their time studying the law (8:9–18).

The festival was followed by a great day of repentance and confession. Some suggest that this may have come before the celebration of the Feast of Tabernacles.[9] The Jews separated themselves from all foreigners and confessed not only their sins but also those of their ancestors (9:2). They alternated hearing the law read with confession of sin. The solemn day was climaxed by Ezra's prayer of confession. In it, in a style common to the Old Testament, he first praised God. Then the reason for the praise was stated by telling again the story of the LORD's mighty act in delivering the people from Egyptian bondage and his mercy on them even though they had sinned so gravely against the LORD (9:1–31).

Finally, he confessed the sins of the generation then present. Like their fathers, they, too, had sinned. As a token of their repentance they entered into a solemn covenant, signed by the princes, Levites, and priests (9:32–38). This was the last mention of the work of Ezra.

Nehemiah, the Builder (Neh. 1:1–7:73; 13:1–31)

The time of Nehemiah's return is not so debated as that of Ezra. He said in his memoirs that he returned to Jerusalem in the twentieth year of Artaxerxes. There is general agreement that Artaxerxes I (465–424) is meant, thus dating Nehemiah's return in 445.

Events Leading to Nehemiah's Return (Neh. 1:1–2:8). Nehemiah, a devout Jewish layman, was cupbearer to the Persian king. The cupbearer's position was one of great honor since it involved great trust on the part of the king for the person who held the job.[10] Messengers came from Jerusalem, telling how the walls and gates of the city were in ruins. Either they had never been rebuilt since the Babylonian invasion, or they had been destroyed by the Persians for some unknown reason. Nehemiah undertook a period of fasting and prayer when he heard the news (1:1–11).

Several months passed. One day while Nehemiah was performing his duties as cupbearer, the king noticed his haggard looks and questioned him about it. When Nehemiah told him the reason, the king made Nehemiah governor of Jerusalem and gave him money and materials to repair the city walls (2:1–8).

The Rebuilding of the Walls (Neh. 2:9–7:73; 12:44–47). Nehemiah was not welcomed by everyone. Sanballat, the governor of Samaria, who had dominated Judah for some time; Tobiah, governor of Ammon in Transjordan; and Geshem (Gasmu), an Arab king, immediately took exception to Nehemiah's presence. They would cause much trouble in the days ahead (2:9–10, 19).[11]

Nehemiah's first action was to make a nighttime survey of the broken walls. Afterwards, he called the Jewish leaders together and told them of his plans to rebuild the walls. He received an enthusiastic response from them. The response from Sanballat, Tobiah, and Geshem, however, was to suggest that he really was trying to stir up rebellion against the emperor (2:11–20).

Organizing the people into construction gangs, Nehemiah proceeded with his plans (3:1–32). When Sanballat and Tobiah heard that constuction was in progress, they immediately began to make threats about what they would do. Nehemiah responded by dividing the Jews into two groups—one to stand guard against an attack and another to carry on construction (4:1–23).

Then, problems arose within the Jewish community. Many of the Jews had abandoned their villages and farms to aid construction. They had borrowed from their rich fellow Jews to have food for their families. When they could not pay their debts because of their contributions to the project, those to whom they owed money began to foreclose on them. Some even had to give their children as slaves to pay their debts.

Nehemiah called the leaders together and told them that such practices must stop immediately. Anyone who was a slave must be freed. He threatened to call the wrath of God down on them if they did not do as he ordered. They believed him and did so (5:1–13).

To show that he would not ask them to do what he would not do himself, never in his first twelve-year term as governor did Nehemiah take a salary paid by tax money. Instead, he supported himself and 150 other Jews from his own resources (5:14–19).

Sanballat and Tobiah kept trying to undermine Nehemiah. They invited him to several meetings outside Jerusalem to discuss matters. Each time, Nehemiah refused to go. In an open letter sent to Nehemiah, Sanballat suggested that the reason the wall was being built was that the Jews intended to revolt and that Nehemiah was going to have himself declared king by some of the prophets. He threatened to tell Artaxerxes what was going on. Nehemiah denied all the charges and continued his work. He also refused any special kinds of precautions for his own safety (6:1–14).

After fifty-two days the construction was finished. Tobiah's sympathizers started a campaign to convince Nehemiah that Tobiah was a nice fellow after all. He had a Jewish father-in-law and a Jewish daughter-in-law. Nehemiah was still unconvinced. He posted trustworthy guards on the city gates with strict instructions about opening and closing hours (6:15–7:4).

When the building was completed, dedicatory services were held, the central feature being a service of sacrifice after a march around the walls. The march ended in the Temple area, where the service of thanksgiving was held (12:27–43).

> They offered great sacrifices that day and rejoiced, for God had made them rejoice with great joy; the women and children also rejoiced. The joy of Jerusalem was heard far away (12:43).

To climax his work, Nehemiah made arrangements for regular services to be carried on by people who were paid by the offerings given, as had been the case in the time of the great kings. Since provisions were made for the regular collection of Temple revenues, the priests could attend to the services instead of working at other jobs for a living (12:44–47).

These were the major accomplishments of Nehemiah's first term as governor, which covered twelve years (445–433). In the thirty-second year of Artaxerxes, Nehemiah returned to Persia (13:6).

Nehemiah's Second Term as Governor (Neh. 13:1–31). Nehemiah later returned to Jerusalem to find some rather disturbing developments. His old nemesis, Tobiah, had been given a room in the Temple itself. That an Ammonite would even be permitted within the Temple precincts was a shock to Nehemiah. The Deuteronomic code contained a law that no Ammonite or Moabite ever be allowed to become a part of Israel since those peoples had opposed Israel's peaceful passage through their territory in the Exodus (Deut. 23:3–5). By the time of Nehemiah, the Torah (Gen.–Deut.)was already the written law (13:1–3).

When Nehemiah discovered that the high priest Eliashib had allowed Tobiah a room in the Temple, he ordered Tobiah thrown out, along with his furniture. A special cleansing of the room took place. It was then restored to its normal use (13:4–9).

He found, furthermore, that because the offerings had fallen off, the pay for the Levites to conduct the services in the Temple had failed. The Levites had to return to farming for a living. Nehemiah immediately began collecting the tithes again for the support of the Temple worship (13:10–14).

A third situation that confronted him in the second term was that many people were no longer observing the sabbath. Instead, they were working on the sabbath as though it was just another day. He ordered the city gates closed on the sabbath so the foreign traders and farmers could not bring their goods to sell on that day. He issued a warning that anyone who violated the sabbath would be punished (13:15–22).

Finally, in a rather severe manner he dealt with the still troublesome problem of mixed marriage. He physically beat Jews who were married to foreign wives, including the son of the high priest Eliashib. He made a decree that no such marriages would be permitted and rooted out foreign influences from Jewish life (13:23–31).

When the community was about to be swallowed up by its neighbors, Ezra and Nehemiah had played a vital role in preserving the religious life and culture of the Jews who had returned from exile. The zeal they inspired would be carried over into the period that, in Jewish historical records, is almost blank. Around 200 B.C.E., the curtain would be lifted, when Palestine once again became the battleground between two powers who were trying to gain control of its territory.

STUDY QUESTIONS

1. How did Cyrus' conquest of the Babylonians affect the Jews in exile?
2. What happened to the Jews who returned from the exile to Palestine?
3. What did Haggai contribute to the Palestinian postexilic Jewish community?
4. What was the purpose of Zechariah's visions?
5. When did Ezra return from the exile?
6. Assess the relative significance of Ezra and Nehemiah to the Jerusalem community.
7. What was significance of the reading of the law described Nehemiah 8?
8. What were Nehemiah's accomplishments as governor?
9. Term to know: *menorah.*

ENDNOTES

1. Noth, *The History of Israel,* 300–302.
2. Bright, *A History of Israel,* 361ff.
3. The Persian version can be found in Pritchard, *ANE,* 206–208.
4. Unlike previous books, where an attempt has been made to follow the order of the material as closely as possible, the order of Ezra and Nehemiah is somewhat confusing. References will be made to the material in chronological order as near as possible.
5. Satan actually is called *the* Satan. It probably would be more accurate to translate the phrase as "the Accuser" (*NRSV*) or "the Adversary."
6. George A. Smith, *The Book of the Twelve Prophets II* (London: Hodder and Stoughton), 200.
7. For a more extended discussion, see Jacob M. Myers, "Ezra-Nehemiah," *AB* 14 (Garden City, NY: Doubleday, 1965), 50–54.
8. Frank M. Cross, "A Reconstruction of the Judean Restoration," *INT* XXIX, 2 (April, 1975), 198. The article has a good summary of the arguments for the three basic dates (187–203).
9. Myers, "Ezra-Nehemiah," 165.
10. Myers, *op. cit.,* discusses the location of Susa and the role of the cupbearer.
11. Cross, "A Reconstruction," 200.

Chapter 13 🌿

A LEGACY OF ISRAEL

Wise Men and Psalm Singers

Israel contributed many things to the world, and its modern descendants (the Jews) are still making invaluable contributions to human society. Of all its literature, the most admired must be the words of its wise men and the songs of its singers. Its proverbs and metaphors spice the speech of many lands. Its greatest literary masterpiece, the Book of Job, ponders the mystery of some of life's deepest questions. Its psalms reflect the full range of human emotion, from abject misery to ecstatic praise. Its love songs, the explicitness of which challenge both Jewish and Christian interpreters alike, sing of the "way of a man with a maiden" (Prov. 30:19). Because all these literary types use poetry as the medium of expression, they will be studied together.

WISE MEN AND WISDOM LITERATURE

Wise Men and Their Work[1]

Wisdom was a product of the people, rooted in the experiences of life and representing the distillation of those experiences. Two of its most important characteristics were: (1) it originated in and was nurtured by the family or tribe, and (2) it was oral in its earliest forms. Its origins are lost in the mists of time, but logic would dictate that it began when leaders began to use their experiences in life to teach the young.

Wisdom in the Ancient Near East. Long before the inhabitants of Israel appeared in history as a separate people, there was a wisdom tradition among the people of the Fertile Crescent. Among the Sumerians, scribes used proverbs in Sumerian and Akkadian, both as a teaching device and as a means of learning a second language. The theme of the righteous sufferer was known in the area long before the Book of Job was written. A Babylonian work, *The Dialogue about Human Misery* (1000 B.C.E.), had echoes of ideas found in both Job and Ecclesiastes.

In Egypt, wisdom literature was commonly used to train young people in morals and for competent work in the court of the king. Especially important is "The Instruction of Amen-em-opet," which many scholars believe influenced Proverbs 22:17–24:22. The fact that Solomon had an Egyptian princess as his chief wife had led to the suggestion that Egyptian wisdom influence entered Israel through Solomon's court.

Wisdom in Israel. Israelite wisdom undoubtedly had its oral stage. Later, however, it seems to have taken on a more formal structure. References to the wisdom of Solomon (1 Kings 4:29–34) probably were reinforced by the fact that: (1) following the tradition of the Egyptians, he established schools of wisdom, and (2) since the Israelites viewed prosperity as evidence of God's blessing and with it, the evidence of wisdom, they equated great wealth with great wisdom. Since Solomon's prosperity was unquestioned, such prosperity would have enhanced any reputation he gained as a wise man. Further evidence of wisdom schools connected to the royal court might be deduced from the reference to the "men of Hezekiah" (Prov. 25:1) who were said to have collected "proverbs of Solomon." Generally it is agreed that the earliest reference to the "wise" as officials of the religious establishment is found in Jeremiah 18:18. Two books whose English names are often confused, Ecclesiastes in the Hebrew Bible and Ecclesiasticus from the Alexandrian Canon, seem to have been schoolbooks. Both are classified as wisdom books.

But wisdom knows no political or national boundaries. This was true especially when those boundaries really did not act as barriers to travel as they do today. Israel's wisdom was part of the larger pool of wisdom of the Near East. The book of Proverbs is a good illustration. In addition to collections of Israelite wisdom, it contains materials that had been brought into Israel from other countries. For example, Proverbs 22:17–24:22 has thirty sections similar to "The Instruction of Amen-em-opet." There are numerous parallels between the two texts, suggesting that the Hebrew writer knew the Egyptian text. This would not be unlikely since Solomon had close relations with Egypt. His scholars, who were concerned with collecting and developing Israelite literature, were undoubtedly influenced by others.[2]

Other examples can be found in Proverbs 30–31. The former is said to have been "the words of Agur son of Jakeh of Massa" (30:1), while the latter chapter is attributed to "Lemuel, king of Massa" (31:1). Massa was not in Israelite territory but was located in northwestern Arabia (Gen. 25:14).

Wisdom teachings were of two types. Practical wisdom was concerned with the problems of everyday living. The form of this wisdom was such that much of it was easily taught. The use of easily remembered literary forms—such as proverbs, fables, and short poetic discourses on some human problem—could be committed to memory. The proverb was a short, easily remembered saying that contained one main point. It could take the form of a comparison or a contrast. The fable (such as Jotham's fable in Judg. 9:7–15) was a story that had a moral, usually giving human characteristics to plants or animals. The short poetic discourses actually were just longer proverbs, still designed to make one main point. This kind of wisdom took a simple and orthodox view of life.

In the postexilic period, the wise men became the schoolmen in Israel. Perhaps the most famous was Ben Sirach, whose teachings were collected in the apocryphal Book of Ecclesiasticus or the Wisdom of Ben Sirach. Practical wisdom was the chief concern of the schoolmen.[3]

Wisdom of a different kind was found in Ecclesiastes (not to be confused with the Wisdom of Ben Sirach) and the Book of Job. These books belong to the realm of philosophical, or speculative, wisdom. These were extended discussions involving many of the deepest questions that confront human beings as they try to live in the world. They challenged many of the most widely held ideas of the time. They questioned things that most people would never dare to question. For them, life was far from simple. Indeed, they posed many unanswerable questions and challenged many traditional values.

Wisdom Books

Proverbs. Proverbs contains a diverse collection of orthodox wisdom. Life was viewed in a very simple manner—the man who followed wisdom would prosper, while the man who ignored wisdom would fail. The first was wise; the second was the fool—there was no middle ground.

The wise man's purpose (Prov. 1:1–7). Solomon's place in the wisdom movement is indicated in Proverbs 1:1, where the whole book was credited to him, even though later parts of the book clearly indicate that he was not the author of all the proverbs. Since Solomon was the most famous of all Israel's wise men, he was looked upon as the father of Israelite wisdom.

The purpose of the Book of Proverbs is stated in 1:2–6. Three groups of people are mentioned—those who needed "wisdom and instruction," those who needed "words of insight," and those who received "instruction in wise dealing, righteousness, justice, and equity" (1:2–3). The simple needed shrewdness, and youths needed "knowledge and prudence" (1:4). The wise person needed to "gain in learning" and to acquire skill to understand proverbs, figures of speech, and the words and riddles of the wise (1:5–6). The section ends with the theme:

> The fear of the LORD is the beginning of knowledge; fools despise wisdom and instruction (1:7).

1. Son, listen to your elders (Prov. 1:8–19). A father pleaded with his son to turn a deaf ear to bad companions. He warned him to avoid their ways. Since violence breeds violence, if he followed the way of robbery, violence, and bloodshed, he would be setting a trap for himself.

2. Wisdom's sermon to the simple (Prov. 1:20–33). Wisdom, pictured as a female, went into the busy places of the city in the role of a prophetess. Her sermon was addressed to the simple—those lacking wisdom. If the simple did not accept her leadership, when calamity came, she would mock them. When judgment fell, she would ignore their pleas for help.

3. Son, listen to wisdom (Prov. 2:1–22). The father called on his son to actively seek wisdom, because it came from the LORD. Because the LORD was the source, wisdom had great benefits for those who lived by it. To follow the path of integrity and justice was to be led by the LORD. Increased understanding of righteousness and justice would result. The ability to make right decisions would help the wise son to avoid evil men and evil ways. Most of all, he would avoid immoral women who would lead him to the grave.

4. Son, let the LORD lead you (Prov. 3:1–35). Loyalty and faithfulness characterized the good life. Loyalty to the LORD was supreme. To trust and follow the LORD was the simplest and best way of life. The wise understood that the LORD's correction was motivated by love. This, in turn, made life pleasant and meaningful. Because the LORD's people were safe, regardless of the disaster, fear was removed from life.

One should live in peace with neighbors, doing whatever was promised promptly. One should not be contentious, nor should one be jealous of evil people. They would come to a bad end.

5. Son, get wisdom and insight (Prov. 4:1–27). The father's father had handed down to him that the supreme aim of life was to get wisdom. With it, one could have protection and great honor. Since with wisdom one learned to avoid the pitfalls of life, the wise person lived a long life. To follow the wicked was to be led astray. Thus they should be avoided because doing wickness was their passion.

The road the righteous traveled got lighter, but the road of the wicked led into darkness. The life lived with care and planning, and characterized by truth and honesty, could be lived without shame.

6. Son, beware of that wild woman (Prov. 5:1–22). One of the most vivid passages in Proverbs contains the warning against consorting with an adulteress. Her smooth and seductive speech sounded sweet, but it led to death. The best thing to do was to keep as far away as possible, since she could only bring ruin.

Instead, a man should "drink water" from his own well and love the wife of his youth. The LORD's eyes were on men, so the wicked man could not escape the consequences of his sin.

7. Son, remember four important things (Prov. 6:1–19). (1) A man should be careful about giving security to another person's debt (6:1–5). (2) The diligence of the ant in its work should be an example to the lazy man (6:6–11). (3) A man should beware of a wicked man's words and ways that are the recipe for disaster (6:12–15). (4) The final warning was a numbers proverb using seven examples of disgusting things that the LORD hated:

> haughty eyes, a lying tongue
>> and hands that shed innocent blood,
> a heart that devises wicked plans,
>> feet that hurry to run to evil,
> a lying witness who testifies falsely,
>> and one who sows discord in a family (6:17–19).

8. Son, wisdom will keep you safe from wicked women (Prov. 6:20–35). A man who listened to the wisdom of his parents would be able to avoid loose women. The adulteress was even more dangerous than a harlot, since a harlot would only take a man's money while an adulteress could cause him to lose his life. A jealous husband would take no payment to soothe his anger. Instead, in his rage he would take a man's life.

9. Son, let's talk some more about wicked women (Prov. 7:1–27). Wisdom could keep a man from trouble involving the wife of another. The father told of a personal observation. He saw a naive young man passing the house of an adulterous woman. She came up to him, kissed him boldly, and told him that she had plenty of delicious food, a waiting bed, and an absent husband:

> With much seductive speech she persuades him;
>> with her smooth talk she compels him.
> Right away he follows her,
>> and goes like an ox to the slaughter,
> or bounds like a stag toward the trap
>> until an arrow pierces its entrails.
> He is like a bird rushing into the snare,
>> not knowing it will cost him his life (7:21–23).

10. Wisdom's sermon to humanity (8:1–36). Wisdom stood in the city gates addressing the passersby. She spoke of her value to humankind (8:1–11); the high position she held in the affairs of life (8:12–16); the rewards that came to those who sought her (8:17–21); and her role in creation as the first of created things and companion to God in creation (8:22–31). The prudent person would eagerly seek wisdom (8:32–36).

11. The two ways: The wise and the foolish (Prov. 9:1–18). To the ancients, prosperity was a sign of the LORD's blessing. Wisdom thus was pictured as having a beautiful house, vast flocks from which to choose animals for sacrifice, and an overflowing table to which she could invite those who lacked her blessings (9:1–6). The verses that follow compare the most foolish of the foolish with the wise person. The prize for the most foolish of all went to the scoffer who thought he knew something, but actually knew nothing. Rebuking a scoffer only made the situation worse, but to rebuke a wise person made that person wiser. The wise knew that the fear of the LORD was the real beginning of wisdom (9:7–12). Listening to the foolish woman led to death (9:13–18).

The "Proverbs of Solomon" (Prov. 10:1–22:16).   This section entitled "Proverbs of Solomon" (10:1) is made up exclusively of what modern comedians call "one liners"; not in the sense that they are jokes, but in the sense that their message is contained in one line of Hebrew (two lines in English translation). These short, pointed sayings each contain a simple truth designed to tell any person who hears them some lesson about how to live in relation to others. They are strung together like beads, each one different; yet each one is concerned with how to live a good life in human society.

The fact that these are called the "Proverbs of Solomon" did not mean necessarily that Solomon spoke all of them. They probably were from many lands and many sources. The belief that Solomon collected proverbs and was noted for his wisdom made it natural that his name would be attached to such collections.

Since it would be difficult to do so, no attempt was made to put these proverbs in any logical order. While antithetical parallelism is the dominant form, other forms were used. Of those that are antithetical, some examples of the contrasts made are as follows:

The wise and the foolish:
>A wise child makes a glad father,
>>but a foolish child is a mother's grief (10:1).

The proud and the humble:
>It is better to be of a lowly spirit among the poor
>>than to divide the spoil among the proud (16:19).

The righteous and the wicked:
>The righteous have enough to satisfy the appetite,
>>but the belly of the wicked is empty (13:25).

Good wives and bad wives:
>A good wife is the crown of her husband,
>>but she who brings shame is like rottenness in his bones (12:4).

Truth and falsehood:
>A truthful witness saves lives,
>>but one who utters lies is a betrayer (14:25).

Others of these proverbs are of a synonymous nature or used formal parallelism:

>Honest balances and scales are the LORD's:
>>all the weights in the bag are his work (16:11).
>In the light of the king's face there is life,
>>and his favor is like the clouds that bring the spring rain (16:15).

The Book of Thirty Sayings (Prov. 22:17–24:22).[4] This probably was a teacher's book of instructions to a pupil about some of life's important relationships. By it, the pupil could see what was "right and true." Then he could give a "true answer" to whomever questioned him (22:17–21). While some of its admonitions follow the one-line pattern of the previous section, for the most part they cover several lines. For instance, there were instructions on eating with a ruler (23:1–3); how to discipline children (23:13–14); the inevitable words about wicked women (23:26–28); a rather long warning about excessive wine drinking (23:29–35); and a warning to "fear the LORD and the king" (24:21–22). One piece of advice was repeated twice, the second time being somewhat longer than the first (22:28):

> Do not remove the ancient landmark
>   or encroach on the fields of orphans,
> for their redeemer is strong;
>   he will plead their cause against you (23:10–11).

The sayings of the wise ended with an appendix that contained condemnation for showing favoritism in judgment (24:23–25); a word on getting ready for work (24:27); a warning against bearing false witness and spite actions (24:28–29); and a description of the lazy man (24:30–34).

More "Proverbs of Solomon" (25:1–29:27). This section, like 10:1–22:16, was composed mostly of individual one-line (Hebrew) sayings. The title suggests that King Hezekiah's time was a time when the interest in wisdom was blossoming since these were said to be Solomonic proverbs collected by "the men of Hezekiah" (25:1). After two longer sections on the power of the king (25:2–7) and one on conduct in court (25:8–10), there follows a mixture of proverbs using *comparison:*

> Like clouds and wind without rain
>   is one who boasts of a gift never given (25:14).

Contrasts:

> Better to be poor and walk in integrity
>   than to be crooked in one's ways even though rich (28:6).

As well as other poetic forms:

> If the king judges the poor with equity,
>   his throne will be established forever (29:14).

The Words of Agur (Prov. 30:1–33).   This chapter is made up of two types of material. Verses 1 to 9 were presented as a conversation. "The man" (30:1), who may have been Agur, told two men named Ithiel and Ucal that he had seen no evidence of God (30:2–4). He, in turn, was told that God's every word was true, and that God protects those "who take refuge in him" (30:5). In 30:6–9, a speaker looks on life's highest gifts as being food and truth.

The second part of the chapter opens with a series of statements beginning, "There are those who." These include those who cursed their fathers (30:11), who were "pure in their own eyes" (30:12), who were proud (30:13), and who were greedy (30:14).

There follows a series of "numbers proverbs" that sound like the formula in the oracles of the prophet Amos: "For three transgressions and for four" (Amos 1:3ff). Most of them use the "three-four" formula, although one (30:15–16) uses two, three, and four, while another lists only four things that "are small but they are exceedingly wise" (30:24). Three shorter proverbs are mixed in with the numbers proverbs.

The Words of Lemuel (Prov. 31:1–31).   This chapter contains a mother's advice to her son (31:1–9) and the Old Testament's highest tribute to a woman—the description of the good wife (31:10–31). The first part is about a queen's advice to her son on how to rule wisely. The tribute to the ideal wife pictured her as being of good reputation, diligent about her work, prudent in her decisions, concerned for her family, compassionate toward the needy, wise in speech, and honored by her family.

The Book of Proverbs would be followed in later Judaism by other books that imitated it somewhat. The most famous of these were the Wisdom of Solomon and The Wisdom of Ben Sirach, or Ecclesiasticus. Proverbs was orthodox in theology and practical in its view of life.

Job: When Orthodoxy Fails.   Job represents the struggle of a person who had accepted orthodox answers to all life's questions, but found them useless when the bottom fell out of his world. To compound his problem, his friends sat around still giving the same old answers, never hearing the entirely new set of questions Job was raising.

The structure of the book.   Job consists of a narrative that includes Chapters 1 and 2, is interrupted by a poetic discourse (3:1–42:6), and then has a prose conclusion (42:7–17). When read together with a bit of imagination, the two prose sections tell a fairly complete story of a righteous man who suffers great personal tragedies, whose friends sit in judgment on him, but who finally is justified and rewarded for his patient suffering. In the poetic discourse, Job carries on a dialogue with three friends, Eliphaz, Bildad, and Zophar. Much of what he has to say, however, is directed to God, complaining about the misfortunes that have befallen him. In contrast to the patient Job of the prose narrative, in this section Job is very impatient, storming at his friends and fearlessly questioning both the justice and the mercy of

God. There are three cycles of dialogue between the characters, the third of which is somewhat scrambled in the present text. Each cycle follows the pattern: Eliphaz-Job, Bildad-Job, Zophar-Job. After the third cycle and a chapter on the wisdom of God (28), Job gives a moving account of his life and a strong defense of his integrity (29–31). Then follows the speech of a new character, Elihu, a young man whose arrogance far exceeds his wisdom (32–37). The poetic section concludes with two speeches by God and Job's submission (38:1–42:6).[5]

Who wrote Job, and when was it written?   While the traditional interpreters of Job have viewed the book as the work of a single author, in recent years the emphasis has been on the book as a composite work. The story of the suffering righteous man is found in other literatures, and, indeed, the story of Job may well have originated outside of Israel, possibly in Edom. That the story is an old one is shown by Ezekiel 14:14,20, where he speaks of "Noah, Daniel, and Job" as great righteous men of the past.

Those who see the book as a composite take one of three positions: (1) the author of the poetic section wrote the prose section also, using older traditions that were common in the Near East; (2) the poetic discourse is the older part, the narrative being added later; and (3) the older prose story of Job was used by the author to introduce his own struggles about one of life's most perplexing problems, namely, the suffering of the righteous. This seems to be the more logical of the three positions outlined here.

What we seem to have is an ancient folk tale about a good and patient man named Job. While it possibly originated in Edom, at an early time it became a part of Israelite tradition. Sometime just before or during the Babylonian exile, an Israelite wisdom writer used the old story to introduce a poetic masterpiece in which he examines the problem of a righteous man's relationship to God in the context of great physical and emotional suffering. Either the author of the poetic discourse, or someone who wished to make the book sound more orthodox, added the ending from the old folk tale.

Chapter 28, a discourse on wisdom, and the Elihu speeches (Chapters 32 to 37) add little to the overall arguments of the book and thus seem not to have been part of the original work. The Elihu speeches could have been added later by the original author after further reflection on the problem.

Some things one needs to know for help in understanding Job.   Some basic ideas common in early Israel form the background of Job. Certain basic assumptions had been made in theology: (1) God was just and gave justice to humankind. (2) This life was all there was. When people died, they went to Sheol, the abode of the dead. There was no life after death with rewards and punishments. (3) If justice was to be done, it had to be done in this life.

These assumptions led to certain conclusions: (1) The good person prospered, while the wicked person failed. (2) Sickness was a sign that a person had sinned. It was a part of God's judgment on sinners. These views of orthodox religion formed the basis of the arguments in the book of Job.

The Book

1. Job, the righteous man: the prose story (Job 1:1–2:13).   According to the old tradition, Job was an extremely wealthy man from the land of Uz. No one really knows where Uz was, although it could have been in Edom. He had seven sons and three daughters and owned vast herds of livestock. He was a faithful worshiper of God (*Elohim*) (1:1–5).

But such bliss was not to continue. Satan (as in Zech. 3:2, he is *the Satan*, literally "the Adversary") challenged the LORD (*YHWH*) about Job, accusing him of giving Job special protection. The LORD agreed to let Satan do what he would to Job, but he was not to touch Job's body (1:6–12). Disaster after disaster struck Job, causing him to lose all his children, as well as his livestock. But through it all, Job did not criticize God in the least (1:13–22).

Satan appeared before the LORD again. The LORD proudly reminded him that Job was still faithful. Satan replied that every man had his limits and that included Job. Satan argued that when the LORD permitted Job to be afflicted personally, Job would break under the pressure and would curse the LORD. The LORD took up the challenge. Satan was permitted to do anything to Job except to kill him (2:1–6).

Job's troubles intensified. He was covered with painful sores from head to foot. He sat on an ash heap and used a piece of pottery to scrape the tops off his sores. His wife urged him to curse God and die so that he would be out of his misery, but Job refused. Then three friends came to see him. When they saw him, they began to wail and to mourn over his condition. Then they sat and looked at him for seven days without uttering a single, solitary word (2:7–13).

This prose version of the story of Job pictured Satan as having easy access to the heavenly realms. He came when the "sons of God came to present themselves before the LORD" (1:6). In later theology, Satan was in violent opposition to the LORD, not someone who could come to visit whenever he took a notion to do so.

Job's wife's advice to curse God and die revealed that there was not a developed doctrine of life after death in that time. The dead all went to Sheol (the grave), so this life was the only life there was. There was a kind of existence after death; but the only thing that could disturb it was when (1) a body was not properly buried or (2) a person had been murdered and his death was unavenged.[6]

2. Job, the frustrated sufferer: The poetic discourse (Job 3:1–42:6).   This section of Job was cast in the form of a dialogue between Job and his three friends Eliphaz, Bildad, and Zophar. There are three cycles or sets of speeches, except that the third cycle is incomplete.

a. Job's complaint (3:1–26).   In contrast to Job's refusal to complain in the prose story, the poetic version began with Job cursing the day he was born. In an extended example of synonymous parallelism (3:1–10), Job piles up phrase after phrase to say what was said in 3:2:

> Let the day perish in which I was born
> and the night that said,
> "A man-child is conceived."

Had he died at birth, then he would have gone to the grave, where he would "be lying down and quiet" (3:13). Sheol was where "the wicked cease from troubling" (3:17), for "the small and the great are there, and the slaves are free from their masters" (3:19). But God had hedged Job in so that he had trouble, not peace and quiet (3:26).

b. The debate: Round one (Job 4:1–14:22).

(1) Eliphaz: the man who has visions (4:1–5:27). The core of the argument of Job's friends was found in the first Eliphaz speech:

> "Think now, who that was innocent ever perished?
> Or where were the upright cut off?
> As I have seen, those who plow iniquity
> and sow trouble reap the same.
> By the breath of God they perish,
> and by the blast of his anger they are consumed" (4:7–9).

For his friends, Job's sickness was clear evidence of his sinfulness. Why else should he be suffering if he had not sinned? Eliphaz's authority for his opinion was that he had a vision in the night which told him that God did not even trust his angels, much less mortal man, who was "born to trouble as the sparks fly upward" (4:1–5:7).

What Job needed was to seek God and to commit himself to him. Though God had afflicted Job, with the proper attitude, Job could be healed. Then he would have the traditional blessings of peace, prosperity, a large family, and a long life (5:8–27).

Perhaps the most distinctive mark of the argument of Eliphaz was his view of God. God did not trust anyone, even the most devout worshipers. God was just waiting for one of his creatures to do wrong so he could destroy the wrongdoer.

(2) Job to Eliphaz: Round one (6:1–7:21). Ignoring Eliphaz's charges, Job complained that God had become his enemy, filling him with arrows and lining up all sorts of terrors against him. All Job wanted was for God to crush him so he would be out of his misery (6:1–13).

As for his friends, they were like wet weather springs that had promised cool water all year long, but had dried up when the hot days of summer came. He had not asked any of them for money. If they could teach him anything, he was willing to listen. Instead of being honest, they were talking nonsense. They did not know the difference between right and wrong (6:14–30).

Since life for him was so trying and tedious, he decided that there was no need to be reluctant to say how he felt:

> "Therefore I will not restrain my mouth;
>   I will speak in the anguish of my spirit;
>   I will complain in the bitterness of my soul" (7:11).

When he sought comfort, he got terror. He had terrifying dreams. He was tired of living under such circumstances. But his God would not leave him alone even long enough to swallow his spittle. God was using him for "target practice" (7:20, *TEV*). Soon he would die and then God could not find him because he would be in the grave (7:1–21).

(3) *Bildad, the traditionalist (8:1–22).* Bildad vigorously defended the justice of God. He suggested that Job's suffering was caused by the sins of Job's children. All that Job had to do, if he were "pure and upright" (8:6) was to seek God and everything would be just fine (8:1–7). Anyone who knew the teachings of the fathers (as Job surely did) would realize the truth of what Bildad was saying. The law of God was that the bad men were destroyed and the good men prospered. If Job would follow that philosophy, happiness would be his (8:8–22).

(4) *Job to Bildad: Round one (9:10–10:22).* Job would not argue about God's power and ability to do what he chose. No man could stand up against God and hope to win. Even if a man were innocent, God could take that man's words and condemn him. Job questioned a basic tenet of orthodox religion since he had begun to doubt that God really was just,

> It is all one; therefore I say,
>   he destroys both the blameless and the wicked.
>   . . . .
> The earth is given into the hand of the wicked;
>   he covers the eyes of the judges—
> if it is not he, who then is it? (9:22, 24).

Job's days were passing swiftly. With them, his hope of receiving justice was also passing. He and God were in separate realms, and there was no mediator who could bridge the gap between them (9:1–35).

He was tired of living. Ignoring Bildad, he spoke to God. God had made him. Now was God going to destroy him? He was sure that God had a purpose in making him, but now life was so confusing. He could not win for losing. Since he had to live, he just wanted to be left alone so he could possibly have a little comfort before he died (10:1–22).

(5) *Zophar, God's right-hand man (11:1–20).* Zophar was tired of Job's nonsense. If Job would just listen, Zophar would give him God's point of view about his problems. God knew all things but Job knew so very little. Job just needed to get rid of his sin, and everything would be all right.

(6) Job to Zophar: Round one (12:1–14:22). Job was tired of the advice of his friends:

> No doubt you are the people,
>> and wisdom will die with you.
> But I have understanding as well as you;
>> I am not inferior to you.
> Who does not know such things as these? (12:2–3).

Anyone could see that his condition was brought on by the LORD. Anyone knew that when God decided to do something, there was no way to stop him (12:1–25). Their defense of God was self-serving. They lied for God, hoping that their sins would be overlooked. But that would not work. They could not deceive God by their actions (13:1–12).

Job, therefore, would speak his mind even if it cost him his life. He fully expected God to kill him for being so bold, but that would not stop him. He had prepared his case. He only wanted two concessions from God: (1) that God would hear him, and (2) that God would not terrify him while he was speaking (13:13–22).

Job then presented his case to God. He wanted to know why God had ignored him and attacked him as though he were an enemy. Since one's time was brief on earth, why was he not allowed to enjoy it? If a tree was cut down, it could sprout again. Not so with man. If man had a hope of life after death, it would make life's misery bearable. This yearning for life after death represented a reaching out for what later became accepted teaching in Judaism and Christianity. When life was seen to be unjust, then the doctrine of the justice of God demanded a future life in which God's justice could be carried out fully. The only other choice was to declare God unjust, an idea both Judaism and Christianity rejected.

But even as Job reached out for the hope of a future life, he turned back in despair. The situation was hopeless. This life was all there was (13:23–14:22).

c. The debate: Round two (Job 15:1–21:34).

(1) Eliphaz speaks again (15:1–35). Job's failure to agree with his friends led to increasingly sharp words being flung at him. Eliphaz charged him with undermining religion by assuming that he knew more than his friends, the elders, and even God (15:1–14). Eliphaz returned to his theme of a God who did not trust anybody:

> God puts no trust even in his holy ones,
>> and the heavens are not clean in his sight;
> how much less one who is abominable and corrupt,
>> one who drinks iniquity like water! (15:15–16).

He then proceeded to tell Job what his fate as a wicked man would be. Since such a person had defied God himself, he would suffer great pain and terror. His wealth would melt away, and destruction would come to him (15:17–35).

(2) Job lambasts his friends and questions God (16:1–17:16). Job's patience wore out with the carping of his friends. They were "miserable comforters" who would sing a different tune if they were in Job's place. Everybody was against him, and God especially was against him. God had worn him out, dried him up, and "gnashed his teeth" at him. He was at ease before, yet God had attacked him, even though he had done violence to no one and had been innocent (16:1–17).

Job 16:18–17:2 represents one of the low places in the Book of Job. The afflicted man cried out for the earth not to cover his blood when he died.[7] His unburied blood, which carried his life, would cry out to be avenged. This was a plea for justice to be done. God knew that Job deserved justice even though his friends scorned him. But death was closing in on him, and justice had not been done. His friends, so sure of their own wisdom, really did not have a wise man among them (17:3–14). Added to their insults was his lack of hope of recovery:

> Where then is my hope?
>   Who will see my hope?
> Will I go down to the bars of Sheol?
>   Shall we descend together into the dust? (17:15:16)

(3) Bildad plays the same record again (18:1–21). Bildad really added little to what had been said.

(4) Job reaches the bottom (19:1–29). Continuing his rebuke of his friends, Job pointed out that even if he had sinned, it had been a personal fault, not a public one. God had put him "in the wrong" (19:6), stripped him of everything, and loosed the divine troops against Job. As if that were not enough, even his closest friends and relatives now shunned him, including his wife. He pleaded with his friends:

> Have pity on me, have pity on me, O you my friends,
>   for the hand of God has touched me!
> Why do you, like God, pursue me,
>   never satisfied with my flesh? (19:21–22)

Job wanted his words to be written in a permanent record. He had confidence that one would come who would prove him right. The "redeemer" of whom he spoke (19:25) would be the one who cleared his name. To biblical people, one's honor and reputation was of supreme importance. Job desired that his name be cleared above all, and somehow he believed God would see that justice was done. At the lowest point, there came a glimmer of hope, another instance of reaching out to the later doctrine of life after death.

(5) Zophar knows the answer (20:1–29). Zophar was insulted by what Job had said. He knew how to reply, however, since he was one of those persons who always had an answer even if he did not know the question. He proceeded to lecture Job

on the fate of the wicked according to traditional wisdom. No matter how he prospered, it only would be temporary. God would wash him away in the flood of divine wrath.

(6) Job replies to Zophar (21:1–34). Job replied that his quarrel was not with them. After all, look what had happened to him. When he compared his condition to that of some of the evil men he knew, they were prospering while he, a righteous man, was suffering. With this argument, Job went completely counter to traditional teaching. As his friends had overstated their case to prove him wrong, Job now overstated the case the other way. His so-called friends were just liars.

d. The debate: Round three (Job 22:1–27:23). The third cycle of speeches is incomplete. Perhaps the text was scrambled over the years. In part of one speech assigned to Job, he sounds like Zophar.

(1) Eliphaz gets nasty (22:1–30). Eliphaz began to make wild charges against Job. According to him, there was no end to Job's sins. He had oppressed his brothers, starved the hungry, and oppressed widows and orphans. His only hope lay in turning to God before it was too late. He could only be delivered if his hands were clean.

(2) Job searches for God (23:1–24:25). Ignoring Eliphaz's charges, Job complained of his inability to find God. He believed God would give him a fair hearing if he could only get a chance to lay his case before God. But no matter how much Job sought, God could not be found. The terrifying thing, however, was that God knew where Job was. He could do to Job whatever he chose, and no one could stop him (23:1–17).

Job 24:18–25 sounds more like the arguments of Zophar than of Job since it argued that the wicked were punished, in contrast to the arguments just stated that sinners escaped their just punishment.

(3) Bildad contrasts God and man (25:1–6). In a short speech, Bildad spoke of God's rule over "a mortal, who is a maggot, and a human being, who is a worm!" (25:6).

(4) Job replies to Bildad (26:1–4). In an abbreviated reply, Job lambasted Bildad for his arrogant attitude toward Job.

(5) The continuation of Bildad's speech on God and humanity (26:5–14). This section was part of Bildad's third speech since it continued to speak of God's rule over the universe. Its theme was God's mastery of the created order of things.

(6) Job ends his part of the debate (27:1–12). To the end, Job defended his point of view, yielding nothing to his friends. He wished that those who opposed him would get the punishment they deserved.

(7) Zophar again? (27:13–23). In another speech that sounded like Zophar's bombastic style, the debate was ended. He spoke as God's supposed authority on the fate of the wicked, which he described in loving detail.

e. The wisdom poem (Job 28:1–28). This poem, which separates the speech cycles from Job's final statement of his innocence, would fit well into the Book of Proverbs. Its theme is the value of wisdom. Men dug deep into the earth for minerals and precious metals (28:1–11). Wisdom, however, could not be found in the depths of the earth; nor could it be bought with humankind's most precious material possessions. Nothing could compare with it in value. Only God knew where wisdom could be found. It was present in creation; its worth had been tested and proven. God declared:

> "Truly the fear of the LORD, that is wisdom
>   and to depart from evil is understanding" (28:28).

f. Job presents his case (Job 29:1–31:40). Job's final argument fell into three divisions: (1) his past prosperity, (2) his present problems, and (3) his code of conduct.

Looking back over his life, Job yearned for the good days he had enjoyed. His family had been around him, his flocks had prospered, and he had an honored place in the community (29:1–10). He had been known in the community for his kindness and generosity toward the poor and oppressed. He had been praised by those around him. They had come to him for advice because he was a leader among those who knew him (29:11–25).

But things had changed. He was ridiculed by the people who were on the very lowest levels of human society, people whom once he would not trust to care for his flocks. Now they spat on him, made him the butt of their ridicule, and harassed him at every turn. He was in pain—both in body and in spirit—for God had cast him down into the dirt (30:1–19).

Turning to God, Job charged God with treating him cruelly and refusing to listen to Job's pleas. Job's skin had turned black and fallen away. He mourned his fate (30:20–31).

As a climax to his speeches, Job set forth his code of conduct. It has been described as the "code of an Old Testament gentleman."[8] Except for the first, each common breach of conduct in society was introduced by the formula, "If I have . . ." followed by a sort of self-curse: "Let [me] . . ." with the appropriate punishment. (1) He had not looked on a virgin with lust in his heart (31:1–4). (2) He had not lied, nor had he coveted the possessions of others (31:5–8). (3) He had not committed adultery (31:9–12). (4) He had been sensitive to the needs and rights of his servants (31:13–15). (5) He had seen to the needs of the less fortunate (31:16–23). (6) He had not put his trust in wealth, nor had he worshiped the sun or the moon (31:24–28). (7) He had not gloated over another man's ruin, failed to be kind to stangers, nor sinned any secret sins (31:29–34). If an indictment against him were written down, he would carry it to God as a prince wore a crown (31:35–37). Finally, he had taken care of his land (31:38–40).

g. The Elihu speeches (32:1–37:24). A new character appears, Elihu by name, who makes four speeches. They reveal a brash young man who possesses more wind than wisdom. The speeches are ignored, both by the previous characters in the drama and by the LORD, who addresses Job following the Elihu speeches. This has led to suggestions that: (1) these speeches are not a part of the original arguments; (2) Elihu is not a real person, but a disguise "adopted by Satan to press his case for the last time."[9] In any case, he plows ahead with such an outpouring of verbiage that Job and his friends could not answer if they had wished to do so. Perhaps the passage that captures the flavor of Elihu's speech better than any other is 36:1–4 where he concluded:

> I have something to say on God's behalf.
> I bring my knowledge from far away,
>   and ascribe righteousness to my Maker.
> For truly my words are not false;
>   one who is perfect in knowledge is with you.

h. The divine speeches (38:1–41:34). God spoke from the whirlwind, chiding Job for questioning divine wisdom. Then followed a series of divine test questions on the mysteries of nature. Beginning with Creation, they were concerned with various aspects of the Creation and the natural order, but especially were concerned with water in nature (38:1–38). Then the questions turned to Job's knowledge of animal life, ranging from wild animals to domestic animals, such as the horse. The answer to all the questions was, "Only God knows these things." Job admitted his ignorance and vowed to speak no more (38:39–40:5).

God was not through with his speech, however. Job was challenged to use his power to bring down all the proud men of the earth. Then God would acknowledge Job's power and wisdom (40:6–14).

The divine speeches were concluded by the description of two legendary animals—Behemoth, which was an exaggerated description of the hippopotamus, and Leviathan, a legendary creature of the sea and rivers that was modeled on the crocodile (40:15–41:34).

i. Job's submission (42:1–6). Job was overwhelmed by the divine outpouring. He admitted that God's power and wisdom far exceeded his own puny efforts:

> Therefore I have uttered what I did not understand,
>   things too wonderful for me, which I did not know (42:3).

But all that did not matter. His obsession with his sufferings was not superseded by a new and different experience of the divine:

> I had heard you by the hearing of the ear,
>   but now my eye sees you:

> therefore I despise myself,
> and repent in dust and ashes (42:6).

Job's previous knowledge of God had been a secondhand knowledge. What he had known of God had been passed on by tradition. Now, he had experienced God personally. The fact that God had taken time to speak to him personally changed his view of himself and his problems.[10]

The traditional ending of the story (42:7–17).   The unorthodox ending of the poetic portions of Job was too much for the traditionalists. To bring it in line with orthodoxy, the ending of the older story was added. In it, Job's friends had to have Job to sacrifice for them because they misrepresented God.

As for Job himself, his health and wealth were restored. His family, who had shunned him in his illness, now gathered to comfort him once the ordeal was over. He lived a long life, accumulated twice as many animals as before his illness, and once again had the perfect number of children, seven sons and three daughters. The names of the daughters were Jemimah ("Dove"), Keziah ("Cinnamon"), and Keren-happuch ("Horn of eye paint").

Job: A summary.   Job has long been regarded as one of the great literary masterpieces of all time. The question with which it deals still intrigues and baffles thoughtful people of our age—the problem of human suffering and, more specifically, the suffering of righteous or innocent people. The problem is crucial especially in the context of the belief in a just and all-wise God. Job really did not solve the problem. Instead, Job's vision of God changed his focus from his own problems to faith in a personal God. The air of mystery surrounding Job and the problem with which the book deals remain. Perhaps that is part of the reason the book is still so fascinating.

Ecclesiastes: Skeptical Wisdom.   Ecclesiastes illustrates how far some Jewish thinkers had strayed from orthodox theology in the postexilic period. Except for occasional orthodox corrections, the book voiced the skeptical, pessimistic feelings of a man who had tried everything but had found nothing satisfying or meaningful in which to invest his life. The main speaker in the book was " the Preacher, the son of David, King in Jerusalem" (1:1). "Preacher" is but one possible translation of the Hebrew title *Qoheleth.* It was used to refer to a schoolmaster, or one who was in charge of an assembly of people.

The reference to the son of David, king in Jerusalem, has led to Solomon being identified as the author of Ecclesiastes. In reality, Solomon's relation to this book probably was the same as Ruth's relation to the Book of Ruth—that is, he was the main character portrayed by the book rather than being the author. The language and thought of the book suggest that it was postexilic in its origin. Like Proverbs, it probably was used as a textbook.

Vanity of vanities (Eccl. 1:1–2:26).   "Vanity of vanities! All is vanity" (1:2). With these words, the writer of Ecclesiastes gives his opinion of the world and life in it. Nothing was lasting—nothing was of real value. While he was not an atheist (one who denied the existence of God), he was a deist, one who believed in God, but who believed that God had little or nothing to do with what went on in the world.

The Preacher had tried many things. He had tried work, but he concluded that it was for nothing. The world was going in circles. Life had no purpose.

> What has been is what will be,
>   and what has been done is what will be done;
>   there is nothing new under the sun (1:9).

So work did not satisfy (1:2–11).

Next he tried wisdom. He acquired great wisdom, but it too was emptiness, for "he who increases knowledge increases sorrow" (1:12–18). Pleasure was tested without restraint; but it, too, proved to be worthless (2:1–11). When he considered wisdom and folly, he realized that both the wise man and the fool died with no lasting memory of their accomplishments and failures (2:12–16). When he realized that what a man gained in this life had to be left to someone else to enjoy, this thought led him to despair (2:17–23). So he concluded:

> There is nothing better for mortals than to eat and drink, and find enjoyment in their toil. . . . For to the one who pleases him God gives wisdom and knowledge and joy (2:24, 26).

The latter verse sounds more like the voice of orthodoxy speaking.

"For everything there is a season" (Eccl. 3:1–15).   These famous lines, a setting out of opposites to stress the paradoxical nature of life, represented the view of history that was strange to the rest of the Old Testament. The general Old Testament view was that history had a beginning and it will have an end. It was moving to a goal under the expert direction of God.

A philosophy of history that saturated the Book of Ecclesiastes—history moving in circles, having no purpose or goal— was clearly expressed in 3:1–15. This view, held in common by the Greeks and a number of Eastern religions (Buddhism, Hinduism, etc.) is not a Hebrew conception of history. This seems to suggest that Ecclesiastes was influenced by the Hellenistic culture that saturated the Near East following the conquests of Alexander the Great (3:1–8).

While God had given people a sense of time as past and future, they were not given the ability to look at life as a whole. Their hope lay in taking life as it came while doing their best (3:9–15).

The question of justice (Eccl. 3:16–4:4).   As far as justice was concerned, it was a matter of chance, too. Wickedness triumphed just as often as righteousness did. Humankind had no advantage over the animals. The oppressed cried out, but no one comforted them. Power was behind the oppressors. As a result, the dead were better off than the living. The unborn were even more fortunate, since they had not had to experience life.

The futility of working alone (Eccl. 4:5–16).   People worked out of the sense of rivalry with others. It was better to work with someone so as to have the protection that a partner could give. It was better to be young, poor, and wise than to be an old and foolish ruler. Being a hero was also just temporary, since heroes were soon forgotten.

Do not fool around with God (Eccl. 5:1–7).   The Preacher warned that a person should avoid calling God's attention to himself. God should be obeyed without question. If one could not keep a vow, it would be better not to make it. Silence was better than chatter that might make God angry.

Life had problems (Eccl. 5:8–6:12).   If the government oppressed people, they had no hope for justice since every official was protected by the one above him (5:8–9). Kings and the rich had money, but life was not a bed of roses for the rich. More riches meant one was responsible for more people. The rich lost sleep worrying about money, while the laborer slept peacefully. If people saved money, they could lose it and leave the world as they came into it—with nothing. The best thing to do was to accept what God gave and not worry about it (5:10–20).

There was no justice in the Preacher's way of looking at life. People could be wealthy and lose it all. They could have large families and long lives and still be disgraced by not having a proper burial. If people could not be happy with how they lived, they would have been better off not to have been born. The best thing to do was take what one saw rather than to desire the unseen thing. Things were already predetermined, so there was no profit in arguing about it (6:1–12).

Thinking about life (Eccl. 7:1–8:1).   Life's end was more important than its beginning. Mourning was better than joy, and sorrow better than laughter. Only a fool laughed. The wise rebuked the fool. Wisdom was the best guarantee that people would keep what they had. The key to life was moderation. Wisdom had shown the Preacher that " wickedness is folly and that foolishness is madness" (7:25). But the worst of all things was woman. A very few men could be trusted, but no woman was worthy of trust.

Watch out for the ruler (Eccl. 8:2–9).   The only safe thing to do in regard to rulers was to stay out of their way. If people were wise enough, they could make the right choices about what to do and when to do it. Unfortunately, no one had that kind of wisdom.

There is no justice in life (Eccl. 8:10–9:12). The wicked prospered as though they were righteous. There was no way the Preacher could understand the ways of God. Even those wise persons who claimed to know God's ways really did not know them. The Preacher had decided that the wise and righteous were controlled by God, however (8:10–9:1).

The righteous and the wicked suffered the same fate. A sinner was just as well off as the saint. Of course, where there was life there was hope. While one was living, he should enjoy life with his wife. He should do what he did with diligence, for there would be no chance to do anything once he went to the grave. His time would come before he knew it (9:2–12).

Wisdom and foolishness (Eccl. 9:13–10:20). This section contains a number of illustrations about wisdom and foolishness. According to the Preacher, a little wisdom would go a long way, but a little foolishness would cancel out the effects of a great deal of wisdom. Foolishness especially was bad when it infected those who had power.

The actions of the wise (Eccl. 11:1–6). A man wise in business spreads his investments around . One who always worried about the weather would never reap a crop. That was just the risk of living.

Advice to the young (Eccl. 11:7–12:8). Long life should be appreciated, but such a life had dark days. A young man should relish his youth, but he should still remember that he had to account to God for it. For that reason, he should take God into account in his youth before the problems of age and death overtook him.

The end of it all (Eccl. 12:9–14). Another person summarized the Preacher's life. He had taught what he had discovered about life with honest conviction. A final word was given to students:

> Of making many books there is no end, and much study is a weariness of the flesh (12:12).

A final orthodox word was added:

> Fear God, and keep his commandments; for that is the whole duty of everyone (12:13).

What about Ecclesiastes? Ecclesiastes revealed that postexilic Jews were not all orthodox in their views of God. The writer of Ecclesiastes believed in God. For him, however, God was not actively involved in the everyday events of life—or, if so, one could not discover how God was involved. The writer did not accept the orthodox view that righteousness was always rewarded with blessing and that sin was always punished.

THE SWEET SINGERS OF ISRAEL

Any complete discussion of Israel's poets and singers would involve every book in the Old Testament. A major portion of the materials in the books of the prophets was in poetic form. Jeremiah and Nahum, especially, excelled as poets. The historical works abound in poetic passages. Two notable examples of such passages are the Song of Deborah (Judg. 5) and David's lament over Jonathan and Saul (2 Sam. 1:19–27). As has been indicated previously, the wisdom materials made extensive use of poetic forms.

There was a reason for this extensive use of poetry. Poetry was much more easily remembered than prose. Putting words in a rhythmic pattern gave an additional device for aiding the memory of a people who had to depend on it as the most common method of preserving and passing along traditions they valued. The words plus the rhythm were easier to commit to memory, just as the words sung to a tune are easier to remember than just words by themselves.

Two books in the Old Testament were devoted exclusively to preserving Israel's greatest poetry. One of them—the Song of Solomon, or Song of Songs— deals with what we would call a secular theme—human love—and, more specifically, love between a man and a woman. It should be pointed out that to the Israelite this was not a secular theme. All of life and its relationships were the concern of the LORD of Israel, a biblical view that somehow has been lost over the centuries.

The second book, the Psalms, represented Israelite worship, both on the personal and on the community level. In it all areas of life were touched, from going to war to praising God. In it were placed poems expressing the full range of Israelite feelings, from their most violent expressions of hatred to their most joyous sense of praise for God's blessings.

The Song of Songs[11]

This book has long been a source of embarassment both to Judaism and to the Christian church. It does not mention God anywhere. This failure has caused its place in the canon to be debated as no other Old Testament book has. Judaism and Christianity both solved the problem by interpreting it allegorically. For Jews the "husband" was the LORD and Israel was his "bride." For Christians, Jesus was the "husband" and the church was the "bride."

The Nature of the Book.   In reality, the book was a collection of love songs, celebrating the joys of physical lovemaking. Its lesson was that sex was God's gift to humankind. Like all such gifts, it could be used properly or abused. But because some abused it, this did not lessen its value or beauty.

The poems cover a wide span of years. They were brought together in their present arrangement in the postexilic period. Solomon was not only noted for his wisdom, but he also seemed to enjoy a reputation for his way with women. He was reputed to have had 700 wives and 300 concubines (slave wives) (1 Kings 11:3). Thus, this book, like Proverbs, was attributed to him. The collector and arranger of the poems thought of Solomon as one of the main characters.

Interpretations of the Book.   There are two basic interpretations of the characters in the book. Some hold that there were two characters: Solomon and the maiden. Others argue that three characters were involved: Solomon, the maiden, and her home-town boyfriend. For the purpose of this discusson, it will be assumed that only two characters were involved.

A Look in the Book

The bride is prepared for her lover (Song 1:1–6).   Before a bride was brought to her husband for the first time, she was carefully bathed and perfumed for the occasion. The poet has skillfully caught the thoughts of the bride as she approaches the time when she will first be brought to the groom. As she was anointed with oils, she anticipated his kisses. Her manner had charmed the maidens who waited on her (1:2–4).

She looked at herself. She was tanned by the sun. She wondered if this would make her less attractive. For this reason, she explained why she was so dark—she had been forced to work in the vineyards by her brothers.

The bride and the groom together (Song 1:7–2:5).   She asked where he was. He answered in a teasing manner that since she did not know, he was following the flock. He praised her beauty, comparing her to "a mare in Pharaoh's chariots" (1:9)! She, in turn praised him. He was like "a cluster of henna blossoms in the vineyards of En-gedi" (1:14), an oasis on the Dead Sea. His next compliment was more appropriate for modern ears:

> Ah, you are beautiful, my love,
>   ah, you are beautiful;
>   your eyes are like doves.
> Ah, you are beautiful, my beloved,
>   truly lovely (1:15–16).

Compliments continued to pass back and forth between the lovers as he brought her to the banqueting house and fed her the finest delicacies (2:1–5).

The bride's memories of love (Song 2:6–17).   She remembered their lovemaking and longed for him to wake up from his sleep. She thought of how he had come to her and how he had used such beautiful words to woo her in that springtime season:

> "Arise, my love, my fair one,
>   and come away;
> for now the winter is past,
>   the rain is over and gone.

> The flowers appear on the earth;
>   the time of singing has come,
> and the voice of the turtledove
>   is heard in our land" (2:10–12).

With these memories, she rested, assured of his love for her.

The bride has a bad dream (Song 3:1–5).   She dreamed that he had gone. She went out to search for him. She had just asked the watchman if he had seen her lover when she found him. She took him home so he would be safe with her.

The king's wedding procession (Song 3:6–11).   The king was borne to the wedding in an elaborate litter or palanquin, preceded by sixty soldiers in battle dress as an honor guard.

The groom describes the bride (Song 4:1–5:1).   This was a twofold description: what the bride looked like to the groom (4:1–8), and how she had devastated his heart (4:9–15). While the groom's description of the bride's features might not suit a modern maid, they were the highest compliments he could give a girl of his time. Her eyes were like doves (4:1); her hair was "like a flock of goats" (4:1); her neck was "like the tower of David" (4:4); her breasts were "like two fawns" of a gazelle (4:5). In short, there was no flaw in her (4:7). She had so captured him that she was like a garden of the most fragrant flowers and spices (4:9–15). The thoughts of her caused him to call her to him (4:16–5:1).

The bride has another dream (Song 5:2–6:3).   In her dream, the bride heard her lover call at her door in the night. She ran to open it; but when she did, he was gone. When she went to look for him, she was attacked by the city's watchmen (5:2–8).

Her dream changed. She was describing her lover to the women of Jerusalem. He was tall, dark, and rugged. They asked her where he had gone. She answered that he had "gone down to his garden, . . . to pasture his flock in the gardens, and to gather lilies" (6:2). The garden probably was an exaggerated expression for the open pasture lands (5:9–6:3).

The groom describes the bride (Song 6:4–10).   Using many of the same terms found in 4:1–7, the groom described the bride. Of all his wives, she was the only perfect one. Even the other wives in the harem praised her beauty.

An invitation to dance (Song 6:11–7:9).   She visited the garden where the fruit and nut trees blossomed. The next she knew she was in her lover's chariot (6:11–12). The she was invited to dance (6:13). Her dance evoked the poetry in the soul of her lover as once again he tried to describe her charms (7:1–9).

The bride invites the groom to a garden tryst (Song 7:10–13).   The bride invites the groom into the garden where she will give herself to him. There grew the mandrake, a fruit believed to promote fertility (see Gen. 30:14–15).

A poem in anticipation of the wedding (Song 8:1–4).   This poem reflected the protected status of women. Strange men were not permitted to have any dealings with them. The bride-to-be wished that her lover were like a brother. Then he would have access to her in her tent as a member of the family.

Please be faithful to me (Song 8:5–12).   Here are some of the Song's most famous lines as she pleads for him to be faithful to her:

> Set me as a seal upon your heart,
>   as a seal upon your arm;
> for love is as strong as death,
>   passion fierce as the grave.
> Its flashes are flashes of fire,
>   a raging flame.
> Many waters cannot quench love,
>   neither can floods drown it.
> If one offered for love
>   all the wealth of his house,
>   it would be utterly scorned (8:6–7).

A final call (Song 8:13–14).   The lovers call to each other as the book ends.

The Book of Psalms

No other book in the Old Testament is better known than Psalms, because no other Old Testament book mirrors human emotions better than Psalms. There are psalms for times of meditation, psalms for times of despair, psalms for times of worship, and psalms for times of joy. Unlike other Old Testament literature—which described what had happened to Israel, which contained messages to Israel from the LORD through the prophets, or which was the distilled wisdom of society—the psalms were Israel's expression of feelings to God. They primarily were messages *to* God, not messages *from* God. As a result, they run the gamut of human emotions.

Who Wrote the Psalms, and When Were They Written?   There are not simple answers to these questions. David, called the Psalmist in Jewish and Christian traditions, undoubtedly wrote some of the Psalms. But even the book itself—if the introductory comments found in some of the psalms are to be taken literally—indicates that David did not write all the psalms. Many names are attached to the psalms by the earliest commentators on psalms—those men who attached titles to individual psalms many years after they were written. Thus the names of Asaph

(Ps. 73–83), the sons of Korah (84, 85, 87), Heman the Ezrahite (88), Ethan the Ezrahite (89), and Moses (90), were attached to the psalms.[12] Many psalms have no one's name attached to them.

In reality, the Book of Psalms was more like a modern church hymnal in that it was a collection of songs that came into existence over a long span of time. A church hymnal today may have hymns whose words go back to the early Christian centuries, while at the same time having hymns that were written especially for that edition of the hymnal. In the Psalms, for example, Psalm 29 was "a Yahwistic adaptation of an older Canaanite hymn to the storm-god Baal"[13]—that is, the Israelites liked the hymn so much they removed Baal's name and inserted the personal name of the God of Israel. Psalm 29 in its original form went back to at least the fourteenth century B.C.E. Similar adjustments are made in songs today when words to popular tunes are changed to give them a religious meaning. On the other hand, psalms such as Psalm 137 reflect an exilic background, and some psalms probably even came from the postexilic period.

Within the Book of Psalms, there are other evidences that the psalms come from different periods in Israel's history. The book, for example, had five divisions, corresponding to the five books of the Torah, or Law (1–41; 42–72; 73–89; 90–106; 107–150). Each of the divisions has its own benediction. Psalm 1 serves as an introduction to the whole book and Psalm 150 serves as the benediction for the whole book. Book 2 (42–72) ends with the statement that "the prayers of David, the son of Jesse, are ended" (72:20). There are some psalms in other sections which are titled "a psalm of David," but it is generally agreed that most of the psalms that might have come from David are in Chapters 1 to 72, and most likely in Chapters 1 to 41.

The title "a psalm of David," furthermore, does not necessarily mean Davidic authorship. The Hebrew language allows it to be translated "in the style of David," or "to David"—that is, "dedicated to David." These and similar titles indicate that there were several smaller sections of psalms before the final edition that we know as the Book of Psalms.

Another evidence of such collections are duplications in the Book of Psalms, the most notable of these being Psalms 14 and 53. They are identical for all practical purposes except for their references to God. Psalm 14 refers to God as *Yahweh* (the LORD), while Psalm 53 uses *Elohim* (God). This must have been a popular psalm that was known in different parts of the country. Since the psalms were collected at local worship centers (shrines), this psalm got into two different collections. When the book was put together, the two collections were merged, ignoring the fact that there were duplicate psalms in them. To conclude: While David is called the psalmist, the psalms actually came from different periods of Israelite history. Before the present Book of Psalms there were a number of smaller collections. Sometime in the postexilc period, these were merged into the larger collection we call the Book of Psalms.

The Study of Psalms.   Studies of the Book of Psalms have changed much in the past seventy-five years. Archaeological discoveries, especially of Canaanite materials, have opened up new avenues of study. Whereas seventy-five years ago the tendency was to date the psalms late in Israelite history, now the trend is for a much earlier dating. Many words and phrases in the poems that once were obscure now have been clarified by the discoveries at Ugarit. One of the latest commentators on the Book of Psalms makes extensive use of those materials.[14]

The most influential work in the recent study of the Book of Psalms was that of Hermann Gunkel, a German scholar of the Old Testament. Before Gunkel's time, each psalm was studied individually. Scholars tried to discover its historical setting by connecting it to some person or event in Israelite history. Since the Book of Psalms contains few historical references, scholars based their interpretations more on guesswork than on evidence.

Gunkel, however, made an important discovery. He concluded that the psalms had to be looked at in the light of their association with Israelite worship services. By looking at the literary form of the individual psalms, he discovered that they could be separated into classes. He concluded that there were five major groups (or classes) into which more than two-thirds of the psalms would fit. There were five other subclasses which would accommodate the rest of the psalms.

Gunkel said that each psalm had a specific setting in life—it was used in a particular form of worship service. Thus, when a person who had been ill and who had recovered wanted to offer a sacrifice to show gratitude, he did not compose a psalm. There were already psalms for that purpose. Or, when a psalm such as a hymn was composed, it followed a rather fixed pattern, so that all hymns shared certain basic characteristics.

While there have been modifications of Gunkel's classifications, they still are accepted today as the basis for most modern study of the psalms. For that reason— and because the length of the Book of Psalms makes a comment on every psalm somewhat difficult—selected psalms following Gunkel's classes will be studied as examples for all the psalms.[15]

Hymns. The key word for the hymns was "Hallelujah," which means "praise the LORD." It is one of the few Hebrew words which, when transliterated, comes over into English virtually unchanged. Hymns usually had three basic parts: (1) a call to praise God; (2) the reason for praising God; and (3) a renewed call to praise God. Other than Individual Laments, this was the largest of Gunkel's classes.[16]

There were two subclasses of the hymn: Songs of Zion (46, 48, 76, 87), which were hymns praising Jerusalem, and Enthronement Psalms (47, 93, 97, 99), which were used in connection with the crowning of the king. This latter group was called New Year's Psalms by Sigmund Mowinckel, a Scandanavian scholar. Mowinckel argued that the Hebrews in preexilic times had a New Year's festival in which the king portrayed the role of God in creation. Psalms 47, 93, 95, 96, 97, 98, 99, and 100 were used, according to Mowinckel, as part of such a festival because they contain the phrase, "the LORD reigns" (47:7).[17]

Communal Laments. These were prayers of petition to God to bring deliverance to the community in time of such disasters as war, famine, or epidemic. The laments usually contained (1) a cry to God for help, (2) a description of the situation which brought on the appeal, (3) a prayer for deliverance, and (4) sometimes an oracle from a prophet or an expression of confidence that the LORD would answer. Not all these elements were always present, nor did they necessarily follow the same order.[18]

Individual Laments.   The lament of the individual had the same basic form that communal laments had. They were used in services in which individuals were asking God to deliver them from personal disaster. This was the largest class.[19]

Since laments contained an expression of confidence that the LORD would answer the plea of the sufferer, a subclass of the individual lament was the Psalms of Confidence. Psalms 4, 11, 16, 23, 27:1–6, 62, and 131 made up this subclass.

Individual Songs of Thanksgiving.   These hymns were used by an individual to praise the LORD for deliverance from trouble. They had (1) an introduction; (2) a narration which told of his trouble, his cry to God, and his deliverance; (3) an acknowledgment of his deliverance; and (4) an announcement of an offering of thanks.[20]

The Royal Psalms.   These psalms were used for special occasions in the religious services for the king. No major activity could be carried out by the king without the proper religious ceremony. Later, when Israel had no king, these psalms began to be interpreted as applying to God's anointed king of the future, the Messiah.[21]

The other psalms.   Not all psalms could be fitted into the five major classes. There were five other classes: (1) songs of pilgrimage (84, 122); (2) community songs of thanksgiving (67, 124); (3) wisdom poetry (1, 37, 49, 73, 112, 127, 128); (4) two types of liturgies—Torah liturgies (15, 24, 121, 134) and prophetic liturgies (12, 14, 50, 53, 75, 81, 82, 85, 91, 95, 132); and (5) mixed poems, the largest group outside the major classes. These psalms often combined characteristics of the major classes (9, 10, 36, 40, 77, 78, 89, 90, 94, 107, 108, 119, 123, 129, 137, 144).

A Look at Selected Psalms.   Due to space limitations, only representative psalms from each category will be studied.

Psalm 1 (a wisdom psalm).   This psalm seems to have been written to introduce the Book of Psalms. Its theme is "the two ways." The psalm tells what the righteous man is (1:1); what he does (1:2); and what he is like (1:3). In contrast, the wicked are like wheat husks that can be blown away by the wind (1:4). They cannot endure the judgment (1:5), for

> the LORD watches over the way of the righteous,
>   but the way of the wicked will perish (1:6).

Psalm 8 (a hymn on the glory of the LORD and the dignity of humanity).   While not opening with a call to praise as was typical of the hymns, Psalm 8 does open with praise to the LORD (8:1). The greatness of the LORD's presence can be seen in the heavenly bodies (8:2–3). They make the psalmist consider humankind, whom the LORD had made as the crown of creation. Humankind had been given dominion or authority over all other creatures—whether the land animals, the birds of the air, or the sea creatures (8:4–8). The psalm closes with a repeat of the psalmist's praise of the LORD.

Psalm 117 (a short hymn). The shortest psalm is a classic example of a hymn. The call to praise begins with "Hallelujah," literally "praise to *Yah(weh)*." Verse 2 gives the reason for praising the LORD:

> For great is his steadfast love toward us;
> and the faithfulness of the LORD endures forever.

The renewed call to praise, "Hallelujah," ends the psalm.

Psalm 74 (a communal lament). The condition that gave rise to this psalm was an attack on the temple. As a lament, it begins with a complaint to God. God had cast off his people. The congregation of Israel had been forgotten, because the Temple, God's dwelling place in Zion, was destroyed (74:1–3).

The psalmist described how the enemy destroyed the Temple woodwork and burned the Temple. There was no prophet to give a word from the LORD (74:4–9). He asked how long Israel had to endure the scoffing of the enemy (74:10–11).

It was not a lack of ability that had caused God not to deliver Israel from the enemy. God had created the heavens and the earth, defeated the great sea monster Leviathan, had set the heavenly bodies in place, and had established the seasons (74:12–17).

God's honor needed to be defended:

> Rise up, O God, plead your cause;
> remember how the impious scoff at you all day long.
> Do not forget the clamor of your foes,
> the uproar of your adversaries that goes up continually (74:22–23).

When God punished his foes for their scoffing, Israel's enemies would be destroyed. Thus, two needs could be met by one activity.

Psalm 22 (an individual lament). The largest class of the psalms was the individual lament. The opening words of this lament are familiar to Christians because, according to Matthew and Mark, they were quoted by Jesus on the cross (Matt. 27:46; Mark 15:34). The opening cry (22:1–2) complains that God had forsaken the sufferer. Instead of an account of his condition, the psalmist recalled God's activity on behalf of the fathers (22:3–5). He had a low opinion of himself, for he said, "I am a worm, and not human." Men mocked and scorned him. They also scoffed at God for not delivering him (22:6–8).

He recalled that he had depended on God from birth. For this reason he still called on God. His enemies were like raging bulls. He was weak from illness, his

Photograph by John H. Tullock.

Figure 13–1.   "The wicked are not so, but are like the chaff the wind
drives away." (Ps. 1:4). Threshing floors, such as this one
in the Judean hill country, were established where the
threshers could take advantage of the late afternoon
breeze that separated the husks, or chaff, from the grain.

strength was all gone, his mouth felt dry, and death seemed near. This encouraged
his enemies to encircle him like a pack of vicious dogs, ready to snap and bite him,
exposing his bones (22:9–18).

From the depths of despair, he moved upward toward assurance that God
would hear him. He repeated his cry for help (22:19–21) and promised that he would
praise God to his brethren. He exhorted those near him to stand in awe of the LORD.
The LORD would hear the cry of the afflicted.

Addressing God again, he pledged to praise him in the assembly (22:25–26).
The remainder of the psalm was an expression of confidence in God. This type of
ending, while not present in all laments, frequently did appear (22:27–31).

Psalm 23 (a psalm of confidence).   The psalms of confidence grew out of the individual laments. This, the most famous of the psalms, is often referred to as "the
Shepherd Psalm." While the figure of the shepherd does introduce the psalm, there
are two other figures in the psalm—the guide and the host.

The psalmist thought of the LORD as a shepherd to lead his flock to the best
pastures where there was tender grass and plenty of water (23:1–3a). The LORD was
like a guide who led the traveler through the deep, dark ravines so common in the

Palestinian hill country. There lurked thieves and wild animals ready to pounce on the unsuspecting traveler. The guide carried both a heavy stick and a weighted club to defend the one he was guiding. The traveler could proceed with assurance that the guide would protect him (23:3b–4).

The LORD was like a Bedouin sheik who took in a man fleeing from his enemies. The law of hospitality in the Near East, especially among the nomadic and semi-nomadic groups, was to take in a stranger, to give him the best of food, and protect him at the cost of the host's own life, if necessary.[22] The practice of anointing the guest's head with oil was an act of hospitality, as was the filling of the cup to overflowing. As the servants of the host would serve the stranger, so goodness and mercy followed the one blessed by the LORD throughout his days (23:5–6).

Psalm 51 (an individual lament).   This is perhaps the most famous of the individual laments. Early Jewish interpreters connected it with David's seduction of Bathsheba and the child born from that act. Its appeal, however, like that of the psalms in general, is that it mirrors the inner conflict of any moral person who has committed a grievous sin of immorality. It contains a varied vocabulary to describe sin and repentance.

Verses 1 and 2 contain a plea for forgiveness based on God's "mercy," "steadfast love," and "abundant mercy." Sin was described in a threefold manner as "transgression" (or rebellion), "sin" (which basically means failing to come up to the accepted standard), and "iniquity" (meaning moral distortion). God's forgiveness also was described as a threefold action: blotting out or erasing, washing thoroughly, and cleansing as in a ceremonial sense (51:1–2).

The psalmist had a deep sense of guilt. He felt that he had sinned against God and that the troubles he had been enduring were just punishment for his failures (51:3–5). He asked God to teach him wisdom. The cleansing he desired was both an outward cleansing of a ceremonial act and an inward cleansing through repentance and forgiveness. He wanted a sense of inner joy. This could only come with the assurance of sins forgiven (51:6–9).

He pleaded with God to create a clean heart within him, for God to keep him in his presence, and for God to restore him to the joy of the salvation which was God's (51:10–12). If these things were done, he promised to proclaim God's ways to sinners (51:13–14). Unlike other psalms, in which animal sacrifices were offered, this one speaks of "a broken and a contrite heart" as the sacrifice most acceptable to God (51:15–17). A later addition by a priestly hand tried to bring it back to priestly orthodoxy by mentioning "burnt offerings and whole burnt offerings" (51:18–19).

Psalm 32 (an individual song of thanksgiving).   This psalm, like others of its class, was used in a service to offer thanks to the LORD when one had recovered from a serious illness. After speaking about the blessedness of being forgiven of his sins, the psalmist told about how his sense of guilt made him physically ill so that his "strength was dried up like the heat of summer" (32:3–4). But he had confessed his sins, and his happiness was restored (32:5). He would recommend that the godly pray to the LORD.

An oracle, probably spoken by a Temple prophet, interrupted the psalmist:

> I will teach you and instruct you in the way you should go;
> I will counsel you with my eye upon you (32:8).

He was not to be like the horse or mule that had to be controlled with "bit and bridle" in order to get it to obey (32:9).

The psalm closes with a call for joy because of the love which the LORD had given to those who trusted him (32:10–11).

Psalm 116 (an individual song of thanksgiving).[23]   This psalm, more clearly than most, gives directions for worship. The individual had been healed from a devastating illness. He came to the Temple to make a sacrifice of thanksgiving. The service opened with an address to the other worshipers in which he described what had happened to him (116:1–4). Praise to the LORD followed because the LORD had delivered him from almost certain death (116:5–11).

Next, the offerings were made. They were introduced by the question, "What shall I return to the LORD for all his bounty to me?" Then followed the drink offering. The cup containing the wine was lifted to the LORD while he recited his vows and commitment (116:12–16). Then the animal sacrifice was made with the proper comments (116:17–19). The service ended with the shout, "Hallelujah!"

Psalm 45 (a royal psalm).   This was a psalm for a royal wedding. It was sung by the court minstrel to celebrate the happy event that was about to take place. First, the singer addressed the king, using exaggerated language to describe him. In verses 6 and 7, especially, there appears the kind of language that led later interpreters to see this as a messianic psalm, particularly in those days when Israel had no king. The king was told that his "divine throne" would "endure forever and ever" (45:1–9).

Next, the queen-to-be was addressed. She was told how fortunate she was to be marrying the king of Israel. She was to forget her people and submit to the king as her lord (45:10–12). As though he were the writer of the bridal column in the Jerusalem *Gazette*, the psalmist described the queen's bridal attire as she was led by her escort to the wedding chamber (45:12–15).

The psalm ended with a forecast that the king would be succeeded by sons more famous than their forefathers. Because of the illustrious sons born to him and his queen, the king's name would be remembered for many generations (45:16–17).

Psalm 139 (a lament of the individual).   This great psalm reflects a more developed theology than some of the earlier poems. It falls into four stanzas of six verses each. The first stanza speaks of God's knowledge of the psalmist's everyday activities and thoughts. He was awed by such intimate knowledge as the LORD possessed (139:1–6).

In the second stanza, he spoke of God's all-pervading presence in the universe. No matter where he might go in the future, God would be there, even in the grave. This was a new idea (139:7–12).

In stanza three, he spoke of God's knowledge of him before he was even born. God had seen his creation in the womb. God knew what he would be before he was. The thoughts of God were beyond his comprehension (139:13–18).

In the fourth stanza (139:–19–24), he turned to his enemies, who were also God's enemies. Since he was powerless to overcome them, he called on God who had all power to do so. Then the thought struck him that his thoughts might not be what they should be. He closed with a plea:

> Search me, O God, and know my heart;
>   test me, and know my thoughts.
> See if there is any wicked way in me,
>   and lead me in the way everlasting (139:23–24).

Special groups of psalms. There are a number of psalm groupings and special psalms. One such group is Psalms 113–118. These psalms are still used today in the celebration of the Jewish feast of Passover. They are known as the Egyptian Hallel. Another such special group is Psalms 120–134. Each psalm in the group bears the title, "A Song of Ascents." They were used in the great pilgrimage festivals. As devout Jews went up to Jerusalem, they sang these "Songs of Ascents" as they moved toward the Holy City.

While they are not distinct groups as such, certain psalms have unique characteristics. Among these are the acrostics, the most famous of which is Psalm 119. It contains twenty-two sections of stanzas, each containing eight verses. All eight verses in a stanza begin with the same Hebrew letter, and all twenty-two stanzas begin with a different letter of the Hebrew alphabet in alphabetical order. Certain of the psalms were antiphonal psalms. They were written so a leader spoke lines that told a story while a choir or the people answered with a refrain. Thus, in Psalm 136, the speaker told the story of the Exodus while the congregation or choir responded with the refrain, "For his steadfast love endures forever." When the refrain is removed, the words of the leader tell the story.

The vengeance psalms. One of the major problems that face interpreters of the psalms are those psalms that express violent hatred toward the nation or of the psalmist. Psalm 137 is an example of such attitudes. After lamenting the conditions that the exiles had to endure, the psalm turns to a violent denunciation of the Babylonians. It ends with the bitter words:

> O daughter Babylon, you devastator!
>   Happy shall they be who pay you back for what you have done to us!
> Happy shall they be who take your little ones
>   and dash them against the rock! (137:8–9).

One must admit that this attitude was a far cry from that expressed by a great teacher of a later time who said, "Let the children come to me and do not hinder them, for to such belongs the kingdom of heaven" (Matt. 19:14). How does one deal with these psalms and what value, if any, do they have? Several things must be understood before these questions can be answered. In the background are certain ideas:

1. They are grounded in ideas from the practice of blood-vengeance. Blood-vengeance was justice in its most primitive form. It arose in a time when there was no state to see that justice was done. Because of this lack of a neutral party to adminster justice, the family or clan had that responsibility. The more specific responsibility fell upon the nearest of kin of the person who had been wronged. Thus, if A^1 killed B^1, then A^1 could expect B^2 to try to avenge B^1. This avenger (or redeemer as he was called) was judge, jury, and executioner. For example, see Gideon's revenge for the death of his brothers in Judges 8.
2. Closely allied with these ideas was the idea of corporate personality. The individual was so bound up with the group that whatever affected the individual affected the group.
3. The concept of covenant was also at work in these psalms. The LORD and Israel were bound together in covenant. In that covenant relationship, the LORD became a part of Israel's "family," so to speak.
4. The belief in the justice of God, and that justice had to come in this life, led to the plea for God to destroy the enemy.

With these ideas in mind, the vengeance psalms reflect a condition in which Israel (or an individual) had been devastated by an enemy. There was no avenger who had survived the devastation or who had strength enough to see that justice was done. God, as Israel's covenant partner, was the only one left who could see that justice was done. Thus, basically, these rather brutal sounding psalms came from a people so brutalized themselves that God was their only hope. In their primitive way, they cried for justice just as oppressed groups still do today.

Summary on the Psalms.   The psalms were the hymns of a people. They represent individual and group worship. For the most part, they reflect the kind of orthodox theology that the Book of Proverbs and the friends of Job reflect: (1) God is just. (2) This life is all there is of real life. (3) Since God is just, the good will prosper and the wicked will suffer. Despite their simple view of life, they continue to speak to every generation because they mirror the full range of human emotion.

STUDY QUESTIONS

1. How was Israelite wisdom related to the wisdom of other countries?
2. How did the Egyptian "Instruction of Amen-em-opet" influence the Israelite Book of Proverbs?
3. Name and define two types of wisdom teachings.
4. What was the theme of the Book of Proverbs?
5. How do Proverbs 1–9 and 10–31 differ?
6. What distinctive proverb form in Proverbs 30 reminds one of the prophet Amos?

7. What does Proverbs 31:10–31 tell us about the status of women in ancient Israel?
8. What are the evidences that the Book of Job is the work of more than one author?
9. What are some things one needs to know to help in understanding the Book of Job?
10. What is the role of Satan in Job 1 and 2?
11. How does Job in Chapters 1 and 2 differ from Job in 3:1–42:6?
12. Who are Job's friends and what are their basic arguments to Job?
13. What are Job's arguments to his friends? to God?
14. Why is Job 31 called the "code of an Old Testament gentleman"?
15. What do the Elihu speeches add to the book?
16. How does God answer Job?
17. What conclusion does Job reach about the meaning of his suffering?
18. Why is Ecclesiastes called "skeptical wisdom"?
19. How does the view of God in Ecclesiastes differ from that in the Book of Job?
20. What sort of philosophy of life does Ecclesiastes advocate?
21. What does Ecclesiastes tell us about the theological views of at least some Jews in postexilic times?
22. What was the purpose of the Song of Songs?
23. How has the Song of Songs been interpreted and why?
24. Who are the characters in the Song of Songs?
25. What basic difference in the nature of the psalms helps to explain some of the attitudes they contain?
26. How do we know that the Book of Psalms is a collection of songs covering a long period of time?
27. How is the Book of Psalms arranged?
28. What does the expression " psalm of David" mean?
29. What did Hermann Gunkel contribute to our understanding of the Book of Psalms?
30. What are Gunkel's five major classes of psalms?
31. What does Psalms tell us about Israelite worship?
32. What was the purpose of Psalm 45?
33. How is one to interpret the vengeance psalms?
34. What is the basic theology of the psalms?
35. Term to know: *Qoheleth.*

ENDNOTES

1. For an excellent short introduction to wisdom literature, see Roland E. Murphy, "Wisdom Literature and Psalms," in *Interpreting Biblical Texts* (Nashville: Abingdon Press: 1983), 13–25. For a longer introduction, see James L. Crenshaw, *Old Testament Wisdom: An Introduction,* rev. and enl. (Louisville: Westminster/John Knox Press, 1998).
2. Pritchard, *ANE,* 237–243.
3. An excellent work that thoroughly examines the development of schools both in Israel and in the rest of the Near East is James L. Crenshaw, *Education in Ancient Israel: Across the Deadening Silence* (New York: Doubleday, 1998). For a discussion of the law as "moral education," see Joseph Blenkinsopp, "Sage, Priest, and Prophet," in *Library of Ancient Israel* (Louisville: Westminster/John Knox, 1995), 38ff.
4. R. B. Y. Scott, *The Way of Wisdom* (New York: Macmillan, 1977), 24, suggests that this section was developed by an

Egyptian-trained Hebrew scribe who copied what he remembered of "The Instruction of Amen-em-opet" and then supplemented it with other sayings to fill out the total of thirty.

5. Samuel Terrien, "The Book of Job: Introduction and Exegesis," *IB* III, 877–902, is a comprehensive introduction to the book of Job.
6. John H. Tullock, *Blood-Vengeance among the Israelites*, 141 ff.
7. See Genesis 4:10; Ezekiel 24:7.
8. I am indebted to the late J. Philip Hyatt of Vanderbilt University for this phrase.
9. David Noel Freedman, "Is It Possible to Understand the Book of Job?" *BR* IV, 2 (April, 1988), 29.
10. Ibid., 30.
11. For all you would ever want to know about this book and more, see Marvin H. Pope, "Song of Songs," *AB*, 7C.
12. The sons of Korah and Asaph were professional singing guilds connected with the Temple (1 Chronicles 25).
13. Mitchell Dahood, "Psalms I," *AB*, 16, 175.
14. Dahood, "Psalms I, II, III," *AB*, 16, 17, 17A.
15. A summary of his views can be found in Hermann Gunkel, "The Psalms," *Facet Books*, 19 (Minneapolis: Augsburg/ Fortress Press, 1967).

16. It included Psalms 8, 19, 33, 65, 68, 96, 98, 100, 103, 104, 105, 111, 113, 114, 115, 117, 135, 136, 145–150.
17. See Sigmund Mowinckel, *The Psalms in Israel's Worship*, 2 vols., trans. D.R. Ap-Thomas (Nashville: Abingdon Press, 1967), esp. Ch. 3.
18. Among the communal laments are Psalms 44, 48, 60, 74, 79, 80, 83, 106, and 125.
19. It included Psalms 3, 5, 6, 7, 13, 17, 22, 25, 26, 27:7–14, 28, 31, 35, 38, 39, 42–43, 51, 52, 54, 55, 56, 57, 61, 63, 64, 69, 70, 71, 86, 88, 102, 109, 120, 130, 139, 140, 141, 142, and 143.
20. Psalm 18 (a Royal Psalm as well), 30, 32, 41, 66, 92, 116, and 138.
21. They include Psalms 2, 18, 20, 21, 45, 72, 101, 110, and 132.
22. See the story of Abraham and the two men (Genesis 18:1–33). Also Lot's attempt to protect the same men (Genesis 19:1–11).
23. The idea for what follows in the discussion of this Psalm came from H. J. Flanders, R. W. Crapps, and D. A. Smith, *The People of the Covenant: An Introduction to the Old Testament*, 3rd ed. (New York: Oxford, 1988), 412f.

Chapter 14 ❦

THE TIME OF SILENCE

Judah in Eclipse

It was as if someone had suddenly put out all the lights on the stage and cut off the sound while a play was in progress. The actors continued to act out their parts, but the audience could not see and hear, for there were neither lights nor sound. Things happened in Palestine between 400 and 200 B.C.E., but our knowledge has to be based largely on what was evident in 200 B.C.E. and what can be gleaned from sources outside Israel.

THE HISTORICAL SITUATION

Persia's Last Days

The Persian Empire continued to control Palestine for the next century and a half. Persia was not without its troubles, however. From the time of Nehemiah on, Persia faced constant problems—first from an Egyptian revolt, then from the Greeks, and finally from the rulers of the western part of the empire.

Real troubles came, however, during the reign of Darius III (Condomannus) (336–331). When Philip of Macedon (359–336) came to power, Macedonia gained control of the Greek states in 338. When Philip was assassinated in 336, that tragedy was not to Persia's advantage because it put Alexander, his son, on the throne of Macedonia.[1]

The Campaigns of Alexander the Great

The young Alexander (336–323) was a military genius. In 334, he invaded Asia Minor and quickly gained control of the entire area. At the battle of Issus (333), he routed the main Persian army, even capturing Darius' wife and family. Moving down the Mediterranean coast, he quickly captured Phoenicia, except Tyre and Palestine. He was welcomed with open arms by the Egyptians in 332. From there he moved eastward until he reached the Indus River. In his wake, he left centers of Greek learning and culture as he required his older soldiers to retire and live in the conquered lands. Because of the influence of Greek culture, over the period of several hundred years the effects of Alexander's action changed the course of civilization.

Ptolemies and Seleucids in Palestine

When Alexander died in 323, his empire was divided among four of his generals. Ptolemy, a Macedonian Greek and founder of the last Egyptian dynasty, was given control of Palestine, while Syria was given to Seleucus.[2] For a century, the Ptolemies dominated Palestine. During that time, Egypt gained a large Jewish population. It has been estimated that one million Jews lived in Alexandria in the first century B.C.E.

But Egyptian domination of Palestine came under direct challenge from the Seleucids when Antiochus the Great (223–187) came to the Seleucid throne. After a number of battles, Antiochus prevailed in the battle of Panium (Baniyas), where the later city of Caesarea Philippi (of New Testament fame) was to be located.[3]

While Antiochus the Great was welcomed by the Jews—especially since he gave special favors to the priests and other leaders—the honeymoon ended when Antiochus IV (Epiphanes) came to the throne.

Antiochus Epiphanes was determined that all his subjects worship Greek gods, speak the Greek language, and follow Greek customs. He infuriated pious Jews by his actions, especially when he interfered in the selection of the high priest. He threw out Onias III, the ruling high priest, and sold the office to Onias's brother Jason. Before long, Menelaus, a priest who did not belong to the high priestly family, paid Antiochus a bigger sum of money. Antiochus deposed Jason in favor of Menelaus.

The high priest became the promoter of Hellenization—the adoption of Greek religion and culture. There followed a number of outrages by Antiochus against the Jews. Among other things he forbade Jewish religous practices (including circumcision), set up an altar to the Greek god Zeus in the Temple, and sacrificed a hog on the sacred altar. Those Jews who resisted him were slaughtered without mercy. When he ordered all Jews to sacrifice to Zeus, he provoked à revolt that would bring Jewish indepedence for the first time in many centuries.

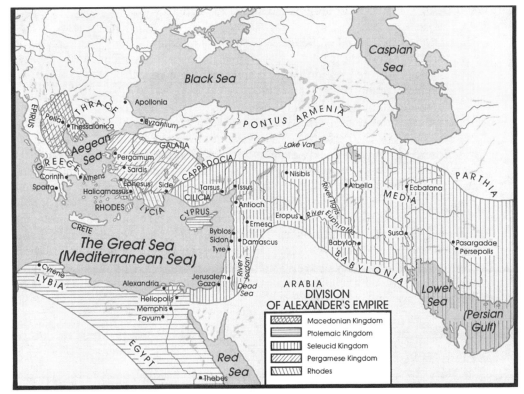

Artwork by Margaret Jordan Brown ©) Mercer University Press.

Figure 14–1. Alexander's Empire.

THE MACCABEAN REVOLT

In 168 B.C.E., a representative of the king went to the village of Modein to enforce the Hellenization decree. He called on a village leader, the priest Mattathias, to set the example by sacrificing to Zeus. Instead, Mattathias killed the king's officer, as well as a Jew who had offered to make the sacrifice. Having done that, he fled into the Judean wilderness with his five sons.

Mattathias soon died, but his son Judas Maccabeus took leadership of the revolt started by his father. Judas and his brothers were joined by pious Jews called the *Hasidim.* Their revolt was so successful that by 165, they had recaptured Jerusalem. In December 165, the Temple was cleansed and rededicated to the worship of the LORD.

Later Judas was killed. His brother Jonathan succeeded him. He, recognizing the power of the high priest, took over that office for himself in 150. In 142, Simon, another brother, led the Jews to independence from the Seleucids and founded the Hasmonean Dynasty that ruled Palestine until the Roman conquest in 63 B.C.E.

THE WORD OF THE LORD IN DIFFICULT TIMES

The period from the end of Nehemiah's governorship until the Maccabean revolt saw much literature of the Old Testament reach the form in which we now have it. As has been indicated previously, we actually know very little about what was going on in Palestine.

There were large Jewish communities outside Palestine, however. Such a community existed in Babylon, where Jews were deeply involved in the business life of the area. In Egypt, the Persians had a Jewish military colony located at Elephantine in southern Egypt. This colony even had its own temple, where regular sacrifices were offered. It was somewhat unorthodox in its doctrine of God, saying, among other things, that God had a wife. It seems that other gods were worshiped as well. Even so, there seems to have been the observance of such traditional Jewish holidays as the Sabbath, Passover, and Unleavened Bread, and contact was maintained with religious leaders in Jerusalem.[4] The Elephantine temple was destroyed by the Egyptians around 410 and the colony appealed to Jerusalem for help in rebuilding. When no help came, they then appealed to Bagoas, the governor of Judah, and the sons of Sanballat, who ruled Samaria. They got the help they requested. This colony was still in existence as late as 399 B.C.E.[5]

The Last of the Prophets

From this time in Jewish history came the last of the prophets and their successors, the apocalyptists.

Obadiah: A Hymn of Hate Against Edom (Obad. 1:1–21).   Nothing is known about the author of this short book. The name means, "the LORD's servant," which may not be a name but just a title. Part of the book almost duplicates sections of Jeremiah (verses 1 to 9 are quite similar to Jer. 49:7–22).

The biblical stories of conflicts between Jacob and Esau found in Genesis 25 to 36 reflect a long-standing animosity between the Israelites and the Edomites. The time of these oracles could be almost any period of Israelite history, but recent archaeological findings indicate Edomite intrusions into Judah's Negev territory just before or after the fall of Jerusalem in 587.[6]

The theme of the book was that Edom was doomed. Petra (or Sela), its capital, was so secure that the prophet compared it to an eagle's nest built on a lofty peak. But the LORD would bring it down (1:1–4). As Edom gloated over the rape and pillage of Jerusalem, so the Jews would have the opportunity to gloat over the ruin of Edom. The day of the LORD was going to be directed toward the enemy, and they would receive just punishment for their sins. When the LORD's kingdom came to pass, the Jews would be triumphant over such enemies as Edom and Philistia (1:5–21).

Malachi: The LORD Questions the Community. Since none of the Israelite historical material mentions Malachi, nor does the book give any sort of biographical information, this prophet, like Obadiah, is anonymous. The name means "my messenger." Malachi 1:1 could be translated, "The oracle of the word of the LORD to Israel by my messenger." The content of the book suggests a time not too far removed from that of Ezra and Nehemiah. Many of the problems were the same concerns with which Ezra and Nehemiah had to deal. It was a time when the hopes of the returned exiles had turned bitter. The people had become cynical and were careless in their acts of worship. The prophet was trying to arouse a disillusioned community, grown cynical with the continued delay of the glorious future Deutero-Isaiah had talked about.

The nature of the book is that of a dialogue. The LORD, through the prophet, made a statement. The statement provoked a question which, in turn, was answered by the LORD:

1. *The statement:* "I have loved you."
   The question: "How have you loved us?"
   The answer: "I chose Jacob instead of Esau to be my people. The Edomites (Esau) will be punished" (1:1–5).
2. *The statement:* "You have not shown proper respect for me."
   The question: How have we disrespected you?"
   The answer: "By offering blemished animals. The priests have failed in their responsibilities to see that proper kinds of sacrifices were made" (1:6–2:9).
3. *The statement:* "The LORD no longer accepts your offerings."
   The question: "Why does he not?"
   The answer: "Because you have been faithless to your wives as you have been faithless to the LORD's covenant. The LORD hates divorce" (2:10–16).
4. *The statement:* "You have wearied me with your words."
   The question: "How have we wearied you?"
   The answer: "By saying that God is unjust. The LORD is coming in judgment upon such sinners" (2:17–3:5).
5. *The statement:* "Return to me, and I will return to you."
   The question: "How shall we return?"
   The statement: "You are robbing me."
   The question: "How are we robbing you?"
   The answer: "In tithes and offerings."
   (This series of questions and answers suggests something of the same kind of situation Nehemiah found at the beginning of his second term as governor of Judah) (3:6–12).
6. *The statement:* "You have spoken harsh words against me."
   The question: "How have we spoken against you?"
   The answer: "By saying, 'It is vain to serve God. Evildoers not only prosper, but when they put God to the test, they escape.' But the LORD keeps a record of the righteous and will reward them according to their righteous deeds. In the judgment, evildoers will be punished" (3:13–4:4).

The book closes with a promise to send the LORD's messenger before the day of the LORD comes to call people to repentance (4:5–6).

Joel: Prophecy and Apocalyptic.   Joel combines characteristics of both prophetic and apocalyptic. For many years, this book was regarded as one of the early books of the prophets, but in recent years, its relationship to apocalyptic literature has caused it to be put in the postexilic era. Its exact date is far from certain, but it does share common themes with Zechariah 9–14 and Daniel. Because of that, it is discussed here.

The locusts are coming! (Joel 1:1–2:27).[7]   The prophet was "Joel, the son of Pethuel" (1:1). Beyond that, nothing personal is known about him. The outstanding feature of the book is its vivid description of one of the most frightening plagues known to ancient peoples—the locusts. Locusts are a large and voracious grasshopper, destructive beyond description (1:4). When they descended by the millions on an area, they literally would devour every living plant.

> It [the locust] has laid waste my vines,
>   and splintered my fig trees;
> it has stripped off their bark and thrown it down;
>   their branches have turned white (1:7).

But the locust plague was only a way for Joel to introduce a bigger and more important idea—the day of the LORD (see Amos 5:18).

> Alas for the day!
> For the day of the LORD is near,
>   and as destruction from the Almighty it comes.
> Is not the food cut off from your eyes,
>   joy and gladness from the house of God? (1:15–16).

Using words sounding as if they were borrowed directly from the prophet Amos, Joel spoke of the day of the LORD as a "day of darkness and gloom, a day of clouds and thick darkness" (2:2). The locusts, who were the LORD's agents for bringing in the great day of the LORD, were like a conquering army sweeping over the land:

> Like warriors they charge,
>   like soldiers they scale the wall.
> Each one keeps to its own course,
>   they do not swerve from their paths (2:7).

The locusts were everywhere, even in the houses.

The whole universe got involved. There was an earthquake, the sun and moon could not be seen, and the stars disappeared (2:10–11). The LORD called on the people to repent and return to him. As in times of calamity, a solemn fast was to be observed, where all the people came together. The priest led the people in prayer for a lifting of the plague (2:12–17).

The LORD heard and would return his blessing to the land. Peace and prosperity would follow. Food would be plentiful, peace would prevail, and the LORD would rule the people (2:18–27).

The great day of the LORD *(Joel 2:28–3:21).* Part of this passage (2:28–32) is well known to Christians because it is quoted in Peter's sermon at Pentecost (Acts 2:17–21). It shows the characteristics of apocalyptic judgment in its references to the darkening of the sun and the moon turning to blood as signs of its approach. Now the other nations would be subject to judgment, but Judah and Jerusalem would be restored to a place of glory. Tyre, Sidon, and Philistia were used as examples of nations which had oppressed Judah. The reference to the Greeks (3:6) seem to give a hint about the time of the prophet's work. If so, the time was somewhere in the fifth or fourth centuries (3:1–8).

The nations would be called to judgment in the valley of Jehoshaphat, a valley whose name meant "the LORD judges." Like a farmer harvesting grain, the nations would be cut down. It would be a time of decision with the multitudes gathered (3:9–15). The words of Amos were quoted:

> The LORD roars from Zion.
> and utters his voice from Jerusalem, (see Amos 1:2)
> and the heavens and the earth shake.
> But the LORD is a refuge for his people,
> a stronghold for the people of Israel (3:16).

For Judah and Jerusalem, the day of the LORD promised a time of unparalleled prosperity. For Egypt and Edom, which long had been thorns in Judah's side, the day would mean drought and desolation for crimes committed against Judah. The LORD would see that justice was done (3:17–21).

The Apocalyptic Writers

Joel marked the transition from prophecy to apocalyptic. Discouraging times produced such men, whose purpose was to give the people hope when the situation seemed hopeless.

Zechariah 9–14. This part of the book of Zechariah differs radically in form from the rest of the work. While Chapters 1 to 8 consist of a series of visionary experiences in which Zechariah plays a major role, no mention is made of him in these chapters. The mention of the Greeks, furthermore, suggests a later time than that of the prophet Zechariah. These matters have led to the conclusion that Chapters 9 to 14 of this book were from someone other than Zechariah, sometime before the Greek or Hellenistic period of Judah's existence (332–63 B.C.E.), since Tyre was still uncaptured (9:3–4). Tyre fell to Alexander in 333 after a seven-month siege.

The day of the LORD means new life for Israel (Zech. 9:1–11:17). With the boundaries of Israel in the days of David and Solomon in mind, the writer envisioned the triumph of the LORD over Israel's enemies. The restored kingdom would stretch from northern Syria to the southernmost borders of David's kingdom (9:1–8). Yet its king would not be warlike. He would ride a small burro, the symbol of peace, instead of the prancing stallion of a warlord (9:9–10).

The Jews would be gathered from the ends of the earth. Judah would even be triumphant over powerful Greece (9:11–13). The reason for this turn of events would be the LORD's leadership:

> Then the LORD will appear over them,
> and his arrow go forth like lightning;
> the LORD God will sound the trumpet,
> and march forth in the whirlwinds of the south (9:14).

The people would be saved and would prosper in a well-watered land. The idols, on the other hand, and their prophets would be powerless to deliver on their promises. God's anger would be directed toward such false leaders (9:10–10:5). But the LORD would raise up leaders for Judah:

> Out of them shall come the cornerstone,
> out of them the tent peg,
> out of them the battle bow,
> out of them every commander (10:4).

Israel would be strong once again because the LORD would gather the people from among the nations where they had been scattered. Egypt and Assyria, representative of the nations that had scattered the LORD's people, would be destroyed (10:6–12). Others who had oppressed the LORD's people would be burnt out like a fire raging in the forest (11:1–3).

As the shepherd had life-and-death control over his sheep, so the Jews' rulers had life-and-death control over them. The prophet, acting for the LORD, took the role of the shepherd of the people. Symbolizing their one-time condition as a united people (Israel and Judah), he took two shepherd's staffs and held them together as one. Three rulers (shepherds) came and went in rapid succession. To express the LORD's unhappiness at the situation, the staff named Grace was broken. As a wage, the prophet was given 30 shekels of silver for being the shepherd. These he gave to the Temple treasury. Then the second staff (Union) was broken, symbolizing the separation of Israel from Judah. The LORD was going to raise up a shepherd (leader) who did not care for the people (11:4–17).

The day of the LORD and the triumph of Jerusalem (Zech. 12:1–14:21). As part of the apocalyptic vision of the day of the LORD, Jerusalem and the cities of Judah would be attacked by their enemies. But they would fall, for Jerusalem would be like an immovable rock straining the back of anyone who tried to lift it. While Jerusalem's people stayed safely within the city, the tide of battle would turn, with Judah's clans destroying the enemy (12:1–6).

Since the descendants of David were among Jerusalem's citizens, Judah's warfare on their behalf assured that all Judah, not just Jerusalem, would receive praise for their success. Any nation that tried to attack Jerusalem would be destroyed. Its defense would be led by the descendants of David. The Jerusalemites and David's descendants would also take on a new spirit of mercy and prayer. They would mourn someone whom they had stabbed to death, possibly because too late they realized he did not deserve such severe punishment. It would be like Baal worshipers mourning in the annual fertility rites in Megiddo. All the Jerusalem families would be mourning (12:7–14).

In the day of the LORD, idols would be banished and false prophets sent out to do useful work, such as farming. Even their former friends would attack them if they tried to prophesy again. To purify the land, the people who were false would be destroyed (13:1–9).

But Jerusalem's troubles would not be over. Its enemies would attack again and it would fall. Then the LORD himself would intervene. He would stand on the Mount of Olives, east of the city. A great earthquake would cleave an east-west valley through the mountain. The LORD with his angels would come, bringing in the ideal age (14:1–5).

The age would bring marvelous changes. There would be ideal weather (24-hour sunshine) and perpetual rivers flowing east and west from Jerusalem to the Dead Sea and the Mediterranean. Over this the LORD would reign in triumph (14:6–9).

To the south, the land would become a plain, with only Jerusalem on a hill, dominating the land. Jerusalem's enemies would suffer horrible diseases. Judah would loot its enemies, becoming immensely wealthy. The enemy would realize that the God of the Jews was to be the LORD of all and would come to worship him in Jerusalem each year during the Feast of Booths or Tabernacles. Those who refused would be wiped out in an epidemic.

Everything would be dedicated to the LORD, even the harnesses of the horses. Jerusalem would become one big worship center, with every pot in town set apart for the services of sacrifice (14:10–21).

Daniel: An Encouraging Word for a Dark Time.   For the Old Testament, Daniel is the most apocalyptic book of all. The name Daniel was well known in ancient Palestine. In Canaanite literature there was a hero Dan'el.[8] Ezekiel mentioned Noah, Daniel, and Job. He said:

> Even if Noah, Daniel, and Job were in it [Palestine], says the LORD God, they would save neither son nor daughter; they would save only their own lives by their righteousness (14:20).

According to Daniel 1:1–7, Daniel was taken to Babylon by Nebuchadnezzar in 606. Ezekiel's oracle was from the period before Jerusalem's fall in 587. While it cannot be said with certainty, since he classed Daniel with Noah and Job, both names from ancient Israelite tradition, Ezekiel spoke of him as though he were a figure of the distant past. It is not impossible, of course, that he could be speaking of Daniel of the Book of Daniel.

The book: Its form.[9]   The book of Daniel was not included among the prophets in the Jewish canon. Instead, it was classed as one of the Writings, the last books to be accepted as Scripture. It was found among the Dead Sea Scrolls, but the way it was copied indicated that the Essenes, who were responsible for the Scrolls, did not consider it to be Scripture. Those books they considered sacred were copied in a special format.

While the stories in the book were set in the background of the Babylonian Exile, as it stands now, evidence suggests that it was put in its present form during the persecution by Antiochus Epiphanes to encourage those who were under persecution. Just as the LORD delivered Daniel, so he would deliver the righteous ones who were being persecuted by the tyrant Antiochus IV.

One other note of interest about the book—a major portion of it was written in Aramaic (2:4–7:8), the language the Jews adopted in Babylon. Only one other book (Ezra 7:12–26) used Aramaic to any extent, and it was a postexilic product.

The book: Its contents.   The book has two major divisions: (1) stories about Daniel, and (2) apocalyptic visions of a brighter future for those under persecution.

1. Stories about Daniel (Dan. 1:1–6:28).   The first story (1:1–21) concerns the captivity of Daniel and his three friends of the Jerusalem nobility. Each of the friends was given a Babylonian name. Daniel was called "Belteshazzar," while the three friends were called Shadrach, Meshach, and Abednego. The king ordered that they were to be educated for three years for court service. As such, they were to be fed from the king's table. "But Daniel resolved that he would not defile himself with royal rations of food and wine" (1:8). Thus he and his friends were resolved to be faithful to the laws of their Jewish faith.

When the servant brought them the rich food, they asked instead for vegetables, since there was no danger of violating Jewish laws concerning food it they ate no meat or milk products. When the three years were up, the Jewish youths were as healthy as any others and much more skilled in wisdom. This said to those whom Antiochus was trying to force to follow Hellenistic customs that they could prosper just as Daniel and his friends if they were faithful to the law.

As in the story of Joseph, in which the pharaoh's dreams were so important, so the second story about Daniel concerns a dream of King Nebuchadnezzar (2:1–49). Nebuchadnezzar had a dream his wisest men could not interpret. Daniel told him the dream had to do with things that would come to pass "in the latter days" (2:28). This emphasis on the last days of history is known as *eschatology* (2:1–30).

In Nebuchadnezzar's dream, he had seen a great image with a head of gold, "breasts and arms of silver," belly and thighs of bronze, legs of iron, and feet "partly of iron and partly of clay" (2:33). The image was broken by a stone that became "a great mountain and filled the whole earth" (2:35). The image represented kingdoms that had dominated the Near East, beginning with Nebuchadnezzar. Others were the Medes, the Persians, and the empire of Alexander. But Alexander's kingdom, the one made of iron, was so divided that part of it was mixed with clay. It (the Seleucids and the Ptolemies) would crumble. Then the kingdom of God would come in and replace all earthly kingdoms (2:31–45). Because of Daniel's success in interpreting the dream, he was given a place of honor in the king's court (2:46–49).

The third story concerned Daniel's companions Shadrach, Meshach, and Abednego. When the king set up an idol and demanded that everyone worship it, the three young men refused. Nothing was said about where Daniel was when all this was going on. When the news of the Jews' refusal to worship reached the king, they were ordered thrown into a fiery furnace. When the king looked in to see what had happened to them, he saw not three, but four, one of whom was like "a son of the gods" (3:25). It was a word of assurance to those who were undergoing the fiery trials of persecution by Antiochus Epiphanes (3:1–30).

Next came the story of another dream by the king. He dreamed of a mighty tree that covered the earth; but, on God's orders, a heavenly being descended and cut down the tree. When Daniel was asked to interpret the dream, he told the king that he (the king) was the tree. He would suffer temporary insanity, during which he would act like an animal because he exalted himself above God. When a year had passed, the king suffered as Daniel said. Then he acknowledged the power of the Most High God (4:1–37). In this story, the apocalyptist was saying what Deutero-Isaiah had said many years before:

> By myself I have sworn,
>   from my mouth has gone forth in righteousness
>   a word that shall not return:
> "To me every knee shall bow,
>   every tongue shall swear" (Isa. 45:23).

That even included the tyrant Antiochus, who called himself "God manifest" (Epiphanes).

Chapter 5 tells the story of Belshazzar's feast. Belshazzar was the son and co-regent of Nabonidus (he was called the son of Nebuchadnezzar in 5:2). Nabonidus was an amateur archaeologist who was more interested in old ruins that he was in the breakdown of his kingdom. While Belshazzar was having a wild drinking bout using sacred vessels from the Jerusalem Temple, he saw a message written on the wall. The words were MENE, MENE, TEKEL, PARSIN. Daniel, when called to interpret them, explained that they pronounced Belshazzar's doom. His days were numbered, for he had been found lacking in leadership qualities. Now, his kingdom would be divided among the Medes and Persians. According to Daniel, the kingdom was taken by "Darius the Mede." According to Persian records, it was Cyrus. Darius the Persian ruler came to the throne succeeding Cambyses (530–522) in 522 (5:1–30).

The final is the most famous of the Daniel stories. Exalted to position of *satrap* or governor over a province of the Persian Empire, Daniel was still the faithful worshiper of the LORD. His fellow governors persuaded the king to make a decree that no one could pray to any god for thirty days. Only the king could be petitioned. Daniel ignored the edict and continued to worship three times a day as was his custom. The result was that he was thrown to the lions.

The king realized what a mistake he had made and worried all night about Daniel. But in the morning, Daniel walked out of the lion's den unharmed. Those who had set the trap for him were fed to the lions.

The object of all these stories was to tell the people who where suffering under persecution that as the LORD delivered Daniel, Shadrach, Meshach, and Abednego, so they would be delivered. This was a common theme in apocalyptic literature—the delivery of the righteous from the fire of persecution and the human animals who were trying to destroy them (6:1–28).

2. Daniel's visions (Dan. 7:1–12:13). In the visions recorded in Daniel, there was typical apocalypse. Unusual beasts, the use of numbers, and the view of the last days, including a messianic figure, were all common themes in such literature. Despite any persecution the saints might have been undergoing, the apocalyptic writer brought a message of hope whose theme was that God would win out over the forces of evil.

a. The four beasts from the sea (Dan. 7:1–28). In the first vision, four beasts arose out of the sea. For Jews, the sea always represented a place of awe and mystery. It was a fearsome place, which had great monsters who swallowed up men who dared to venture out into it. This was not unusual for them to conceive of evil creatures coming from the sea. The beasts in the vision represented the strong empires of the time: the Babylonian; the Median, which lay east of Mesopotamian region; the Persian; and finally the Greek or Hellenistic empire of Alexander and his successors. The ten horns represented the ten kings who followed Alexander. Since the horn was a symbol of power, the writer showed his contempt for Antiochus Epiphanes by referring to him as a little horn, a button with a big mouth "that spoke arrogantly" (7:20). But God ("the Ancient One" 7:22) would put an end to his persecution and his mouthings.

> The kingship and dominion
>> and the greatness of the kingdom under the whole heaven
> shall be given to the people of the holy ones of the Most High;
> their kingdom shall be an everlasting kingdom,
>> and all dominion shall serve and obey them (7:27).

b. The ram and the he-goat (Dan 8:1–27). The ram was the Persian Empire, which owed much of its strength to an alliance with the Medes. Alexander (the he-goat) defeated the Medo-Persian Empire. At his death, four of his generals (the four horns) inherited his empire (8:22). Antiochus (a king of bold countenance, 8:23) persecuted the Jews. The 2,300 "mornings and evenings" were three-and-one-half years of the period from the beginning of the Maccabean revolt until the cleansing of the Temple in December, 165.

c. The seventy weeks (Dan. 9:1–27). Numerology came into full play in this vision, along with the introduction of the angel Gabriel as the chief messenger for God. Daniel was pondering Jeremiah's prophecy of the seventy weeks "in the first year of Darius, the son of Ahasuerus . . . who became king over the realm of the Chaldeans" (9:1). This verse holds problems, since Persian records currently available know nothing of such a king. The Chaldeans, furthermore, were the Babylonians, not the Persians.

After a long prayer of repentance and confession, both of his sins and the sins of the people (9:3–19), Daniel was visited by the angel Gabriel. Gabriel's purpose was to reveal the meaning of the seventy weeks, which were explained as "seventy weeks of years" or 490 years. Unfortunately, the meaning of what was revealed to Daniel has not been passed on to us, either by written or oral tradition, making this passage one that has brought interpretations ranging from something less than sublime to the ridiculous. Seemingly, if the historical context is of any value, it referred to the period from the return (538) to the Maccabean era (about 168). It would end when one would come (the Messiah) who "desolates, until the decreed end is poured out on the desolator" (9:27). Again, this seems to refer to Antiochus Epiphanes, who profaned the altar by sacrificing a hog on it. That this interpretation is widely disputed can be readily admitted. One can find all sorts of contrary interpretations, including some current best sellers, applying this to some future event. History is full of such interpretations (9:20–27).

d. The last days (Dan. 10:1–12:13). A favorite theme of apocalyptists was the last days, when the Lord would bring an end to evil and bring in the Kingdom of God. It has always been tempting, especially in trying times, for Jewish and Christian interpreters to apply this passage to their own time. A notable example occured in the 1840s, when a sincere preacher convinced thousands that the end would come in 1843. When it did not come, he changed the date to 1844. There were still many who believed him. But when the end did not come, he died a disillusioned and broken man. This vision, like the others, seems best to be understood as referring to the events from 538 B.C.E. to the Maccabean period. References such as 11:31, "Forces from him (Antiochus Epiphanes) shall occupy and profane the temple and fortress. They shall abolish the regular burnt offering," seem to point to Antiochus and his atrocities against the Jews. For Daniel, this was the prelude to the coming of the Messiah who would deliver the righteous Jews. After a clear reference to a belief in life after death, with rewards and punishment (12:1–4), Daniel closed the veil so that what came after was hidden from view.

The Great Debate: How to Deal with the World

In the postexilic period, there developed a strong conflict among the Jews over how to deal with the non-Jewish world. Second Isaiah had spoken glowingly of Israel's responsibility to be a "light to the nations" (Isa. 49:7). Two poles of opinion grew up on that subject. One said that the Jews' responsibility was to be closed to the world around them, to be exclusively the people of God. Such people undoubtedly would have argued that the nations would be drawn to Israel's God if Israel was faithful in their commitment. This view has been designated as *particularism*.

On the opposite end of the spectrum was the view that the Jews were to be the people of God, but they were to seek actively to bring others to the knowledge of their God. This missionary outlook encompassed all people and, as such, is known as *universalism*. Expression of these contrasting viewpoints are stated nowhere more clearly than in three short books: Esther, Ruth, and Jonah.

Esther: Jews Should Look after Themselves.[10]   This book, set in the background of the Persian Kingdom in the mid-fifth century B.C.E., was a strongly nationalistic tract of the times. God was not mentioned in the book. Its purpose seems to be to explain the origin of the Jewish feast of Purim.

According to the story, Ahasuerus (Xerxes I 485–464), king of Persia, had a banquet for his friends. When he asked his queen Vashti to appear at the banquet, she refused. In retaliation, Ahashuerus deposed her as queen and set up a national search for a replacement (1:1–2:4).

At this point, Esther, the heroine of the story, was introduced. She was a beautiful Jewish girl who had been reared by her elderly cousin, Mordecai. It is said that Mordecai sat "in the king's gate"(2:19, 21; 5:13; 6:10). Rather than meaning that he was just a "hanger-on," it implies that he was a government official, perhaps even the head of the Persian version of the secret service, since the gate was the site of the government offices. This would explain how he found out about a plot against the king and why he did not have to bow to Haman, the prime minister.[11]

When the national beauty contest was conducted, Esther (who concealed her Jewish background) was chosen as the new queen. Not long afterward, Mordecai heard of a plot against the king, and through Esther, was able to warn him. The conspirators were punished, but Mordecai was not rewarded, although his action was noted in the king's chronicles (2:5–23).

The villain of the story was Haman the Agagite, prime minister to Ahasuerus. Mordecai refused to bow to Haman when Haman went out the palace gate, so Haman decided to get rid of Mordecai. Since he hated Jews, he would get rid of all the other Jews as well (3:1–6).

Casting lots (Purim) to determine the best time for getting rid of the Jews, Haman finally felt that the time was right to approach the king. Using persuasion and an enormous bribe, Haman convinced the king to make a decree that on a certain day, all Jews were to be killed. The king, of course, did not realize that Esther was a Jew (3:7–15).

When the decree was published, Mordecai immediately went into mourning. When word got to Esther that Mordecai was in mourning, she sent to ask him why. Since she stayed in the king's harem, she would have been ignorant of the decree. Mordecai sent Esther a copy of the decree, asking her of go to the king and to ask him to lift the death sentence against the Jews. She was reluctant, but she finally agreed to do so, even though it meant risking her life (4:1–17).

Courtesy of A. Griffin/H. Armstrong Roberts.

Figure 14–2. "In the days of Ahasuerus . . ." (Est. 1:1). This
was Xerxes (485–464 B.C.E.) of the Book of Esther.
These ruins of Xerxes Porch are at his capital,
Persepolis.

When she went to the king, he granted her the privilege to speak to him. She asked him to invite Haman to a dinner for the three of them. The king granted her wish. Haman, sure that his moment of glory had arrived, rejoiced until he happened to see Mordecai at the palace gate. He went home and ordered carpenters to build a gallows in his garden so he could personally hang the Jew he hated most (5:1–14).

Meanwhile, the king was having a sleepless night. Looking for something to read, he happened to read in his chronicles how Mordecai had saved his life. The next morning, when Haman arrived, he was asked what would be a proper reward to be given to a man whom the king wanted to honor. Thinking that he was the one the king intended to honor, Haman suggested that such a man should be clad in the king's robes, put on the king's own horse, led through the streets of the capital, and have it proclaimed that the man was being honored by the king. The king liked the suggestion, ordered Haman to find Mordecai, and do to him as Haman had suggested. Haman did it, but, at the same time, felt rather sick about the whole affair (6:1–14).

The day of Haman's dinner with the king and queen came. Ahasuerus asked Esther what it was that she wanted him to do. Then she revealed that she was Jewish. She pleaded for her own life, as well as for the lives of her people. When the king (who seemed to have problems with his memory!) asked who had caused all the trouble, she pointed an accusing finger at Haman. In anger, the king left the room for the cool of the garden. Haman fell at the queen's feet as she lay on the dining couch. When the king returned to the room, " Haman had thrown himself on the couch where Esther was reclining" (7:8). He took what he saw as an attempt of Haman to rape the queen. That did it. Haman was hanged on the gallows he had built for Mordecai (7:1–10).

Since he could not revoke his decree about the slaughter of the Jews, he sent out another decree that gave the Jews the right to defend themselves against anyone who might attack them (8:1–17). The Jews took it as an opportunity to rid themselves of their enemies throughout the kingdom. The tenth day of the month of Adar was designated the day for celebration of the Feast of Purim, which would commemorate the event (9:1–32). Mordecai replaced Haman as prime minister (10:1–3).

Ruth and Jonah: The Jews Have an Obligation to Others.   Two other books carry the arguments of the universalists.

The Book of Ruth (Ruth 1:1–4:18).   The setting for Ruth was the period of the Judges. A postexilic author composed a beautiful short story about Ruth, King David's grandmother, to say that the Jews had no right to be narrow in their view of other nations.

Naomi, who was Jewish, had been taken by her husband, Elimelech, to live in Moab during a time of famine in Israel. Elimelech died in Moab, leaving Naomi with two sons, Mahlon and Chilion. Eventually, the sons married two Moabite women, Orphah and Ruth. Then the sons died, leaving the three widows with no one to look after them.

Naomi decided to return to Israel to be among her own people. The daughters-in-law were determined to go with her, but she tried to persuade them to return to their own people. Orphah did so, but Ruth insisted on going with Naomi:

> Do not press me to leave you
>   or turn back from following you!
> Where you go, I will go;
>   Where you lodge, I will lodge;

> your people shall be my people,
>   and your God, my God (1:16).

These words, often used as a bride's vow to her husband in a wedding ceremony, were addressed to a mother-in-law, not a husband (1:6–18).

At the time of the barley harvest, the women arrived in Bethlehem, where Naomi's husband had rights to ancestral property. As a widow, Naomi had no rights to the property, since in reality, she was part of the property rather than owner of it. Whoever got the property had to assume responsibility for Naomi and Ruth (1:19–22).

Elimelech's property was to go to his nearest male relative. Boaz, a wealthy landowner at Bethlehem was a relative of Elimelech; but there was another who was closer kin than Boaz. Naomi took Ruth to the barley fields to glean scattered heads of grain left by the reapers for the poor. Ruth happened to be gleaning in Boaz's field when he noticed her. When told who she was, he ordered that extra grain be scattered where she could find it. Calling her to him, Boaz told her to follow his reapers closely so she would not miss the extra grain. She was allowed, furthermore, to drink water from the vessels of Boaz. When she asked why she was so favored, she was told that it was because of her kindness to her mother-in-law, Naomi (2:1–14).

After being fed by Boaz, she gathered a large amount of grain because of his generosity. When Naomi heard this, she was pleased with what Boaz had done (2:15–23).

Naomi began to plan. She told Ruth to clean up and put on her nicest perfume and prettiest clothes. Then she was to go down to the threshing floor where Boaz was threshing his grain. Such work was done late in the afternoon when the breezes arose. When Boaz had finished eating and had laid down to sleep, Ruth was to go up and lie at this feet, pulling his cover over her. In those days, this was a woman's way of proposing to a man (3:1–5).

Ruth did as she was told. When Boaz awoke to find her lying at his feet, he was pleasantly surprised, especially since she was a beautiful young woman and he was an older man. As if to answer her proposal, the next morning, he gave her a sackful of grain to carry home (3:6–18).

There were complications, however. Since Boaz was not the nearest relative, he had to get the right to inherit the property. He found the nearest relative in the town gate, where all legal transactions took place. When told about the property, the man said he would claim the right of inheritance. But when he found that the two women went with the property, he changed his mind. Since he would have had to marry Ruth, the first son born to her would be credited to her first husband, and thus would have the right to inherit Ruth's first husband's property.[12]

Boaz then claimed the right of inheritance since he was next in line. He married Ruth and they, according to the story, were the great-grandparents of King David. The point of the story was that the Jews could not claim to be an exclusive group since the great-grandmother of their greatest king was a foreigner (4:1–22).

The Book of Jonah (Jonah 1:1–4:11).[13]   The tragedy of the Book of Jonah is that a great missionary plea is known largely as a fish tale. The fish was not a major character—it only played a supporting role!

The historical character Jonah was a fiercely nationalistic prophet who lived in the days of Jeroboam II (2 Kings 14:25). The book that bears his name is about Jonah, not by him. Unlike the other prophetic books that contain the oracles of the prophet, the book contains only one oracle of Jonah that has only five Hebrew words.

The importance of this book did not lie in what the prophet said. Instead, the important thing was what the book said. Arguments about whether a man could survive three days in the belly of a fish, while they may be interesting, really miss the point. It is tragic that most people get so fascinated by the story of the fish that they never get to Chapter 4, where the real purpose of the book is unfolded.

1. Jonah, the stubborn prophet (1:1–7).   There are interesting parallels between Jonah and Israel. In Chapter 1, Jonah, called by God to go to Nineveh, was stubborn and rebellious. He decided to do things his way, so he went down to Joppa to board a ship to Tarshish (probably Spain). That was the extreme opposite to where Jonah was supposed to be going. The next thing he knew, a storm was tossing the ship. Jonah ended up being tossed into the sea, where a great fish swallowed him.

As it was with Jonah, so it had been with Israel. Her prophets constantly had called on her to do the LORD's will, but Israel had been stubborn and rebellious. The Babylonians, to use Isaiah's figure about the Assyrians (Isa. 8:7), had overflowed the land. Israel had been swallowed up in the exile.

2. Jonah, the prophet in the depths (2:1–10).   To symbolize Jonah's despair over his condition, a psalm of lament comprises Jonah 2. Such psalms undoubtedly were common in the exile as the Israelites poured out their feelings of despair. These psalms often ended with a note of renewed commitment and with praise to the LORD. As Jonah came out of the depths, so Israel came out of Babylon.

3. Jonah, the reluctant prophet (3:1–10).   When Jonah finally decided to do what he was called to do, he met with unusual success. The king ordered that even the animals should wear sackcloth as a symbol of mourning and repentance. With high hopes Israel had returned to the land. The people of the land offered to join with them to rebuild the Temple, but the particularistic Jews had rejected all such offers. They did not want to contaminate their faith, which had been purified by the exile in Babylon.

4. Jonah, the angry prophet (4:1–11).   God's failure to destroy Nineveh was frustrating to Jonah. He wanted his problem solved by the annihilation of Nineveh, not by God transforming it. Particularistic Jews wanted their enemies wiped out rather than taken in by God's grace.

There was a stinging satire in the description of Jonah's vigil on the hill overlooking Nineveh as he waited for its hoped-for destruction. The LORD who had already "provided a great fish to swallow up Jonah" (1:17), now "appointed a bush" to shade Jonah's head (4:6). Just as Jonah was beginning to relax in its shade, "God appointed a worm" who attacked the bush and caused it to wither (4:7). If that were not enough, God "prepared a sultry east wind," which combined with the sun beaming down on his head, adding to his exterior discomfort and his inner turmoil. Jonah begged to die so he would not be so miserable (4:8). In return, the LORD chided Jonah for being more concerned with plants than he was with people, even the hated Ninevehites.

The universalists felt that the particularists were more concerned with their own "plants" than they were concerned with people, the most important of God's living creatures. They could not be "a light to the nations" by the Jonah method. Instead, they had to be concerned enough about other people to gladly carry the word to them. In short, the book of Jonah was a missionary tract that proclaimed the views of postexilic Jews who believed that they had to be active examples in a non-Jewish world.

STUDY QUESTIONS

1. How important for subsequent history were the conquests of Alexander the Great?
2. Identify: Ptolemies, Seleucids, Antiochus the Great, Antiochus Epiphanes.
3. What were the causes of the Maccabean revolt, who were its leaders, and what were its long-term effects on Jewish history?
4. What was Elephantine?
5. How does one justify Obadiah's intense hatred for the Edomites?
6. What is unique about the form of the Book of Malachi?
7. What does the Book of Malachi tell us about the conditions in the time of its formation?
8. What natural catastrophe does Joel use to describe the coming Day of the LORD?
9. How does Zechariah 9–14 differ from Zechariah 1–8? What are possible ways to explain these differences?
10. What evidence does Ezekiel present to show that Daniel was a character from ancient times?
11. What do you see as the purpose of the Book of Daniel?
12. What are the two major divisions of the Book of Daniel?
13. How is Antiochus Epiphanes symbolized in the Book of Daniel?
14. What were the viewpoints of the "universalists" and the "particularists" in postexilic Judaism? What conditions gave rise to these opposing views?
15. What does the Book of Esther argue for?
16. What is the main point of the Book of Ruth?
17. Who was the original Jonah?
18. What was the Book of Jonah designed to say?
19. Term to know: *Hasidim.*

ENDNOTES

1. John Bright, *A History of Israel*, 3rd ed. (Philadelphia: Westminster, 1981), 412f.
2. I am grateful to Professor Kathryn Larch, Pima County Community College, for correcting my identification of Ptolemy.
3. Bright, *A History of Israel*, 414–416. See also Martin Noth, *The History of Israel*, 2nd ed. (New York: Harper and Row, 1960), 346–351.
4. For an excellent short discussion of this community, see J. Maxwell Miller and

John H. Hayes, *A History of Ancient Israel and Judah* (Louisville: Westminster/John Knox Press, 1986), 435–436.

5. Bright, *A History of Israel*, 406f.

6. Itzhaq Biet-Arieh, "New Light on the Edomites," *BAR* XIV, 2 (March-April, 1988), 41.

7. For an excellent discussion of the implications of a locust plague, see Harold Brodsky, "An Enormous Horde Arrayed for Battle—Locusts in the Book of Joel," *BR* VI, 4 (August, 1990), 32–39.

8. See "The Tale of Aqhat" in James B. Pritchard, *ANET,* 118–132.

9. For a balanced introduction to Daniel, see Robert A. Anderson, "Signs and Wonders," *ITC* (Grand Rapids: Wm. B. Eerdmans, 1984).

10. Cary A. Moore, "Eight Questions Most Frequently Asked About the Book of Esther," *BR* III, 1 (Spring, 1987), 16–31.

11. Michael Heltzer, "Esther—Where Does Fiction Start and History End?" *BR* VIII, I (February, 1992), 29.

12. This was the law of the Levirate marriage (Deut. 25:5–6).

13. David Noel Freedman, "Did God Play a Dirty Trick on Jonah in the End?" *BR* VI, 4 (August, 1990), 26–31, gives some insights into this book.

Chapter 15 ❦

EPILOGUE

The Continuing Story

The Old Testament story comes to an end, but it would be a grave error to suppose that religious people ceased to write. Indeed, if the literature that has survived is any indication, there were numerous religious literary works, many of which never became part of any canon of Scripture. Their work, nevertheless, played an important role in the lives of religious people of their times. All that remains for us is to examine briefly some important changes in the religious life of the Jewish community, to discuss the rise of some factions within Judaism that were to play important roles in later history, and to look at some of the more important other religious literature from the time of the Babylonian exile and the beginning of the Christian era.

LIFE IN THE JEWISH COMMUNITY

Except for the freedom they gained during the Maccabean revolt, Palestinian Jews, as well as those outside of Palestine, were the pawns of foreign rulers. Most Jews, in fact, did not live in Palestine. The Babylonian, Persian, and Greek conquests of Palestine had had the effect of scattering Jews all over the Middle East. Babylonia and Egypt in particular had large Jewish communities. Those Jews who lived outside of Palestine were said to be part of the *Diaspora*.

While Israel was no longer a nation, it was still a people, spread from Babylon to Alexandria and to Rome, yet bound together by a love for God, a love for God's teaching (*Torah*), and a love for God's city, Jerusalem. No matter how far one lived from Jerusalem, every devout Jew vowed to go to that city to worship at least once in his lifetime. This love for Jerusalem is expressed in the words of a lonely poet during the Babylonian Exile:

> How could we sing the LORD's song
>> in a foreign land?
> If I forget you, O Jerusalem,
>> let my right hand wither!
> Let my tongue cling to the roof of my mouth,
>> if I do not remember you,
> if I do not set Jerusalem
>> above my highest joy (Ps. 137:4–6).

As a consequence of their loss of political independence, certain important changes took place in the Jewish community that had their effects not only in Palestine but also in the Jewish communities of the Diaspora. First, the chief priest increasingly assumed both religious and political roles in the Palestinian Jewish community, with his power in many ways extending to Jewish communities everywhere. An important step in this rise in political power came when Jonathan, the brother of Judas Maccabeus, combined the office of political ruler and high priest (circa 150 B.C.E.).

Second, the voice of the prophet, so powerful in Israelite life before and during the Babylonian Exile, faded to a whisper as the written Torah gradually became the standard for life and conduct. Since Torah basically means "teaching," the teacher or rabbi became a major force in Jewish life. More and more the synagogue was where the teaching took place. While the Temple, located in Jerusalem , was Judaism's most sacred shrine, every Jewish community that had a minimum of ten Jewish men—a *minyon*—had a synagogue as the very center of community life. Since the synagogue was an institution controlled by laypersons and the rabbi was a layperson, the lay interpreters of the Torah became the most important influence in the life of the ordinary Jew, wherever he lived. So while the political power of the high priest was increasing, the religious power of the priesthood as a group was decreasing.

Two important things grew out of this situation. First, since teaching became primarily a function of laymen, by 200 B.C.E. there were two great lay interpreters (rabbis) in each generation whose authority in scriptural interpretation became preeminent. Second, oral tradition came to have equal status with the written Torah. This was based on the belief that (1) it, like the written Torah, had its origins in the time of Moses, and (2) it had been passed along over the centuries by word of mouth until it came to be entrusted to the *zugoth*, the pair of great rabbis whose word was law for that day.

THE RISE OF PARTIES AND SECTS

This period also saw the rise of numerous parties within Judaism that were to have major roles in its future. Before the Maccabean revolt, the Samaritans, descendants of the inhabitants of the territory of the northern kingdom that Assyria had conquered in 722/21 B.C.E., became a distinct group. Assyria had brought in foreign colonists who intermarried with the poor Israelites left in the land. In the Babylonian conquests, the poor also were left in the land while most of those in the leadership classes were carried into exile. Open hostility developed between those who remained in the land and the Jews who returned after the Babylonian Exile. The people of the land still looked upon themselves as true followers of the God of Israel, but the Jews who returned felt that those who had stayed in the land had a corrupted faith and that their mixed heritage disqualified them from being a part of Judaism. Eventually, the Samaritans, so named because Samaria was their chief city, built a temple on Mount Gerizim, one of the mountains that overlooks the site of Shechem, the old Israelite capital. Later, John Hyrcanus, the Hasmonean ruler, forcefully converted the Samaritans to his version of Judaism, destroyed their temple, and earned their undying enmity both for himself and Judaism of the Jerusalem variety.[1]

The extremely orthodox *Hasidim* who had supported the Maccabean revolt in its beginnings became disenchanted when the revolt became more of an attempt to gain political power than a struggle for freedom. It is likely, though not proven, that two political groups important to later Judaism, the Pharisees and the Essenes, had roots in this movement. They predominantly were a group made up of laymen who wanted to interpret the law so that its meaning was clear to each generation. They were the party that emphasized oral tradition and that produced the great rabbis who were to dominate later Judaism. The Pharisees accepted the Pentateuch (*Torah*), the Prophets (*Nebi'im*), and the Writings (*Kethubim*) as authoritative. While they would have strongly affirmed their religious orthodoxy, they were in fact the religous liberals of their day, introducing into Judaism such ideas as the belief in resurrection of the dead and the belief in angels.

The Essenes, whose best known settlement was the Qumran community near the Dead Sea, produced the now-famous Dead Sea Scrolls. Many interpreters believe that the Essenes withdrew from Jerusalem initially when Jonathan, the brother of Judas Maccabeus, seized the high priesthood (circa. 150 B.C.E.). Frequent reference is made in their literature to the "wicked priest." Of the known historical personages, Jonathan best fits this description.

Their theology was similar to that of the Pharisees in many respects but had important differences. The Essenes believed they were to prepare for the coming of the end of the age. Their literature was dominated by the idea that a great final struggle was approaching, the war of the "Sons of Light" (themselves) and the "Sons of Darkness" (all who opposed them). Everything they did was aimed at preparing for the day when God would intervene on their behalf and make them victorious over their enemies. They were attempting to make real the things about which apocalyptic writers wrote.[2]

Jonathan's attempt to combine the office of high priest and ruler was further carried out by the Hasmoneans, who ruled the country after the Maccabean revolt gained freedom for the Jewish people in 142 B.C.E. The priestly party, the Sadducees, dominated the political and economic life of the country but lost much of their religious influence over the common people. They were quite conservative religiously, accepting only the first five books of the Bible as Scripture, those books that describe the responsibilities of the priests. In contrast, since the prophets frequently attacked the priesthood, this would not have endeared them to the Sadducees. The Sadducees' political and economic power as well as their religious views led to a struggle between them and the Pharisees. This situation, in turn, led to severe persecution of the Pharisees during the days of the Hasmonean rule.

While there would be other parties and sect groups that would arise later in Judaism, these were the most important. Their existence illustrates that as the Old Testament story closes, Judaism was not a unified religion in which everyone believed the same doctrines and interpreted God's will for their lives in the same way. Instead, the Jews were a diverse people whose society and religion mirrored that diversity.

LITERARY ACTIVITY

As the period that produced the Old Testament came to a close, literary activity did not cease among religious people. Four major groups of literature need to be examined briefly: the Apocrypha, the Pseudepigrapha, the Dead Sea Scrolls, and the oral tradition of the Jews that eventually produced the Talmud.

The Apocrypha

To speak of the Apocrypha as extrabiblical literature is not entirely accurate since Catholic canon (both Roman and Eastern Catholicism) accepts these books as sacred Scripture. In these traditions they are called "Deuterocanonical" since their canon basically follows the Alexandrian Canon. The Apocrypha may be defined as those accepted by the Jews of Alexandria as part of their sacred writings that were not accepted as part of the Hebrew canon. They may be grouped as follows:[3]

1. Additions to biblical books

Apocryphal Book	*Related Biblical Book*
1 Esdras	2 Chronicles, Ezra, Nehemiah
Baruch	Jeremiah
The Letter of Jeremiah	Jeremiah
The Prayer of Azariah and the Song of the Three Young Men	Daniel
Susanna	Daniel
Bel and the Dragon	Daniel
The Prayer of Manasseh	2 Chronicles

2. An apocalypse—2 Esdras
3. Two stories of Jewish piety
   Tobit
   Judith

4. Two books of wisdom
 > The Wisdom of Solomon
 > Ecclesiasticus, or the Wisdom of Jesus,
 >   the Son of Sirach
5. Historical books
 > 1 Maccabees
 > 2 Maccabees

The books that are supposed to be additions to biblical books are varied. First Esdras essentially duplicates portions of the biblical books of 2 Chronicles (35:1–36:23), all of Ezra, and that part of Nehemiah that tells of Ezra reading the Torah to the Jews (7:38–8:12). The only original part of the book is a delightful story of three guards in the palace of the Persian king who compete for a prize by giving answers to the question, "What one thing is strongest?" (1 Esd. 3:5). One argues for wine; the second for the king himself; and the third, who is identified as Zerubbabel, wins the argument and the prize by praising women and truth. As his reward, he is allowed to return to Jerusalem to rebuild the Temple (1 Esd. 4:61–63). Of the books listed in the first category, Baruch, the Letter of Jeremiah, and The Prayer of Manasseh also can be classified as wisdom literature.[4]

Second Esdras differs drastically from 1 Esdras in that it is an apocalypse. The introduction and conclusion show evidence of being the work of Christian editors, while the core of the book is from a Jewish writer. While it wrestles with the problem of how a just God can permit such an evil world (as do some of the wisdom books), its emphasis on revelations, angels, and the final judgment puts it in the category of the apocalyptic.

Tobit and Judith are contrasting stories that illustrate Jewish piety in postexilic times. Tobit is a man who is unusually sensitive to the hurts of his fellow Jews. He even risks the wrath of the governing authorities because of his concern to see that the dead receive proper burial. After many reverses, including blindness, his faithful service to God is rewarded. Tobit's son, Tobias, carries out a mission for his father that secures the family's wealth, cures his father's blindness, and frees a beautiful woman from domination by a demon. The woman, Sarah, also becomes the wife of Tobias.

The story of Judith, on the other hand, is not nearly so romantic. When her native city is surrounded by the Assyrian army, she follows God's guidance and uses her feminine wiles to cut off the head of the enemy general. The siege is lifted and the people are freed. Internal evidences within both books confirm that both Judith and Tobit are fictional characters.[5]

The Wisdom of Solomon and Ecclesiasticus are two of the finest books in the Apocrypha. Had they come at an earlier time, they undoubtedly would have been included in the Hebrew canon. The Wisdom of Solomon is from the Alexandrian Jewish community, probably from the first century B.C.E. It deals with the themes of the righteous and the wicked, immortality, the judgment of the wicked, and the importance of wisdom as the guide for life. In this book, wisdom takes on even more of the characteristics of a person than it does in earlier wisdom books. Chapters 10 to 12 illustrate how wisdom guided the great persons and events in Israel's history.

Ecclesiasticus, or the Wisdom of Jesus the Son of Sirach, is the work of a Jewish schoolmaster who lived around 200 B.C.E. It sets out rules for getting along in this world. Unlike the Book of Proverbs, in which sayings are not grouped according to subject matter, Ecclesiasticus tends to group material in a topical arrangement.

Of the two historical works, 1 Maccabees is the more valuable as history. It is an unusually reliable history that begins with the reign of Antiochus Epiphanes (175 B.C.E.) and ends with the beginning of the reign of John Hyrcanus, the first Hasmonean ruler (135 B.C.E.). Its major concern is the Maccabean revolt. Second Maccabees covers a shorter time period and concerns itself primarily with the exploits of Judas Maccabeus. Its writer has a strong bias against the Hasmonean rulers.

The earliest books in the Apocrypha come from the late third century, while the latest would be dated as late as the first century B.C.E. They came from a time when many changes were taking place in the Near East and did their part to encourage the faithful during unsettled days.

The Pseudepigrapha

Pseudepigrapha literally means "writings with false superscriptions." They have certain characteristics: (1) they primarily are Jewish or Christian in origin; (2) they "are often attributed to ideal figures in Israel's past"; (3) they claim to be the bearer of God's message; (4) they usually use Old Testament ideas and narratives as a starting point; and (5) they usually are dated in the period 200 B.C.E. to 200 C.E. The number of known pseudepigraphical writings are now in the hundreds. They undoubtedly will increase in number as more of the Dead Sea Scrolls are translated into English.[6]

None of the writings classed as pseudepigraphical is found in either of the major canons of Scripture. This does not mean that they are of no value. As evidence of the regard with which some were held, the New Testament Book of Jude quotes the Assumption of Moses (Jude 8) and Enoch (Jude 13–14). Another pseudepigraphical work, The Psalms of Solomon, was included among one of the most important collections of biblical manuscripts.[7] Some of the other prominently mentioned writings are The Letter of Aristeas, The Book of Jubilees, The Martyrdom of Isaiah, Fourth Maccabees, The Sybylline Oracles, The Book of Enoch, Fourth Ezra, The Apocalypse of Baruch, The Testaments of the Twelve Patriarchs, The Life of Adam and Eve, and the Damascus Document. The major value of the pseudepigrapha is that it shows the many currents of thought that were present at the end of the Old Testament era.

The Dead Sea Scrolls

In 1947, a young goat herder's curiosity led to one of the greatest archaeological discoveries of all time. A Bedouin boy threw a rock into a hole in a cliff that overlooks the Dead Sea. When he heard the sound of something breaking, he climbed up the cliff to investigate. Inside the caves were clay jars filled with manuscripts.

Most of these manuscripts eventually would fall into the hands of biblical scholars, who recognized their great value. This led to an investigation of a number of other caves in the area and the excavation of a nearby ruin. The result of these investigations was the finding of a large number of manuscripts and manuscript fragments from almost every Old Testament book, as well as manuscripts of numerous religious writings. The latter finds furnished a wealth of new information about the people known as the Essenes, a Jewish sect that existed in the early part of the Christian era and about whom little was known previously. Qumran, the community that produced the manuscripts, was located on the northwestern shore of the Dead Sea. It existed from Maccabean times off and on until the Roman conquest of Palestine around 70 C.E.

The most famous biblical manuscript found at Qumran is commonly known as the St. Mark's Isaiah Scroll. It is at least one thousand years older than any previously known manuscript of Isaiah, yet its discovery led to no radical changes in the translations of the Book of Isaiah. Of the nonbiblical manuscripts, the best known is The Manual of Discipline, a rulebook for the conduct of the members of the sect; The Thanksgiving Scroll, which contains songs similar to the Book of Psalms; and The War of the Sons of Light and the Sons of Darkness, a book describing a great battle to take place between the community members (the Sons of Light) and the Kittim or Romans (the Sons of Darkness). The latter work illustrates the apocalyptic nature of the community. Another major manuscript, the Temple Scroll, was published for the first time in 1978.[8]

The Dead Sea Scrolls and the people who produced them are just another illustration of the diverse character of Judaism as this period comes to a close.

JUDAISM'S ORAL TRADITION

The final body of literature we must mention is the growing body of oral tradition being developed by the rabbinic interpreters of the Hebrew scriptures. The aim of the great rabbis was to translate the principles in the Torah and the Prophets into rules for everyday living. Because of this felt need, a pair (*zugoth*) of outstanding rabbis, one representing the more orthodox or conservative viewpoint, and one of a more liberal persuasion, interpreted the Scriptures for the people of their day. As was mentioned previously, they believed that this oral tradition extended all the way back to Moses, who, according to their view, received both an oral and a written Torah.

The time of the great rabbis began around 200 B.C.E. and would continue until 500 C.E. There were two types of oral literature: (1) *halakah*, or rules for living based on the interpretation of the legal portions of the Old Testament, and (2) *haggadah*, a more sermonic and illustrative kind of material that consisted of such things as fanciful expansions of the narrative parts of the Old Testament. It was designed to encourage the ordinary Jew to be diligent in observing *halakah*. By the end of the second century C.E., this material would be collected and organized into six divisions by the great rabbi Judah ha-Nasi. This was called *Mishnah*. Following this, a commentary on the *Mishnah* was developed that would be known as the *Gemara*. The *Mishnah* and the

Gemara were then joined to form the *Talmud.* There eventually were two Talmuds—a Palestinian and a Babylonian Talmud. One truly amazing thing about this was that each generation of rabbis memorized the interpretations of the previous generations, added their own interpretations, and passed them on to the succeeding generation. Nothing was preserved in writing until the fifth century C.E.! But these developments were only in their beginnings as the Old Testament story closes.

THE END OF THE MATTER

This version of the Old Testament story comes to an end. Perhaps it had opened a few eyes to the treasures of the Old Testament. If so, the telling has been worth it. It may even inspire some to look again at the story and to try to make it theirs so they can experience the thrill of walking in the steps of its characters; experiencing their joys, sorrows, and frustrations; tasting their foods; and savoring some of the smells of that world. If so, that is even better. But this version closes with the hope that even those who may never look at it again will in some way be a bit richer than before because they came this way to listen to the story.

STUDY QUESTIONS

1. What event symbolized the increasing political involvment of the High Priest?
2. Why were laypersons increasingly influential in religious matters in postexilic Jewish communities?
3. How were the Samaritans related to Judaism?
4. What were the distinct beliefs of the Pharisees?
5. Why is it said that the Essenes were an apocalyptic group?
6. What best illustrates the diverse nature of Judaism as it was developing?
7. Why is it not completely accurate to speak of the Apocrypha as extrabiblical literature?
8. Briefly state the nature of the following books of the Apocrypha: (a) 1 Esdras; (b) 2 Esdras; (c) Tobit; (d) The Wisdom of Solomon; (e) Ecclesiasticus, or the Wisdom of Jesus the Son of Sirach; (f) Maccabees.
9. What illustrates the importance of the pseudepigraphical literature?
10. What do the Dead Sea Scrolls contribute to our knowledge of the Bible and of the Essenes?
11. How did the Talmuds develop?
12. Terms to know: *Diaspora, zugoth, Hasidim, Halakah, Haggadah, Mishna, Gemara, Talmud.*

ENDNOTES

1. R. J. Coggins, *Samaritans and Jews,* rev. ed. (Garden City, N.Y.: Doubleday, 1964), is a good up-to-date discussion of the Samaritans and their relationship to the Jews. The Samaritan temple was destroyed circa 128 B.C.E.

2. T. H. Gaster, *The Dead Sea Scriptures,* rev. ed. (Garden City, N.Y.: Doubleday, 1964).

3. For the most part this classification is that of Robert C. Dentan, *Apocrypha: Bridge to the Testaments* (New York: Seabury, 1954, 1964).

4. Robert C. Dentan, *Apocrypha*, 76–92.

5. Carey A. Moore, "The Case of the Pious Killer," *BR* VI, 1 (February, 1990), discusses the reasons why Judith was not in the canon of the Old Testament.

6. James H. Charlesworth, *The Old Testament Pseudepigrapha*, vols. 1 and 2 (Garden City, N. Y.: Doubleday, 1983, 1985).

7. The Sinaiticus manuscripts.

8. Jacob Milgrom, "The Temple Scroll," *BA* 41, 3(1978), 105–120.

FOR FURTHER STUDY

CHAPTER ONE

Biblical Archaeology

Archaeology. A bi-monthly magazine published by the Archaeological Institute of America that has occasional articles relating to Biblical archaeology. (*ARCH*)

Bible Review. A bimonthly magazine published by the Biblical Archaeology Society. It majors on biblical interpretation using both archaeological and geographical information. (*BR*)

Biblical Archaeologist. (now *Near Eastern Archaeology*). A quarterly of the American Schools of Oriental Research. Its purpose is "to provide the general reader . . . with an interpretation of the meaning of new archaeological discoveries for the biblical heritage of the West."(*BA* or *NEA*)

Biblical Archaeology Review. A bimonthly magazine also published by the Biblical Archaeology Society. It has a popular magazine format and excellent photography. (*BAR*)

Books on Archaeology

Avi-Yonah, Michael, and Ephraim Stern, eds. *Encyclopedia of Archaeological Evacuations in the Holy Land.* 4 vols. Englewood Cliffs, N.J.: Prentice Hall, 1975–78.

Coogan, Michael D., J. Cheryl Exum, and Lawrence E. Stager, eds. *Scripture and Other Artifacts: Essays in Honor of Philip J. King.* Louisville: Westminster/John Knox, 1994. An excellent series of essays relating archaeology to biblical interpretation.

Dever, William G. "Archaeology, Syro-Palestinian and Biblical," in *ABD*, I. Garden City, NY: Doubleday, 1992, 354–366. A thorough discussion of the strengths and weaknesses of present-day archaeology.

Drinkard, Joel F. Gerald L. Mattingly, and J. Maxwell Miller, eds., *Benchmarks in Time and Culture: An Introduction to Palestinian Archaeology.* Atlanta: Scholars Press, 1988. A book of practical essays on the "how-to" of archaeology.

Hoerth, Alfred J. *Archaeology and the Old Testament.* Grand Rapids: Baker Books, 1998. A very conservative yet helpful book of the relation of archaeology and the Old Testament.

Mazar, Amihai, *Archaeology of the Land of the Bible: 10,000–586 B.C.E. ABRL.* New York: Doubleday, 1990.

Biblical Criticism

The first four titles are in the *Guide to Biblical Scholarship Series*, edited by Gene M. Tucker, Published by Minneapolis: Augsburg Fortress, 1971, and are designed for the beginning student.

Habel, Norman C. *Literary Criticism of the Old Testament.*

Krentz, Edgar. *Textual Criticism of the Old Testament: From the LXX to Qumran.*

Rast, Walter E. *Tradition History and the Old Testament.*

Tucker, Gene M. *Form Criticism of the Old Tes-*

tament.

Mays, James Luther, David L. Petersen, and Kent Harold Richard, eds. *Old Testament Interpretation: Past, Present, and Future. Essays in Honor of Gene M. Tucker.* Nashville: Abingdon, 1995.

Soulen, Richard N. *Handbook of Biblical Criticism.* Louisville: Westminster/John Knox, 1976. A handbook of technical terms and tools.

Appropriate articles in such works as *MDB* and *ABD.*

Other Books and Articles on Old Testament Subjects

Bright, John. *The Authority of the Old Testament.* Nashville: Abingdon, 1967. An excellent discussion on the relevance of the Old Testament for modern life.

Harrelson, Walter. "The Hebrew Bible," in *MCB,* 13–22.

Harrington, Daniel J., S.J. "Introduction to the Canon," in *NIB,* I,7–13.

Hoerth, Alfred J, Gerald L. Mattingly, and

Edwin M. Yamauchi, eds. *Peoples of the Old Testament World.* Grand Rapids: Baker Books, 1994. An excellent guide to peoples of Old Testament times.

Matthews, Victor H. *Manners and Customs in the Bible: An Illustrated Guide to Daily Life in Bible Times.* Peabody, Mass.: Hendrickson, 1988. Gives insight into societies in biblical times.

Extrabiblical Texts

The most famous series on extrabiblical texts is edited by James B. Pritchard and published by Princeton University Press. These include:

_____. *Ancient Near Eastern Texts Relating to the Old Testament* (3rd edition with supplements), 1969. (*ANET*)

_____. *The Ancient Near East: An Anthology of Texts and Pictures,* 1958, and *Vol. II: A New Anthology of Texts and Pictures,* 1976. These are paperback condensations of Pritch-

ard's longer works. (*ANE*)

Martinez, Florentino Martinez, trans. *The Dead Sea Scrolls Translated: The Texts in English.* Leiden, The Netherlands: Brill, 1994.

Shanks, Hershel. *The Mystery and Meaning of the Dead Sea Scrolls.* New York: Random House, 1998.

Vermes, Geza. *The Dead Sea Scrolls in English,* 4th ed. New York: Penguin, 1995. This paperback edition is edited by Vermes.

CHAPTER TWO

Bible Atlases

Aharoni, Yohanan, and Michael Avi-Yonah. *The MacMillan Bible Atlas,* rev. ed. New York: Macmillan, 1977. An atlas that emphasizes the military aspects of Old Testament history using clear maps and appropriate archaeological illustrations. (*MBA*)

May, Herbert G., ed. *Oxford Bible Atlas,* 3rd ed. New York: Oxford University Press, 1974. A good atlas in paperback. (*OBA*)

Pritchard, James B., ed. *The Harper Bible Atlas.* New York: Harper and Row, 1987. (*HBA*)

Geography

Aharoni, Yohanan. *The Land of the Bible*. trans. Anson P. Rainey. Louisville: Westminster/John Knox, 1980.

Baly, Dennis. *The Geography of the Bible*. New York: Harper and Row, 1974. A thorough study of all aspects of Palestinian geography.

Frank, Harry Thomas. *Discovering the Biblical World*. ed. James F. Strange. Maplewood, N.J.: Hammond, 1988.

In addition there is an excellent series of short articles entitled "Bible Lands" appearing periodically in *BR*.

CHAPTER THREE

Blenkinsopp, Joseph. "The Pentateuch: An Introduction of the First Five Books of the Bible," in *ABRL*.

Brueggeman, Walter. "Genesis," in *INT*, 1982.

Freitheim, Terence E. "The Book of Genesis: Introduction, Commentary, and Reflections," in *NIB*, I, 1994.

Hamilton, Victor P. "The Book of Genesis: Chapters 1–17," in *NICOT*, 1990.

_____. "The Book of Genesis: Chapter 18 in *NICOT*, 1995.

Matthews, Victor H. *Manners and Customs in the Bible: An Illustrated Guide to Daily*

Life in Bible Times. Peabody, Mass: Hendrickson, 1988.

Smith, David A. "Curse and Blessing," in *MDB*, 188–189. A good brief discussion of this subject.

Speiser, E. A. "Genesis," in *AB*, I, 1964. One of the best volumes in this series.

Urbrock, William J. "Blessings and Curses," in *ABD*, I, 755–761. An extensive article on this important subject.

Vawter, Bruce. *On Genesis: A New Reading*. Garden City, N.Y.: Doubleday, 1977.

The Patriarchal Period

The most convenient source for continuing discussions of this important period are *BA* (now *NEA*), *BAR*, and *BR*. More technical dicussions may be found in such publications as the *JBL*. Articles in the major Bible dictionaries are also helpful.

CHAPTER FOUR

Anderson, Bernhard. "Liberation from Bondage" and "Covenant in the Wilderness," in *Understanding the Old Testament*. 4th ed. Chapters 1 and 2. Englewood Cliffs, N.J.: Prentice Hall, 1986. A good discussion of the Exodus in light of modern scholarship.

Ashley, Timothy R. "The Book of Numbers" in *NICOT*, 1993.

Beegle, Dewey M. *Moses: The Servant of Yahweh*. Grand Rapids: Wm. B. Eerdmans, 1972. A thorough discussion of Moses by a responsible conservative scholar.

Brueggemann, Walter. "The Book of Exodus," *NIB*, I. Nashville: Abingdon, 1994.

Buber, Martin. *Moses: The Revelation and the Covenant*. New York: Harper & Row, 1958. A Jewish perspective on Moses' life.

Childs, Brevard. "The Book of Exodus," *OTL*. Louisville: Westminster/John Knox, 1974.

Craigie, P. C. "The Book of Deuteronomy," *NICOT*. Grand Rapids: Wm. B. Eerdmans, 1976.

Durham, John I. "Exodus," *MCB*. Macon: Mercer University Press, 1995.

Kaiser, Walter C., Jr. "The Book of Leviticus," *NIB*, I. Nashville: Abingdon, 1994.

Levine, Baruch A. "Numbers 1–20," *AB*. Garden City, N.Y.: Doubleday, 1993.

Mayes, A. D. H. "Deuteronomy," *NCBC*. Grand Rapids: Wm. B. Eerdmans, 1979.

Milgrom, Jacob. "Leviticus 1–16," *AB*. Garden City, N.Y.: Doubleday, 1991. This commentary is especially concerned with the significance of the tabernacle.

Noth, Martin. "Numbers: A Commentary,"

trans. James D. Martin. *OTL*. London: SCM Press, 1966.

Rad, Gerhard von. "Deuteronomy," trans. Dorothea Barton. *OTL*. Louisville: Westminster/ John Knox, 1966. A classic commentary on Deuteronomy.

Weinfeld, Moshe. "Deuteronomy 1–11," *AB*, Garden City, N.Y.: Doubleday, 1991.

Since the Exodus and Conquest are two of the most popular themes in biblical studies at present, frequent articles on these subjects appear in such publications as *BA, BAR*, and *BR*.

Law, Covenant, and Worship

Alt, Albrecht. "The Origins of Hebrew Law," *Essays on Old Testament History and Religion*, trans. by R. A. Wilson. Garden City, NY: Doubleday, 1967.

De Vaux, Roland, *Studies in Old Testament Sacrifice*. Cardiff: University of Wales Press, 1964.

Kraus, Hans-Joachim. *Worship In Israel*. Louisville: Westminster/ John Knox, 1966.

Mendenhall, George. *Law and Covenant in Israel and the Ancient Near East*. Pittsburgh: The Biblical Colloquium, 1955. See also his article on "Covenant" in *ABD*, I. Garden City, N.Y., 1994, for an update on his views.

Trueblood, Elton. *Foundations for Reconstruction*. New York: Harper & Row, 1946. A good, sound discussion on the relevance of the Ten Commandments.

In addition, appropriate articles on specific subjects can be found in such Bible dictionaries as *ABD, IDB*, and *MDB*.

CHAPTER FIVE

Albright, W. F., *Yahweh and the Gods of Canaan*. Garden City, N.Y.: Doubleday, 1969. An Anchor paperback.

Boling, Robert G. "Judges: A New Translation with Introduction and Commentary," in *AB*, 6A.

Boling, Robert G., and G. Ernest Wright. "Joshua: A New Translation with Notes and Commentary," in *AB*, 6.

Bright, John. "The Book of Joshua: Introduction and Exegesis," in *IB*, II.

Coogan, Michael D. "Joshua," in *NJBC*.

Dunstan, Robert C. "Judges," in *MCB*.

Gottwald, Norman K. *The Hebrew Bible: A Socio-Literary Introduction*. Philadelphia: Fortress, 1985.

Gray, John. "Joshua, Judges, and Ruth," in *NCBC*.

Hamlin, E. John. "At Risk in the Promised Land," in *ITC*.

_____. "Inheriting the Land," in *ITC*.

Meyers, Carol. "The Roots of Restriction: Women in Early Israel," *BA* 41 (1978), 91–102.

Rad, Gerhard von. *Holy War in Ancient Israel*. Grand Rapids: Wm. B. Eerdmans, 1991. Paperback.

In addition, read articles on pertinent subjects in such Bible dictionaries as *ABD, IDB*, and *MDB* and in *BA, BAR*, and *BR*.

CHAPTER SIX

Bright, John. *A History of Israel*. 3rd ed. Louisville: Westminster/John Knox, 1981, 183–228.

Grizzard, Carol Stuart. "First and Second Samuel," in *MCB*.

McCarter, P. Kyle, Jr. "I Samuel: A New Translation and Commentary," in *AB*, 8.

_____. "II Samuel: A New Translation and Commentary," in *AB*, 9.

Miller, J. Maxwell, and John H. Hayes. *A History of Ancient Israel and Judah*. Louisville: Westminster/John Knox, 1986, ch. 4.

Robinson, Gnana. "1 & 2 Samuel: Let Us Be Like the Nations," in *ITC*.

In addition, read appropriate articles in previously cited Bible dictionaries or their equivalents.

CHAPTER SEVEN

Gray, John. "I and II Kings," 2nd ed., *OTL*.

McCarter, Kyle M., Jr. "II Samuel: A New Translation and Commentary," in *AB*, 9.

Meyers, Carol M. "I Chronicles: Introduction, Translation and Notes," in *AB*, 12.

Rad, Gerhard von. *Old Testament Theology*, 1. Trans. D. G. M. Stalker. New York: Harper and Row, 1962. See pages 312ff for a discussion of the Court History of David.

Smothers, Thomas G. "First and Second Kings," in *MCB*.

Snaith, Norman H. "The First and Second Books of Kings," in *IB*, 3.

CHAPTER EIGHT

Chronology

Thiele, E. R. *The Mysterious Numbers of the Hebrew Kings*. Chicago: University of Chicago Press, 1951. An in-depth study of the problems of biblical chronology.

The Prophets

Blenkinsopp, Joseph. *A History of Prophecy in Israel: From the Settlement of the Land to the Hellenistic Period*. Philadelphia: Westminster, 1983.

_____. "Sage, Priest, and Prophet: Intellectual Leadership in Ancient Israel," *LAI*. Louisville: Westminster/John Knox, 1995.

Gray, John. *I and II Kings*. Philadelphia: Westminster, 1963.

Heschel, Abraham J. *The Prophets*. New York: Harper & Row, 1963. A classic work on the prophets.

Koch, Klaus. *The Prophets*. 2 vols. Trans. Margaret Kohl. Philadelphia: Fortress, 1984.

Scott, R. B. Y. *The Relevance of the Prophets*. Rev. ed. New York: MacMillan, 1968. Old but good.

Amos and Hosea

Anderson, Francis I., and David Noel Freedman. "Amos: A New Translation with Introduction and Commentary," in *AB*, 24A.

Beeby, H. D. "Hosea: Grace Abounding," *ITC*.

King, Philip J. *Amos, Hosea, and Micah: An Archaeological Commentary*. Philadelphia: Westminster, 1988.

Mays, James L. "Hosea," in *OTL*. A fine commentary on Hosea.

Paul, Shalom M. "Amos," in *HER*.

Ward, James M. *Hosea: A Theological Commentary*. New York: Harper & Row, 1966.

Wolff, H. W. "Joel and Amos," in *HER*.

CHAPTER NINE

Isaiah 1–39

Blank, Sheldon H. *Prophetic Faith in Isaiah*. New York: Harper & Row, 1958. Isaiah as viewed by a leading Jewish scholar.

Clements, Ronald E. "Isaiah 1–39," in *NCBC*.

Hayes, John H., and Stuart A. Irvine. *Isaiah, the Eighth-Century Prophet: His Time and His Preaching*. Nashville: Abingdon, 1980.

Kaiser, Otto. "Isaiah 1–12." Trans. R. A. Wilson. *OTL*.

_____. "Isaiah 13–39." Trans. R. A. Wilson. *OTL*.

Kelly, Page H. "Isaiah," *BBC*, 5.

Oswalt, John N. "The Book of Isaiah: Chapters 1–39," *NICOT*.

Scott, R. B. Y. "Isaiah 1–39: Introduction and Exegesis," *IB*, V.

Watts, John D. W. "Isaiah," *MCB*.

Widyapranawa, S. H. "Isaiah 1–39, The Lord is Saviour: Faith in Crisis," *ITC*.

Wright, G. Ernest. "Isaiah," *LBC*.

CHAPTER TEN

Habakkuk, Zephaniah, Nahum

Berlin, Adele. "Zephaniah: A New Translation with Introduction and Commentary," *AB*, 25A.

Steeger, William P. "Nahum," *MCB*, 773–784. See the general works on the prophets.

Jeremiah

Bright, John. "Jeremiah: Translated with Introduction and Notes," *AB*, 21.The introductory material especially is helpful.

Brueggemann, Walter. "Jeremiah 1–25: To Pluck Up, To Tear Down," *ITC*.

_____. "Jeremiah 26–52: To Build, To Plant," *ITC*.

Holladay, William L. "Jeremiah 1," *HER*.

_____. "Jeremiah 2," *HER*. A massive two-volume work on Jeremiah.

Hyatt, J. Phillip, "Jeremiah: Introducton and Exegesis," *IB*, VI.

Jones, Douglas Rawlinson. "Jeremiah," *NCBC*.

Skinner, John. *Prophecy and Religion*. New York: Cambridge University Press, 1922. A standard work on Jeremiah.

CHAPTER ELEVEN

Lamentations

Gottwald, Norman K. "Lamentations," *Studies in Biblical Theology*, 14. Napierville, Ill.: Alec C. Allenson, 1954.

Hillers, Delbert R. "Lamentations: A New Translation with Introduction and Commentary, *AB*, 7A.

Ezekiel

Eichrodt, Walter. "Ezekiel." Trans. Crosslet Quin. *OTL*.

Greenburg, Moshe. "Ezekiel, 1–20," *AB*, 22.

Vawter, Bruce, and Leslie J. Hoppe. "Ezekiel: A New Heart," *ITC*.

Zimmerli, Walther. "Ezekiel 1," *HER*.

_____. "Ezekiel 2," *HER*.

Isaiah 40–66

Knight, George A. F. "Isaiah 40–55: Servant Theology," *ITC*.

_____. "Isaiah 56–66: The New Israel," *ITC*.

Mckenzie, John L. "Second Isaiah," *AB*, 20. Excellent discussion on the Servant's identity.

North, Christopher R. *The Second Isaiah: Introduction, Translation, and Commentary on Chapters XL–LV*. Oxford: The Oxford University Press, 1964.

Rowley, H. H. *The Servant of the Lord and Other Essays on the Old Testament*. 2nd ed. Oxford: Blackwell, 1956.

Smart, James D. *History and Theology in Second Isaiah: A Commentary on Isaiah 35, 40–66*. Louisville: Westminster/John Knox, 1965.

Whybray, R. N. "Isaiah 40–66," *NCBC*.

CHAPTER TWELVE

Ackroyd, Peter. *Exile and Restoration: A Study of Hebrew Thought of the Sixth Century B.C.* Philadelphia: Westminster, 1968.

Holmgren, Frederick Carlson. "Ezra-Nehemiah: Israel Alive Again," *ITC*.

Meyers, Carol L., and Eric M. "Haggai-Zechariah 1–8," *AB*, 25B.

Myers, Jacob M. "Ezra-Nehemiah," in *AB*, 14.

———. "I and II Chronicles," *AB*, 12, 13.

Snaith, Norman. *The Jews from Cyrus to Herod.*

Walling, England: The Religious Education Press, 1949.

Stern, Ephraim. *Material Culture of the Land of the Bible in the Persian Period: 538–332 B.C.* Warminster, England: Aris and Phillips, 1982. An excellent book on the Persian Period.

Stuhlmueller, Carroll. "Haggai and Zechariah: Rebuilding with Hope," *ITC*.

CHAPTER THIRTEEN

Wisdom

Blenkinsopp, Joseph. "Sage, Priest, and Prophet: Religious and Intellectual Leadership in Ancient Israel," *LAI*.

———. *Wisdom and Law in the Old Testament*. London: Oxford University Press, 1983.

Brueggemann, Walter A. *In Man We Trust: The Neglected Side of Biblical Faith*. Louisville: Westminster/John Knox, 1972.

Crenshaw, James. *Old Testament Wisdom*. rev. and enl. ed. Louisville: Westminster/John Knox, 1998.

———. *Theodicy in the Old Testament*. Minneapolis: Augsburg Fortress, 1983.

———. *Education in Ancient Israel: Across the Deadening Silence*. New York: Doubleday, 1998.

Gammie, John G., and Leo G. Perdue, eds. *The Sage in Israel and in the Ancient Near East*. Winona Lake, Wis.: Eisenbrauns, 1990.

Rad, Gerhard von. *Wisdom in Israel*. Trans. James D. Martin. Nashville: Abingdon, 1973.

Scott, R. B. Y. *The Way of Wisdom in the Old Testament*. New York: Macmillan, 1971.

Proverbs

Fritsch, Charles T. "Proverbs: Introduction and Exegesis," *IB*, IV.

McKane, William. "Proverbs: A New Approach," *OTL*.

Job

Gordis, Robert. *The Book of God and Man: A Study of Job*. Chicago: University of Chicago Press, 1965.

Hartley, John E. "The Book of Job," *NICOT*.

Janzen, J. Gerald. "Job," *Interpetation: A Bible Commentary for Teaching and Preaching*. Louisville: Westminster/John Knox, 1985.

Murphy, Roland E. "Wisdom Literature: Job, Proverbs, Ruth, Canticles, Ecclesiastes, Esther," *FOTL*, XXVIII.

Perdue, Leo G., and W. Clark Gilpin. *The Voice from the Whirlwind: Interpreting the Book of Job*. Nashville, Abingdon, 1992.

Pope, Marvin H. "Job," *AB*, 15.

Rowley, Harold H. "The Book of Job," *NCBC*.

Terrien, Samuel. "Job: Introduction and Exegesis," *IB*, III. One of the best commentaries on Job.

Watts, John D. W., Jr., J. J. Owens, and Marvin Tate. "Job," *BBC*, IV.

Ecclesiastes

Gordis, Robert. *Koheleth, the Man and His World*. New York: Jewish Theological Seminary of America Press, 1951. Revised edition in Schocken paperback, 1967.

Seow, Choon-Leong. "Ecclesiastes: A New Translation with Introduction and Commentary," *AB*, 18C.

The Song of Songs

Meek, T. J. "The Song of Songs," *IB*, V.

Pope, Marvin, H. "Song of Songs: A New Translation with Introduction and Commentary," *AB*, 7C.

Rowley, H. H. "The Interpretation of the Songs of Songs," in *The Servant of the Lord and Other Essays*. Oxford: Blackwell, 1965, 195–245.

Psalms

Allen, Leslie C. "Psalms 101–150," *WBC*, 21.

Anderson, Bernhard W. *Out of the Depths: The Psalms Speak to Us Today*. Louisville: Westminster/John Knox, 1974.

Craigie, Peter C. "Psalms 1–50," *NICOT*, 19.

Dahood, Mitchell. "Psalms, I, II, III," *AB*, 16, 17, 17A.

Durham, John I. "Psalms," *BBC*.

Gunkel, Hermann. *The Psalms: A Form-Critical Introduction*. Trans. T. M. Horner. Louisville: Westminster/John Knox, 1967. This is a Facet paperback giving the essentials of Gunkel's pioneering work in Psalms.

McCann, J. Clinton. *A Theological Introduction to the Book of Psalms: The Psalms as Torah*. Nashville: Abingdon, 1993.

Mowinckel, Sigmund. *The Psalms in Israel's Worship*, 2 vols. Trans. D. R. Ap-Thomas. Nashville: Abingdon, 1962. Mowinckel is second only to Gunkel in his influence on modern studies in the Psalms.

Weiser, Artur. "The Psalms." Trans. Herbert Hartwell. *OTL*.

Westermann, Claus. *The Living Psalms*. Grand Rapids: Wm. B. Eerdmans, 1984.

CHAPTER FOURTEEN

Apocalyptic

Collins, John J. "Early Jewish Apocalypticism" in *ABD*, 282–288.

Gowan, Donald. *Eschatology in the Old Testament*. Minneapolis: Augsburg Fortress, 1986.

Mowinckel, Sigmund. *He That Cometh*. Trans.

G.W. Anderson. Nashville: Abingdon, 1956. A classic work on eschatology.

Russell, D. S. *The Method and Message of Jewish Apocalyptic*. Louisville: Westminster/John Knox, 1964.

Joel, Obadiah, Jonah, Zechariah 9–14, Malachi

Crenshaw, James L. "Joel: A New Translation with Introduction and Commentary," *AB*, 24C.

Hill, Andrew E. "Malachi: A New Translation with Introduction and Commentary," *AB*, 25D.

Knight, George A. F., and Friedann W. Golka. "The Song of Songs and Jonah," *ITC*.

Meyers, Carol L., and Eric M. Meyers.

"Zechariah: A New Translation with Introduction and Commentary," *AB*, 25C.

Raabe, Paul R. "Obadiah: A New Translation with Introduction and Commentary," *AB*, 24 D.

Sasson, Jack M. "Jonah: A New Translation with Introduction and Commentary," *AB*, 24B.

Daniel

Anderson, Robert A. "Signs and Wonders," *ITC*.

Collins, John J. "Daniel," *HER*.

Hartman, Louis F., and Alexander A. Di Lella. "The Book of Daniel: A New Translation with Introduction and Commen-

tary," *AB*, 23.

Lacocque, Andre. *The Book of Daniel.* Louisville: Westminster/John Knox, 1979.

Towner, W. Sibley. "Daniel," *Interpretation: A Bible Commentary for Teaching and Preaching.* Atlanta: John Knox, 1984.

CHAPTER FIFTEEN

The Dead Sea Scrolls

Cross, Frank M. *The Ancient Library of Qumran and Modern Biblical Studies.* Rev. and enl. ed. Minneapolis: Augsburg Fortress, 1995.

Shanks, Hershel. *The Mystery and Meaning of the Dead Sea Scrolls.* New York: Random House, 1998.

Stegemann, Hartmut. *The Library of Qumran: On the Essenes, Qumran, John the Baptist, and Jesus.* Grand Rapids: Wm. B. Eerd-

mans, 1995.

Vanderkam, James C. *The Dead Sea Scrolls Today.* Grand Rapids: Wm. B. Eerdmans, 1995.

Vermes, Geza. *The Dead Sea Scrolls in English,* 4th ed. Baltimore: Penguin Books, 1995.

With the recent publication of the texts of all the Dead Sea material, the literature in this area will change rapidly over the next few years.

The Samaritans

Coggins, R. J. *Samaritans and Jews: The Origins of Samaritanism Reconsidered.* Louis-

ville: Westminster/John Knox, 1975.

Judaism

Berquist, John L. *Judaism in Persia's Shadow: A Historical and Social Approach.* Minneapolis: Augsburg Fortress, 1995.

Charlesworth, James H., ed. *The Old Testament Psuedepigrapha.* Vols. 1 & 2. New York: Doubleday, 1983, 1985.

Neusner, Jacob. *Rabbinic Judaism: Structure and System.* Minneapolis: Augsburg Fortress, 1995.

All the major modern translations of the Bible, such as the NRSV, now contain translations of the books of the Apocrypha.

Other Old Testament Studies

The following is a select list of other introductions to the Old Testament, each taking a different approach to the subject than the one taken here.

Alter, Robert, and Frank Kermode, eds. *The Literary Guide to the Bible*. Cambridge, Mass.: The Belknap Press, 1987. While not an introduction in the traditional sense, nevertheless it is a good example of one of the major trends in present-day Biblical study.

Anderson, Bernhard W. *Understanding the Old Testament*. 5th ed. Englewood Cliffs, N.J.: Prentice Hall, 1998. A work that is in a class by itself.

Carmody, John, et al. *Exploring the Hebrew Bible*. Englewood Cliffs, N.J.: Prentice Hall, 1988.

Childs, Brevard S. *Introduction to the Old Testament as Scripture*. Minneapolis: Augsburg Fortress, 1979.

Dick, Michael B. *Introduction to the Hebrew Bible: An Inductive Reading*. Englewood Cliffs, N.J.: Prentice Hall, 1988.

Gottwald, Norman K. *The Hebrew Bible: A Socio-Literary Introduction*. Minneapolis: Augsburg Fortress, 1985.

La Sor, William Sanford, et al. *Old Testament Survey: The Message, From, and Background of the Old Testament*. Grand Rapids: Wm. B. Eerdmans, 1982.

Matthews, Victor H. and James C. Moyer. *The Old Testament: Text and Context*. Peabody, Mass: Hendrickson, 1997. An up-to-date approach to the Old Testament.

Pfeiffer, Charles F. *Old Testament History*. Grand Rapids: Baker Book House, 1973. Very conservative but comprehensive introduction.

Weiser, Artur. *The Old Testament: Its Formation and Development*. Trans. Dorothea M. Barton. New York: Association Press, 1961.

HEBREW HISTORY	THE LARGER WORLD

EARLY BRONZE AGE 3000-2200 B.C.E.

First Sumerian Empire 2800-2350
Egyptian Old Kingdom 2900-2300
Akkadian Empire 2360-2180
Ebla 2400-2250

MIDDLE BRONZE AGE 2200-1550 B.C.E.

Sumerian resurgence 2060-1950
Amorites enter the Fertile Crescent
  Hammurabi c. 1728-1686
The "Mari Age" 1750-1697
Hyksos Rule in Egypt 1720-1570

LATE BRONZE AGE 1500-1200 B.C.E.

Hurrian kingdom (Mitanni)

The sojourn in Egypt

Egypt
  Amarna Age 1500-1370
    Amenhotep IV 1370-1353
    19th Egyptian Dynasty 1305-1200
    Seti 1305-1290
    Rameses II 1290-1224

The Exodus 1290-1250 (?)
  Wilderness wanderings 1290-1250 (?)
  Conquest and settlement 1250-1200 (?)

Merneptah invades Palestine 1224
State of Merneptah 1220

IRON AGE I 1200-900 B.C.E.

Period of the Judges 1200-1020 B.C.E.
  Fall of Shiloh 1050
  Samuel and Saul 1020-1000
The United Kingdom 1000-922 B.C.E.
  David 1000-961
  Solomon 961-922
  Solomon dies—the kingdom divides 922

Philistines settle in Palestine
  12th century

THE DIVIDED KINGDOMS

JUDAH	ISRAEL	
Rehoboam 922-915	Jeroboam 922-901	Egypt
Abijah 915-913		Shishak invades Palestine 918

IRON AGE II 900-600 B.C.E.

Assyria
Assyrian power increases

Asa 913-873	Nadab 901-900	
	Baasha 900-877	
	Elah 877-876	

	Zimri (7 days) 876	
	Omri 876-869	
Jehoshaphat 873-849	Ahab 869-850	Shalmaneser III 859-825
	(Elijah)	Battle of Qarqar 853
Jehoram 849-842	Jehoram 849-842	
	Jehu's rebellion 842	
(Athaliah 842-837)	Jehu 842-815	
Joash 837-800	Jehoahaz 815-801	
Amaziah 800-783	Jehoash 801-786	
Uzziah (Azariah) 783-742	Jeroboam II 786-746	
	(Amos)	
	Zechariah 746-745 (6 mo.)	Tiglath-Pileser III 745-727
	(Hosea)	
	Shallum (1 mo.)	
Jotham 742-735	Menahem 745-738	Israel pays tribute to Assyria
(Isaiah)		
	Pekehiah 738-737	
Ahaz 735-715	Pekah 737-732	
(Micah) Syro-Ephraimitic		
Crisis 735-732		
	Hoshea 732-724	Shalmaneser V 727-722
	Samaria falls to Assyria	Sargon II 722-705
	722-721	
The Kingdom of Judah 722-587		
Hezekiah 715-687/86		Sennacherib 705-681
Sennacherib's invasion 701		
Sennacherib's second invasion (?) 690		
Manasseh 687/86-642		Rise of the Babylonian Empire
Amon 642-640		
Josiah 640-609		
(Zephaniah, Nahum)		Fall of Nineveh 612
(Habbakuk, Jeremiah)		
Jehoahaz 609		Final defeat of Assyria at Haran 609
Jehoiakim 609-598		Nebuchadnezzar 605-562
		Battle of Carchemish 605
		Period of Babylonian dominance

Jehoiachin 598-597
    Jerusalem falls—first deportation of the Jews 597
Zedekiah 597-587/86
    2nd fall of Jerusalem—2nd deportation 587/86
    Governorship of Gedaliah 586-582
    3rd deportation 582

IRON AGE III 600-? B.C.E.

Babylonian Exile 587-538
    (Ezekiel 593-573)

Nabonidus 556-538
    (father of Belshazzar)
Rise of Persia
    Cyrus II 550-530 conquers
    Media (550) and Lydia (546) and
    Babylon (539)

Deutero-Isaiah (540)
Edict of Cyrus—First return of Jews (538)
   Second return (520)
   Rebuilding of Temple 520-515—(Haggai and Zechariah)

   (Malachi c. 500-450)
   (Ezra's mission 458 [?])

Nehemiah's first governorship 445-433
   (Ezra's mission 428 [?])
Nehemiah's second governorship 30f (?)

   (Ezra's mission 498 [?])

Cambyses 530-522
Darius I 522-486
Persia controls Egypt 525-401
Xerxes (Ahasuerus) 486-465
Artaxerxes I (Longimanus)
   465-424

Xerxes II 423
Darius II 423-404
Artaxerses II (Mnemon) 404-358
Artaxerxes III 358-336
Darius III 336-331

EMPIRE OF ALEXANDER THE GREAT 336-323

At Alexander's death, his empire was divided among four of his generals. Of these, Ptolemy, who controlled Egypt, and Seleucus are important for Old Testament history and Jewish history.

Ptolemies and Seleucids

400-198 B.C.E. Palestine was controlled by Egypt and the Ptolemies. Antiochus III (223-187) wrested control of Palestine from Ptolemy V (203-181) in 198 B.C.E.

Maccabean Revolt (168/67)
Judas (the Maccabee) 166-160
Jonathan, 160-143

Simon, 143-134 (Jewish independence won)
John Hyrcanus 134-104

Seleucid Rulers
Antiochus III (the Great), 223-187
Seleucus IV, 187-175
Antiochus IV (Epiphanes), 175-163
Antiochus V, 163-162
Demetrius, 162-150
Alexander Balas, 150-145
Demetrius II, 145-138

63 B.C.E.—Pompey conquers Jerusalem, ending Jewish independence

*Note: Names of kings are underlined to indicate a change in dynasty. Athaliah is parenthesized (1) because she was the only woman ruler and (2) she was the only non-Davidic ruler in Judah. Other parentheses indicate significant events during a king's reign.

INDEX

M

N